Y0-AJP-355

APOCALYPTIC GEOGRAPHIES

Apocalyptic Geographies

RELIGION, MEDIA, AND THE
AMERICAN LANDSCAPE

JEROME THARAUD

PRINCETON UNIVERSITY PRESS
PRINCETON & OXFORD

Copyright © 2020 by Princeton University Press

Requests for permission to reproduce material from this work should be sent to permissions@press.princeton.edu

Published by Princeton University Press
41 William Street, Princeton, New Jersey 08540
6 Oxford Street, Woodstock, Oxfordshire OX20 1TR

press.princeton.edu

All Rights Reserved

Library of Congress Cataloging-in-Publication Data

Names: Tharaud, Jerome, 1980– author. Title: Apocalyptic geographies : religion, media, and the American landscape, 1820–1860 / Jerome Tharaud.
Description: Princeton : Princeton University Press, 2020. | Includes bibliographical references and index. | Identifiers: LCCN 2019059666 (print) | LCCN 2019059667 (ebook) |
ISBN 9780691200101 (paperback) | ISBN 9780691200095 (hardcover) | ISBN 9780691203263 (epub)
Subjects: LCSH: American literature—19th century—History and criticism. | Apocalypse in literature. | Landscapes in literature. | Evangelicalism in literature. | Landscape painting, American—19th century. | Apocalypse in art. | Spirituality in art.
Classification: LCC PS217.A66 T43 2020 (print) | LCC PS217.A66 (ebook) | DDC 810.9/382—dc23
LC record available at https://lccn.loc.gov/2019059666
LC ebook record available at https://lccn.loc.gov/2019059667

British Library Cataloging-in-Publication Data is available

Editorial: Anne Savarese and Jenny Tan
Production Editorial: Debbie Tegarden
Text Design: Leslie Flis
Jacket/Cover Design: Leslie Flis
Production: Erin Suydam
Publicity: Alyssa Sanford and Katie Lewis

Jacket/Cover Credit: Frederic Edwin Church, *Cotopaxi*, 1862. Oil on canvas (48 × 85 in., 121.9 × 215.9 cm.), Detroit Institute of Arts Purchase 76.89.

This book has been composed in Arno

Printed on acid-free paper. ∞

Printed in the United States of America

10 9 8 7 6 5 4 3 2 1

For Rebecca, Marie, and Serena

CONTENTS

Illustrations ix
Acknowledgments xiii
Abbreviations xvii

Introduction   1

PART I. EVANGELICAL SPACE   27

1 Thomas Cole and the Landscape of Evangelical Print   29

2 Abolitionist Mediascapes: The American Anti-Slavery Society and the Sacred Geography of Emancipation   67

3 The Human Medium: Harriet Beecher Stowe and the *New-York Evangelist*   110

PART II. GEOGRAPHIES OF THE SECULAR   145

4 Pilgrimage to the "Secular Center": Tourism and the Sentimental Novel   147

5 Cosmic Modernity: Henry David Thoreau, the Missionary Memoir, and the Heathen Within   184

6 The Sensational Republic: Catholic Conspiracy and the Battle for the Great West   214

Epilogue   254

Notes 273
Selected Bibliography 321
Index 327

ILLUSTRATIONS

1. Frederic Edwin Church, *Twilight in the Wilderness* (1860)	8
2. Frederic Edwin Church, *The Heart of the Andes* (1859)	9
3. John Bunyan, *The Pilgrim's Progress* (185–?)	11
4. Jasper Francis Cropsey, *Starrucca Viaduct, Pennsylvania* (1865)	12
5. Detail of Frederic Edwin Church, *The Heart of the Andes* (1859)	13
6. Frederic Edwin Church, *New England Scenery* (1851)	14
7. Frederic Edwin Church, *Cotopaxi* (1862)	25
1.1. William James Bennett, *Niagara Falls* (1829)	30
1.2. Thomas Cole, *View from Mount Holyoke, Northampton, Massachusetts, after a Thunderstorm—The Oxbow* (1836)	31
1.3. Thomas Cole, *Expulsion from the Garden of Eden* (1828)	37
1.4. Detail of Thomas Cole, *View from Mount Holyoke*	38
1.5. John Martin, *Adam and Eve Driven out of Paradise* (1827)	39
1.6. Thomas Cole, *The Subsiding of the Waters of the Deluge* (1829)	40
1.7. Joseph Alexander Adams after J. G. Chapman, *Garden of Eden* (1846)	42
1.8. Detail of Thomas Cole, *View from Mount Holyoke*	44
1.9. Alexander Anderson, "I walked abroad alone"	47
1.10. Asher B. Durand after George Miller, American Tract Society Certificate (detail)	50
1.11. Abel Bowen, "Go Ye into All the World," *The Christian Almanack, for 1825* (1824)	51
1.12. Harvest scene, *The Family Christian Almanac* (1840)	52
1.13. Family reading, *Evangelical Family Library*	53
1.14. "The Warning Voice"	56
1.15. "The Life and Conversion of the Dairyman"	57

1.16. "The Seaman's Chart" — 58
2.1. "Printing Press," *Slave's Friend* (1838) — 80
2.2. "Consequences of Emancipation," *The American Anti-Slavery Almanac, for 1837* ([1836]) — 84
2.3. "The Fugitive Slave," *Slave's Friend* (1838) — 85
2.4. "Moral Map of U.S.," Julius Rubens Ames, *The Legion of Liberty!* (1844) — 86
2.5. Phillis Wheatley [and George Moses Horton], *Memoir and Poems of Phillis Wheatley, A Native African and a Slave* (1838) — 90
2.6. "St. Thomas and Antigua," *Slave's Friend* (1838) — 99
2.7. "An Emancipated Family," *The American Anti-Slavery Almanac, for 1836* ([1835]) — 100
2.8. Asher B. Durand, *Sunday Morning* (1839) — 101
2.9. "Emancipation, Ruin—Slavery, Salvation!!" *The American Anti-Slavery Almanac, for 1839* ([1838]) — 102
2.10. "My Country is the World; my Religion is to do good," Julius Rubens Ames, *The Legion of Liberty!* (1844) — 105
3.1. Hammatt Billings and Baker and Smith, *Little Eva Reading the Bible to Uncle Tom in the Arbor* (1852) — 133
3.2. Robert S. Duncanson, *Uncle Tom and Little Eva* (1853) — 134
3.3. George Cruikshank and William Measom, *Tom and Eva in the Arbour* (1852) — 135
4.1. Jasper Francis Cropsey, *Catskill Mountain House* (1855) — 148
4.2. Thomas Cole, *A View of the Two Lakes and Mountain House, Catskill Mountains, Morning* (1844) — 148
4.3. Jasper Francis Cropsey, *The Millennial Age* (1854) — 149
4.4. Detail of Jasper Francis Cropsey, *Catskill Mountain House* (1855) — 170
4.5. Detail of Jasper Francis Cropsey, *The Millennial Age* (1854) — 171
4.6. John Rubens Smith, *Catskill Mountain-House* (ca. 1830) — 181
5.1. William Channing Woodbridge, *Moral and Political Chart of the Inhabited World* (1835) — 186
5.2. "Memoir of Mrs. Harriet Newell, Wife of the Rev. Samuel Newell, Missionary to India" — 195
5.3. James Craig, gravestone of Harriet Ruggles Loomis (1861) — 196

6.1. Asher B. Durand, *Progress (The Advance of Civilization)* (1853)   215

6.2. Klauprecht & Menzel, *Cincinnati in 1841* (1841)   216

7.1. "An Apparent Success," Mark Twain, *The Innocents Abroad; or, The New Pilgrim's Progress* (1869)   261

7.2. Albert Bierstadt, *Yosemite Valley* (1868)   264

7.3. Albert Bierstadt, *Sunset in the Yosemite Valley* (1868)   265

Color Plates of Figures 1, 2, 7, 1.2, 3.2, 4.1, 7.2, and 7.3 follow page   130

ACKNOWLEDGMENTS

WORKING ON THIS BOOK has indebted me to many people and connected me to many places over the years, and it could not have been written without them.

At the University of Chicago, Bill Brown, Janice Knight, and Eric Slauter gave me a broad, eclectic education in American culture and helped me become the kind of scholar I wanted to be. Along the way Neil Harris fed my fascination with American landscapes, and W. Clark Gilpin and the other members of the American Religious History workshop taught me a great deal. The participants at the Newberry Library's seminar on art history and visual culture provided another intellectual home, welcoming me into their lively, interdisciplinary conversations. Gregory S. Jackson and Alan Wallach read versions of chapter 1 and offered feedback and encouragement.

At the University of Wisconsin-Madison, my colleagues in the English Department and the UW-Madison Center for the Humanities, including Monique Allewaert, Russ Castronovo, Susan Stanford Friedman, Sara Guyer, and the late Jeffrey Steele, as well as Jonathan Senchyne at the Center for the History of Print and Digital Culture, offered valuable feedback on portions of this project. The fellows and faculty participants of our monthly Mellon workshops offered thoughtful, engaged attention to portions of the manuscript. Trish Loughran persevered through a broken-down car and icy roads to join us as a guest respondent to an early draft of chapter 6; her insightful comments helped me to better articulate the main claims of that chapter. During my entire time in Madison, David Zimmerman was a kind and rigorous guiding presence, the best mentor any young scholar and teacher could ever ask for. I'm proud to call him a colleague and a friend.

My wonderful colleagues at Brandeis University not only gave me a warm welcome but offered encouragement and advice as I wrestled the manuscript into shape and looked for a publisher. John Plotz and Caren Irr gave excellent advice and guidance on both counts, and John Burt gave insightful feedback on chapter 2. Jordan Clapper, SarahGrace Gomez, and Miranda Peery were diligent research assistants. Maura Jane Farrelly, Dan Perlman, Elizabeth Ferry, and Brian Donahue provided mentorship and inspiration through their conversation, scholarship, and teaching. During the three summers I spent molding my material into a complete manuscript, I might have easily gone for days without speaking to another soul if not for the cheerful, skilled presence of Lisa Pannella, Rebecca Mahoney, and Leah Steele, who not only fielded countless questions and helped me navigate administrative and logistical hurdles but also were always willing to listen and to commiserate or celebrate with me. Wai Chee Dimock, David Morgan, and John Stauffer read the entire manuscript and came to campus for a daylong book workshop sponsored by the Brandeis Faculty Mentoring Program (planned with the help of Lisa Pannella and Carina Ray). Their feedback, meticulously transcribed by Jenny Factor, helped me revise the book and address some of its weaknesses. Those that remain, of course, are mine alone.

Several other institutions provided invaluable assistance along the way. The Andrew W. Mellon Foundation generously funded my research at two critical junctures through fellowships. The staffs at the University of Chicago Library, the Newberry Library, the New-York Historical Society, the Center for Research Libraries, the American Antiquarian Society, and the University Library at the University of Illinois at Urbana-Champaign, Elizabeth Burgess of the Harriet Beecher Stowe Center, Anthony Speiser of the Newington-Cropsey Foundation, and Ida Brier at the Olana Partnership graciously offered their time and expertise to help track down and digitize materials. At Princeton University Press, Anne Savarese patiently shepherded the manuscript through the review and publication process, and Jenny Tan fielded numerous questions about permissions and formatting with unfailing good humor. Earlier versions of chapters 1, 3, and 5 appeared in *American Art*, *Arizona Quarterly*, and *ESQ: A Journal of the American Renaissance*, respectively.

Finally, I want to extend thanks of a more personal nature. A small circle of generous friends has given me intellectual and moral support over the years and helped me think beyond the boundaries of my discipline: Paul Steinbeck, who dragged me to jazz clubs all over Chicago in our college years and whose mantra, taped to his dorm-room wall, I came to adopt as my own: "No more shit. Love and effort"; Aidan Johnson, who in graduate school introduced me to Stoicism and the work of Martha Nussbaum (among many other passions), and then had the courage to change course and pursue the active life to serve others; Ethan Jewett, whose conversations over Wisconsin beer on Thursday nights kept me grounded with an outsider's perspective on academia; Daegan Miller, who enlivened many runs through the arboretum in Madison with talk of trees, Thoreau, family, and much else—who helped me become a better writer and a better parent; Emily Warner and Will Selinger, who schlepped out to Waltham and Arlington to visit us all those times, who reminisced with us about Chicago, talked painting and politics and publishing, and took good care of our children. You have all challenged me and enlarged me, and I will always be grateful.

My parents, Barry Tharaud, Cynthia Harrison, and Robert Harrison, taught me to love books and ideas as much as they do and gave me my first real-world education in geography from the car window as we crisscrossed the continent from Colorado to New Jersey to Montana, and many places in between. My brothers John Harrison and Brian Harrison kept things fun along the way.

Most of all, I want to thank my wife, Rebecca, for her love and patience. This project began before we were married and has been with us through many moves and milestones, including the birth of our daughters. Willa Cather once said a book represents "cremated youth." Well, this one is mine—ours. Whatever light and warmth it gave is nothing compared to what you have given me.

ABBREVIATIONS

    A *American Anti-Slavery Almanac.*

  AASS American Anti-Slavery Society.

ABCFM American Board of Commissioners for Foreign Missions.

   ABS American Bible Society.

   ACS American Colonization Society.

    AJ James D. Knowles. *Memoir of Mrs. Ann H. Judson, Late Missionary to Burmah.* 3rd ed. Boston: Lincoln & Edmands, 1829.

    AR *Anti-Slavery Record.*

   ATS American Tract Society.

     C Henry David Thoreau. *The Correspondence of Henry David Thoreau.* Ed. Walter Harding and Carl Bode. New York: New York University Press, 1958.

    CB Charles Ball. *Slavery in the United States: A Narrative of the Life and Adventures of Charles Ball, A Black Man.* 1836. New York: John S. Taylor, 1837.

  CGW *Columbian & Great West.*

  CMW Emil Klauprecht. *Cincinnati; or, The Mysteries of the West.* Trans. Steven Rowan. Ed. Don Heinrich Tolzmann. 1854–55. New York: Peter Lang, 1996.

     E *Emancipator.*

   EWI James A. Thome and J. Horace Kimball. *Emancipation in the West Indies: A Six Months' Tour in Antigua, Barbadoes, and Jamaica, in the Year 1837.* New York: American Anti-Slavery Society, 1838.

   GW *Great West.*

   HN Leonard Woods. *A Sermon, Preached at Haverhill, (Mass.) in Remembrance of Mrs. Harriet Newell, Wife of the Rev. Samuel Newell, Missionary to India.* 4th ed. Boston: Samuel T. Armstrong, 1814.

HO [Edwin W. Dwight and] Henry Obookiah. *Memoirs of Henry Obookiah, A Native of Owhyhee, and a Member of the Foreign Mission School; who Died at Cornwall, Conn. Feb. 17, 1818 Aged 26 Years.* Philadelphia: American Sunday School Union, 1830.

HR *Human Rights.*

IA Mark Twain. *The Innocents Abroad; or, The New Pilgrim's Progress.* Hartford, CT: American Publishing Company, 1869.

IN William Apess. *Indian Nullification of the Unconstitutional Laws of Massachusetts Relative to the Mashpee Tribe; or, The Pretended Riot Explained.* In William Apess, *On Our Own Ground: The Complete Writings of William Apess, A Pequot*, ed. Barry O'Connell, 166–274. Amherst: University of Massachusetts Press, 1992.

J *The Journal of Henry D. Thoreau.* Ed. Bradford Torrey and Francis H. Allen. 14 vols. bound as 2. 1906. New York: Dover, 1962.

JTW [Susan DeWitt?], *Justina; or, The Will; A Domestic Story.* 2 vols. New York: Charles Wiley, 1823.

JW James Williams. *Narrative of James Williams, An American Slave.* New York: American Anti-Slavery Society, 1838.

KP William Apess. *Eulogy on King Philip, as Pronounced at the Odeon, in Federal Street, Boston.* In William Apess, *On Our Own Ground: The Complete Writings of William Apess, A Pequot*, ed. Barry O'Connell, 277–310. Amherst: University of Massachusetts Press, 1992.

L [Maria S. Cummins.] *The Lamplighter.* Boston: John P. Jewett, 1854.

LCB Angelina Grimké. *Letters to Catherine [sic] E. Beecher.* Boston: Isaac Knapp, 1838.

LIM Rebecca Harding Davis. "Life in the Iron-Mills." *Atlantic Monthly* (April 1861): 430–51.

ME William Ellis. *Memoir of Mrs. Mary Mercy Ellis, Wife of Rev. William Ellis, Missionary in the South Seas.* Boston: Crocker & Brewster, 1836.

MM [C. P. Bickley.] *The Mock Marriage; or, The Libertine's Victim: Being a Faithful Delineation of the Mysteries and Miseries of the Queen City.* Cincinnati: E. Mendenhall, [1855].

NY George Lippard. *New York: Its Upper Ten and Lower Million.* Cincinnati: H. M. Rulison. 1853.

NYE   *New-York Evangelist.*

PATS *Publications of the American Tract Society.*

PJ   Henry D. Thoreau. *Journal.* Ed. Elizabeth Hall Witherell et al. 8 vols. Princeton: Princeton University Press, 1981–2002.

PW   Phillis Wheatley [and George Moses Horton]. *Memoir and Poems of Phillis Wheatley, A Native African and a Slave; Also, Poems by a Slave.* 3rd ed. 1833. Boston, Isaac Knapp, 1838.

R   *Annual Report of the American Anti-Slavery Society.*

RI   Mark Twain. *Roughing It.* Hartford, CT: American Publishing Company, 1872.

RP   Henry D. Thoreau. *Reform Papers.* Ed. Wendell Glick. Princeton: Princeton University Press, 1973.

SF   *Slave's Friend.*

UTC   Harriet Beecher Stowe. *Uncle Tom's Cabin; or, Life among the Lowly.* 2 vols. Boston: John P. Jewett, 1852.

W   Henry D. Thoreau. *Walden.* Ed. J. Lyndon Shanley. 1854; Princeton: Princeton University Press, 1971.

WW   Elizabeth Wetherell [Susan Warner]. *The Wide, Wide World*, 2 vols. New York: George P. Putnam, 1851.

APOCALYPTIC GEOGRAPHIES

Introduction

BEGIN AT THE END.

In April 1861, the same month Confederate batteries opened fire on Fort Sumter, readers of the *Atlantic Magazine* found a story titled "Life in the Iron-Mills" that opens by asking, "Is this the end?"[1] From its epigraph to its final image of a carved korl woman pointing to the horizon where "God has set the promise of the Dawn" (*LIM*, 451), Rebecca Harding Davis's story telegraphs its concern with last things. After the Welsh iron-mill worker Hugh Wolfe dies, his korl sculpture's lips "seem to tremble with a terrible question. 'Is this the End?' they say,—'nothing beyond?'" (450). Davis even suggested to the magazine's assistant editor, James T. Fields, changing the title to "Beyond" in order to convey "the subdued meaning of the story," amplifying this apocalyptic motif and its inscription onto physical space.[2] But Fields put his foot down, selecting the title that would cement the story's reputation as a bellwether of realism and a repudiation of an antebellum religious and literary world that to many later critics seemed as obsolete in industrial America as the smoke-begrimed "little broken figure of an angel pointing upward from the mantelshelf" (430).[3] Like some relic displaced from Little Eva's bedroom, the angel seems to signal that in this emerging modern world, there will be no triumphant deathbed scenes offering glimpses of heaven—just "the End" with "nothing beyond."

Fields's editorial control over the story's title and his censorship of a crucial passage in which a working-class Christ appears before Wolfe suppressed the religious dimensions of the text, essentially turning "Life in the Iron-Mills" into a document of American secularization.[4] Yet as scholars have shown, Davis's engagement with debates over the role of Protestant churches in confronting urban poverty and labor strife persists in the text's religious imagery, biblical allusions, and narrative structure.[5] The most fundamental medium of the story's religious imagination, however, lies not in these diegetic elements but in its setting—in the incandescent, spiritually charged spaces the characters look and move through. Most spectacular is the hellscape that Hugh's cousin, Deborah, observes as she approaches the mill:

> Fire in every horrible form: pits of flame waving in the wind; liquid metal-flames writhing in tortuous streams through the sand; wide caldrons filled with boiling fire, over which bent ghastly wretches stirring the strange brewing; and through all, crowds of half-clad men, looking like revengeful ghosts in the red light, hurried, throwing masses of glittering fire. It was like a street in Hell. (*LIM*, 433)

Balancing this infernal vision is the sunset Hugh first sees reflected in the river, "a glimpse of another world than this." Lifting his gaze, the picture "became strangely real," as "overhead, the sun-touched smoke-clouds opened like a cleft ocean,—shifting, rolling seas of crimson mist, waves of billowy silver veined with blood-scarlet, inner depths unfathomable of glancing light. Wolfe's artist-eye grew drunk with color. The gates of that other world!" (444). Finally there is the glowing landscape across the river that a kind Quaker woman points out to Deborah through the window of the jail cell where Hugh lies dead. Likened to "the hills of heaven," where "the light lies warm . . . and the winds of God blow all the day" (450), the Quaker settlement that becomes Hugh's final resting place and Deborah's home wavers between an earthly place and an eschatological promise. From hellish industrial scenes to heavenly pastoral landscapes, space is the primary means through which Davis's text activates readers' apocalyptic imagination, their sense of what lies beyond this world. Such use of represented space by a variety of writers and artists in the antebellum United States in order to visualize Christian sacred history—the vast arc of God's plot of redemption from the Creation to the Last Judgment narrated in the Bible—and ultimately to make moral claims on their audiences is central to what this book terms apocalyptic geographies.

While those spaces are just as likely to express hopeful, millennial visions as they are to prophesy catastrophe, they can be considered apocalyptic in the word's literal sense (derived from the Greek *apokalypsis*) as an "unveiling" or "uncovering."[6] In the genre of apocalyptic texts that includes the Book of Daniel (ca. 164 BCE), the Book of Revelation (ca. 90 CE), and the Persian *Bundahishn* (1000–1100 CE), an angel or other supernatural being offers a vision that reveals "a transcendent world of supernatural powers and an eschatological scenario, or view of the last things, that includes the judgment of the dead." Though in popular usage apocalypse typically connotes the end of the world, John J. Collins notes that apocalypses "are not exclusively concerned with the future" but "may also be concerned with cosmology, including the geography of the heavens and nether regions as well as history, primordial times, and the end times."[7] An apocalyptic geography in this sense refers to the cosmic architecture revealed through a supernatural vision—whether the relationship of Earth to heaven and hell or one particular site within that cosmography—that functions to convey and reinforce a particular narrative of sacred history.

Nineteenth-century Americans typically used the word "apocalypse" to refer not to an event but to a single text: the Book of Revelation, also known as the Apocalypse of John.[8] But given the distinctive configuration of space and time that Michael E. Vines calls the "apocalyptic chronotope"—the "temporal and spatial unboundedness" that enables "a God's-eye view on human history and activity"—a number of antebellum literary texts can be understood to participate in the apocalyptic tradition.[9] Indeed, as Douglas Robinson has argued, not only can major works by Emerson, Poe, Melville, and others be considered apocalypses, but "the whole question of the apocalyptic ideology, of the historical transformation of space and time from old to new, from corruption to new innocence, from death to rebirth, is fundamental to American literature."[10] This highlights a second meaning of apocalyptic geography: just as for antebellum Americans an "apocalypse" meant not primarily a cataclysmic event but a particular kind of text, Martin Brückner has argued that in early America and well into the nineteenth century, "geography" referred not only to the physical structure of the Earth but to "a broadly defined genre consisting of many vibrant textual forms: property plats and surveying manuals, decorative wall maps and magazine maps, atlases and geography textbooks, flash cards and playing cards, paintings and needlework samplers."[11] An apocalyptic geography in this sense refers to a text—a geography—that "purport[s] to unveil to human beings secrets hitherto known only in heaven."[12]

To recognize "Life in the Iron-Mills" as animated by a pervasive form of religious spatial imagination at work in antebellum culture is to restore it to an archive of apocalyptic geographies threaded through American literary history and beyond. It is to register, for instance, the long shadow of Harriet Beecher Stowe's *Uncle Tom's Cabin* (1852), in which Tom and Eva (like Hugh) witness the "sea of glass, mingled with fire" described in the Book of Revelation reflected in the waters of Lake Pontchartrain, and the gates of the "new Jerusalem" in the sunset clouds; and in which Eliza (like Deborah) finds a vision of "Paradise" in a Quaker settlement across the Ohio River.[13] So too, it is to recognize Davis's debt to more obscure figures like Presbyterian minister and social reformer George Barrell Cheever, whose sensational 1835 temperance tale "Inquire at Amos Giles' Distillery" takes place in a rum distillery that glows as if "one of the chambers of hell had been transported to earth, with all its inmates."[14] Reaching back further, it is to find echoes of the Oriental tales that filled eighteenth-century American magazines, in which angelic guides lead protagonists to mountaintops or other heavenly perches where the universe (and typically the errors of Calvinist orthodoxy) can be encompassed at a glance.[15] Further still, it is to recognize in the iron mill not only, as the overseer Kirby and his privileged guests do, an image of "Dante's Inferno" (436) but also the ancient tradition that stretches behind it, back through the Revelation of John and the Jewish apocalyptic books to the "Underworld Vision of an Assyrian Crown Prince," the seventh century BCE Neo-Assyrian text that scholars consider the "oldest known visionary journey to hell."[16] So while "Life in the Iron-Mills" represents a seminal moment in what Gregory S. Jackson has termed "the spiritualization of American realism"—the seed of the "spiritual sight" that will become literalized in a multimedia text like Jacob Riis's *How the Other Half Lives* (1890)—the story might just as accurately be captioned as the materialization of American sentimentalism, or the fictionalization of Protestant evangelicalism—or the modernization of apocalypse.[17]

The historical and global reach of literary apocalypse lends itself to the enlargement of perspective that Wai Chee Dimock calls "deep time," in which literature breaks free of the confines of national history and continental geography and becomes "a crisscrossing set of pathways, open-ended and ever multiplying, weaving in and out of other geographies, other languages and cultures" across "millennia."[18] For the Protestant evangelicals who are the focus of this book, apocalyptic time enabled a way of imagining modern social life distinct both from the "homogenous, empty time" that Benedict Anderson associates with the "imagined communities" of the modern nation-state and from the corresponding secular conception of geopolitical space that emerged with the Treaty of Westphalia in 1648, which Elizabeth Maddock Dillon notes "sought to replace an earlier map of the world on which religion, rather than the sovereign state, served as the organizing principle for grasping the globe in its entirety."[19] Indeed, for many antebellum Protestants, apocalyptic expectation (including optimistic forms that anticipated a peaceful earthly millennium) became the primary lens for understanding the emerging form of modernity known today as globalization.

Even as the apocalyptic imagination dislodges texts like "Life in the Iron-Mills" from secular time and space and highlights "imagined spiritual communities" beyond the nation, its multisensory and above all visual mode of expression bursts the bounds of print itself and restores the literary to a broader field of religious media.[20] The traditional manifestation of apocalyptic revelation in visions encouraged a number of antebellum painters including Thomas Cole, Asher B. Durand, Frederic Edwin Church, Robert S. Duncanson, and Jasper Francis Cropsey to explore apocalyptic themes in works that depict scenes from scripture as well as volcanic eruptions and other cataclysmic geological phenomena.[21] Other artists went further, translating sacred history into immersive multimedia spectacles. In New York and elsewhere, audiences flocked to "sacred dioramas" of *The Creation of the World* and *The*

Deluge, attractions that combined painted scenes with light and sound effects, and sometimes mechanical figures.[22] In the 1830s, visitors to the Infernal Regions exhibition at the Western Museum in Cincinnati found themselves transported to Dante's Inferno, where they confronted some thirty life-size wax figures carved by the sculptor Hiram Powers and presided over by a giant mechanical Beelzebub.[23] Like the texts they evoked, these spectacles purported to disclose a realm beyond appearances, enabling viewers to perceive the material world as embedded in a larger cosmic framework. In short, in Davis's America (as in our own) learning to think apocalyptically meant thinking not just about disasters or the end of the world but about media: the medium of scripture, the penumbra of printed texts and images emanating from it, popular visual media, and matter itself—nature, the body, the land—as conduits through which sacred power passes into the world. In the fullest sense, then, an apocalyptic geography is more than a vision of cosmic space and more than a text that reveals that vision: it encompasses the entire media system in which such visions and texts circulate.

Apocalyptic Geographies studies the relationship of religious media and the landscape in the antebellum United States in order to rethink the meaning of space in American culture. As it traverses a range of genres and media including sermons, landscape paintings, aesthetic treatises, abolitionist newspapers, slave narratives, novels, and grave markers, it traces the birth of a distinctly modern form of sacred space at the nexus of mass print culture, the physical spaces of an expanding and urbanizing nation, and the religious images and narratives that ordinary Americans used to orient their lives. The book's central case study investigates the efforts of Protestant evangelical publishing societies to teach readers to use the landscape to understand their own spiritual lives and their role in sacred history. This "evangelical space," I argue in the first part of the book, ultimately spread beyond devotional culture to infuse popular literature, art, and politics by the 1850s; in turn it was appropriated, challenged, and parodied in several major secular print cultures that are the focus of the book's later chapters.

For an earlier generation of Americanists, the phrase "American space" likely conjured up images of Puritans carving settlements out of the "wilderness" or Leatherstocking passing from the forest onto the prairie; for scholars today it might evoke a cosmopolitan *letrado* embarking from Cuba to New York or a slave ship plying the "black Atlantic."[24] *Apocalyptic Geographies* showcases a different set of spaces: painters contemplating creation from mountaintop hotels; slaves kneeling in Caribbean churches to await the Jubilee of emancipation; Native and white families gathered around religious newspapers on the shores of the Great Lakes; Protestant missionary women in Asia writing memoirs about their journeys; Jesuit priests watching cathedral spires rise in the heart of the Mississippi Valley. By foregrounding such scenes, I argue that the landscape meant more than physical territory to be conquered or new markets to be exploited: it signified an arena of intense spiritual longing and struggle that was shaped decisively by religious media. Indeed, the land was itself a medium through which antebellum Americans looked to see the state of their souls and the fate of the world unveiled.

As it explores these spaces, *Apocalyptic Geographies* intervenes in several scholarly conversations. It recontextualizes studies of antebellum print culture by Trish Loughran, Meredith L. McGill, and others to emphasize the ways many Americans understood print not simply as a secular medium connecting (or dividing) an expanding republic but as a sacred conduit linking a community of believers spread across time and space to each other and to God. In the process it highlights a religious dimension often missing from the various transatlantic, hemispheric, and global reframings of American literature that have emerged as part of the "spatial turn" of the last two decades.[25] I argue that the "literary geographies" mapped by scholars including Brückner, Paul Giles, and Hsuan L. Hsu can be deepened by attending both to theories of sacred space and to the study of what cultural geographers call "moral geographies," or the ways people invest particular places and landscapes with value and map moral categories and conceptions of obligation onto physical space.[26] Finally, because of the importance of landscape as a medium of spiritual vision in antebellum America, this book seeks to add nuance to critical scholarship that sees landscape representation chiefly as an expression of expansionist political desire—what Angela Miller calls "the empire of the eye."[27] Running alongside that imperial vision, at times reinforcing it and at others ignoring or even resisting it, runs a tradition of using the landscape to imagine new forms of selfhood, community, and agency suited to the modern world.

The remainder of this introduction provides an overview of a few key concepts that anchor the chapters that follow. First I relate landscape to geography through the concept of "mediascapes." Next turning to accounts of American sacred space, I use the work of cultural geographers, spatial theorists, and scholars of religion to lay the groundwork for understanding the modern form of sacred space produced by religious media. I conclude by sketching a map of the rest of the book.

Excavating Sacred Mediascapes

In nineteenth-century America the landscape told many stories. It told of the rise of a vast continental empire; of a market economy shouldering aside traditional patterns of production, consumption, and exchange; of dizzying advances in transportation and communication that prompted one midcentury observer to marvel that "fifty years ago, there were no steamboats, no locomotives, no railroads, and no magnetic telegraph. Now time and space are absolutely annihilated."[28] By registering such momentous changes (even if by concealing or distorting them) the landscape—understood both as the physical environment perceived and shaped by humans and as the representation of that environment in words and pictures—helped narrate the emergence of the modern world. But the landscape told other stories as well, ones scholars are less likely to recognize as modern. For many Americans it told of a cosmic struggle between good and evil, and the diffusion of the Gospel around the globe; it told of the individual's spiritual quest to find God and the attempt to make sense of suffering; most dramatically it heralded the dawn of a millennial age when the enslaved would go free and warned of an impending day of doom when God would return to punish the wicked. These were stories in which the annihilation of space and time took on a different meaning: apocalyptic stories.

For much of the twentieth century this latter group of stories seemed to many observers in the West poised to wither away before the advance of a more enlightened, secular age. But in recent decades, thanks to a resurgent Protestant evangelicalism in Africa and the Americas and the global spread of radical Islamist ideologies, the holes in that secularization narrative have become glaringly apparent. We now live in what some scholars call a "postsecular age," one in which the accounts that Charles Taylor calls "subtraction stories"—triumphalist narratives of the gradual emancipation of humankind from religious dogma—no longer seem convincing.[29] In a new millennium convulsed by climate crisis and religious conflict, as apocalyptic futures increasingly grip the public imagination, it is perhaps this second group of stories that we most urgently need to understand.

When Hugh Wolfe beholds that otherworldly sunset with his "artist-eye," he enacts a form of spiritualized landscape perception that had been cultivated in the United States since the 1820s through numerous popular media forms, from paintings and sermons to novels and moving panoramas.[30] For the more than 100,000 largely middle-class *Atlantic* readers who encountered Davis's story in 1861—a readership centered in New England but extending to London, the Midwest, and California—the most prominent nodes in this media network were undoubtedly the spectacular "Great Pictures" of Frederic Church, the most popular landscape painter in the nation.[31] Inspired by the success of British painter John Martin's *Last Judgment* triptych when it was exhibited in New York in 1856, Church launched a series of single-painting exhibitions on both sides of the Atlantic in the late 1850s and early 1860s that translated Martin's apocalyptic vision into a naturalistic idiom.[32] As audiences flocked, opera glasses in hand, to see Church's huge, gemlike canvases, they

FIGURE 0.1. Frederic Edwin Church, *Twilight in the Wilderness*, 1860. Oil on canvas, 40 × 64 in. (101.6 × 162.6 cm). The Cleveland Museum of Art, Mr. and Mrs. William H. Marlatt Fund, 1965.233.

encountered pyrotechnic sunsets drenched in carmine and cadmium yellow in works like *Twilight in the Wilderness* (1860), luminous depictions of the divinely ordered processes of creation and destruction in tropical landscapes like *The Heart of the Andes* (1859) and *Cotopaxi* (1862), and anxious meditations on political crisis in arctic scenes such as *The North (The Icebergs)* (1861) and *The Aurora Borealis* (1865).

Viewers had plenty of help deciphering what they were seeing. In pamphlets and broadsides distributed at the exhibitions as well as published art reviews and sermons delivered in nearby churches, art critics, ministers, and other arbiters of taste interpreted Church's canvases as visualizations of sacred history and dramatizations of personal spiritual life. In 1860 the *New York Albion* described *Twilight in the Wilderness* (fig. 0.1; see plate 1) in terms that anticipate Wolfe's sunset prospect: "the heavens are a-blaze," the reviewer wrote, as "the clouds sweep up in flaming arcs, broadening and breaking toward the zenith, where they fret the deep azure with the dark golden glory." Where this reviewer used lush description to evoke a "natural apocalypse" (in David C. Huntington's words), others invited viewers into Church's pictures, immersing them in spiritually charged moral landscapes.[33] Writing in the *Christian Intelligencer*, New York Presbyterian minister Theodore Ledyard Cuyler described *The Heart of the Andes* (fig. 0.2; see plate 2) as a spiritual allegory that visualized John Bunyan's *The Pilgrim's Progress* (1678), in which the hero, Christian,

FIGURE 0.2. Frederic Edwin Church, *The Heart of the Andes*, 1859. Oil on canvas, 66⅛ × 119¼ in. (168 × 302.9 cm). The Metropolitan Museum of Art, bequest of Mrs. David Dows, 1909.95.

undertakes a perilous journey from the "City of Destruction" to the "Celestial City," encountering obstacles like the "hill Difficulty" along the way.[34] "The 'Heart of the Andes' is a picture for young men," Cuyler wrote. "It is luxuriant in rapid growths. It has a glassy river flowing on under o'er-arching verdure until it plunges over a precipice—an allegory of the sensualist's career." Noting the "flashing peak of alabaster brightness in the far-away distance, which recalls the Apocalyptic visions of heaven," Cuyler urged "the aspiring youth who gazes at this matchless picture [to] bear in mind that it is only he who spurns the seductive waves of temptation, and bravely masters the 'Hills of Difficulty' for Christ's sake, that shall yet make good his entrance to the golden glories of the New Jerusalem."[35] Cuyler's mapping of Bunyan's great Puritan allegory onto Church's tour-de-force of naturalistic observation might seem farfetched until we recall that Church himself painted two scenes from *The Pilgrim's Progress* in the late 1840s and contributed a design to a moving panorama based on the book in 1850.[36] More to the point is the way Cuyler uses print media to fuse the picture's exotic setting with an evangelical literary text in order to visualize the spiritual development of an assumed white male viewer, in effect transforming a Catholic landscape into a Protestant spiritual medium, what Rebecca Bedell calls "a tropical version of *Pilgrim's Progress*."[37]

Viewers who saw *The Heart of the Andes* in any of the eight U.S. cities where it toured between October 1859 and May 1861 would have encountered similar messages.[38] They might have heard the Rev. Z. M. Humphrey of the First Presbyterian Church in Chicago compare navigating the uneven terrain of *The Heart of the Andes* to the increasingly strenuous stages of an individual's

"Christian progress," from "the Cross" to the banks of "the River of Life," and on toward "the unreached summits of human perfection which are still infinitely below the absolute perfection of the heavenly world."[39] They might have heard the Rev. Dr. Richard Newton, in a sermon delivered at St. Paul's (Episcopal) Church in Philadelphia, use the painting as an object lesson in how to contemplate the lives of great biblical figures (in this case the Old Testament character of Abigail), telling listeners that the details were "the episodes of the painting, and you must take them into the account before you can do justice to it as a whole."[40] They might have even heard the famous Congregationalist minister Henry Ward Beecher declare from his Brooklyn pulpit that "it was a sin for any man in the country to miss seeing Church's Heart of the Andes, when it could be inspected for twenty-five cents."[41]

As Protestant ministers used landscape paintings as visual aids to bring home the realities of sin and salvation, their audiences brought the landscape home in a literal sense, not only in engravings like the one William Forrest produced of *The Heart of the Andes* in 1862 (ensuring that prints of the painting could be found hanging in parlors across the country) but in the books they read.[42] The title page of an American Tract Society (ATS) edition of *The Pilgrim's Progress* (fig. 0.3) from the 1850s that depicts Christian kneeling against a backdrop of conical peaks that bear a striking resemblance to Church's Andes signals just how intimate and self-reinforcing the association between landscape imagery, print, and Protestant piety had become. When the ATS used the same image to illustrate a Dakota translation of Bunyan's allegory in 1858, it demonstrated how evangelical fervor to spread that sacred landscape could conspire with colonial designs to appropriate physical territory.[43] While art historians have traced the transatlantic itineraries of Church's paintings and literary scholars have charted the "transnational circulation" of texts like *The Pilgrim's Progress* to illuminate the global contours of the "evangelical Protestant public sphere," bringing those objects together highlights another form of mobility: how spatial images and narratives move across media to create vivid imagined landscapes where viewers could rehearse their own spiritual journeys.[44]

Jennifer L. Roberts has argued that pictures in the late eighteenth and nineteenth centuries "register the complications of their own transmission" across physical space through the pictorial language deployed within the frame: in her words, "geography *inhabits* pictures rather than simply surrounding them."[45] *The Heart of the Andes*, with its transatlantic and continental itineraries, might seem to epitomize the spectatorial economy Roberts describes, yet the picture itself presents a puzzle. Unlike contemporary Hudson River School paintings that depict transportation and communications technologies integrated harmoniously into pastoral landscapes, from the canal and telegraph

THE
PILGRIM'S PROGRESS
FROM

THIS WORLD TO THAT WHICH IS TO COME;

DELIVERED

UNDER THE SIMILITUDE OF A DREAM.

BY JOHN BUNYAN.

PUBLISHED BY THE
AMERICAN TRACT SOCIETY,
150 NASSAU-STREET, NEW YORK

FIGURE 0.3. John Bunyan, *The Pilgrim's Progress, from This World to That Which Is to Come; Delivered Under the Similitude of a Dream* (1678; New York: American Tract Society, [185–?]), title page. The University Library, University of Illinois at Urbana-Champaign.

poles that lead the eye toward a glorious future on the horizon in Asher B. Durand's *Progress (The Advance of Civilization)* (1853) (see fig. 6.1) to the graceful parallel curve of river and railroad in Jasper Francis Cropsey's *Starrucca Viaduct* (1865) (fig. 0.4), Church's composition permits no such smooth navigation. The rocky falls in the middle ground impose a barrier that denies any upstream passage. Likewise, the footpath in the left foreground beckons the viewer into the picture, leading to the shrine where two pilgrims have stopped

FIGURE 0.4. Jasper Francis Cropsey (American, 1823–1900), *Starrucca Viaduct, Pennsylvania*, 1865. Oil on canvas, 22⅜ × 36⅜ in. (56.8 × 92.4 cm). Toledo Museum of Art (Toledo, Ohio). Purchased with funds from the Florence Scott Libbey Bequest in Memory of her Father, Maurice A. Scott, 1947.58.

to pray (fig. 0.5); once there, the white cross directs the eye toward a church basking in the well-lit pastoral upland, but the overgrown bank of trees descending from the left interrupts the visual trail, rendering the route uncertain. Instead of depicting travelers moving parallel to the picture plane across bodies of water as he had done in *Hooker and Company Journeying through the Wilderness in 1636 from Plymouth to Hartford* (1846) and *New England Scenery* (1851) (fig. 0.6), here Church has scooped out the foreground and emphasized the chasm with the perilously overhanging cluster of trees on the right side. Paradoxically, this most mobile of paintings arrests the viewer's movement through its lush inner geography at every turn.

Yet if *The Heart of the Andes* fails to "register the complications of [its] own transmission" in Roberts's sense, a kind of "geography" nonetheless "*inhabits*" the picture. Clearly many viewers did find a form of transit enacted there, one in which the plunge of the young "sensualist" into perdition was of greater concern than the passage to London and the way to the "New Jerusalem" was more real than the road to Chicago. Here the spatial challenges famously posed by the picture—the physical ordeal of navigating Andean terrain to produce a composite view of an entire region (as Church and Alexander von Humboldt before him had done), the aesthetic task of integrating the painting's obsessive detail into a harmonious whole—converge with Protestant eschatological imperatives: completing the individual Christian pilgrimage toward the New

FIGURE 0.5. Detail of Frederic Edwin Church, *The Heart of the Andes*, 1859. Oil on canvas, 66⅛ × 119¼ in. (168 × 302.9 cm). The Metropolitan Museum of Art, bequest of Mrs. David Dows, 1909.95.

Jerusalem and contemplating the sweep of sacred history from Edenic lowland to apocalyptic peak.[46] The transit dramatized in Church's canvas, in other words, is through *sacred* geography, the collection of holy places (some historical, others mythological) referenced in the Bible and other religious texts that provides the setting where dramas of individual and collective salvation play out.

The interplay of physical and spiritual itineraries in *The Heart of the Andes* epitomizes the confluence of two distinct forms of space in antebellum America: the sacred geographies Protestants had long used to chart their spiritual journeys within the unfolding design of sacred history, and the emerging modern spaces of a globalizing capitalist economy and an expanding nation. That is, in addition to mediating modernity's "horizontal" networks—the uneven spread of goods, people, and information across the Earth's surface—the landscape facilitated "vertical" circuits, connecting people to powers and realities

FIGURE 0.6. Frederic Edwin Church, *New England Scenery*, 1851. Oil on canvas, 36 × 53 in. (91.4 × 134.6 cm). George Walter Vincent Smith Art Museum, Springfield, Massachusetts. George Walter Vincent Smith Collection. Photography by David Stansbury.

they conceived to exceed the earthly realm. The concept of a "mediascape" is particularly useful for capturing this dual process of mediation. As defined by anthropologist Arjun Appadurai, the term refers both to the material media networks used to "produce and disseminate information" and to "the images of the world created by these media."[47] In this case, the antebellum mediascape encompassed the network of magazines, newspapers, books, churches, exhibition halls, and art galleries through which words and images were disseminated *and* the verbal and visual landscape images disseminated through those media. While the concept thus helps relate the material and representational dimensions of modern media, several scholars of religion have adapted Appadurai's taxonomy of "scapes" (a suffix intended to convey the cultural instability and disjunction wrought by globalization) as a model for thinking about the role of religion within globalizing modernity.[48] What Thomas A. Tweed terms "sacroscapes" represent "*religious* flows" that enable not only "*terrestrial*" and "*corporeal crossings*" through physical space but also "*cosmic crossings*" that transport believers across "the ultimate horizon of human life." "Religions," Tweed explains, "travel vertically back and forth between transcendence and immanence. They bring the gods to earth and transport the faithful to the heavens. And they move horizontally, back and forth in social space."[49]

One example of such a religious mediascape is the "ethical soundscape" analyzed by anthropologist Charles Hirschkind, who argues that the circulation of cassette sermons through the Middle East beginning in the Islamic Revival of the 1970s had the effect of "reconfiguring urban space acoustically through the use of Islamic media forms." Hirschkind describes the experience of riding in a Cairo taxi as the words of the *khatib* (preacher) coming through the speakers mixes with the beat of Western pop music percolating in from the street, the visual blare of passing billboards and storefronts, and the canny commentary of fellow passengers. The cassette sermon is significant, Hirschkind argues, not primarily for the theologies or ideologies it inculcates but because of "its effect on the human sensorium, on the affects, sensibilities, and perceptual habits of its vast audience."[50]

Despite its radically different historical and cultural context, *Apocalyptic Geographies* charts a similarly vibrant confluence of traditional and modern, a mediascape in which the Word spilled out of churches and into packed exhibition halls where crowds gawked at spectacular Holy Land panoramas and biblical paintings, and mass-produced Bibles and tracts were carried by pious volunteers through city streets and backwoods settlements. Caught up in their own wave of religious revivals, antebellum Americans experienced a religious mediascape that shaped the human sensorium in equally dramatic ways. But this one privileged vision as a tool for living a Christian life in the modern world. Protestants who practiced the discipline of devout looking that David Morgan terms "visual piety" carved out an alternative to the secular "scopic regime" that equated vision with Enlightenment, imperial control, and the "instrumental rationality" of modern science.[51] In doing so they contributed to a counter-Enlightenment project of cultivating the "spiritual senses" that engaged a diverse range of believers on both sides of the Atlantic.[52] Those senses included hearing as well as the kinesthetic sense of moving through physical space. But vision took special prominence, as a Protestant tradition of spiritual sight rooted in the eighteenth-century revivalism of Jonathan Edwards intersected with the rise of mass visual culture in which, in Michael Leja's words, "a world in which pictures were rare and remarkable began to give way to one permeated by them."[53]

Given W. J. T. Mitchell's axiom that landscape is "a medium" that facilitates "exchange between the human and the natural, the self and the other," it is no surprise that the landscape emerged as a privileged nexus within this religious mediascape.[54] As a visual medium (even when evoked through language), landscape deals with what can be seen; geography, by contrast, describes a spatial order that exceeds immediate perception. But in the nineteenth century, landscape art often aspired to transcend the limits of the senses and provide access to those encompassing realities—in essence to become a form of geography. Whether that meant using a landscape painting to represent the nation, Humboldt's cosmos, or the Christian universe, the landscape became a medium between the senses and geography. It became a tool for thinking across geographical scale, for linking regional, national, global, and cosmic spaces. For Protestants who learned to use the landscape as a tool for what geographers term "cognitive mapping"—mentally orienting oneself within one's spatial environment—modernity's horizontal and vertical itineraries converged in spectacular moments of vision that carried viewers beyond their immediate experience in multiple senses.[55] Restoring landscapes to the religious mediascape in which audiences encountered them—learning to read them not only as meditations on physical mobility but as maps for spiritual transit—is crucial to understanding the new form of sacred space that antebellum evangelicals created.

Evangelicals and the Production of American Sacred Space

Many accounts of how Americans "sacralized the landscape"—made it holy—focus on churches and other religious buildings.[56] Historians have traced the proliferation of Anglican churches in colonial Virginia, the transformation of New England Congregationalist meetinghouses into steepled churches, the construction (and destruction) of Roman Catholic cathedrals and convents during the antebellum period, and the rise of auditorium-style churches during the same years to house a new generation of Protestant revivalists.[57] Other scholars have broadened the frame to consider an array of natural and built landscapes that communities have constructed (and contested) as sacred, including mountains, battlefields, national parks, and even amusement parks.[58] At its most capacious, this conception of sacred space encompasses the entire continent, as a Puritan tradition of projecting the biblical Holy Land onto New World terrain grounds exceptionalist tropes of "redeemer nation" and Promised Land that continue to echo in the national imagination to this day.[59] The diversity of scope, scale, and definition on display in such accounts has led one scholar to declare "a renaissance" of sacred space, and another to argue that the concept has become so capacious and "politicized" that it has "los[t] its value as an analytical category" and should be abandoned altogether.[60]

Despite their differences, nearly all of these accounts emphasize contiguous physical spaces. But as geographer David Harvey points out, space is not limited to the "absolute space" of buildings and national territory—physical spaces demarcated by "bounded territorial designations."[61] It also includes the "relative space-time" generated as transportation and communication networks warp the rational, Cartesian order of absolute space into new configurations of proximity and distance. And it includes the "relational spacetime" that occurs when space is absorbed in the mind and infused with "dreams, daydreams, memories, and fantasies."[62] In antebellum America, a period often narrated in terms of the triumph of absolute space (reflected in the extension of the Jeffersonian survey grid and the consolidation of national territory), people experienced modern space in all three forms. In 1835, from his post as president of Lane Theological Seminary near Cincinnati, prominent evangelical minister Lyman Beecher marveled at the relative space-time taking shape around him in "the West," where as a result of "24,000 miles of steam navigation, and canals and rail roads, a market is brought near to every man, and the whole is brought into near neighborhood":

> When I perceived the active intercourse between the great cities, like the rapid circulation of a giant's blood; and heard merchants speak of just stepping up to Pittsburgh—only 600 miles—and back in a few days; and others just from New Orleans, or St. Louis, or the Far West; and others going thither; and when I heard my ministerial brethren negotiating exchanges in the near neighborhood—only 100 miles up or down the river—and going and returning on Saturday and Monday, and without trespassing on the Sabbath;—then did I perceive how God, who seeth the end from the beginning, had prepared the West to be mighty, and still wieldable, that the moral energy of his word and spirit might take it up as a very little thing.

Not only does Beecher reveal how steam travel was changing people's lived experience of American geography, but his fusion of that networked landscape with postmillennial eschatology—a prevalent form of sacred history that held that God was working through human means to usher in the 1,000-year period of peace and prosperity prophesied in scripture—turns the Mississippi Valley into a sacred spacetime in which Protestants are summoned to unite behind a common mission to "evangelize the world." While such "providential developments" convince Beecher of the truth of Jonathan Edwards's prediction that "the millennium would commence in America," he warns that European immigration threatens that prospect, setting the stage for an impending battle of Catholic "superstition" and "despotism" versus "evangelical light" and "liberty."[63] In short, the sacred space that Beecher and his clerical brethren helped create was not limited to the churches where they ministered; rather, their spoken and printed words generated a more expansive apocalyptic geography by assembling a dispersed community of devout listeners and readers and transforming the Mississippi Valley into the setting of a "cosmic drama" in which the fate of the West, the nation, and the world hung in the balance.[64]

Then as now, evangelicalism was a vibrant religious movement characterized by considerable denominational, regional, and racial diversity but united by a common theology "characterized by a stress on conversion, the Bible as supreme religious authority, activism manifest especially in efforts to spread the Christian message, and a focus on Christ's death on the cross as the defining reality of Christian faith."[65] This book focuses on a small but influential subset of that movement: the highly literate, largely middle-class Congregationalists and Presbyterians like Beecher who dominated the interdenominational voluntary associations that arose in the 1820s in the Northeast to promote causes such as Bible distribution, foreign missions, temperance, and eventually abolitionism. In Mark Noll's terms, these evangelicals were "formalists" (they retained greater respect for order and institutions than "antiformalists" like Methodists and Baptists who stressed "spiritual liberty"), predominantly northern white men and women whose leadership of the Benevolent Empire helped sustain the explosive growth of evangelical churches that occurred between the 1780s and the Civil War.[66]

This group, which included preachers, artists, reformers, novelists, editors, and publishers, illuminates the encounter between traditional Protestant sacred geographies and the emerging spaces of modern America. Not only did these evangelicals possess a rich tradition of sacred geography drawn from the Puritan past; they also proved adept at using modern methods to spread their message, combining technologies such as steam presses, stereotypography, and new forms of illustration.[67] In the process they adapted a number of traditional Christian topoi (formulaic images that recur across media and through time) and narratives to interpret the modern world taking shape around them.[68] That world included a capitalist economy rooted in industrial methods of exploiting land and labor, virulent forms of racial hatred and violence, newly popular modes of cultural expression, and an emerging mass media that would give rise to the condition of ubiquitous mediation that contemporary theorists have termed "media culture."[69] By bringing religious ideas and practices to bear on these conditions, I argue, these evangelicals created a modern, networked form of Protestant sacred space that I call evangelical space. As they mapped sacred geography onto terrain being transformed by modern flows of goods, information, and people, landscape representation emerged as a crucial tool for teaching audiences to inhabit a particular moral geography and to adjust their actions accordingly.

Of course this form of spatial imagination represents just one version of evangelical space. Methodist circuit-riders, anti-mission Baptists, and black Christians in the so-called invisible church of the Slave South all created their own sacred mediascapes through their words, songs, and movements. By focusing on this particular form, I am less concerned with comparing different flavors of piety than with tracing a particularly consequential model of media distribution and its corresponding theory of how texts change readers and shape the course of history. That faith in the agency of religious words and images to circulate universally and almost instantaneously across vast stretches of physical and social space, sparking mass conversions, calling on readers to act on behalf of distant strangers, and hastening the coming of the millennium, is what marks this space as evangelical. While evangelical space originated in religious texts and organizations, it did not remain confined to them but spread through a broad swath of American popular culture, influencing everything from novels and paintings to tourism.

The apocalyptic geography condensed in Beecher's 1835 tract figures prominently in countless literary works of the antebellum period, perhaps nowhere more forcefully than in the best-selling novel penned by his daughter Harriet Beecher Stowe less than two decades later. In its breathtaking claims to summon into being a national "family" of devout readers, its plot that propels readers through national and international geographies while simultaneously guiding them on a spiritual tour of Christian cosmography, and its scenes in which characters gaze across landscapes that disclose visions of a world to come, *Uncle Tom's Cabin* represents the triumph of evangelical space as American space. As the novel proliferated across a transatlantic mediascape through illustrated editions, paintings, and popular theatrical shows, what emerged was an immersive sensory environment—a space that was socially "produced" in the sense described by spatial theorist Henri Lefebvre. Lefebvre's influential spatial "triad" captures how modern space is not simply given or inert but is actively created through the dialectical interaction of three spatial registers. The first is "spatial practice," the ways people negotiate their physical environment: Lefebvre gives the example of a modern city-dweller's daily commute to work, but one could also think of the physical printing of Stowe's novel and its circulation through "material space" as it was carried on foot or by railroad car, perused in parlors and reading rooms, and enacted onstage. Next is *"representations of space"* or "conceived space," the maps, blueprints, and other images created by "scientists, planners, urbanists," and "artist[s]" that represent the "dominant" form of space designed by powerful elites; this might include the various landscapes and geographies described and depicted within Stowe's novel, such as the panoramic view of the plantation South that Tom famously witnesses from the deck of a Mississippi steamboat. Finally there is the emotionally rich *"representational spaces"* or "lived" spaces people experience as they infuse the material spaces around them with the "images and symbols" existing in their mental worlds; for our purposes this is the space of the reader, who may feel compelled to inhabit the novel's expansive moral geography, weeping with love for distant strangers and trembling with apocalyptic dread, or who may resist it as many readers did, especially in the South.[70]

While Lefebvre's theory gives a sense of how evangelicals used media to produce sacred space, applying it to the religious world of the nineteenth century requires some retrofitting, since he considered "religio-political space" to be an archaic vestige of "pre-capitalist societies," from ancient "Greek temples" to the "tombs" and "crypts" of medieval Catholicism. With the rise of "nation states," such spaces gave way to "the space of a secular life, freed from politico-religious space."[71] In Lefebvre's Marxist subtraction story, religious space is by definition a premodern mystification of "real" (i.e., material) forces, and to become modern is to be liberated from it. Kim Knott has attempted to correct this bias and adapt Lefebvre's theory to the study of contemporary religious space, noting that "religion, which is inherently social, must also exist and express itself in and through space."[72] But this points to a broader methodological issue. Jeanne Halgren Kilde, in her overview of approaches to "religious space," describes a key shift in how scholars theorize religion. "Hermeneutical approaches" influenced by the mid-twentieth-century work of Mircea Eliade assume an "ontological or substantive" orientation, which means they privilege the meanings that religious insiders ascribe to religious spaces. Eliade, for example, interpreted the "*axis mundis*" or sacred center as the place where the divine erupts into ordinary existence, while Victor and Edith Turner explored the transformative sense of collective identity or "*communitas*" experienced by believers during Christian pilgrimages. Then in the 1980s a group of "socio-historical approaches" emerged that emphasize sacred spaces as social constructs, human products that reflect the power dynamics and exclusions of the societies that produced them. In the work of Jonathan Z. Smith, David Chidester, and Edward T. Linenthal, religious space is viewed not as a manifestation of divine presence but as the result of a social process through which human actors "sacralize" a given space through rituals and stories. Closely related to this approach is an eclectic cluster of "critical-spatial approaches" by theorists influenced by poststructuralist theory, including Lefebvre and Edward Soja. While religion per se is not a central concern of these thinkers, scholars of religion have applied their theories to interpret religious spaces as products of social power rather than manifestations of sacred power. A final category of "critical-spatial approaches from inside the study of religions" in effect reverses that flow of influence, as scholars such as Tweed, Knott, and Robert M. Hayden have recently developed theories that "ask how the study of specifically religious spaces can contribute to the broader discussion of human spatiality rather than the other way around."[73]

While the current study draws insights from each of these camps, I maintain that even as the turn from hermeneutical to socio-historical and critical-spatial methods has enabled a deeper understanding of sacred space as the product of historical forces, it has also made it difficult to see sacred spaces as anything *other* than human constructs. As Belden C. Lane notes, the socio-historical approach considers "sites as neutral and indifferent objects" and "fails to recognize place itself as a participant"; he proposes a "phenomenological approach" that stresses how "places themselves participate in the perception that is made of them."[74] Extending Lane's insight, one might say that media is another crucial component in the sacralization process that has been reduced to a "neutral and indifferent object." While the historical turn in the study of sacred space was marked by secularist assumptions, the postsecular approach pursued here emphasizes the ways antebellum Americans understood media networks (and the forces of modernity more broadly) as instruments of God acting through history—the sort of sacred media that Beecher perceived unfolding around him in the West and that Stowe later claimed she herself became as her great novel poured forth from her pen. In other words, American modernity did not replace sacred geographies with secular ones: it created spaces that were both modern and sacred, and media was a crucial player in that process.

As this project aims to redefine our sense of sacred space, it seeks to intervene in discussions of American space more broadly. American Studies has used space as an organizing theme since its inception, in classic studies of Puritan sacred geography—what Cotton Mather called "Christiano-graphy"— and the subsequent development of a national origin myth centered on westward expansion and tropes of wilderness and garden.[75] In recent decades the field has moved beyond the continent and the frontier, emphasizing the global reach of American power and raising vital questions about the spatial scale appropriate to the study of American cultures. Yet something has been lost in that shift. Despite scholarly investment in the religious origins of the "American Mind" for much of the twentieth century, by the turn of the millennium religion had largely receded from critical concern even as it assumed an increasingly prominent role in national culture and politics and in geopolitics, prompting Lawrence Buell to wonder if Americanists were, like the characters in the popular evangelical novel series, "in danger of being 'left behind.'"[76] The recent flowering of scholarship on what Michael Warner has termed the "evangelical public sphere" offers an opportunity to catch up.[77] As a transatlantic enterprise that sought national and global influence, the evangelical mediascape examined here offers an ideal lens through which to combine the insights of classic accounts of American space with important newer work on its transnational dimensions. Together they provide a fuller understanding of America's role in the rise of global modernity, including the apocalyptic geographies that now confront us all.

Time grows short: we need a map. Each of the six chapters that follow revisits a familiar antebellum cultural object—landscape painting, abolitionism, the sentimental novel, tourism, Transcendentalism, sensational fiction—and restores a sense of its numinous strangeness by reconstructing its place within the religious mediascape. The book's first part narrates the emergence of evangelical space in the 1820s and early 1830s, its adaptation to new ends in the abolitionist press of the late 1830s, and its spread to American popular culture by the 1850s. Chapter 1 defines the book's central concept, evangelical space, by showing how the evangelical print that flooded the nation in the 1820s and 1830s combined with an emerging landscape art culture to produce spectacular visualizations of the evangelical spatial imagination. Reading illustrated religious tracts, almanacs, and Bibles alongside one of the most iconic landscape paintings of the period—Thomas Cole's *View from Mount Holyoke, Northampton, Massachusetts, after a Thunderstorm—The Oxbow* (1836)—reveals that landscape art enacted a symbolic synthesis of two competing impulses in northern evangelical culture: the individual believer's inward pilgrimage toward God and the collective work of global missionary activism. Chapter 2 traces how American abolitionists took up evangelical media strategies in the mid- and late 1830s, launching circulating antislavery libraries that adapted evangelical space to the geographies of slavery. Like its evangelical forerunners, the American Anti-Slavery Society urged readers to extend their "ethical horizon" beyond the local, but it also used events in the Caribbean and elsewhere to refocus evangelical zeal from Asia to the U.S. South. In the process, it transformed the world missionary enterprise into a model for national reform. Chapter 3 examines Harriet Beecher Stowe's work for one of the nation's most prominent evangelical newspapers, the *New-York Evangelist*, as a literary apprenticeship that recasts the cultural significance of the most popular book in nineteenth-century America. The dozens of pieces Stowe published in the *Evangelist* between 1835 and 1852 reframe *Uncle Tom's Cabin* as a sustained reflection on modern media that dramatizes mass print as a sphere where evangelical piety and an emerging democratic society converge, a prospect that raises both millennial promise and apocalyptic peril. By crafting a novel that scrutinizes the problems of apocalyptic interpretation—a meta-apocalypse—Stowe theorizes the human itself as a medium through which information, feeling, and divine power circulate.

While the first part of *Apocalyptic Geographies* tells a story of direct influence and continuity, the second part turns from this linear account, shifting its focus from emulation and continuity to contestation and rupture. These chapters reveal a mediascape strikingly different from evangelicals' idealized sphere of universal print diffusion and irresistible conversion—one characterized instead by patchy distribution, perishable paper, and resistant or indifferent readers. While evangelical space retains a prominent cultural presence, these chapters trace its mediation by an archive of ostensibly secular objects with the help of several scholars whose work probes the meaning of secular modernity, including Charles Taylor, Tracy Fessenden, Bruno Latour, and Talal Asad. Chapter 4 revises standard accounts of the secularization of antebellum culture by examining the widespread practice among Protestant travelers of using physical landscapes as media for visualizing sacred history. Using tourism literature, aesthetic treatises, and best-selling sentimental novels by Susan Warner and Maria Cummins to uncover the clash of religious and secular interpretations in tourist landscapes, this chapter redefines what one critic calls the "secular center" of the American 1850s—not as a cultural space from which religion has been evacuated but one in which the proliferation of religious "options" plays out.[78] Chapter 5 reads Henry David Thoreau's *Walden* (1854) as a parody of a popular evangelical genre, the missionary memoir, in order to recover a conception of "cosmic modernity" that challenges recent accounts of a secularized global modernity. Thoreau's polemical engagement with missionary culture in the context of the Transcendentalist project of comparative religion dramatizes how the modern encounter with global religious difference catalyzed new conceptions of the local and new spiritual communities while shaping the deepest, most private experiences of the self. Chapter 6 descends into the profane depths of antebellum literary culture to probe the ways religious difference haunts the sensational public sphere. Excavating a neglected body of popular fiction circulating in the "Great West" in the 1840s and 1850s, I argue that these violent, quasi-pornographic novels stage vivid scenes of vision across the landscape that articulate a regional strain of republican ideology. The Catholic conspiracies and corrupt Protestant elites that constantly threaten the body politic in this fiction dramatize the dilemmas of political mediation in an expanding federal republic, anticipating Asad's critique of secularism's fictions of "direct access" and exposing the roots of the convulsions that grip Western liberal democracies today as a crisis not of deliberation but of mediation.[79]

I conclude by looking beyond the Civil War to consider the ways evangelical space continued to shape how Americans saw the landscape and themselves in cultural arenas from literary realism to the conservation movement. Mark Twain, in his riotous, irreverent travels through the Holy Land and the Far West, becomes a representative figure of how a secularizing America remained haunted by a sense of sacred presence rooted in the soil itself.

While the first part of this book tells a story of the rise of white Protestant evangelicals within U.S. national culture—of how their form of evangelical space became American space by the eve of the Civil War—the second tells an ironic story about how that space escaped their control as writers and artists from other traditions reconfigured the relationship between landscape representation, media, and the sacred to produce their own apocalyptic geographies. There were, of course, many other mappings that are not fully explored here, including those from within African American, Native American, and African diaspora communities. While figures including William Apess, Frederick Douglass, Phillis Wheatley, Robert S. Duncanson, and Henry Obookiah all appear in the chapters that follow, a more complete account of how they and others appropriated and adapted evangelical space must await its own study. The decision not to attempt such an account here is partly owing to my emphasis on mass media and popular culture: whites tended to control the printing presses, galleries, and other means of cultural production necessary to generate the widespread middle-class cultural phenomena studied here. In addition, expanding this study beyond its current focus on a particular evangelical tradition would require crossing into other traditions (particularly Methodism) and other forms of evangelical space that I feared would quickly outrun my expertise (not to mention my word limit) and threaten the coherence of the story I had to tell. Finally, a number of other scholars have already begun to explore subaltern evangelical mediascapes in greater detail, particularly in the case of scholarship on the "evangelical black Atlantic."[80] So while this book largely offers an account of antebellum culture's dominant spaces rather than its resistant ones—of evangelical "strategies" as opposed to "tactics," to borrow Michel de Certeau's terminology—the existence of those alternative spaces is always implied and awaits further elaboration.[81]

In June 1861 Frederick Douglass delivered a lecture before the Spring Street AME Zion Church in Rochester, New York, in which he reflected on "The American Apocalypse." Slavery, he told the audience, "is not an earthquake swallowing up a town or city, and then leaving the solid earth undisturbed for centuries. It is not a Vesuvius which, belching forth its fire and lava at intervals, causes ruin in a limited territory; but slavery is felt to be a moral volcano, a burning lake, a hell on the earth, the smoke and stench of whose torments ascend upward forever."[82] His metaphor made explicit the parallel many observers at the time and since have drawn between the "apocalyptic" imagery of Frederic Church's *Cotopaxi* (fig. 0.7; see plate 3) of the following year and a nation convulsed by Civil War.[83] But as Douglass described the "war in heaven" captured in John's "apocalyptic vision," he invoked a specific sense of the relationship between apocalypse and geography that most modern-day critics fail to recognize. Declaring that "the human heart is a constant state of war," Douglass reminded his listeners that "what takes place in individual human hearts, often takes place between nations, and between individuals of the same nation. Such is the struggle now going on in the United States."[84] In this light, Church's refulgent scene symbolizes more than political conflict: it becomes a vehicle for individual moral and religious scripts of the sort that

FIGURE 0.7. Frederic Edwin Church, *Cotopaxi*, 1862. Oil on canvas, 48 × 85 in. (121.9 × 215.9 cm). Detroit Institute of Arts, Founders Society Purchase, 76.89.

The Heart of the Andes had activated a few years earlier. Douglass's address, which appeared in the pages of *Douglass' Monthly* the following month, signaled the pervasive use of the landscape to help Americans mediate between individual and collective dramas of redemption, and between this world and a world to come. The story of how the landscape became the nation's most powerful apocalyptic medium begins decades earlier with the rise of a new evangelical mediascape.

PART I
Evangelical Space

1

Thomas Cole and the Landscape of Evangelical Print

ONE FRIDAY EVENING in February 1835, the most famous evangelical revivalist in the United States, Charles Grandison Finney, called on an audience of at least two thousand listeners in New York's Chatham Street Chapel to imagine themselves standing on the brink of Niagara Falls:

> As you stand upon the verge of the precipice, you behold a man lost in deep reverie, approaching its verge unconscious of his danger. He approaches nearer and nearer, until he actually lifts his foot to take the final step that shall plunge him in destruction.—At this moment you lift your warning voice above the roar of the foaming waters, and cry out, *Stop*. The voice pierces his ear, and breaks the charm that binds him; he turns instantly upon his heel, all pale and aghast he retires, quivering, from the verge of death.

Finney used this harrowing scene to illustrate the forces at work in "the conversion of a sinner," explaining that while God "is the agent in changing the mind," "he is not the only agent." The minister plays a crucial role through his words, but, most important of all, "a change of heart is the sinner's *own act*."[1]

For the economically diverse and racially mixed audience who attended Finney's Second Free Presbyterian Church as well as the national readership of the *New-York Evangelist*, the prominent evangelical weekly newspaper that first published Finney's popular "Lectures on Revivals," the scene at Niagara was an invitation to use a well-known image from an emerging national landscape culture to imagine more vividly the dramatic (and controversial) process of religious conversion that Finney sought to spark in his audiences.[2] Those who visited Niagara in person might experience its sublimity in similar terms, as did an *Evangelist* correspondent later that year who described how her visit to the falls helped her "learn to fear and obey that wo[n]der-working God who is not less merciful to his friends than he is terrible to his enemies."[3] But they

FIGURE 1.1. William James Bennett, *Niagara Falls. To Thomas Dixon Esq. this view of the American Fall taken from Goat Island*, 1829. Aquatint and etching, color. Popular Graphic Arts Collection, Prints & Photographs Division, Library of Congress, LC-DIG-pga-00206.

could also enter this spiritualized space by immersing themselves in a burgeoning body of landscape illustrations and prints (fig. 1.1) or by paying a visit to public art exhibitions like the ones put on every spring by the National Academy of Design in New York, where no fewer than eight views of Niagara Falls were displayed during the 1830s.[4] Over the next decade visual art increasingly became a tool for nurturing evangelical piety and morality. The *Evangelist* promoted exhibitions of Frederick Catherwood's panoramas of Niagara and Jerusalem, encouraged readers to support a campaign to purchase Luman Reed's art collection for "a public gallery of paintings" because of the "moral uses" it would provide, and even called visiting the academy's annual exhibitions an "obligation resting upon the moral and religious community."[5] For the reform-oriented Protestant evangelicalism that connected preachers like

FIGURE 1.2. Thomas Cole, *View from Mount Holyoke, Northampton, Massachusetts, after a Thunderstorm—The Oxbow*, 1836. Oil on canvas, 51½ × 76 in. (130.8 × 193 cm). The Metropolitan Museum of Art, Gift of Mrs. Russell Sage, 1908, 08.228.

Finney, publications like the *Evangelist*, and the Benevolent Empire of voluntary associations devoted to causes including missions, temperance, and abolition, "visual piety" extended beyond explicitly religious images and themes to encompass a broadly moralized and sacralized art culture.[6]

This evangelical art culture helped fuel the rise of a new class of bourgeois art patrons and led to the purchase of one of the most iconic American landscape paintings of the nineteenth century: Thomas Cole's *View from Mount Holyoke, Northampton, Massachusetts, after a Thunderstorm—The Oxbow* (fig. 1.2; see plate 4).[7] Here again evangelicalism mediated the consumption of the landscape. While Finney brought his rapt audiences to the edge of Niagara, a colleague in New York's evangelical free church movement, the Reverend Erskine Mason, instructed his congregation at the Bleecker Street Church in a similar form of spatial imagination.[8] In a typical sermon he described the spiritual condition of a sinner who "resist[s] the Holy Ghost" in terms of what Mason called the "moral landscape": "though he may live amid scenes of spiritual beauty, and though the refreshing showers of heavenly grace may brighten and give new verdure to the moral landscape around him—there he is—a spot blasted by heaven's fire, which can never be cultivated, a tree scathed by heaven's lightning, ready to be cut down as fuel for the burning."[9] The visual and pictorial sensibility that Mason infused into his sermons at the

Bleecker Street Church from 1830 until his death in 1851 intersected with the New York art world in 1836, when a prominent member of his congregation, the New York merchant and long-time American Bible Society (ABS) board member Charles N. Talbot, visited the National Academy and decided to purchase *The Oxbow* for five hundred dollars.[10] Riven by lightning and sunlight, life-giving rain and wrathful storm, Mason's moral landscape uncannily evokes the painting's celebrated clash of pictorial and meteorological elements and translates them into a cosmic drama of sin and salvation. Cole's lone entry at the exhibition that year, *The Oxbow* was a "well known" prospect from Mount Holyoke that Cole considered "the finest scene I have in my sketchbook." Although it depicted an actual site, Cole intended the painting to be more than just a "view" in order to attract more attention at the exhibition. As he explained to his patron Luman Reed, "understanding there will be some dashing landscapes there, I thought I should do something that would tell a tale."[11]

The tale that *The Oxbow* and landscapes like it might have told to Talbot and countless others swept up in the "evangelical surge" of the early nineteenth century is the subject of this chapter.[12] Deciphering that tale requires bringing evangelical culture, and in particular evangelical print culture, into dialogue with landscape art in a way that has eluded literary scholars and art historians alike. More fundamentally, it requires using that religious mediascape to complicate the way we think about space itself in antebellum America. In the constellation of meaning that crystallizes around places like Niagara and Mount Holyoke, we glimpse what this chapter defines as "evangelical space," a pervasive form of imagined space that emerged at the tumultuous confluence of popular visual culture, the antebellum "revolution" in transportation and communications technologies, and the period of religious mobilization known as the Second Great Awakening.[13] Evangelical space was "produced" (to adopt the terms of spatial theorist Henri Lefebvre) through the interaction of "material spaces" like churches, art galleries, and tourist sites; the "represented space" evoked in sermons, pamphlets, Bibles, and paintings; and the "lived space" of believers who used religious narratives to orient their lives.[14] To recognize landscape art as a crucial node within this layered, interactive spatial field is to unsettle an entrenched scholarly account that interprets landscape representation as a transparent manifestation of expansionist ideology and political imperialism; it is to begin to restore texture to a landscape that performed a much more complex role in mediating the tensions and contradictions that gripped evangelical culture and American culture as a whole during the period.[15] Landscape paintings were not simply real-estate ads for the appropriation of physical land; they were immersive spaces where viewers learned to cultivate a particular kind of self, defined by distinctive moral perceptions and imperatives, directed toward a concrete set of practices and habits, and oriented toward an overarching vision of a good society. It is within this more capacious moral geography, which includes but exceeds the literal space of the continent, that American landscape painting assumes its most compelling and luminous cultural presence.

After a brief discussion of why Cole's work is particularly appropriate for studying evangelical modes of vision, I turn to *The Oxbow* as a case study of evangelical space. Situating the painting in the context of Cole's exhibition record at the National Academy, contemporary published accounts of Mount Holyoke, and developments in American Bible illustration, the chapter reconstructs an immersive form of looking closely tied to evangelical reading practices and shows how devout viewers used the landscape to orient themselves in sacred history. Next delving into the illustrated pamphlets of one of the period's most prolific evangelical publishing societies, I show how picturesque landscape aesthetics became a tool to guide spiritual life within an apocalyptic framework drawn from the work of Jonathan Edwards, the eighteenth-century theologian and revivalist who became a touchstone for many antebellum evangelicals, particularly the Presbyterians and Congregationalists who led the print distribution efforts intended to bring about the earthly millennium Edwards had predicted.[16] In this light, Cole's famous split composition takes on a significance that goes beyond its innovative combination of the aesthetic modes of the sublime and the beautiful, and beyond its dramatization of the historical clash between wilderness and settlement.[17] Though perhaps not the "tale" Cole had in mind, *The Oxbow* tells a neglected story about how popular religion, mass media, and visual culture combined in antebellum America to create an apocalyptic geography in which viewers could use the landscape to envision the unfolding of sacred history and to rehearse their roles in hastening the millennium. Meanwhile other observers including Catharine Maria Sedgwick and the Methodist Pequot preacher William Apess contested that evangelical vision from Mount Holyoke, using fiction and oratory to expose a terrain scarred by a history of colonial violence and dispossession.

Thomas Cole and the Evangelical Eye

Scholars have explored revealing links between Cole's work and evangelical culture. Alan Wallach has documented the artist's ties to the Protestant "dissenting tradition" of emblems, Bunyanesque allegory, and other formal devices that influenced nineteenth-century evangelicals; more recently, Michael Gaudio has explored Cole's interest in revivalism in the late 1820s.[18] Turning to *The Oxbow* itself, Mark R. Stoll interprets the painting as a proto-environmentalist statement that reflects "the vital place of nature and landscape in the Reformed Protestant tradition in which Cole was raised," while

David Bjelajac has read the painting as "an imaginative Christian allegory" that spoke to Talbot's religious and philanthropic commitments.[19] As Cole catered to devout patrons including Samuel Ward, Luman Reed, and Talbot throughout his career, his personal background and intellectual temperament seem to have positioned him well to speak to their religious concerns through his art. Certainly Cole's own version of the moral landscape surfaces frequently in his writings, perhaps nowhere more explicitly than in his "Essay on American Scenery" of 1835, which describes how "in gazing on the pure creations of the Almighty," the viewer "feels a calm religious tone steal through his mind, and when he has turned to mingle with his fellow men, the chords which have been struck in that sweet communion cease not to vibrate."[20] While this formulation lacks the dramatic spiritual rupture that marks the landscapes of Finney and Mason as evangelical, in the paintings themselves Cole's romantic idiom, with its stark juxtapositions of sublime storms and waterfalls with clear skies and placid valleys, provides an apt visualization of what David Morgan calls the "evangelical sublime"—nowhere more clearly than in *The Oxbow*.[21]

This chapter locates *The Oxbow* at the intersection of two major thematic threads of Cole's career that align with a tension at the heart of antebellum evangelical thought. The first is his persistent effort to visualize sacred history, from the Old Testament scenes of his early career to his later interest in apocalyptic themes reflected in the series *The Course of Empire* (ca. 1834–36) and a proposed sequel called "The Future Course of Empire," in which he planned to depict the rise of "a *Christian* Civilization" filled with the "Glory, Beauty & Peace" that Cole associated with "the millennium."[22] The second thread is his allegorical portrayal of individual Protestant piety, stretching from the illustrations he produced in 1819 for an edition of John Bunyan's 1682 allegory *The Holy War*, through two versions of his hugely popular series *The Voyage of Life* (1839–42), to the unfinished *The Cross and the World* series that was interrupted by Cole's death in 1848.[23] *The Oxbow* might seem an unlikely place to find such a convergence. After all, it represents neither a historical scene nor religious allegory in any conventional sense. Yet the painting is illuminating precisely because it reveals how the landscape, even in the absence of explicit religious symbolism or artistic intent, becomes legible as a vehicle for religious and ethical meanings when restored to the evangelical mediascape in which it originally circulated.

Cole's beliefs and intentions, accordingly, are not the focus here. Where earlier accounts approached *The Oxbow* by considering sources that directly influenced the artist's formal choices, this chapter turns to a less obvious source: the illustrated evangelical publications that flooded the nation in the years surrounding the painting's production and reception.[24] The claim is not that Cole necessarily read the tracts, almanacs, and books discussed here or that they had a conscious influence on his painting but, rather, that they exerted a formative (if unquantifiable) influence on the way Talbot and other evangelicals who saw the painting at the National Academy or in Talbot's home would have interpreted it. From the 1820s to the 1840s, as increasing numbers of Americans saw landscapes in art exhibitions and gift books, art engravings and dinner plates, many more were exposed to religious publications filled with landscape depictions and descriptions.[25] Simply put, these printed sources helped teach antebellum Americans how to read the landscape. Piecing together an evangelical version of what Michael Baxandall calls "the period eye" is an admittedly speculative enterprise.[26] The scarcity of direct evidence of the viewing practices of ordinary people requires a creative act of interpretation that combines close formal analysis of particular images, attention to the material settings of looking, and immersion in the dense system of spatial images and tropes circulating in evangelical print culture. The goal is not to achieve a definitive reading but to reconstruct a plausible one from the perspective of an ideal viewer steeped in a religious worldview shared by a large and increasing number of antebellum Americans.

The Alpha and the Omega: *The Oxbow* and Sacred History

The Oxbow depicts an elevated foreground mountaintop of dense, storm-ravaged forest that recedes diagonally from the viewer toward the left side of the painting, where dark clouds and rain shroud the distant ridgetops. In the right half of the painting the mountainside abruptly falls away to reveal a sweeping view of a pastoral valley basking in sunlight. The green valley is covered with neat, rectangular fields and pastures dotted with trees. Sheaves of harvested grain stand in some of the fields, and thin plumes of smoke rise from the chimneys of a few homes on the valley floor. From the lower right-hand corner a wide, placid river enters the picture space parallel to the mountainside and sweeps in a dramatic curve through the valley, enclosing a cultivated, balloon-shaped peninsula within its banks before disappearing behind the mountains. The middle ground recedes to meet a low, mostly wooded mountaintop in the central distance. In the right foreground a camp chair and closed umbrella sit on a rocky outcropping; just below it to the left an artist in a hat and jacket stands before his easel. He has interrupted his plein air painting of the scene before him to turn toward the viewer, whom he confronts with a barely perceptible smile.

With its unusual split composition, dramatic contrasts of meteorological phenomena, and enigmatic self-portrait of the artist, *The Oxbow* has long invited narrative readings. In one influential account, Angela Miller argues that the painting compresses the process of social development depicted serially in Cole's *The Course of Empire* series into a single canvas in which nature itself dramatizes "the confrontation between wilderness and the colonizing energies of American agriculture at a particular moment in history." The painting, she contends, refuses a harmonious pastoral account of the nation's divinely ordained march across the continent in favor of one that foregrounds conflict and human "choice."[27] One need not interpret the painting in primarily political terms nor necessarily agree with Miller's reading of Cole's ambivalence toward the agricultural scene on the valley floor to accept her general point that history is being represented spatially here. The question then becomes, what sort of history is it?

One way to approach that question is to consider how the painting would have appeared to a viewer familiar with Cole's earlier work at the National Academy. In terms of its institutional setting and its status as a speculative painting (one offered for public sale rather than executed for a patron), *The Oxbow* belongs to a sequence of uncommissioned landscapes Cole exhibited there starting in 1827. These works tended to be compositions (as opposed to views) depicting narratives typically drawn from the Bible—what Cole would famously call "a higher style of landscape."[28] After exhibiting a scene from James Fenimore Cooper's novel *The Last of the Mohicans* in 1827, the next year Cole offered *The Garden of Eden* and *Expulsion from the Garden of Eden*, followed by *The Subsiding of the Waters of the Deluge* in 1829, *Christ and the Woman of Samaria* in 1833, and *The Dead Abel* in 1834.[29] His decision to "try the public taste" (as Luman Reed put it) in 1836 with a work that would "tell a tale" was only the latest in a string of narrative landscapes Cole exhibited at the National Academy stretching back nearly a decade.[30]

Of these narrative works, *Expulsion from the Garden of Eden* (fig. 1.3) is most similar in composition to *The Oxbow*. As critics have noted, the division of *Expulsion* between the radiant, pastoral scene of Eden on the right and the storm-engulfed, sublime, postlapsarian landscape on the left seems to anticipate the split composition of the 1836 view.[31] Indeed, Cole's characteristic anthropomorphic trees bent before the storm's fury in the lower left foreground of *The Oxbow* (fig. 1.4) echo the blasted trees in *Expulsion*, which themselves seem to mimic the tiny fleeing figures of Adam and Eve in the center of the composition as if to forecast their passage through the picture space. This figural rhyming is even clearer in the image Cole was accused of plagiarizing, John Martin's *Adam and Eve Driven out of Paradise* (fig. 1.5).[32] This figural allusion, which recalls Mason's description of the sinner as "a tree scathed by heaven's lightning," reinforces the parallel between the sunny valley of *The Oxbow* and Cole's earlier depictions of Eden. Whether intentional or not, Cole's subtle compositional and iconographic transpositions link his 1836 view

FIGURE 1.3. Thomas Cole, *Expulsion from the Garden of Eden*, 1828. Oil on canvas, 39¾ × 54½ in. (100.96 × 138.43 cm). Museum of Fine Arts, Boston, Gift of Martha C. Karolik for the M. and M. Karolik Collection of American Paintings, 1815–1865, 47.1188. Photo © 2020 Museum of Fine Arts, Boston.

to an Old Testament narrative of creation, sin, and exile that he had been presenting at the National Academy for years.

Cole's implicit equation of the Connecticut River Valley with Eden visualized the tendency of the prospect from Mount Holyoke to elicit pious commentary on God's creation of the world from visitors who "found the scene fitted for the indulgence of devotional feelings" and "spoke solemnly of the power and sovereignty of HIM, 'who stretched out the north over the empty place, and hung the earth upon nothing.'"[33] For "the Moralist," one writer explained, "the different piles of mountains and hills, the extended surface of plains and vallies below him, teach him that *the hand that made them is divine.*"[34] Just how reflexive the site's association with the account of Creation in Genesis had become by the mid-1830s is nicely suggested by an 1836 school primer whose entry for "prospect" reads, "Eden, and all the coast, in *prospect* lay. We had a delightful *prospect* from the summit of Mount Holyoke."[35]

While many visitors to Mount Holyoke compared the prospect with Eden, others scrutinized the mountaintop for evidence of history after the Fall. In 1833 the prominent geologist Edward Hitchcock argued that boulders and other "diluvium" were traces not of gradual geological processes but of "a

FIGURE 1.4. Detail of Thomas Cole, *View from Mount Holyoke, Northampton, Massachusetts, after a Thunderstorm—The Oxbow*, 1836. Oil on canvas, 51½ × 76 in. (130.8 × 193 cm). The Metropolitan Museum of Art, Gift of Mrs. Russell Sage, 1908, 08.228.

FIGURE 1.5. John Martin, *Adam and Eve Driven out of Paradise*, 1827. Mezzotint, proof, 10 × 13⅞ in. (25.4 × 35.2 cm). Museum of Fine Arts, Boston, Gift of Samuel Glaser, 69.1326. Photo © 2020 Museum of Fine Arts, Boston.

general deluge" commonly thought to be "identical with the one described in the Christian Scriptures" by pointing to the Connecticut River Valley and to Mount Holyoke in particular, where "we find a very powerful diluvial agency to have been at work."[36] As Rebecca Bedell notes, Cole frequently incorporated "U-shaped valleys," "diluvial drift," and other supposed traces of the Deluge in his landscapes—a habit displayed most explicitly in the "erratic boulders" strewn about *The Subsiding of the Waters of the Deluge* (fig. 1.6).[37] It is not surprising, then, that just as Cole's earlier depictions of Eden and the Expulsion uncannily resurfaced in his 1836 view, traces of the Deluge reappeared there as well in the row of mountaintop boulders running rightward from the foot of the trees in the foreground, down the mountainside to the rocky ledge above the river. Hence, through its deployment of weather, topography, and geology, *The Oxbow* recapitulates Cole's earlier speculative biblical history paintings and in the process condenses a large swath of sacred history into a natural drama set in a specific contemporary landscape—a "higher style of landscape" indeed.

FIGURE 1.6. Thomas Cole, *The Subsiding of the Waters of the Deluge*, 1829. Oil on canvas, 35¾ × 47¾ in. (90.8 × 121.4 cm). Smithsonian American Art Museum, Washington, D.C. Gift of Mrs. Katie Dean in memory of Minnibel S. and James Wallace Dean and museum purchase through the Smithsonian Institution Collections Acquisitions Program, 1983.40.

Clearly, the aura of sacred history generated by the intertextual play of *The Oxbow* with Cole's earlier work at the National Academy was strengthened by the cluster of biblical associations that had built up around Mount Holyoke itself since the early 1820s, associations that reflected a tradition of projecting Holy Land geography onto the New England landscape.[38] That aura was bolstered by the inclusion of landscape illustrations in American Bibles during the 1830s. Although Talbot's ABS did not include illustrations in its Bibles, opting instead for a pared-down product that could be reproduced cheaply and distributed as widely as possible, the society's unprecedented output spurred for-profit publishers to differentiate their own editions through fancy bindings, editorial apparatuses, and lavish illustrations. Unlike the illustrated Bibles published by Isaiah Thomas and Mathew Carey a few decades earlier, which tended to depict well-known scenes from scripture but not the surrounding terrain, by the 1830s landscapes and maps featured prominently in popular American Bibles including the lushly illustrated editions that businessman John Holbrook published in Brattleboro, Vermont. This trend culminated in 1846 with the massive Harper and Brothers' *Illuminated Bible*, which boasted "Sixteen Hundred Historical Engravings," including many images of Holy Land terrain. With these illustrations, packaged in a volume that sold seventy-five thousand copies in its first year alone, the devoutly Methodist Harper brothers taught readers to use landscapes as visual aids for accessing the historical truth of the events and places recounted in scripture, beginning with Eden itself (fig. 1.7) and continuing through the history of the ancient Israelites.[39]

The point is not that Cole was familiar with these illustrations but that the Bible-reading public was and that this religious print culture represents a significant element of the context in which an evangelical like Talbot would have interpreted *The Oxbow*. Those who had seen Cole's earlier religious landscapes at the National Academy (or at least knew of the critical praise and controversy they had garnered) were even more likely to interpret the painting in biblical terms; for those familiar with the religious associations of Mount Holyoke and Northampton, it would have been almost unavoidable. At this convergence of the galleries and tourist sites people visited, the represented spaces they encountered in paintings, guidebooks, and Bibles, and the biblical narratives they used to orient their spiritual lives, evangelical space begins to emerge.

Specifically what emerges is a distinctive way of entering and inhabiting the picture space. This mode of looking corresponds to a Protestant theory of reading in which the text becomes a transparent medium that offers direct access to spiritual reality—access frequently expressed in terms of the immediacy of physical sight.[40] In 1832 Jacob Abbott, the popular evangelical author of *The Young Christian*, promoted a version of this method of visualizing scripture. Noting that "each reader can, if he will task his imagination, paint *for himself* the scenes which the Bible describes," Abbott instructed readers to

> turn to the fifth chapter of the gospel according to St. Luke, and picture to yourself as vividly as possible the scene described there. Do not think of a shore in general, but conceive of some particular shore. Give it shape and form. Let it be rocky or sandy, or high or low, bordered with woods, or with hills, or with meadows. . . . Let it assume either of these forms, or any other which your fancy may portray, and which may suit the circumstances of the narrative; only let it be *something distinct*—clear and distinct in all its parts; so that if you had power to represent upon canvass by painting the conceptions of your mind, you might execute a perfect picture of the whole scene.

Abbott next applies this visualization of scripture to an actual painting as he describes a hushed encounter with Benjamin West's *Christ Rejected* (1814) in

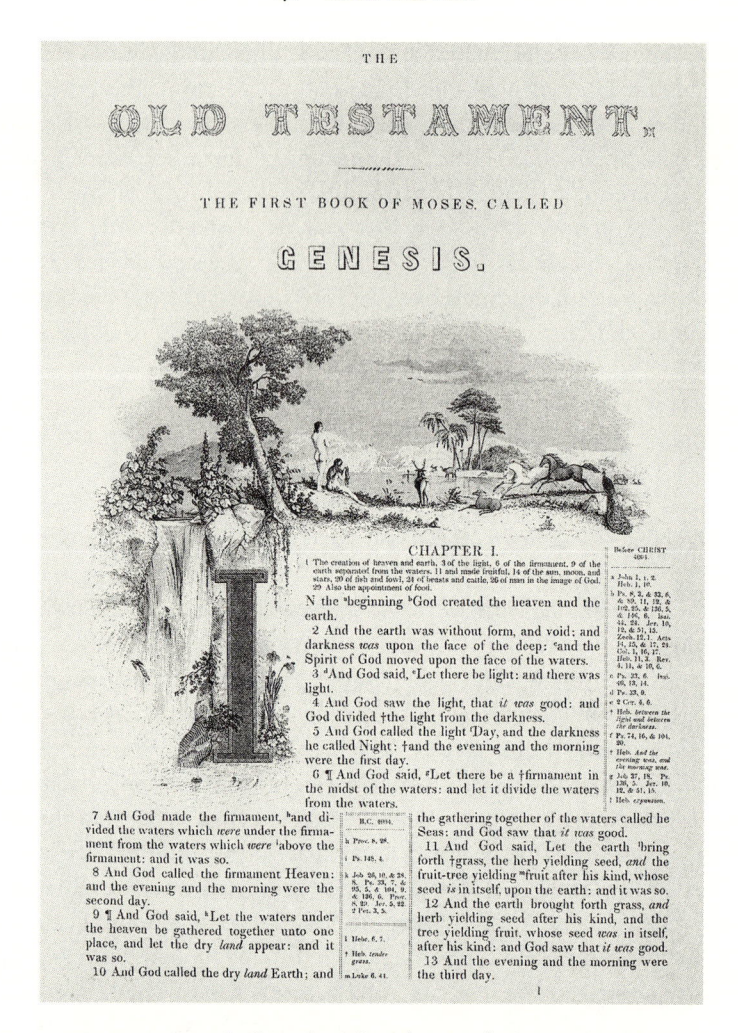

FIGURE 1.7. Joseph Alexander Adams (engraver) after J. G. Chapman, *Garden of Eden*. Wood engraving. From *The Illuminated Bible, Containing the Old and New Testaments, Translated out of the Original Tongues, and with the Former Translations Diligently Compared and Revised* (New York: Harper & Brothers, 1846), 1. Special Collections Research Center, University of Chicago Library.

the Boston Athenæum: "Yes; there stood the Savior in the middle of the picture, passive and resigned, and with a countenance whose expression plainly said that his thoughts were far away. The Roman governor stood before his palace endeavoring to persuade the mob to consent to their prisoner's release."[41] As Abbott lingers over the details of the picture, he becomes immersed in the events depicted there. The painting as a formal construct vanishes and becomes instead a space the viewer imaginatively enters to experience firsthand the truth of the biblical event—a stunning instance of how "visual piety" transforms the images believers see into "untrammeled visualizations of what they profess."[42] Abbott's account reveals a reciprocal process in which evangelical reading facilitates the direct apprehension of divine knowledge that Jonathan Edwards called "spiritual sight," while physical looking becomes a method of rereading that seeks to recapture a sense of the immediacy of scripture that has been lost through repetition and overfamiliarity.[43] This process serves to remedy a condition in which, as Abbott says, "we stop with merely repeating once more the words, instead of penetrating fully to the meaning beyond."[44] This visual sensibility, combined with the practice of inscribing Holy Land sites onto American geography, meant that landscape could serve as a medium through which the biblical text mingled with the lived present.

A viewer attempting to apply this evangelical mode of looking-as-reading to *The Oxbow* might begin in that Edenic valley on the right half of the painting and follow the path of the storm leftward into the foreground wilderness to the blasted trees—driven from paradise, as it were. But here the composition pivots, mirroring the curve of the river below, as the swirling arc of storm clouds and the slant of the tree trunks funnel the eye rightward, back down the slope and along the row of boulders (those traces of the Deluge) before finally arriving at the rock outcropping with the artist's camp chair and umbrella, where an observant viewer might note the distinct cross formed by the legs of the chair (fig. 1.8). Thus as the evangelical eye moves through the picture space, the viewer retraces the path of mankind from Eden through the wilderness of the world toward the cross and experiences spatially the typological fulfillment of the expulsion and the covenant in Christ's crucifixion and resurrection.

But here we encounter a problem, for having arrived at the outcropping, our visual trail is interrupted by the mountainside's vertiginous drop to the river below, leaving the viewer to gaze across the valley, where, as Matthew Baigell and Allen Kaufman first observed, the name of God the "Almighty," *Shaddai*, appears mysteriously emblazoned upside down in Hebrew letters on a low mountainside, while from another perspective "Noah" also seems to be written there.[45] In addition to these figures, at least one other divine symbol appears in the landscape that has gone unmentioned: the oxbow in the river traces a giant omega (Ω), the last letter of the Greek alphabet. Its presence alongside the name of God is significant given that both are invoked in Revelation 1:8 to describe the arc of sacred history: "I am Alpha and Omega, the beginning and the ending, saith the Lord, which is, and which was, and which is to come, the Almighty."[46] In fact, Jonathan Edwards famously cited this

FIGURE 1.8. Detail of Thomas Cole, *View from Mount Holyoke, Northampton, Massachusetts, after a Thunderstorm—The Oxbow*, 1836. Oil on canvas, 51½ × 76 in. (130.8 × 193 cm). The Metropolitan Museum of Art, Gift of Mrs. Russell Sage, 1908, 08.228.

passage in this very valley in what would later become one of the nineteenth century's most influential accounts of apocalyptic history, *A History of the Work of Redemption*.[47]

As we stand in a wilderness gazing at a paradise on the other side of the omega, the painting's abrupt compositional break between foreground and background space takes on a cosmic significance that recalls Washington Allston's use of architectural space to represent the ruptures of apocalyptic history in his biblical paintings of the 1820s.[48] The gap between mountaintop and valley floor could be said to inscribe into the landscape what Thomas H. Luxon has described in the Puritan context as a "two-world dualistic ontology," in which the present world is separate from the world to come, a "really real" realm that exists on a higher plane of being.[49] This was the sort of cosmic dualism the prospect evoked for one visitor to Mount Holyoke who described how "the beauty of the plains, the grandeur of the mountain scenery, and the wide extent of the prospect dilate the mind, and fill it with delightful emotions; and then the sight of so many spires pointing to the heavens, and designating places where the living God is worshipped, and the hopes of a blissful immortality are cherished, gives solemnity to the whole feeling, and turns the thoughts to that better, that heavenly country, of which the earthly Canaan was but a type."[50] In this context, the aesthetic and spatial problems we confront in Cole's composition—Can the painter effectively unify the landscape? Can the viewer successfully bridge the gap?—become theological and ethical ones. What is the relation between this world and the next? Is a passage from the wilderness of the world to the "heavenly country" across the river possible, and, if so, how? Is it achieved primarily through a pious private journey through life to death or through collective efforts to bring about the millennium? Can it be reached through human agency within history or only after an apocalyptic judgment that providentially ends history?

By the time *The Oxbow* was exhibited in 1836, these questions and the spatial terms in which they are posed had filled the pages of evangelical publications for more than a decade. Illustrated tracts and almanacs inscribed a cosmic drama onto the landscape and represented individual and collective participation in that drama in terms of movement through space and changes in the land itself. This evangelical mediascape tied the arrival of the millennium to the willingness of ordinary Christians to minister to distant others—a practice often described in terms of vision across the landscape. While a sense of the sacred past was shared by many Christians, this intense concern for the millennial future—for what lay beyond the omega and how it could be reached—is what makes Cole's landscape resonate so powerfully with antebellum evangelical culture.

That millennial concern began, in a sense, in Northampton, where Jonathan Edwards lived and ministered for nearly twenty-five years and where he led a series of famous revivals before being ousted by his own congregation in 1750. Edwards reportedly even claimed that the millennium had already begun in Northampton, sparked by the revivals he had led from his Northampton pulpit in the 1730s.[51] Although Protestant theologians had revised Edwards's Calvinism substantially by the early nineteenth century, he became an enormous source of religious inspiration and authority for a diverse array of antebellum evangelicals during the Second Great Awakening thanks to a "cultural revival of Edwards" promoted by many of the same Congregationalists and Presbyterians who led the Benevolent Empire.[52] He provided a venerable precedent for a new army of missionaries and revivalists (including Finney himself), and his exposition of millennial history combined with a new theological emphasis on human agency to fuel the benevolent work of countless evangelicals. They included Mary Lyon, founder of the Mount Holyoke Female Seminary, who situated her work within Edwards's millennial framework and often preached with a copy of *A History of the Work of Redemption* in her hand.[53] They included two of the most powerful leaders and backers of organized benevolence, the wealthy New York merchants Arthur and Lewis Tappan, who hailed from Northampton.[54] And they included Talbot himself, who spent his summers in Northampton and bought a home for his father there not long before purchasing *The Oxbow*.[55] Each of these luminaries was intimately familiar with the place Cole chose to depict, and they were undoubtedly aware of its connection to the man who loomed so large in the evangelical tradition they claimed as their own.

But it was not only people with local ties who associated Edwards with the valley. By the nineteenth century the Puritan divine had become one of the area's greatest claims to fame, as demonstrated by the many accounts that identify Northampton as the home of "the celebrated President Edwards."[56] That legacy transformed the Connecticut River Valley and Northampton itself into a kind of pilgrimage site for evangelical tourists. While in town visitors could also pay their respects at the grave of David Brainerd, the young missionary whose piety and selfless concern for others (his "disinterested benevolence") Edwards had immortalized in a memoir that became his most popular work in the nineteenth century.[57] This association with Edwards is crucial for understanding the appeal of Cole's painting to an evangelical viewer. Edwards connects the painting's retelling of biblical history to an account of sacred history that saw the ancient past flowing through the evangelical present and into the millennial future through the medium of print. It is within this apocalyptic geography of evangelical print distribution that *The Oxbow* becomes fully visible as evangelical space.

The American Tract Society and the Landscape of Evangelical Print

In "Conversion of President Edwards," a tract edition of Edwards's 1739 conversion narrative that the American Tract Society (ATS) published in about 1830, Alexander Anderson's wood engraving of a man gazing out over a wooded scene (fig. 1.9), captioned by a passage from Edwards's text, "I walked abroad alone, in a solitary place, for contemplation," highlights the role of the landscape in the protagonist's spiritual development. In the narrative, Edwards recalls that as a young man he often experienced a "calm, delightful abstraction of the soul from all the concerns of this world" and imagined himself "alone in the mountains, or some solitary wilderness, far from all mankind, sweetly conversing with Christ, and rapt and swallowed up in God." As Edwards's piety deepens, he increasingly sees the divine presence shining through nature, as "God's excellency, his wisdom, his purity, and love, seemed to appear in every thing; in the sun, moon, and stars; in the clouds, and blue sky; in the grass, flowers, and trees; in the water, and all nature." By the time he accepts a call to the ministry in Northampton, the text's pattern of linking spiritual experience to the visual perception of natural scenery is firmly established, and it continues there in a way that anticipates Cole's painting. When Edwards confesses, "Often since I lived in this town [Northampton], I have had very affecting

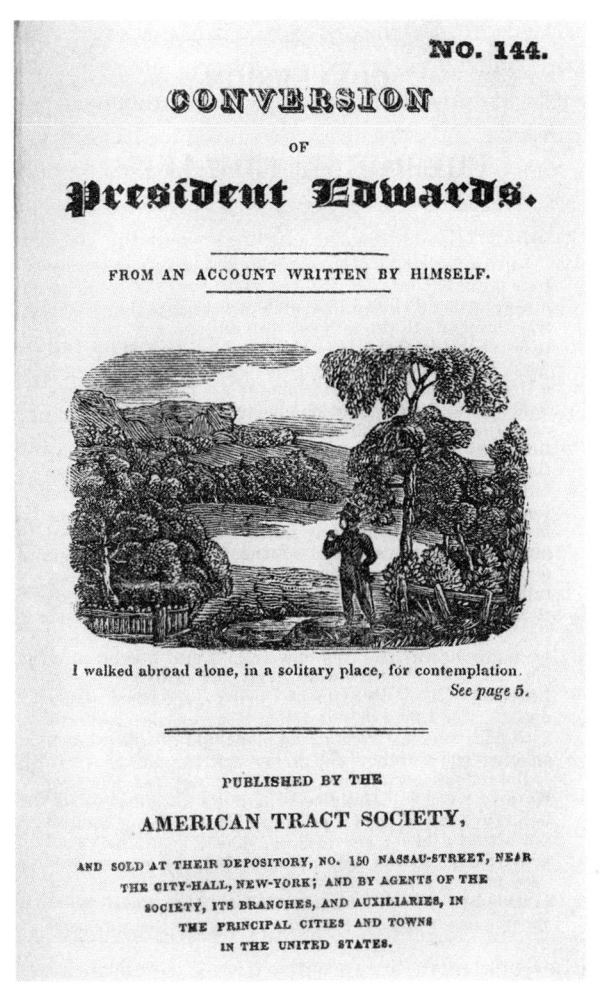

FIGURE 1.9. Alexander Anderson, "I walked abroad alone." Wood engraving. From *Publications of the American Tract Society* (New York: American Tract Society, n.d.), 5:249. Photo courtesy of The Newberry Library, Chicago, call no. C 691.033.

views of my own sinfulness," which he imagines "swallowing up all thought and imagination; like an infinite deluge, or mountains over my head," the passage cues the reader to envision a sublime mountain landscape that materializes Edwards's spiritual condition. Likewise, when he declares that "the doctrines of the Gospel . . . have been to my soul like green pastures" and that "the sweetest joys and delights I have experienced, have been in a direct view of the glorious things of the Gospel," the effect is to picture Edwards gazing from the "mountains" of sin into the "green pastures" of the Gospel—to envision, in short, a moral landscape like the one evoked in Mason's sermon and depicted in *The Oxbow*.[58] Anderson's engraving, produced nearly a century after Edwards penned his narrative, literalizes this visual sensibility using the conventions of picturesque landscape aesthetics. It demonstrates how antebellum evangelicals combined landscape imagery and the medium of mass print to revitalize classic texts and genres, popularizing "a romantic version of evangelicalism" in which "the landscape could serve as the site for evangelical conversion."[59]

In illustrated texts like "Conversion of President Edwards," the ATS offered antebellum readers a kind of instruction manual for using the landscape as a spiritual aid: for reading God's presence in nature, withdrawing from the world for spiritual reflection, reflecting on the progress of sacred history, and scrutinizing the state of their souls. As the ATS emulated the ABS by launching a massive effort to distribute tracts throughout the entire nation in the late 1820s, it contributed to the production of evangelical space by using landscape imagery to promote national and global evangelization and to visualize an ideal of personal piety that transcended worldly concerns. These represented spaces and the narratives they conveyed gave evangelicals a cultural lens through which to read landscape painting as a form of sacred media in which the dawning millennium and the pilgrimage of personal holiness could be merged into a single cosmic drama.

A sense of a divine presence in nature of course was not exclusive to evangelicals: similar views were held by many groups in nineteenth-century America, including liberal Christians, Transcendentalists, and Romantics like Cole.[60] But Edwards's narrative reflects a distinctly evangelical fusion of that presence with sacred history. When he describes his wont, while living in New York as a young man, "to retire into a solitary place, on the bank of Hudson's river," where he would often discuss with a friend "the advancement of Christ's kingdom in the world, and the glorious things that God would accomplish for his church in the latter days," he references his practice of scrutinizing current events for signs prophesied in scripture.[61] Edwards held what antebellum Protestant theologians would term a postmillennial interpretation of sacred history: rather than expecting the Second Coming to be a literal, physical advent that would decisively interrupt secular time and space and inaugurate a new world, Edwards emphasized a figurative interpretation of the millennium that expected Christ's spiritual kingdom to be achieved gradually on Earth and within history through human means.[62] Among these means were coordinated efforts to spread the Gospel through revivals, prayer meetings, and missions that would spread around the globe until, as Edwards predicted in *A History of the Work of Redemption*, "all the world [shall] be united in peace and love in one amiable society; all nations, in all parts, on every side of the globe, shall then be knit together in sweet harmony, all parts of God's church assisting and promoting the knowledge and spiritual good one of another."[63] While the dawning of this new age could be traced in news reports and personal correspondence, Edwards's meditations above the Hudson hint that it was also revealed in the landscape itself.

By the early nineteenth century, postmillennialism had emerged as the dominant form of millennial interpretation among American Protestants.[64] Evangelicals seeking to hasten the arrival of the millennium adopted modern methods to carry out Christ's injunction to "Go ye into all the world, and preach the gospel to every creature" (Mark 16:15).[65] Using stereotypography, steam-powered presses, and new forms of corporate organization, the ABS as well as the ATS and the American Sunday School Union produced millions of publications, culminating in what they termed "general supply" campaigns from 1829 to 1833 that aimed to place Bibles, tracts, and Sunday school books in every home in the country.[66] As the Reverend Justin Edwards, a member of the ATS publishing committee, told delegates at the society's first annual meeting in 1826, "These are the truths ... stamped in bold relief on the face of Religious Tracts, and extended to every city, and town, and village, and family, and soul; by which this Society is to aid in renovating a world, and preparing a 'multitude that no man can number,' to shine in the beauty of holiness, and shout the triumphs of grace to everlasting ages."[67] This faith in the power of print to create an expanding community of believers that transcended physical and social distance is vividly captured in an ATS contribution form engraved by Asher B. Durand (fig. 1.10). A diverse group of individuals iconographically identified with different continents, races, and faith traditions are brought together through the power of the radiant printing press in their midst. The press stands in the central position that in earlier images had been reserved for the preaching missionary (see fig. 1.11) or even Jesus himself, signaling the heightened sense of divine agency and sacred "aura" print assumed within the evangelical public sphere.[68] This centrifugal diffusion of Christian truth around the world became a favorite theme in ATS publications. In an indication of the continuing relevance of Edwards's millennial eschatology to its efforts, those publications included forty thousand copies of *A History of the Work of Redemption*.[69]

Landscape imagery offered a way to condense the complex, shifting, and far-flung network of benevolent enterprises into a comprehensible image of global evangelization. In 1822 the New England Tract Society's *Christian Almanack* captured the proselytizing impulse reflected in its many lists and statistical tables by predicting that "when all men are supplied with Bibles; when the Gospel is proclaimed from every mountain, in every valley and on every plain; when the children of every land are properly instructed; when war is

FIGURE 1.10. Asher B. Durand (engraver) after George Miller, American Tract Society Certificate (detail), n.d. Line engraving on paper, 10⅛ × 8⅜ in. (25.7 × 21.3 cm). Collection of The New-York Historical Society, Asher B. Durand Print Collection, PR.221.13, New-York Historical Society. Photography © New-York Historical Society.

ended, the prisoner liberated, and the bondman freed;—then, but not till then, will the Sabbath of rest, and peace, and righteousness, shed its heavenly light over the nations of the earth."[70] Abel Bowen's wood engraving (fig. 1.11), which graced covers of the *Almanac* throughout the 1820s, visualizes this process of information diffusion and spatial compression in a manner similar to Durand's contribution form, with a group of American Indians, African slaves, and Asians gathered at the feet of a white missionary.[71] Here, however, the mountainous, tropical backdrop signals the geographic scope of missionary efforts promoted in the *Almanac*. This landscape offered readers access to a moral geography far more expansive than the one charted by organizations like the Connecticut Missionary Society during the previous two decades as they encouraged Christians to settle Ohio's Western Reserve. Such home missions on the western "frontier" and the foreign missionary efforts urged in the *Almanac* were complementary projects: both were inspired by Edwards's revivalism and millennial expectations, and both used the landscape to promote their agendas.[72]

Indeed, pastoral landscape imagery became a telling verbal and visual cue for foreign missionary efforts. Harvest scenes depicted in the *Almanac* from the 1820s through the 1840s (fig. 1.12) drew on comparisons of benevolent Christians to field laborers sowing the Gospel and reaping a harvest of souls.

FIGURE 1.11. Abel Bowen (engraver), "Go Ye into All the World." Wood engraving. From *The Christian Almanack, for the Year of Our Lord and Saviour Jesus Christ, 1825* (Boston: Lincoln & Edmands, 1824), cover. University of Chicago Library.

"'The field is the world,'—how wide! how vast! six hundred millions, and probably more, who have never heard of the Gospel," the 1836 *Almanac* declared. "If we have a great harvest to gather, we do not content ourselves with merely thinking of it occasionally—just looking at it, and then turning away. No, we thrust in the sickle, and make it our *business* till it is all secured. So we must do in the great harvest of nations."[73] This agrarian symbolism was literalized in the "missionary fields" that many New England communities tended

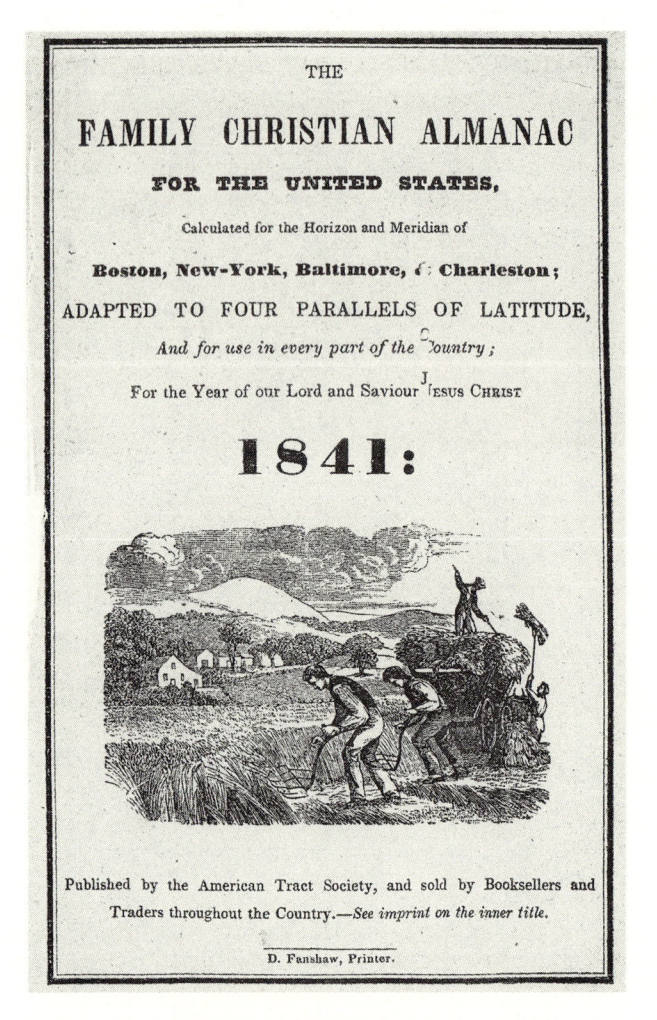

FIGURE 1.12. Harvest scene. Wood engraving. From *The Family Christian Almanac* (New York: American Tract Society, 1840), cover. University of Chicago Library.

beginning in the late 1810s, plots of land where crops were grown and sold to raise funds for foreign missions or donated to feed students boarding at the Foreign Mission School in Cornwall, Connecticut. There Pacific Islanders, American Indians, and others studied to return to their homelands as Protestant missionaries (training that included farm labor as part of its civilizing mission).[74] As ATS publications used the landscape to envision evangelical fervor sweeping the globe and drawing the millennium nearer, they urged readers to expand their sphere of ethical concern beyond the local through benevolent activity, an act that was often likened to looking across the

FIGURE 1.13. Family reading. Line engraving. From *Evangelical Family Library* (New York: American Tract Society, n.d.), vol. 3, frontispiece. University of Chicago Library.

landscape. The 1825 *Christian Almanack* praised a devout farming family full of "so much benevolence" that even the children "look beyond the bounds of their own village, and interest themselves in the welfare of the world" by keeping charity boxes for American Indian children; the family's efforts to achieve "the enlargement of Christ's kingdom" contrast with the narrow self-interest of "farmer Holdfast," who refuses to participate in missions and other benevolent causes.[75] As they drew attention to distant strangers, evangelical publications paradoxically sought to expand believers' ethical attention by gathering them into the home to read—a dynamic captured in the frontispiece to the ATS *Evangelical Family Library* (fig. 1.13), in which the landscape painting hanging behind the family nicely suggests the spatial nature of the cognitive work being performed as they read.[76]

At the culmination of this reciprocal expansion of evangelization and ethical awareness, the land itself indicates the dawning millennium. One tract compared the combined efforts of "Bible, and Missionary, and Education, and Tract Societies" to the tributaries of "a mighty river, destined to penetrate every moral desert, and carry fertilization to every province of our desolated world; fed with the showers of heaven, and every day flowing on with deeper and broader channel, the wilds of Arabia, the heaths of Africa, and the plains of Siberia, can oppose no effectual barrier to its influence."[77] Another likened the contemplation of God's "scheme of redemption" to the prospect of the traveler who "leave[s] his home, and his country" and from an "enchanted spot" surveys "the long extended valley, where vegetation, in her varied forms, puts forth all her magnificence and beauty—where the burning mountain is casting up its liquid flames—or the cataract is thundering amidst the solemn stillness of deserted declivities."[78] Similar to Edwards's meditations above the Hudson River and Northampton, the incandescent character of this landscape suggests that the human community is not all that is transformed as benevolence spreads and the Kingdom draws nearer: the land itself begins to glow with divine presence, becoming a form of sacred media.

The pervasive presence of what might be called the "millennial landscape" in evangelical print provides a crucial context for understanding what *The Oxbow*'s cosmically charged prospect would have signified to an evangelical viewer. With its elevated view of a "mighty river" flowing through a glowing valley, its fields dotted with neatly harvested sheaves of wheat, and the Word literally written on the landscape, the painting gains heightened legibility alongside the literary and visual images displayed in the pages of evangelical publications. As the viewer gazes simultaneously across the omega into a harmonious millennial future and into a valley celebrated as a birthplace of American evangelicalism, the pastoral valley floor resonates strongly with a convention of using the landscape to represent missionary enterprise and millennial activism that was well established by the mid-1830s.

Yet evangelical publications reveal another, more inward dimension to evangelical space, one that Edwards, Finney, and Mason all expressed when they used the landscape to dramatize the individual's struggle with sin. What might be termed the "homiletic landscape" drew on a Protestant tradition of spatial narratives that Gregory S. Jackson calls "homiletic templates."[79] The roots of this tradition reach back to the Christian *peregrinatio*, the journey of faith that finds its scriptural source and ethos in Paul's account of the faithful as "strangers and pilgrims on the earth" who patiently await the fulfillment of God's promises in "a better country, that is, an heavenly" one (Hebrews 11:13–16).[80] This tradition was best known in nineteenth-century America through its Puritan-derived strain exemplified by John Bunyan's *The Pilgrim's Progress* (1678), which appeared in numerous editions throughout the century, including in the ATS *Evangelical Family Library* beginning in the early 1830s.[81] The encounter between Christian's small group of pilgrims and the worldly merchants of "Vanity Fair" captures the ethos at the heart of the homiletic landscape: "The men told them they were pilgrims and strangers in the world, and that they were going to their own country, which was the heavenly Jerusalem, Heb. 11: 13–16; and that they had given no occasion to the men of the town, nor yet to the merchandisers, thus to abuse them, and to let them in their journey." To attain salvation, the pilgrims must hew to the "narrow way" and constantly guard against being detained or distracted from their destination.[82] Their unwillingness to become attached to specific places on their journey reinforces the distinction between "inward and outward" reality that Luxon identifies as a marker of "two-world ontology" in *The Pilgrim's Progress*.[83] In addition to publishing *The Pilgrim's Progress* in its entirety and excerpted as tracts, the ATS adapted the homiletic plot to a variety of settings, from the Holy Land to steamboats and turnpikes in the United States.[84]

Landscape illustration provided a way to visualize the spatial conceit at the heart of the homiletic plot. A tract warning of "the utter vanity and insufficiency, and emptiness of this present world" showed Israelites winding their way through the landscape beneath a storm-engulfed Mount Sinai (fig. 1.14).[85] A sequel to Legh Richmond's popular tract "The Dairyman's Daughter," which chronicled the elderly dairyman's effort to "learn the holy art of walking with God" amidst the "delusions of the world" after his daughter's death, displayed on its cover a casket being carried through the landscape (fig. 1.15), literalizing the Pauline injunction to become "dead to the world" that appeared in countless evangelical devotional manuals and memoirs.[86] A tract that previewed Cole's *Voyage of Life* series, "The Seaman's Chart," tells readers they are "embarked in frail vessels, on the dangerous voyage of life; a voyage, which you are even now pursuing, and which will terminate, either in the Port of Heaven, or in the Gulf of Perdition."[87] The tract's cover illustration (see fig. 1.16) depicts a coastal landscape divided between the "Gulf of Perdition" on the left and the "Port of Heaven" on the right, a scene reminiscent of both the vertical compositional split of Cole's *Expulsion from the Garden of Eden* and the elevated perspective of *The Oxbow*. In each case, the landscape functions as a script for the individual quest for personal holiness. Visual piety converges with the Protestant mode of reading that Matthew P. Brown calls "heart piety," in which

FIGURE 1.14. "The Warning Voice." Wood engraving. From *Publications of the American Tract Society* (New York: American Tract Society, n.d.), 1:65. Photo courtesy of The Newberry Library, Chicago, call no. C 691.033.

the "pious reader incorporates the text and its spiritual tenets, to the neglect of his worldly life."[88]

The homiletic and millennial landscapes imply two different relationships to the sacred and distinct forms of agency. The millennial landscape is infused with a sense of God's immanence as the millennium approaches and the ontological gap between this world and the next diminishes; the homiletic landscape, by contrast, preserves the gap and emphasizes God as distant and transcendent. Whereas the millennial landscape registers the collective efforts of believers to create a Christian community that spans the globe, the homiletic landscape figures the believer's internal state in relation to a corrupt world that cannot be redeemed but only endured. The two spatial imaginaries were not mutually exclusive but instead represented complementary moods of piety and religious practice. As Finney insisted, the individual's conversion and subsequent "growth in grace" led directly to a life of sustained participation in organized benevolence.[89] Even so, in ATS tracts these moods tended to remain relatively discrete, perhaps reflecting the difficulty of integrating them in practice.

THE
LIFE AND CONVERSION
OF THE
DAIRYMAN.

BY REV. DANIEL TYERMAN,
Since one of the Missionary Deputation to the South Seas, China, India, &c.

FIGURE 1.15. "The Life and Conversion of the Dairyman." Wood engraving. From *Publications of the American Tract Society* (New York: American Tract Society, n.d.), 3:349. Center for Research Libraries.

One visual mode gaining popularity in the United States, however, was well suited to signify both. The panoramic sweep of many American landscape paintings, combined with the romantic tendency to elevate nature to an alternative form of scripture, enabled them to express the expansive scope and divine immanence of the millennial landscape. At the same time, the narrative potential of the picturesque visual trail as well as the human figures and other pictorial elements invited the translation of the homiletic journey into visual landscapes—as indeed it was by painters including Cole, Frederic Church, and Jasper F. Cropsey, all of whom painted works inspired by *The Pilgrim's Progress* in the 1840s and 1850s.[90] The ATS seized on this dual potential, using landscape illustrations both to visualize a sphere of ethical obligation and

FIGURE 1.16. "The Seaman's Chart." Wood engraving. From *Publications of the American Tract Society* (New York: American Tract Society, n.d.), 5:177. Photo courtesy of The Newberry Library, Chicago, call no. C 691.033.

agency that stretched beyond the viewer's immediate experience and to represent the narrative unity of the individual Christian life unfolding over time. Indeed, the conventions of the beautiful and the sublime provided a visual grammar that roughly corresponded to these spatial imaginaries. The beautiful evoked a sense of the divine presence in nature and the pastoral harmony of the dawning millennium (as in Anderson's engraving of Edwards and the harvest scenes in the *Christian Almanac*), while the sublime captured the homiletic vision of life as a perilous journey through a hostile world (as in "The Warning Voice" and "The Seaman's Chart"). To be sure, the ATS did not always use landscape imagery to illustrate these two ideas. Images of domestic interiors often accompanied tracts that deployed homiletic tropes; depictions of biblical figures like Adam and Eve or Jesus sometimes were pictured in tracts about millennialism and benevolence; and in some cases, no images were used at all. But only landscape imagery was used consistently to represent both.

Landscape representation, then, functioned within evangelical print culture to mediate between two rhetorical modes that expressed divergent ideals of activism and piety. Scholars have indirectly related Cole's art to each of these modes by discussing his attempts to grapple with American millennial optimism and his affinity for allegory. The religious publications that circulated around *The Oxbow*, though, suggest that for an evangelical viewer like Talbot, Cole's painting would likely have spoken (even if unconsciously) to a fundamental tension at the heart of antebellum evangelical culture—what Candy Gunther Brown calls "the struggle of nineteenth-century evangelicals to balance purity with presence" in the world.[91] Through that lens, the sweeping course of sacred history we have traced through *The Oxbow* from Eden to the millennium serves as a reminder of the ongoing collective labor required to realize the universal harmony and divine presence embodied in the millennial landscape. Concurrently, the path through the wilderness toward the cross (the camp stool) and, beyond that, the fair country across the river, as well as the painting's vivid depiction of the sublime natural forces that revivalists used to represent the inner drama of sin and conversion, evoke the homiletic landscape's emphasis on personal piety and otherworldly detachment. The spectacular combination of both landscapes in a single canvas in such legible terms is what makes *The Oxbow* a paradigmatic example of evangelical space. In other words, the "dramatic synthesis of the Sublime and the Beautiful" that Ellwood C. Parry III (among others) has observed in the painting represents a form of cultural mediation that reached beyond the elite discourse of landscape aesthetics to encompass the concerns of ordinary people whose ministers, newspapers, and books told them repeatedly that the landscape was a spiritual medium that conveyed vital truths about their souls and their world.[92]

Talbot and other evangelicals who saw *The Oxbow* had been prepared by the places they visited, the words and pictures they encountered, and the religious narratives they lived to understand the painting as a meditation on millennial history and their role in it. While it is certainly true that for many Americans this history, with its typological echoes of Chosen People and Promised Land, served to legitimate a process of territorial conquest and settler colonialism, the evangelical mediascape explored in this chapter demonstrates that expansion was just one of many imperatives encoded in the landscape. Indeed, it is precisely because of this polyvalence that for some viewers Cole's landscape would have evoked an altogether different story than the one promoted by Edwards's evangelical descendants.

The Oxbow in Native Space

In Catharine Maria Sedgwick's popular 1827 historical romance *Hope Leslie; or, Early Times in the Massachusetts*, set in Puritan New England of the 1630s and 1640s, a party that includes the eponymous heroine sets out from the frontier settlement of Springfield on "an excursion to a new settlement on the river, called Northampton." There they hire an Indian guide to take them "to the summit of a mountain, which rises precipitously from the meadows, and overlooks an ocean of forest."[93] Having reached the spot that Cole would immortalize in his painting, "Mr. Holioke" and Hope's adopted father, William Fletcher, use the prospect to survey "the sites for future villages, already marked out for them by clusters of Indian huts." As they plot dispossession and conquest, Hope makes a different sort of inventory of the landscape, which she later relates in a letter to her adopted brother, Everell: "I observed that the highest rock of the mountain was crowned with a pyramidal pile of stones, and about them were strewn relicts of Indian sacrifices. It has, I believe, been the custom of people, in all ages, who were instructed only by nature, to worship on high places." This excursus on natural religion prompts an exchange between Hope and the two men:

> I pointed to the rude altar, and ventured to ask Mr. Holioke if an acceptable service might have been offered there?
> He shook his head at me, as if I were little better than a heathen, and said, "it was all worship to an unknown God."
> "But," said your father, "the time is approaching, when through the vallies beneath, and on this mount, incense shall rise from christian hearts."[94]

Even as Fletcher prophecies a holy commonwealth on the Connecticut that antebellum evangelicals would invest with such nostalgia and cultural authority—a vision that harmonizes with the pastoral order of Cole's vision, right down to the smoke rising from the valley floor—Hope affords a competing view. Her sympathetic attention to Native religiosity challenges the Puritan patriarchs' insistence on the necessity of revealed religion (that is, absorbed through the Bible, not intuited from nature), affording glimpses of an alternative moral landscape. For Sedgwick, one of several "New England liberals" during the period who used fiction to challenge Calvinist dogma and puncture the myths being constructed about the Puritan past, the site presented an opportunity to remind readers of a colonial past in which not only land but also the religious truths and practices it manifested were fiercely contested.[95] In doing so she followed published accounts that noted the area's original inhabitants and recounted the bloody contest for the valley during King Philip's War (1675–78), which included Indian "attacks" on Northampton and surrounding towns.[96]

Sedgwick's revision of the prospect from Mount Holyoke anticipates the critical "countermapping" of New England sacred geography performed by Pequot author and orator William Apess in the 1830s as he promoted a vision of the region as what Lisa Brooks terms "Native space."[97] Apess, who was born in Colrain, Massachusetts, and endured an impoverished and abusive childhood in Connecticut, converted to Methodism in 1813 and became an itinerant exhorter (a lay preacher) before being ordained in 1829 as a minister in the Protestant Methodist Church, a group that broke away from the Methodist Episcopal Church in the belief that it had become too elitist and hierarchical. In addition to spreading the Gospel through his preaching, Apess entered the religious mediascape through print, selling Methodist tracts and books as well as his self-published spiritual autobiography, *A Son of the Forest* (1829), to support his preaching tours in the 1820s and 1830s.[98] Over the next several years Apess's evangelical zeal converged with his growing commitment to indigenous rights. After serving as a missionary to the Pequots in Connecticut, Rhode Island, and Massachusetts in the early 1830s, he came to the Indian town of Mashpee on Cape Cod, where in addition to leading the Mashpee Revolt in 1833 to demand Native rights to self-governance and local resources, he "organized a small Methodist meeting," held camp meetings, and formed a temperance society.[99] If, as Brooks argues, in the revolt "the Mashpee Wampanoags declared their reserve Native space," for Apess it was clearly a form of evangelical space as well, in which he endeavored "to say something to my poor brethren that might be for their advantage in time and eternity."[100]

As Apess recounted in his 1835 account of the Mashpee revolt, when he first arrived at Mashpee to preach in May 1833 he expected to see the congregation "thronging around their missionary in crowds," a fantasy reminiscent of the image on the cover of the *Christian Almanack* (see fig. 1.11). The "charming landscape" that greets Apess only heightens his anticipation: a "noble forest" surrounding "an Indian burial ground" and a meetinghouse that resembles "Solomon's temple" or "some ancient monument set upon a hilltop, for a landmark to generations yet unborn" (*IN*, 170). But if the picturesque setting and elevated prospect initially seem to promise the providential success of Apess's mission, the largely white audience assembled there deflates his expectations. He soon learns that the Native congregants, discontented with the tepid preaching style of the white Congregationalist missionary—the aptly named

Mr. Fish—have decamped for the ministry of Blind Joe Amos, a Wampanoag Baptist preacher. When Apess suggests that Fish "imitate Blind Joe" in his delivery and even invite Joe to preach at the meetinghouse in order to "unit[e] the people," he is rebuffed because "Joe was not qualified to preach and instruct"—a reflection of Fish's classism and denominational prejudice if not of outright racism. So Apess himself decides to address Amos's followers. When he does, however, he assumes Fish's benevolent mantle, lecturing on "temperance and education" and, most tellingly, criticizing the community's agricultural landscape as a sign of their moral condition: "[I] plainly told them what I had heard from their missionary, viz., that it was their general disposition to be idle, not to hoe the cornfields they had planted, to take no care of their hay after mowing it, and to lie drunken under their fences. I admonished them of the evil of these, their ways" (171). Such rhetoric had long been used by white Congregationalist leaders of home missionary societies in New England to criticize unchurched whites on the frontier in the belief that "settlers who manifested laziness through their crops and fields were unlikely to exert much energy regarding their souls."[101]

This practice of scrutinizing people's land use practices to decipher their moral condition—reading their spiritual estate through their real estate, so to speak—heightens the legibility of the neatly mowed fields and tidy grain sheaves of *The Oxbow* as a moral landscape. But if Apess to this point views Mashpee land through the lens of the dominant white version of evangelical space, his views would shift markedly during the ensuing weeks in Mashpee after convening "several meetings" to hear the people's "grievances" (*IN*, 173). In late May he helped draft a petition addressed to the state government of Massachusetts and to leaders of Harvard College (who had appointed Phineas Fish as missionary to the tribe), declaring "that we will not permit any white man to come upon our plantation, to cut or carry off wood or hay, or any other article, without our permission, after the 1st of July next." The wooded landscape that had so impressed Apess upon his arrival now appears in a different light, for Fish "had possession of five or six hundred acres of the tribe's best woodland, without their consent or approbation, and converted them to his own exclusive use" (175). Yet Apess does not simply abandon his spiritual mission to the Mashpee to pursue political advocacy. When the tribal council agrees to adopt him, they are interested not only in his legal assistance but in the "religious instruction" he will provide. Once the details are ironed out (including his agreement to "unite my labors" and share his allowance with Blind Joe), Apess describes his relationship with the Mashpee not in terms of land use or rights but in the spiritual terms of the homiletic landscape: "It was then agreed that we should unite and journey together on the road toward heaven" (174). Apess has not replaced evangelical space with Native space so much as he has merged them into an alternative version of evangelical space that combines indigenous struggles to assert their rights to property and resources with the "spiritual liberty" prized by Methodists, Baptists, and other "antiformalist" evangelicals.[102]

By the time Cole's *Oxbow* appeared in 1836, Apess had expanded this alternative moral landscape—one that revealed not spiritual decay but Native dispossession—into a regional and ultimately continental geography. That year he delivered his most direct and forceful attack on settler accounts of New England history in his *Eulogy on King Philip*, a lecture he gave twice in Boston in 1836 and subsequently published in two separate editions. In it Apess countered the sort of whitewashed account of King Philip's War that Edward Everett had delivered the previous year at a gathering in South Deerfield to commemorate the Battle of Bloody Brook.[103] There Everett claimed that "no wars, literally, of extermination, at any time, were waged" in New England; rather, "with the advance of civilization, the native tribes receded." In the Connecticut River Valley, as "Deerfield, Hadley, Northampton, and Springfield" were established, "the Indians, that hunted and fished on the river, retired before the advancing settlements, united themselves with their brethren farther west and north, . . . and easily incorporated among them." This was easy for them, he explained, because such "barbarous tribes" subsisted "by hunting and fishing" rather than "agriculture" and thus had no special attachment to particular places. Everett folded his account of peaceful Native withdrawal into a broader narrative of missionary efforts in New England: English settlers "regarded the aboriginal inhabitants as heathen" and "bestowed unwearied pains to christianize them"; despite some success, "the mass remained unconverted, and an ominous inference was drawn from the expulsion of the native races of Canaan."[104] In implying that the conquest of Native peoples was a providential consequence of their failure to convert, the equivalent of God's decision to "drive out the Canaanites" (Josh. 3:10) and other tribes from Jordan to make way for the Israelites in the Hebrew Bible, Everett used Christian sacred history and geography to legitimize settler colonialism.

If Everett's account represents the peaceful valley depicted in Cole's *Oxbow* as a sign of God's favor for his chosen people, Apess's *Eulogy* evokes an altogether different landscape in which settlers "wreak their vengeance upon whole nations and communities, until the fields are covered with blood and the rivers turned into purple fountains, while groans, like distant thunder, are heard from the wounded and the tens of thousands of the dying."[105] But Apess is not simply content to contest the settler historiography of King Philip's War and the Puritan sacred geography of New England. Rather, he challenges the ongoing association of Protestant missionary enterprise, landscape imagery, and territorial expansion. He quotes a letter published in the *New-York*

Evangelist in which the Rev. Nahum Gould, "a humble divine of the Far West," celebrated "what God has wrought" in Union Grove, Illinois, where in just three years "the savage has left the ground for civilized man," and "the rich prairie" now "brings a harvest of corn and wheat to feed the church." Declaring the place "God's vineyard," Gould describes how God "gathered out the stones thereof, and drove the red Canaanites from trampling it down," so that "the desert becomes an Eden" (*KP*, 287). Elsewhere in the letter Gould boasts of a successful revival, thriving Sunday schools, and the community's donations to "the Tract Society," "the Bible society," and the American Home Missionary Society.[106] In short, Union Grove has become an outpost of the Benevolent Empire in the West. This is precisely the confluence of missionary zeal and colonial violence that Apess attacks: "Why, my brethren, the poor missionaries want money to go and convert the poor heathen, as if God could not convert them where they were but must first drive them out. If God wants the red men converted, we should think that he could do it as well in one place as in another." Instead the missionaries have succeeded in "degrading us as a people, in breaking up our governments and leaving us without any suffrages whatever, or a legal right among men." Apess tells "the ministers and people [to] use the colored people they have already around them like human beings, before they go to convert any more," and urges "the benevolent" to "withhold your hard earnings from them, unless they do do it" (287).

As a result of men like Gould, King Philip's "prophecy" (*KP*, 307) that "these people from the unknown world will cut down our groves, spoil our hunting and planting grounds, and drive us and our children from the graves of our fathers" (295) has come to pass. Following Philip's gaze "from Maine to Georgia, and from the ocean to the lakes," Apess declares, "Had the inspiration of Isaiah been there, he could not have been more correct. Our groves and hunting grounds are gone, our dead are dug up, our council fires are put out," and the people's "rights" (306) have been stripped. His comparison of Philip to the prophet Isaiah is apt, for the continental geography revealed here is indeed apocalyptic. When Apess likens the "crimes" of white "Christians" to "mountains filled with smoke, and thick darkness covering them all around" (300), his imagery is reminiscent of the sin-blasted moral landscape of Edwards's personal narrative but without the solace of those "green pastures" of the Gospel. By 1836 Apess is still mobilizing a version of the homiletic landscape, but he rejects the equation of settled pastoral spaces with the peaceful, racially harmonious millennium envisioned in ATS print, severing the spatial synthesis at the heart of the evangelical space explored in this chapter. While Clayton Zuba has argued that the engraved frontispiece to the *Eulogy*, which depicts "King Philip Dying for His Country," demonstrates Apess's "Native visualcy"— his canny ability to appropriate settler visual culture for his own ends—the landscape is a visual mode far more central to Apess's aesthetics and politics than the iconography of Indian captivity that Zuba explores.[107] Of course it is unlikely that Apess ever saw *The Oxbow*, and there is no evidence to suggest that he did. But considering the full range of spatial imagery in his preaching and writing, one might speculate that seen through the eyes of an indigenous evangelical like Apess, *The Oxbow* might have evoked a conflicted response, torn between recognizing the valley floor as a sign of Christian moral order *and* as a site of genocidal conquest and erasure—a response, in other words, as divided as Cole's painting itself.

The writings of Sedgwick and Apess reveal that the evangelical mediascape created by organizations like the ATS had no exclusive purchase on *The Oxbow*. As much as the painting spoke to Talbot's millennial optimism, Cole's romantic idiom enables the painting to speak to the kind of "imperialist nostalgia" for the "vanishing" Indian that characterized the historical fiction of liberal Christians like Sedgwick and Lydia Maria Child.[108] For Apess, operating within the itinerant, insurgent evangelical mediascape of antebellum Methodism and addressing racially mixed audiences, the painting likely would have symbolized stolen land and resources as much as personal salvation or evangelical activism. Without losing sight of the many possible meanings that may inhere in a single picture, then, *The Oxbow* illuminates the process by which evangelicals in the Benevolent Empire combined religious texts with ostensibly secular images to produce hybrid objects that flicker between the sacred and the secular. Beyond that, it reveals their production of a distinctly modern form of sacred space through the circulation of print, pictures, and people. Evangelical space resided not simply on the gallery wall, in the open air, on the printed page, or in the heart of the believer but in the relational space generated between them. As antebellum preachers, writers, artists, and others filtered traditional Protestant sacred geographies of evangelization and pilgrimage through the popular medium of picturesque landscape representation, they fashioned the landscape into a spiritual tool that believers could use to imaginatively extend ethical concern from the local to the distant while simultaneously rehearsing personal journeys of faith and contemplating sacred history.

The geography they produced was apocalyptic in the sense that it revealed the unfolding of postmillennial eschatology as a spatial process that required the dissemination of print media across the nation and around the globe, and the parallel extension of ethical awareness by ordinary people to encompass distant strangers in need of the Gospel. The vision of sacred history promoted by the evangelical print of the ATS in the 1820s and 1830s was thus by and large characterized by cosmic optimism, not the prospect of impending doom. Not coincidentally, it also largely sidestepped the issue of slavery, relegating it to such anodyne tracts as "The Happy Negro," in which slavery is portrayed as a humane instrument of Christian conversion, which in turn renders slaves submissive and content.[109] By the mid-1830s, however, a new abolitionist mediascape emerged from within the Benevolent Empire that aimed to change that. As abolitionists strategically reshaped evangelical space to encompass the national, hemispheric, and transatlantic contours of enslavement and emancipation, they produced an apocalyptic geography in which the outpouring of divine wrath across the land increasingly seemed more likely than a millennial dawn.

2

Abolitionist Mediascapes

THE AMERICAN ANTI-SLAVERY SOCIETY AND
THE SACRED GEOGRAPHY OF EMANCIPATION

IN AN EXTRAORDINARY letter dated March 19, 1835, a woman in Putnam, Ohio, identified only as "Mrs. Sturges" wrote to Theodore Dwight Weld to describe a vision she had recently experienced after attending one of his fiery abolitionist lectures. Returning home distressed but still "vacillating as to duty," she threw herself into a chair and fell into a "reverie": "I seemed to have been suddenly transported, by some invisible agency, into a remote part of the system, from whence, as from a tower, I beheld the whole terrestrial world on which we live, spread out, as a map beneath my feet." She saw Asia's "lofty minarets & gorgeous palaces" tainted by "the darkness of heathenism," Europe's "halls of learning" overshadowed by "the dark walls of the Inquisition," and Africa's "proud monuments of science & the arts" degraded "by the cries of her captured sons, as they rose to heaven for vengeance." At last her eye came to rest on America, where she beheld a bustling nation of "cultivated farms, flourishing manufactures, schools of learning, & emporiums of commercial enterprise sprung up beneath the fostering hand of her unrivalled Constitution." Alongside this material progress were signs of spiritual advancement: not only had churches been "erected in almost every village," but "the hand of Christian benevolence, was scattering the bread of life among the famishing & destitute of every land."

Enraptured by this millennial scene, Sturges was about to burst into praise when a mysterious figure appeared and directed her eye to the "southern border," where she saw "multitudes of sable figures, bending beneath a schorching [*sic*] sun—their backs lacerated by the whip, scourged, maimed, loaded with irons—subject to every insult—& exposed to every gust of despotic passion." Worse than slavery's physical effects were its spiritual effects, for "no man cared for their souls—Few thought they had any." Suddenly the network of "Christian benevolence" that had seemed a sign of America's holiness and

Christ's imminent return became a reproach: "The hand of benevolence, spreading its diffusive charities to the Islands of the Sea, & the shores of farther Asia seemed to pluck with ruthless grasp—the bread of the water of life, from the famishing mendicants at her door." Sturges wept as a voice from heaven warned, "Vengeance is mine[.] I will repay saith the Lord." Then she watched in horror what came next:

> Spreading like wildfire from plantation to plantation & from cane-brake to cane-brake, a mighty army of infuriated blacks, goaded to madness by inhuman taskmasters & unheard of wrongs, without knowledge, without moral principle, without the restraints of conscience or of law, rose upon their oppressors, & massacred without mercy, all within their reach. And now, the land was indeed deluged with blood, & as the yell of the assassins, & the shrieks of his expiring victims, peirced [sic] my ear—my imagination started from her reverie, exclaiming, "Is this fancy or is it fact?"

Though relieved to find that this cataclysm had not yet come to pass, Sturges feared that the recent emancipation in the British West Indies would only make an uprising among American slaves more likely. She concluded, "Slavery *will* come to an end, for the mouth of the Lord hath spoken it—& who among us can look upon the signs of the times, & hope that the ushering in of the millennial morning is at hand, without trembling for ourselves?"[1]

Sturges's dream shared key features with the evangelical spatial imaginary explored in the previous chapter: its God's-eye-view of world geography, its vivid evocation of the landscape, and its visualization of the spread of Protestant "benevolence" around the globe, culminating in the millennium. As I have argued, this "evangelical space" emerged during the 1820s and early 1830s, as revivalists like Lyman Beecher and Charles Grandison Finney, religious publishing organizations like the ATS, and artists like Thomas Cole created an evangelical mediascape of words and pictures that used the landscape to convey how ordinary Christians could hasten the gradual, peaceful dawn of Christ's Kingdom. Sturges clearly was deeply invested in this postmillennial version of sacred history. But as her letter vividly reveals, by the mid-1830s slavery had begun to exert new pressures on the cognitive maps of many American evangelicals, foregrounding spaces such as Africa and the Caribbean and revising the basic plot of redemption history in which those spaces were embedded. By casting the United States as both the millennial beacon of Protestant modernity and the hellish stronghold of human bondage, Sturges showed how slavery threatened to transform America from a "redeemer nation" into the corrupt harbinger of impending apocalypse.[2]

As Weld's potent antislavery message, forged in the crucible of Finneyite revivalism, catalyzes in Sturges an apocalyptic vision that combines the "visionary mode" of popular fiction with the bloody "great day of judgment" enacted in Nat Turner's 1831 slave uprising, and then rebounds to Weld in an account that pours forth for four pages, the incident hints at how abolitionists would take up evangelical space, filter it through a variety of cultural forms and media, and produce a powerful new apocalyptic geography.[3] That process began with preaching but continued in a widening orbit through print and pictures. After being converted by Finney at an 1826 revival in Utica (Weld would later recall how "for an hour, he just held me up on his toasting-fork before that audience"), Weld had taken up the evangelical banner, traveling through upstate New York as a revivalist and temperance lecturer in Finney's "holy band" before becoming a renowned abolitionist orator in the mid-1830s, the most famous of Finney's many converts.[4] But though Weld initially gained notoriety for his preaching, he arguably achieved his greatest influence through print, as the anonymous author of pamphlets including *The Bible Against Slavery* (1837), *The Power of Congress over the District of Columbia* (1838), and above all *American Slavery as It Is* (1839), the exposé that he and the Grimké sisters compiled from their exhaustive survey of slaveholder "testimony" printed in Southern newspapers.[5] These works were among the most luminous strands of a vast, now largely forgotten abolitionist mediascape that Weld helped build as an author and editor for the American Anti-Slavery Society (AASS).[6]

Following the example of the ATS and other evangelical publishing societies, in the 1830s the AASS embarked on a national print campaign to change the hearts and minds of the American public.[7] Beginning with illustrated periodicals, shifting to pamphlets and books, and culminating with a system of circulating libraries, it assembled an antislavery canon of diverse voices from around the Atlantic world in literary forms including essays, slave narratives, and poetry. In curating, reprinting, and distributing these works, the AASS approximated what Ryan Cordell has defined as a "network author," "a model of authorship that is communal rather than individual, distributed rather than centralized."[8] These texts became the centerpiece of the society's efforts to convert the nation to abolitionism. As the AASS used its own agents and the U.S. postal system to carry this literature from northern publishing centers to towns and school districts across the North, West, and (sporadically) the South, it built a geographically dispersed network of abolitionist texts and readers.

While this network can be interpreted under the rubric of what Robert Fanuzzi dubs the "abolitionist public sphere," I adopt the term "mediascape" for two reasons.[9] The latter encompasses the entire range of media forms through which information was conveyed—print and the spoken word but also the bodies of fugitive slaves and AASS agents, crafted objects produced by women to sell at antislavery fairs, and the landscape itself. Second, because mediascapes encompass not only media networks but also the images they contain, the term offers a framework in which to analyze the landscapes and moral geographies represented in antislavery publications in relation to those texts' trajectories through physical space. As Arjun Appadurai notes, mediascapes "tend to be image-centered, narrative-based accounts of strips of reality, and what they offer to those who experience and transform them is a series of elements (such as characters, plots, and textual forms) out of which scripts can be formed of imagined lives, their own as well as those of others living in other places."[10] This describes well the abolitionist project of using media to convey the lived realities of slavery to distant readers. But while one critical tradition emphasizes the representation of the slave's suffering body, I argue that another consistent feature of the scripts promoted by the abolitionist mediascape is their reliance on the landscape.[11]

That landscape reveals a sacred geography of enslavement and emancipation distinct from the spatial paradigms that scholars have developed to understand modern slavery, from the transnational scope of "the black Atlantic" and the "plantation zone" to more regional and local formulations such as the "Slave South" and West Indian "provision grounds."[12] While each captures vital aspects of "the global socioeconomic and cultural matrix" that Amy Clukey dubs "plantation modernity," they seldom engage in a substantive way with religion, and thus they perpetuate a common conception of global modernity as an essentially material, secular process.[13] Likewise, recent accounts of "abolitionist geography," drawing on a more general "critical remapping" of American literary geography, tend to replicate the invisibility of religion within the broader paradigm of transnational American studies.[14] This chapter corrects that lacuna by showing how abolitionists adapted traditional sacred geographies to chart the global contours of modernity's cruelest and most insidious institution. In the language coined by scholars of religion to highlight the spiritual dimensions of globalization, the geography of slavery and emancipation is also a "religioscape," a term that "draws attention to the integration of and the relationships among sites, social imaginaries, and religious groups across landscapes and over time."[15] When abolitionists set out to redraw readers' moral cognitive maps—telling Northerners, for instance, of their complicity in slave economies of sugar and cotton—they did not just reframe economic and moral geography: they showed how that complicity threw evangelicals' confident predictions of an impending millennium into radical doubt. In sum, abolitionists were building the stage on which a looming political crisis would be widely understood as a cosmic drama, an "American apocalypse."[16]

As it maps the cosmic contours of the abolitionist spatial imagination, this chapter intervenes in scholarly debates surrounding the history of abolitionism, religious reform movements, and American literary and cultural studies.

In recent decades historians have drawn attention to the indispensable roles played by African Americans, women, and workers in the abolitionist movement.[17] They have also increasingly shifted focus from the movement's origins in the 1830s to later decades, tending to see the print campaigns of the 1830s as a failed precursor to political abolitionism. I have chosen to return to the 1830s and to the evangelical New York wing of abolitionism that occupied much of the field's early attention primarily because the AASS's institutional setting within the Benevolent Empire and the sheer scale and ambition of its print campaign offer the best opportunity to study how the spatial practices of evangelical reformers influenced abolitionism and antebellum culture as a whole. Despite the prominent role of wealthy white men like the Tappan brothers in the society's leadership, a more diverse group filled the ranks of its members and agents, its contributors and subscribers, and most importantly (for our purposes) its authors.[18] Timothy Patrick McCarthy and John Stauffer note that abolitionist scholarship remains largely divided between "an older story dominated by white, mostly well-to-do men, and two newer ones told from the perspective of African Americans and women," and that not enough attention has been paid to the "meaning and function" of abolitionist print—to its "art of persuasion."[19] This chapter demonstrates that these gaps can help illuminate each other—that closer attention to the form of abolitionist print can provide a common language with which to unite the "fragmented" narratives of abolitionist history. In other words, abolitionism operated as "a radical, interracial movement" (in Manisha Sinha's words) on the page as well as on the lecture platform and in the streets.[20] More broadly, I argue that the abolitionist mediascape became a vital conduit through which the material and representational strategies developed in the evangelical public sphere passed into American popular culture.

I begin by excavating the material contours of the abolitionist mediascape, using the AASS *Annual Reports* and other publications to reconstruct its media strategy and challenging scholarly accounts that see the print campaign as a relatively brief and unsuccessful episode. Then turning to the represented space in AASS publications, I show how the abolitionist mediascape revised evangelical space to fit an antislavery agenda. Writers such as Angelina Grimké, Charles Ball, and John Greenleaf Whittier translated the millennium into a "jubilee" of immediate emancipation and drew upon picturesque landscape aesthetics to portray the nation as a starkly divided moral geography in which the land itself reflected a cosmic contest between slavery and freedom. Broadening the frame beyond national borders, I show how the AASS's decision to reprint the works of black authors challenged Anglo-American evangelical ideas about Africa that reached back to the First Great Awakening. Its edition of Phillis Wheatley's poems offers a revealing look at how writers from what

Michael Warner terms the "evangelical black Atlantic" both advanced AASS efforts to remap Africa within abolitionist sacred geography and complicated its anticolonization agenda.[21] Meanwhile, the unfolding spectacle of emancipation in the British West Indies captivated abolitionists, prompting a highly publicized fact-finding expedition and deep soul-searching about the United States' role in the world that together served to turn the missionary impulse inward, away from foreign missions and toward domestic reform. Finally returning to Weld, a closer look at *American Slavery as It Is* brings Sturges's apocalyptic warning full circle, as the book's authors mounted a last-ditch effort to stave off impending doom.

"To sow the good seed of abolition": Antislavery Libraries and the AASS Print Campaign

As Weld made his transition to antislavery activism in the early 1830s, critics of slavery increasingly moved away from colonization and other schemes of "gradual" emancipation and sought to add "immediate" abolition to the list of reform causes in which many evangelicals placed their hopes for the coming of the millennium.[22] With the establishment of the American Anti-Slavery Society in 1833, immediatists gained a place alongside the existing eight "national" benevolent societies.[23] The AASS was religiously diverse—liberal Christians, Quakers, and others joined its ranks—but evangelicals were heavily represented, and over the next few years they built a media operation designed to harness the immense energy and resources of organized benevolence and direct it toward eradicating slavery.[24] As the AASS built the infrastructure to circulate millions of texts as well as engraved prints, handcrafted objects, and lectures, it showcased abolition not simply as a "material practice" but a spiritual practice as well.[25]

From its inception the AASS signaled its intentions to build a sacralized mediascape based on evangelical models. The pledge in its 1833 "Declaration of Sentiments" to "circulate, unsparingly and extensively, anti-slavery tracts and periodicals," recalled the print campaigns undertaken a few years earlier by the ABS, the ATS, and the American Sunday School Union.[26] At the AASS's first anniversary meeting in May 1834 in New York's Chatham Street Chapel, delegates hastened to draw parallels between their work and evangelical efforts to spread the Gospel. James A. Thome, a Kentucky slaveholder's son who had been converted to abolitionism during the famous slavery debates Weld led at Lane Seminary in 1834, reminded delegates that "we have no abolition paper in the west or south," related several instances of emancipation resulting from slaveholders reading abolitionist periodicals, and concluded that "it is as unquestionably the province of the north to labor in this cause, as it is the duty of the church to convert the world."[27] Such calls soon coalesced into a national print campaign. At the society's annual meeting in May 1835, delegates approved Lewis Tappan's proposal to raise $30,000 to support a "very lucid and practical plan for a much larger issue of Anti-Slavery publications"; they asked supporters to contribute 12½ cents to "get the [Anti-Slavery] Record [sic] into extensive circulation" and urged "young men," "ladies," and "children" for help "disseminating the Society's publications" (R 1835, 30, 48–50, 52). Initially the campaign "to sow the good seed of abolition thoroughly over the whole country" would focus on four monthly periodicals: the *Emancipator, Human Rights*, the illustrated *Anti-Slavery Record*, and the illustrated children's periodical the *Slave's Friend*.[28] Leaders envisioned a system of broad but targeted distribution in which individuals sympathetic to the cause would receive the publications through the mail and then distribute them in their local communities to those deemed open to persuasion. As Elizur Wright Jr., the society's secretary for domestic correspondence, wrote to Weld on June 10, "We are now making arrangements with all possible expedition to use the press on a larger scale—shall issue gratuitously from 20,000 to 50,000 of some publication or other every week. What seems now the greatest difficulty is to get the *names* of the right persons to whom we may send them. We want names of *inquiring, candid, reading* men who are not abolitionists."[29] The mailing lists compiled that summer included more than 20,000 Southerners.[30]

The mailings that began in late July 1835 provoked swift responses in both the North and the South, including denunciations of the campaign in the press, anti-abolition meetings and rallies, new laws against abolitionist print in several Southern states, and public violence.[31] Rioters in Charleston looted the city's central Post Office, seized the recently arrived bundles of pamphlets, and publicly burned them with effigies of antislavery leaders. In August, Ohio antislavery activist Amos Dresser was publicly flogged in Nashville when copies of the *Emancipator* were discovered in his luggage. The backlash forced the AASS to retreat from its Southern campaign and focus on the North, but it continued to claim its publications were reaching white Southerners and quietly turning public opinion against slavery.[32] In its 1836 *Annual Report*, the AASS claimed that in the previous year it had published 385,000 copies of the *Anti-Slavery Record*, 240,000 copies of *Human Rights*, 210,000 copies of the *Emancipator*, and 205,000 copies of the *Slave's Friend*, together accounting for the vast majority of the publications published by the society that year (35).

In 1837 the focus of the abolitionist print campaign began to shift from periodicals to bound volumes and pamphlets.[33] According to AASS reports, the number of bound volumes it published quadrupled between 1836 and 1839 to 19,958 volumes, and the number of tracts and pamphlets rose by many times that number to top 300,000 even as the circulation of its monthly periodicals dwindled and in some cases stopped altogether.[34] From the start the AASS had promoted individual works, but in 1837 its state antislavery societies began encouraging local branches to purchase the most popular books and pamphlets and circulate them within a given county, township, or school district. In September 1837 the *Emancipator* enthusiastically reported requests for "a complete collection of books and pamphlets to establish an Anti-Slavery Circulating Library" from societies in New York, Rhode Island, and Ohio, and hailed the libraries as the solution to the movement's challenges: "A good circulating library, faithfully loaned out, together with the monthly concert of prayer and the monthly distribution either of the *Human Rights* or the *Record*, to every family, would set every local society on its feet at once; and with the Divine blessing, might be expected in a few months to abolitionize any village or township in the land" (*E* 9/7/37, 73).

Soon the national organization swung into action. In February 1838 John G. Whittier presented a proposal for a school district antislavery library to the AASS executive committee, which approved a resolution appointing Weld to help Whittier "prepare one or more volumes as soon as convenient."[35] At the anniversary meeting that May, the committee reported it had "already made arrangements to issue a series of small volumes which shall embrace, within moderate size and price, the most important facts and arguments which are to be found in our numerous publications" and passed a resolution "immediately to call the attention of abolitionists to the enterprise of establishing libraries, containing a complete assortment of Anti-Slavery books, in all the cities, towns and villages, and school districts throughout the country, and to devise means to accomplish this object" (*R* 1838, 126, 9). The following month the society directed its corresponding secretaries to write to the state societies urging them to establish libraries "in every town, village & school district."[36] By the end of 1838 state societies in Maine, Massachusetts, Vermont, New Hampshire, and Ohio had passed library resolutions of their own; New Jersey and Illinois followed suit the following year.[37] Local societies in Ohio, Massachusetts, Connecticut, Indiana, and Iowa passed similar resolutions.[38] Not only would people in all of these places be reading a common body of antislavery literature, but the library resolutions printed in papers like the *Emancipator* encouraged those readers to be conscious of belonging to a spatially dispersed abolitionist reading public.

As the libraries gained momentum, the list of recommended works grew and the outlines of an antislavery canon began to emerge. In early 1838 the New York Anti-Slavery Society recommended eleven works for a school district library, including Lydia Maria Child's *An Appeal in Favor of that Class of Americans Called Africans* (1833), the slave narrative of Charles Ball, a volume of

Whittier's poems, George Bourne's illustrated *Picture of Slavery in the United States of America* (1834), and the *Anti-Slavery Record*.[39] A few months later the Massachusetts Anti-Slavery Society listed fourteen works, including James Thome and J. Horace Kimball's *Emancipation in the West Indies* (1838), the slave narrative of James Williams, John Rankin's *Letters on American Slavery* (1833), Amos A. Phelps's *Lectures on Slavery, and Its Remedy* (1834), and the *Slave's Friend* (E 6/21/38, 30). The most comprehensive list came in August 1839 when AASS publishing agent R. G. Williams plugged six different libraries, beginning at $5 for twelve bound volumes and eleven pamphlets and tracts for $5, going all the way to $30 for forty-eight bound volumes and seventy-one pamphlets and tracts, "nearly a complete set of all the anti-slavery publications" (E 8/1/39, 55).[40] The works, many of them illustrated, comprised a variety of genres including essays, letters, slave narratives, travelogues, spiritual autobiographies, literary miscellanies, and volumes of poetry. These works represented a diverse group of authors from around the Atlantic, including black writers from Phillis Wheatley and Olaudah Equiano to Charles Ball, as well as white women such as the British philanthropist Elizabeth Heyrick, Quakers Abigail Mott and the Grimké sisters, and the Boston reformer and novelist Lydia Maria Child.

Just as the ATS had assembled a group of classic devotional works in its Evangelical Family Library to unify its diverse readership, antislavery libraries provided a textual common ground for a large and unwieldy movement.[41] Unlike their evangelical predecessor, however, the AASS collections were libraries by virtue of their mode of circulation rather than their format. They were not produced in sets with uniform bindings and numbered volumes but were assembled from imprints by several different publishers—the AASS itself as well as independent houses such as Isaac Knapp in Boston, J. S. Taylor and S. W. Benedict in New York, and Merrihew and Gunn in Philadelphia—and then sold at cost to state and local societies. R. G. Williams described how the system would work:

> The plan is simply this: Let the friends of the cause in each town and village, and so far as practicable in each school district, raise what money they can by subscription, purchase a library, put it into the hands of a proper person, who will act as librarian without charge; and then draw out the books and pamphlets, read them themselves, and put them into the hands of their friends and neighbors who are not abolitionists, (who will read them,) exchanging them every two weeks, until every person in the district has had an opportunity to read them all. . . . Those who can be induced to read, will most assuredly be converted, and well indoctrinated into the principles of the cause. (E 8/1/39, 55)

How close his vision approximated reality is difficult to know, but evidence does suggest considerable demand for books.[42] In New York, plans were announced to supplement the existing book depository in Utica with one in the western part of the state (*E* 3/1/38, 170); agent J. B. Wilcox wrote AASS recording secretary Joshua Leavitt that "I could dispose of a great many anti-slavery books if I had them," citing orders for libraries in Buffalo, Lancaster, Alexander, and Bethany (*E* 3/15/38, 178). From Illinois, abolitionist editor Benjamin Lundy wrote to the society requesting books to establish a book depository there (the request was granted), and the Maine society appointed a library agent and directed him to establish book depositories in Augusta, Bangor, and Portland (*E* 3/14/39, 185).[43] Writing in the *Emancipator*, an agent for the New York society related the story of a man who started a circulating library and made 26 friends and neighbors "thorough and intelligent abolitionists"; the editor concluded, "Suppose, now, every one of these 26 new converts should be equally successful in *their* efforts, and so on. What a harvest would ultimately be gathered from a single seed!" (*E* 7/19/38, 48). The exponential growth of "converts" through grassroots distribution of antislavery libraries epitomizes the process of social mobilization AASS leaders envisioned when they called on readers to "abolitionize" their communities.

Regardless of whether the libraries were as effective as their supporters claimed, they offer a revealing glimpse of the movement's efforts to use media to transcend the limits of face-to-face contact. An agent of the Maine society estimated "that it would take him seven years to visit and lecture in all the towns in the State, and that then, by reason of prejudice, non-attendance, and other causes, not more than one-tenth of the population would be thoroughly abolitionized. He therefore urges the free circulation of publications and the establishment of Anti-slavery circulating libraries, as the only means of penetrating the mass of the people with the principles of equal and impartial liberty" (*E* 8/16/38, 62). R. G. Williams promised that "two or three working abolition men or women, may abolitionize almost any town or village without the aid of a single lecture, and at a trifling expense.... Plant an anti-slavery library in every place and you have established a PERMANENT influence, which will *live*, and *work*, long after the influence of a public lecture will have died away" (*E* 8/1/39, 55). He might have added long after the influence of the AASS itself had waned. Executive committee member Joshua Leavitt recalled years later that in 1839 the society, expecting the economy to rebound after the Panic of 1837, had planned a new surge of print aimed at establishing libraries in western states with the help of $10,000 donated by New York abolitionist Gerrit Smith; but the recovery failed to materialize, and the schism that split the AASS in 1840 combined with the society's declining influence and mounting debt to prevent further efforts.[44] In 1842 the successor to the *Emancipator*, the *Emancipator and Free American*, announced that the "publications and stereotype plates of the American Anti-Slavery Society" were being put up for auction: "These publications embrace the whole of the anti-slavery literature of this country, and much of that of Great Britain, and should be put in circulation. If small depositories were established in different places, or if different individuals would supply themselves with anti-slavery libraries, and lend the books to their neighbors, much good might be done."[45] Old dreams, it seemed, died hard. But even as the influence of the AASS waned in the late 1830s and gave way to local control, the thousands of volumes it had distributed remained, exerting a significant if unquantifiable influence into the 1840s.[46]

Scholars have long debated the scope and significance of the AASS print campaign. Most limit the campaign to the initial efforts to distribute periodicals through the mail in 1835; almost without exception, all note its failure to achieve its stated goals.[47] But clearly the 1835 mailings were only the first wave of a broader strategy that continued right up to the 1840 schism and beyond in the minds of some abolitionists, a strategy that remained remarkably consistent in its faith in the power of print to change hearts and mobilize entire communities against slavery. It is crucial to understand that strategy within its broader cultural context: the evangelical belief, enacted in revivals since the 1730s, that social regeneration would issue from the concert of deeply felt individual responses to preternaturally vivid, revelatory language. In the early nineteenth century, as another great wave of revivalism washed over America, benevolent societies added mass-produced print to the spoken word as a medium capable of conveying that catalytic language. Now in the 1830s, the AASS worked to expand the kinds of social change that language could spark. Far from a brief, unsuccessful precursor to the petition drives of the late 1830s and the formation of the Liberty Party in 1840, the sustained effort of the AASS to distribute print as widely as possible reflects a creative adaptation of a strategy of moral suasion with deep roots in evangelical culture—a strategy subsequently extended to new media and new causes throughout the nineteenth century.

When they established libraries, antislavery societies were building networks of texts and readers, not physical structures. But if, following David Harvey, we accept that spatial production is not limited to the "absolute space" of the built environment but includes the "relative space-time" created by flows of goods and information and the "relational spacetime" generated through reading (among other practices), it becomes clear that abolitionists were engaged in a project of "landscape sacralization" just as significant as physical church-building.[48] That effort required assembling a reading public modeled on the "evangelical textual community" and teaching those readers to reimagine the spaces they inhabited through vivid accounts and illustrations that both drew upon and revised evangelical space.[49] In particular it meant revising the moral geography according to which, as one ATS tract declared, "more than half the earth's surface is covered with moral darkness. Almost the whole of the vast regions of Asia and of Africa, extensive portions of North and South America, together with numerous islands of the sea, belong to the empire of paganism."[50] In antislavery libraries, this image of the United States as a beacon of Christianity surrounded by "heathen" or "pagan" space is simultaneously recapitulated and reshaped. That reframing began with U.S. geography but ultimately extended to the broader Atlantic world.

Slavery and the National Landscape

In 1836 Angelina Grimké published her first abolitionist pamphlet, urging Southern Christian women to exert their moral influence against slavery even if it meant breaking the law. Grimké's *Appeal to the Christian Women of the South* envisions the abolitionist message as "light" whose "rays strike the rock bound coasts of New England and scatter their warmth and radiance over her hills and valleys, and from thence travel onward over the Palisades of the Hudson, and down the soft flowing waters of the Delaware and gild the waves of the Potomac." Grimké, who had grown up in a slaveholding family in Charleston until a crisis of conscience prompted her to flee to Philadelphia to join her older sister Sarah in 1829, wrote that Southerners would like to "build a wall of adamant around the Southern States whose top might reach unto heaven, in order to shut out the light which is bounding from mountain to mountain and from the hills to the plains and valleys beneath, through the vast extent of our Northern States." But she assured readers that it was "utterly fruitless" to resist the "moral . . . light" that "overleap[s] all human barriers." She predicted that the "wheels of the millennial car" would "be rolled onward" by "*woman; it is through their* instrumentality that the great and glorious work of reforming the world is to be done." Benevolent organizations—"the Bible and peace societies, anti-slavery and temperance, sabbath schools, moral reform, and missions"—were instruments of this "*moral power.*" But, Grimké warned, "if these societies were broken up, their constitutions burnt, and the vast machinery with which they are laboring to regenerate mankind was stopped . . . the black clouds of vengeance would soon burst over our world, and every city would witness the fate of the devoted cities of the plain." Next pivoting to a rural scene of judgment, she related the story of a Virginia Quaker who, finding herself excommunicated for testifying against slavery, uttered a dire prophecy: "waving her hand toward a very fertile and beautiful portion of country which lay stretched before her window, she said with great solemnity, 'Friends, the time will come when there will not be friends enough in all this district to hold one meeting for worship, and this garden will be turned into a wilderness.'"⁵¹

By turns a medium of persuasion, promise, and prophesy, landscape is the figural engine of Grimké's pamphlet. As she imagines truth spreading across the continent, personified benevolent organizations striding around the globe, and bondage blighting a land of plenty, Grimké adapts the spatial images popularized in the evangelical press to a national landscape riven by slavery. The resulting sacred geography, as divided between millennium and apocalypse as it is between freedom and slavery, complicates two ways of thinking about the geography of American slavery. At the national level, Jennifer Rae Greeson has described the 1830s as a turning point between two dominant images of the South: from the "Plantation South" of the Early Republic, when the plantation's associations with the British Empire led many writers to cast the South as a premodern throwback to the colonial past, to the "Slave South" of the antebellum period, in which abolitionists (led by Grimké herself) repurposed the lurid imagery of the urban exposé to represent the plantation as the repressed "southern double" of the northern industrial city, fully complicit in "the ills of industrial modernity."⁵² Meanwhile at the local level, by the 1830s Southern slaveholders had developed a comprehensive system of patrols, curfews, and passes that Stephanie M. H. Camp describes as a "geography of containment." In response, enslaved people forged a "rival geography" of resistant spaces, not only through their own illicit movements but by circulating forbidden goods and information, including antislavery print. Camp uncovers tantalizing evidence that slaves hung illustrated abolitionist publications in their cabins, indicating that "a vibrant, if rare, part of the rival geography was the occasional use of antislavery print culture."⁵³ Here again, Grimké provides a touchstone: her 1836 *Appeal* defended abolitionists' use of visual images from Southern critics, arguing that they were the most effective way to make Northerners aware of the cruelties of slavery.

Grimké's pamphlets thus represent a nexus where abolitionist "strategy" meets slave "tactics" on the ground—where the spatial imagery disseminated by abolitionists intersects with the material spaces where slaves lived, worked, and exerted a measure of control over their surroundings.⁵⁴ But her God's-eye-view of the spread of "light" across the continent juxtaposed with landscapes devastated by divine judgment highlights a cosmic dimension to that geography that exceeds both national and local scales. Grimké's deployment of what the previous chapter defined as the millennial landscape suggests that the urban exposé was not the only literary model she drew from the evangelical reform scene. While still in Charleston in the late 1820s, Grimké recorded in her diary being often "called to attend the anniversary of a Bible or a Tract or a Missionary Society" and on several occasions distributing religious tracts to

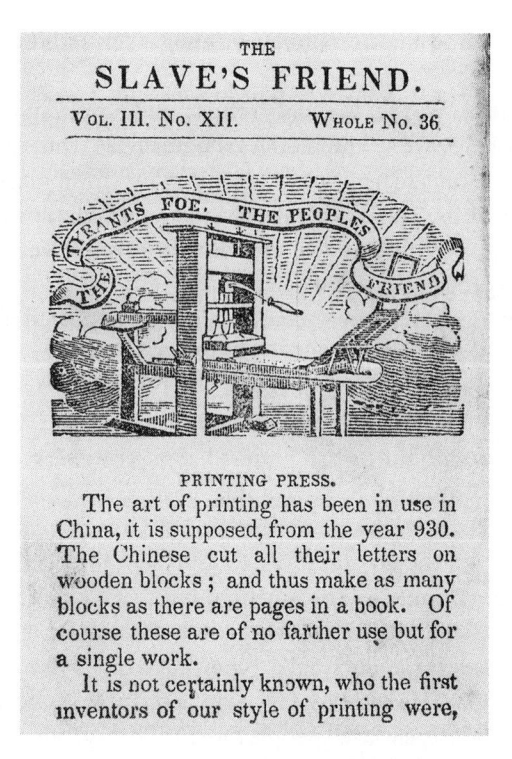

FIGURE 2.1. "Printing Press." *Slave's Friend* 3, no. 12 (1838): 1. Special Collections Research Center, University of Chicago Library.

friends and acquaintances.[55] By the mid-1830s she had begun to translate the evangelical space of those publications into abolitionist terms, contributing to a process of spatial production that would transform the geography of slavery into an apocalyptic geography.

A crucial step of this process involved placing immediate emancipation within a millennial framework. Rev. Elon Galusha, a Baptist from Rochester, moved a resolution at the AASS's annual meeting in 1836 that "slavery, as it exists in the United States, is repugnant to the spirit of the gospel, and must cease before the millennium can come" (*R* 1836, 4). Print circulation remained the central engine of this millennium: the radiant printing presses that had adorned ATS tracts and contribution forms to signal the spread of religious print across continents (see chapter 1, fig. 1.10) now reappeared in abolitionist publications (fig. 2.1).[56] But key elements of the evangelical narrative underwent translation to fit an antislavery agenda. Adopting rhetoric used in the 1830s by abolitionist ministers in Britain and black churches in the North to describe emancipation in the British West Indies, the AASS translated the millennium into the "jubilee," a term that in the Bible refers to the one year of every fifty when servants of the ancient Hebrews were granted their freedom under Mosaic Law but which now came to signify permanent mass-emancipation.[57] A piece in the *Slave's Friend* about a child distributing antislavery tracts on a steamboat concluded that if children "all feel and act right on the subject of slavery, all the people in the United States will be immediate abolitionists one of these days. Then there will be a jubilee over the land. . . . May the Lord hasten the time!" (*SF* 1.6, 6–7). In such passages, words, phrases, and images from evangelical publications served as formal patterns or "templates" that encouraged readers to activate familiar Protestant "masterplots"— shared narratives that guided spiritual development—and apply them to slavery.[58]

Landscape representation provided a particularly important template. Just as the older benevolent societies inscribed their eschatological visions onto landscapes that reflected the approaching millennium, the AASS represented emancipation in spatial terms. Whittier envisioned it as a geographical event as much as a political one:

When not a slave beneath his yoke shall pine,
From broad Potomac to the far Sabine:
When unto angel-lips at last is given
The silver trump of Jubilee in Heaven;
And from Virginia's plains—Kentucky's shades,
And through the dim Floridian everglades,
Rises to meet the angel trumpet's sound,
The voice of millions from their chains unbound. (*HR* 6/38, 4)

Whittier's jubilee could easily be the culminating moment of Grimké's description of the light of truth beaming irresistibly across the continent. Zooming in from such panoramic views of emancipation, abolitionists frequently envisioned a rejuvenated landscape where people would live in peace with each other and the land, a blend of divinely sanctioned natural abundance and social harmony that Ian Frederick Finseth calls "antislavery pastoral."[59] The *Anti-Slavery Almanac* predicted that "by persuading our Southern brethren voluntarily to remove 'the curse entailed upon them' by their own criminal consent, we hope to see the entire South budding and blossoming as the rose, and becoming as the garden of God."[60] Endlessly reiterated, such scenes produced an identifiable spatial image—what we might call the landscape of freedom—that made the jubilee tangible in the same way that ATS print used the millennial landscape to represent the dawning Kingdom. The apocalyptic geography evoked in Grimké's 1836 *Appeal* belonged to a widespread abolitionist adaptation of evangelical space that hinged upon a narrative of media saturation, mass conversion, and environmental restoration.

This future landscape of freedom stood in sharp contrast to the degraded landscape of slavery in the present, reflecting a more general tendency to view Southern land as a symbol and symptom of the institution.[61] In one of several slave narratives published by the AASS, Charles Ball described being forced to march in a coffle for days through abandoned Virginia farmland, where a crumbling brick church in a "wilderness of cedars" prompts him to reflect "that this earthly dwelling of the Most High, now so desolate and ruinous, was once the resort of a congregation of people, gay, fashionable, and proud; who had disappeared from the land, leaving only this fallen edifice, and these grassy tombs, as the mementos of their existence." As if witnessing the fulfillment of the prophesy uttered by Grimké's Virginia Quaker, Ball continues, "As I sat musing upon the desolation that surrounded me, my mind turned to the cause which had converted a former rich and populous country, into the solitude of a deserted wilderness."[62] Ball describes the process by which colonial planters bought slaves, cleared huge tobacco plantations, and built refined homes and churches, only to exhaust the soil, forcing them to sell out and move to Kentucky, "again to act the same melancholy drama, leaving their native land to desolation and poverty. The churches then followed the fate of their builders" (CB, 48). Evoking a cycle of civilizational rise and fall similar to the one Cole completed that same year in *The Course of Empire* (which culminates in a moonlit scene titled *Desolation*), Ball shifts the culprit from commerce, luxury, and political demagoguery to slavery, anticipating free black painter Robert S. Duncanson's ruin-filled landscapes of the 1850s, which warn of the threat of slavery to the American republic.[63] Yet beyond the republican idiom of Cole and Duncanson, Ball's emphasis on churches suggests that this "wilderness" is spiritual as well as natural. Ball's account of the degradation of the landscape joined a contemporary discourse that documented the wasteful and exploitative nature of plantation agriculture, but he highlighted how such accounts were more than economic arguments about the profitability of slave versus free labor.[64] They were also theological arguments about the souls of slaveholders, the fate of the nation, and God's presence in the landscape—about land that had been rendered "barren, desolate, and seared as it were by the avenging hand of Heaven" (A 1843, 28). Whereas postmillennial evangelicals expected the divine presence to infuse the landscape as benevolent activism drew His kingdom to Earth, AASS publications warned that slavery chased that presence from the land and threatened to derail the millennium.

The landscapes of freedom and slavery played an ongoing counterpoint in AASS print. The 1836 *Anti-Slavery Almanac* envisioned an allegorical figure of slavery stalking the landscape: "Wherever she sets her foot, the land is cursed.

Thorns and briers spring up around her.... Decay and ruin mark her path....
Churches and schools shrink away from her approach" (33). The following
year a companion vignette described liberty redeeming that blighted land and
sowing the seeds of the millennium:

> Light and truth go before her: peace and plenty follow in her path. In one
> hand she brings a key to unlock the prison doors: in the other she bears the
> open volume of the word of life.... Churches and schools spring up around
> her. The ground on which she treads assumes new verdure and beauty. She
> builds again "the old waste places." The land which had been gloomy and
> desolate, becomes "as a watered garden," and "as a spring of water, whose
> waters fail not." (*A* 1837, 44)

The phrases from Isaiah 58:11–12 that punctuate the passage situate emancipation firmly within that book's promise of a righteous God who will "let the oppressed go free," and "break every yoke" (Isaiah 58:6). The almanac's cover illustration (fig. 2.2) accentuates this apocalyptic dimension, depicting a densely populated landscape of freed people dancing, working, and praying. The tree that stands as a traditional enframing *repoussoir* in the right foreground is adorned with a sign announcing "EMANCIPATION" and a pair of shackles, while the body of water that typically fills the middle-ground of Claudean landscape compositions has been shunted to the side and into the distance to make way for a large neoclassical building, perhaps the U.S. Capitol. The caption, identifying the image as "A sketch from God's description of the 'Consequences of Emancipation,' Isa. 58," casts emancipation as the typological fulfillment of the Lord's promise to free Jerusalem from captivity under the Assyrians, a striking example of how the AASS combined words and images to place American slavery within the arc of biblical sacred history and geography.

As the *Almanac*'s cover suggests, picturesque landscape aesthetics provided a means to visualize the geographies of slavery. Those who read about the landscape of freedom in abolitionist pamphlets could envision the beautiful pastoral landscapes they witnessed in increasing numbers at public art exhibitions; likewise, audiences who encountered sublime landscapes in the gallery and then read about the blasted landscape of slavery in AASS publications would have ready pictures for the mind's eye. Illustrations depicting runaway slaves being pursued through tangled swamps or gazing toward distant mountains (fig. 2.3) would have only reinforced the parallel. Whittier made this link explicit when he wrote that Southern slavery "has made desolate and sterile one of the loveliest regions in the whole earth," while free labor had transformed New England from "a landscape wild and savage as the night scenery of Salvator Rosa into one of pastoral beauty."[65] Whittier divides the national

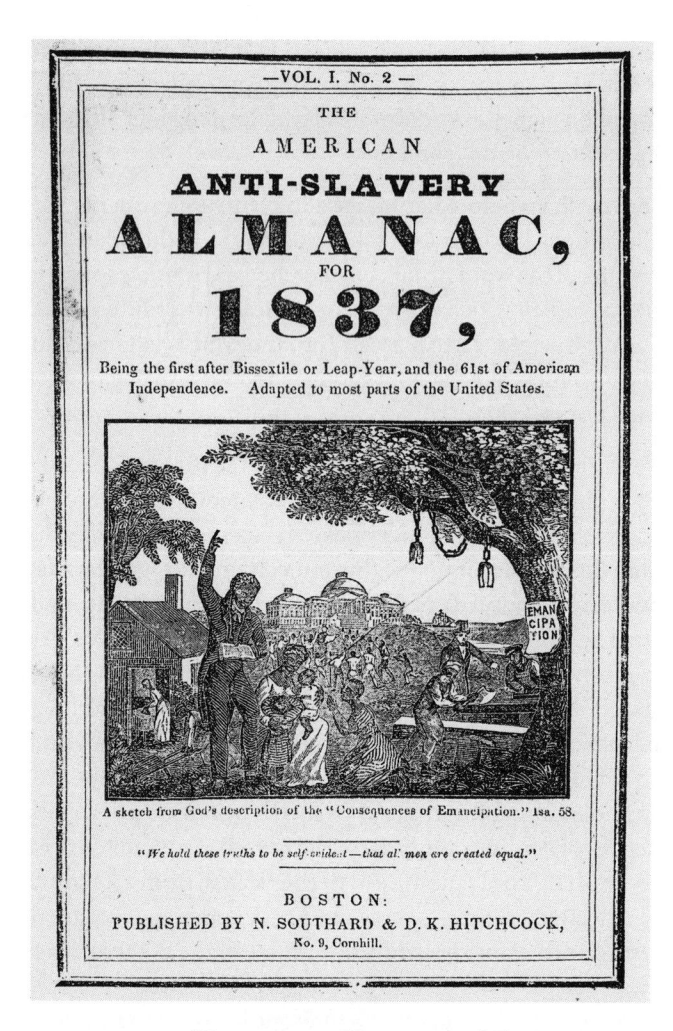

FIGURE 2.2. "Consequences of Emancipation." *The American Anti-Slavery Almanac, for 1837* (Boston: N. Southard & D. K. Hitchcock, [1836]), title page. Special Collections Research Center, University of Chicago Library.

canvas between the sublime and the beautiful in a manner that echoes the dramatic split compositions of Cole's *The Oxbow* and *Expulsion from the Garden of Eden*. But in the abolitionist version, each of these spatial registers is materialized in a specific sectional geography, and the burden of achieving the synthesis of evangelical space shifts from the aesthetic realm to the political arena.

While the bifurcated national landscapes of Grimké and Whittier helped produce the stark moral geography depicted in Julius Rubens Ames's "Moral

THE
SLAVE'S FRIEND.

VOL. III. No. IX.   WHOLE No. 33.

THE FUGITIVE SLAVE.

I am now going to tell you a story about some fugitive slaves that I assisted in getting their freedom.

One day a letter was brought to me from the Post Office. I opened it, and saw that it was written by a gentleman

FIGURE 2.3. "The Fugitive Slave." *Slave's Friend* 3, no. 9 (1838): 1. Special Collections Research Center, University of Chicago Library.

Map of U.S." (fig. 2.4), the slave narratives of Ball and others placed readers on the ground, enabling them to vicariously navigate that treacherous terrain. The controversial *Narrative of James Williams* (1838), which Whittier transcribed from Shadrach Wilkins's account of his life on an Alabama cotton plantation and his escape to Pennsylvania, and which the AASS distributed to every member of Congress before retracting the narrative when an Alabama newspaper editor uncovered factual inaccuracies in Williams's story, reveals how slave narratives in AASS libraries infused abolitionist moral geography with a distinctive African American sacred geography.[66] Early in his narrative, Williams recalls a sermon that his brother, a Baptist exhorter, preached during the 1832 cholera epidemic in Richmond, "in which he compared the pestilence to the plagues, which afflicted the Egyptian slave-holders, because they would not let the people go."[67] Such rhetoric, which was alarming enough in the wake of the Nat Turner rebellion to get the speaker banned from preaching to his mixed-race congregation, activates the Exodus story as a masterplot of Williams's narrative. Popularized over the previous decade through sermons,

Slavery is a dark spot on the face of the nation! —*Lafayette.*

FIGURE 2.4. "Moral Map of U.S." Julius Rubens Ames, *The Legion of Liberty! And Force of Truth, Containing the Thoughts, Words, and Deeds, of Some Prominent Apostles, Champions, and Martyrs* (New York: American Anti-Slavery Society, 1844), frontispiece. Photo courtesy of The Newberry Library, Chicago, call no. H 57.497.

pamphlets like David Walker's *Appeal to the Coloured Citizens of the World* (1829), and black newspapers, the biblical story of how the Israelites escaped from bondage under Pharaoh through the intervention of an avenging God, wandered through the wilderness with Moses for forty years, and at last crossed the River Jordan to enter the Promised Land of Canaan had been figured as "an account of African American slavery and eventual deliverance" that was swiftly becoming "the predominant political language of African Americans."[68] As James is driven from Virginia to Alabama through a country "wild and forbidding, save to the eye of a cotton-planter" (*JW* 38), endures the torments of his "fiendish" (41) overseer Huckstep ("the demon of that Sabbathless hell" [63]), escapes and flees by night through a tangled wilderness studded with "dreary and frightful place[s]" (88) like "Wolf Valley" (87) (where wolves indeed attack him), until he at last "on the 5th of December, stepped across the line which divided the free state of Pennsylvania from the land of slavery" (97), he inscribes Exodus onto a divided national landscape. At the same time, his religious imagery casts his ordeal as a kind of Bunyanesque allegory in which salvation is recoded as freedom, connecting the slave narrative to the homiletic landscape so familiar to evangelical readers.[69] In addition to anticipating the devilish figures of Covey in Frederick Douglass's 1845 *Narrative* and Legree in Stowe's *Uncle Tom's Cabin*, Williams thus highlights strands of sacred geography that more popular authors would develop with such panache over the next two decades: Douglass would amplify Williams's homiletic undertones through the names of his characters (Mr. Severe, Mr. Gore, etc.) and use Christian symbolism to figure his ascent from slave to man as a kind of spiritual rebirth, while Stowe would project the Exodus narrative across the national canvas of her novel, most famously through Eliza's intrepid leap onto the Ohio River that takes her, as one character exclaims, "clar 'cross Jordan" to "the land o' Canaan."[70]

The two distinct conceptions of deliverance embedded in Williams's narrative—a collective migration toward a physical place of refuge and a solitary pilgrimage toward an otherworldly salvation—parallel the tension between millennial and homiletic landscapes explored in the previous chapter. Here again the location of the Promised Land and the nature of deliverance remain unsettled. Recalling the "sympathy and kindness" he experienced from his abolitionist hosts in New York, Williams says, "The slaves are always told that if they escape into a free state, they will be seized and put in prison, until their masters send for them"; but if they knew "that thousands in the free states are praying and striving for their deliverance, how would the glad tidings be whispered from cabin to cabin, and how would the slave-mother as she watches over her infant, bless God, on her knees, for the hope that this child of her day of sorrow, might never realize in stripes, and toil, and grief unspeakable, what it is to be a slave!" (*JW*, 98–99). The "deliverance" envisioned here implies not an act of immediate, self-willed escape or revolt but mass emancipation through the influence of benevolent Northern abolitionists. While that might suggest a millennial model of moral suasion akin to Grimké's rays of truth irresistibly spreading across the South, Whittier's concluding "Note by the Editor" reveals that shortly after Williams's arrival in New York, abolitionists there learned he was being pursued by slave catchers; determining "that he would not be safe in any part of the United States," they decided "to send him to England." Thus, Whittier concludes, "America has no place too sacred from the profaning presence of slavery. It pervades the whole land,—an active and almost omnipresent despotism" (101). Suddenly it is as if the dark southern half of the "Moral Map of U.S." has bled across the entire nation. While Williams's closing words evoke the jubilee described and depicted throughout AASS print, Whittier's editorial framing portrays not a collective millennial dawn but the assisted escape of individual fugitives beyond national borders. With the North revealed not as the Promised Land but as part of Egypt (and hence a target of God's righteous wrath), it seems that the answer is not print but the Underground Railroad. So as Williams's narrative formally anticipates the sacred geographies of Douglass and Stowe, it forecasts a changing political landscape (driven partly by the actions of fugitive slaves themselves) that would render both fugitives and free blacks in Northern states increasingly vulnerable to kidnapping, a condition codified in the Fugitive Slave Act of 1850.[71]

In a range of literary and visual registers, then, abolitionists adopted the basic contours of evangelical space—its millennial narrative of universal print distribution as well as its tension between the millennial and homiletic landscapes—and projected them onto national geography.

That process of spatial production highlights the dual nature of the geography of slavery: the secular geographical imaginary that Greeson traces, of a corrupt capitalist order being exported from the Slave South over the entire nation, exists alongside a sacred geography in which abolitionist print joins a wave of evangelical media sweeping across the nation and around the globe. In this latter register, the South, far from being fully modern (i.e., Protestant), remains a dark space on the map awaiting redemption—an outpost of heathen space. Likewise, excavating the religious dimensions of the abolitionist mediascape recasts the struggle between the geography of containment and the rival geography of the enslaved. Camp judges it "unlikely" that slaves ever encountered "liberatory image[s] of black people." Any pictures they saw, she argues, probably "represented enslaved people in degraded, abused, and exploited terms," and thus would not have offered dreams of freedom but only "a glimpse of the struggle for emancipation being waged in the North." To the contrary, a closer examination of AASS print uncovers numerous scenes of liberation in the United States and elsewhere. Crucially, the achievement of that freedom, whether through a collective jubilee or the solitary flight of the fugitive, is seldom figured simply as a physical escape from bondage but is cast in terms of a spiritual transformation that reflects the evangelical roots of the AASS media campaign. Just as the Slave South was both a material geography and a sacred one, the world-shattering moment when the geography of containment was escaped or overturned took place in sacred history as well as secular. It is in this sense that the unidentified "Amalgamation prints" hanging on the wall of a slave cabin in Mississippi in 1842, put there by a woman named California who, according to her overseer, "has an idea that she is free," can be said to have contributed to a new form of lived space—one in which legal freedom and spiritual redemption are one and the same.[72]

Phillis Wheatley and the Remapping of the Evangelical Black Atlantic

A copy of the 1838 Isaac Knapp edition of the *Memoir and Poems of Phillis Wheatley* in the American Antiquarian Society displays traces of two forms of movement on its title page (fig. 2.5). Most obvious is the handwritten heading, which reads "Quechee Village A.S. Library" and "May be out 1 wk," evidence of the volume's local circulation in an antislavery library in Quechee, Vermont. But the printed epigraph below the title references another form of transit through what is undoubtedly the most famous instance of Wheatley's geographical imagination, her poem "On being brought from Africa to America":

> Some view the sable race with scornful eye—
> Their color is a diabolic dye;
> But know, ye Christians, Negroes black as Cain,
> May be refined, and join the angelic train.

This process of conversion is premised on the poem's opening image of the forced movement of slaves across the Atlantic, which Wheatley's speaker infamously declares an expression of God's "mercy."[73] As the project of national conversion to abolitionism rubs uncomfortably against a providential narrative justifying slavery as an instrument of global evangelism, the volume hints at the challenge the American Anti-Slavery Society faced as it sought to marshal evangelical energies to the abolitionist cause. As the AASS used antislavery libraries to recast national space as sacred geography, it remapped an Atlantic world long defined by a set of morally charged spatial gradients that cast transatlantic itineraries as movements from illness to health, enslavement to freedom, tyranny to liberty, paganism to Christianity (and vice versa). At the heart of that project was an effort to redefine the place of Africa in sacred history and geography.

The earliest sustained attempts by English-speaking Protestants to locate Africa in Christian sacred geography coincided with the launch of Anglican missions to the continent under the auspices of the Society for the Propagation of the Gospel in Foreign Parts (SPG) in the 1750s.[74] The Church of England's first missionary to Africa, Thomas Thompson, spent several years stationed in New Jersey before going to Africa's Gold Coast in 1752, and the

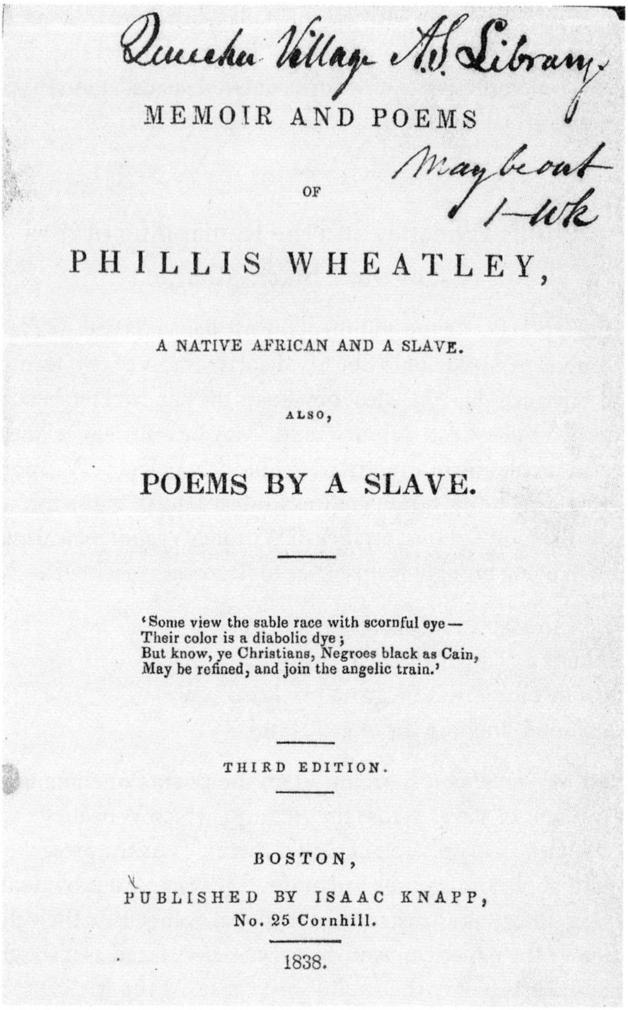

FIGURE 2.5. Phillis Wheatley [and George Moses Horton], *Memoir and Poems of Phillis Wheatley, A Native African and a Slave. Also, Poems by a Slave*, 3rd ed. (Boston: Isaac Knapp, 1838), title page. Courtesy, American Antiquarian Society.

memoir he subsequently published about his voyages drew a parallel between America and Africa as sites of "Heathen Superstition," holding up the successes of the "*Indian* Mission in *North America*" as evidence that "the *Gold Coast Negroes* may be brought to receive the Christian Religion."[75] Jonathan Edwards, who launched his own mission to the Stockbridge Indians in Massachusetts the year before Thompson left for the Gold Coast, similarly expressed confidence in the conversion of Africa to Christianity, which he saw as a key turning point in millennial history. In *A History of the Work of Redemption* (1739), Edwards described how in the millennium, "the many nations of Africa, the nations of Negroes and others—heathens that chiefly fill that quarter of the world, that now seem to be in a state but little above the beasts in many respects and as much below them in many others—[shall] be enlightened with glorious light, and delivered from all their darkness, and shall become a civil, Christian and an understanding and holy people."[76] Such was the depth of African "darkness" that the continent's redemption would not occur for some time: as Edwards elaborated in *An Humble Attempt* (1747), the millennium would dawn gradually around the globe in stages, from Protestant lands to Catholic ones to Islamic and Jewish ones, until finally after 250 years "the whole *heathen* world should be enlightened and converted to the Christian faith, throughout all parts of Africa, Asia, America and Terra Australis."[77]

Reflecting that sense of deferral, Africa did not become an active target of American missionary zeal until the early 1770s when one of Edwards's New Divinity disciples, Samuel Hopkins, devised a plan to purchase the freedom of local slaves and send them to Africa to preach the Gospel, beginning with two converts from his Newport, Rhode Island, congregation named Bristol Yamma and John Quamine, both natives of Guinea.[78] Wheatley, by then an internationally known poet and a regular attendee at Hopkins's First Congregational Church, wrote Hopkins that year that she believed the plan marked "the beginning of that happy period foretold by the Prophets, when all shall know the Lord from the least to the greatest."[79] Though in the end the plan was frustrated by the Revolutionary War and a scarcity of funds, Hopkins continued to advocate African colonization until his death in 1803, and like Wheatley he conceived of the project in millennial terms (though the millennium he envisioned was less imminent and more marked by God's wrath than Wheatley's).[80]

African colonization as a means of evangelizing the continent ascended to prominence in the Benevolent Empire with the establishment of the American Colonization Society (ACS) in 1816. Although the ACS and several state colonization organizations managed to secure a foothold in Liberia, which sustained a population of more than one thousand by the end of the 1820s, in the following decade the AASS's fervent opposition to colonization led it to question the inexorable diffusion of the Gospel across Africa.[81] That friction was on full display in 1834 as the AASS sponsored a series of public meetings on colonization in the Chatham Street Chapel, the first two of which featured the testimony of Thomas C. Brown, a free black carpenter from South Carolina who had recently returned from Liberia after spending more than a year there.[82] Brown faced hostility from supporters of colonization and foreign missions alike as he painted a dispiriting picture of life in a colony where illness was rampant, alcohol flowed freely, Sabbath schools had languished, missionaries had failed to win converts because they didn't speak the native tongue, and Bibles and tracts lay neglected because most settlers could not read. When asked, "Do the colonists pray much about the conversion of Africa to God? And do those who are professing Christians act as if they considered themselves missionaries among the heathen," Brown could only respond, "I cannot say they do."[83] Clearly this was not the millennium Hopkins and Wheatley had envisioned.

While one strategy to revise the Edwardsian narrative about Africa involved undercutting colonization as a means to spread Gospel light across the "dark continent," another involved dispelling the notion of African darkness in the first place by reclaiming the cultural and intellectual achievements of African civilizations.[84] Lydia Maria Child chronicled the history of African societies and cultures since "ancient times," when "Africa was the centre, from which religious and scientific light had been diffused." The "degraded condition" of modern Africans, she argued, was not due to "laws of nature" but to European colonialism, specifically the simultaneous emergence of "the *art of printing*" and "modern slavery," and the decision to export the slave trade to Africa and print everywhere else.[85]

The most eloquent testament to African cultural and intellectual potential, however, came from Africans themselves. Works by Equiano and Wheatley (as well as Chloe Spear's ghostwritten memoir) were featured in antislavery libraries under titles that identified their authors as "African" or African "Native[s]." The prominence of Africa in these works varies widely. Equiano famously (and controversially) describes a childhood in the West African kingdom of Benin and his travels through surrounding nations in considerable detail; Spear's narrative, by contrast, opens with a brief scene of her childhood kidnapping (which is also depicted in the volume's frontispiece) before quickly moving to Boston, while Wheatley, according to the "Memoir" that prefaced all three editions of her poems published in the 1830s, remembered nothing of her African past except for a single image of her mother pouring out water every morning to greet the rising sun.[86] Nonetheless, each text is pulled between the impulse to disavow their subject's African origins and Africa's continuing claims on their identities and feelings. Spear, arriving in New England having been "divided from all she held dear in this life, and knowing nothing of a better, . . . sighed, and wished for *death*," believing that her spirit would return to Africa and be reborn into her family.[87] While such scenes have provided fodder for scholarly debates over how much African culture survived the Middle Passage, when read within the abolitionist mediascape they raise a different set of issues.[88] Circulated by an organization intent on discrediting colonization but eager to avoid alienating evangelicals who supported the foreign missionary enterprise, these texts face east across the Atlantic: they ask not only what religion slaves brought with them from Africa to America but what they might carry away from America after emancipation. Surprisingly it is Wheatley, the figure in whom the providential erasure of African origins would appear to be most complete, who presents the most complex and challenging answer to that question.

"'Twas mercy brought me from my heathen land." This, as it turns out, is the only line quoted in the "Memoir" that prefaces the 1838 Knapp edition of Wheatley's poems. Penned by Margaretta Matilda Odell, Wheatley's first biographer (and the great-grandniece of Wheatley's mistress, Susanna Wheatley), the memoir declares the poem "On being brought from Africa to America" "a beautiful expression of [Wheatley's] religious sentiments, and a noble vindication of the claims of her race," while at the same time noting the impossibility of reading it "without emotions both of regret and admiration" (*PW*, 16–17).[89] Odell's regret, presumably, is for the existence of a transatlantic slave trade that kidnapped Wheatley as a child and brought her to Boston decades earlier, even as Odell admires the providential result in an individual who showed "African genius, sustained by Christian benevolence, and guided by Christian faith" (9). Odell negotiates this ambivalence by constructing a kind of amnesia dividing Wheatley's African nativity from her subsequent life in America. Odell writes, "She does not seem to have preserved any remembrance of the place of her nativity, or of her parents, excepting the simple circumstance that her mother *poured out water before the sun at his rising*—in reference, no doubt, to an ancient African custom" (12–13). But this claim presents a difficulty for Odell, who notes that "the memories of most children reach back to a much earlier period than their seventh year," the approximate age at which Wheatley was kidnapped. One possible explanation, Odell surmises, is that Wheatley's memory was poor and "did not equal the other powers of her mind" (13)—a possibility she infers from Wheatley's need to record her compositions in writing as soon as they entered her head, whether in the middle of the night or in the midst of domestic tasks, before they "vanished" (18). But if "faithlessness of memory" is not the culprit, the child may have been kidnapped at an age much younger than seven and endured a long period of captivity before entering the Wheatley household in Boston; that intervening period, combined with the traumatic nature of the experiences Wheatley endured, "might naturally enough obliterate the recollection of earlier and happier days" (13). This preoccupation with Wheatley's memories of Africa bespeaks a certain anxiety that the poet might have recalled more than she let on; the mental and temporal gap Odell constructs ensures that the African past really is past—that Wheatley's life and poetry represent the bold inscription of Christianity on the blank slate of racialized "African genius."

The poetry itself, however, tells a far more complex story. The opening invocation in "To Maecenas" playfully foregrounds Wheatley's African origins by drawing a parallel between Wheatley's relationship to her British patron, Selina Hastings the Countess of Huntingdon, and that of the African poet Terence to his Roman patron Maecenas, thus dignifying the British Empire while displaying Wheatley's fondness for what Odell calls "Heathen Mythology" (PW, 20). After pivoting to Christian allegory in "On Virtue," Wheatley immediately confronts the Middle Passage in "On being brought from Africa to America." Significantly, the only change in the order of the poems in the Knapp edition from the 1773 London edition of Wheatley's Poems is that "On being brought from Africa to America" has been moved up from the sixth position to the third, placing it immediately before "To the University of Cambridge, in New-England," in which the speaker declares,

> 'T was not long since I left my native shore,
> The land of errors and Egyptian gloom:
> Father of mercy! 't was thy gracious hand
> Brought me in safety from those dark abodes. (48–49)[90]

While it's impossible to know how deliberate this editorial rearrangement was, the effect is a sense of narrative continuity that reinforces Wheatley's figuration of the Middle Passage as a means of "redemption" and stresses that experience as the source of the spiritual authority claimed by the speaker of "To the University of Cambridge" to warn her audience of white male Harvard students to reject "sin" (49).

The narrative thrust created by placing two poems that reference the poet's forced removal from Africa to America together at the beginning of the collection fulfills the expectation already raised by the volume's prefatory material, from the title page's identification of Wheatley as a "Native African" and its epigraphic allusion to the Middle Passage to the opening sentence of Odell's "Memoir": "Phillis Wheatley was a native of Africa; and was brought to this country in the year 1761, and sold as a slave" (PW, 11). This in turn heightens the significance of "A Farewell to America" near the end of the collection, creating a symmetrical frame of arrival and departure in which the initial affirmation of America as instrument of divine "mercy" is balanced by the ambivalent prospect of leaving a land of "health denied" (112) for England, a place where not only "Health appears" (113) but where, as Wheatley likely knew, a slave could not be held against her will thanks to the Somerset decision of the previous year (1772).[91] Between these poles, the poems repeatedly interrogate and recalibrate the relationships of Africa, England, the United States, and the Caribbean within overlapping Atlantic geographies of grace, health, and freedom. In one of Wheatley's most famous poems, her elegy "On the Death of the Mr. Rev. George Whitefield.—1770," the great English revivalist serves as an equalizer for an audience marked by diverse geographical origins but united by the need for Christ:

Take him, my dear Americans, he said,
Be your complaints on his kind bosom laid:
Take him, ye Africans, he longs for you;
Impartial Saviour is his title due:
Washed in the fountain of redeeming blood,
You shall be sons, and kings, and priests to God. (53)

The parallel structure of Whitefield's exhortations implies not only the equivalence in God's sight of "Americans" and "Africans" (who shall equally become "kings" by accepting Jesus) but also that conversion promises to reverse their shared marginal position as colonial subjects. Wheatley uses Whitefield's evangelism to equate America and Africa, subtly undermining America's centrality in Edwards's redemption history.

While some of Wheatley's poems destabilize the sacred geography that represented America as a unique site where God's grace manifested itself, others remap the Atlantic contours of what Conevery Bolton Valencius calls "the geography of health."[92] In "To a Lady on coming to North America with her Son, for the recovery of her health," the lady's voyage from "Jamaica's fervid shores" to "northern milder climes" to let her "health revive" (*PW*, 86–87) in Boston proleptically reverses one of the popular "itineraries of illness" that in the 1830s would bring Anglo-American consumptives (including prominent abolitionists) to the British West Indies to convalesce.[93] The poem's closing scene of the return of the lady and her young son, their "health revive[d]," to be reunited with his father while "With shouts of joy Jamaica's rocks resound, / With shouts of joy the country rings around" (87), preview the joyous scenes that filled AASS publications following emancipation in the British West Indies in 1834. The anachronism created by the circulation of eighteenth-century poems alongside accounts from the 1830s gives Wheatley's scene of Caribbean family reunification a new valence in the context of antebellum abolitionist politics. Similarly when Wheatley swivels the recuperative itinerary eastward, first in "To a Gentleman, on his Voyage to Great Britain for the Recovery of His Health" and then in "A Farewell to America," the journeys gain added resonance in light of victories in the British abolitionist movement (particularly the 1833 Slavery Abolition Act) that drew U.S. abolitionists like William Lloyd Garrison to England in the 1830s to raise support for the American movement.[94] So if Vincent Carretta is correct that "A Farewell to America" "anticipat[es] the speaker's arrival in England, the restoration of her health, and ... the possibility of the restoration of her freedom," the poem's publication in abolitionist libraries in the 1830s amplifies its emancipatory overtones, remapping the Atlantic geography of health as a geography of freedom.[95]

As a bookend to the forced departure from Africa recounted in "On being brought from Africa to America" and "To the University of Cambridge, in New-England," what is striking about "A Farewell to America" is the relative absence of the Christian rhetoric that infuses the earlier pair. No divine "mercy" attends this departure, and the all-powerful "Father" (*PW*, 49) has been replaced by the sun, that "Celestial maid of rosy hue" whose "reign" the speaker longs to "feel" (112). Wheatley's turn back across the Atlantic toward the sun recalls the image of her mother pouring out her daily oblation to the dawn; the "crystal shower" (112) of tears her mistress sheds at her departure in the next stanza poignantly suggests the ways Susanna Wheatley might have served as a surrogate for the mother's love irreparably stolen from a child of seven on the shores of Africa. In this light, the scandal of Wheatley's poetry is not so much that it affirms slavery as God's instrument to Christianize Africans, an argument that had been common since the beginning of the European slave trade (and that Samuel Hopkins himself had promoted) and that white and black colonization advocates would continue to make in the 1850s.[96] Rather, it is that after opening with an unambiguous declaration of that providential outlook, Wheatley proceeds to complicate, ironize, and undercut it with an unfolding series of Atlantic itineraries that gradually remap the contours of evangelical sacred geography.

Yet there is one final wrinkle in Wheatley's geographical gymnastics. Appended to the Knapp edition of the *Memoir and Poems* is a second work titled *Poems by a Slave*, a collection of twenty-one poems by an enslaved field hand from North Carolina named George Moses Horton. Originally published in Raleigh in 1829 under the title *The Hope of Liberty*, the collection was intended to raise money to purchase Horton's freedom and send him to Liberia.[97] Its inclusion alongside Wheatley's poems, complete with the original "Explanation" introducing Horton and soliciting funds to free him, in effect completes the circuit begun by Wheatley's "On being brought from Africa to America": from enslavement and conversion to emancipation and return to Africa.[98] The decision to publish Horton's collection seems to present a startling contradiction to the AASS's opposition to colonization. Perhaps the proof of intellectual ability provided by the poetry of a Southern slave was simply too compelling for the editors to pass up. Whatever the reason, the point is that a close examination of a single volume among the dozens circulating in antislavery libraries reveals neither a simple recapitulation nor an outright reversal of traditional evangelical mappings of the Atlantic world; instead, it shows how those narratives were refracted and reframed by the shifting and often contradictory abolitionist geographies of the 1830s.

Paul Gilroy's seminal formulation of the "black Atlantic" has little to say about religion; evangelical figures like Wheatley and Equiano are scarcely mentioned.[99] But while scholars including Joanna Brooks, Cedric May, and Michael Warner have since charted the diverse currents of the evangelical black Atlantic, they have tended to focus on individual authors' immediate historical and theological milieus, and (in the book-length studies) to produce narratives that unfold chronologically from the 1760s to an end point somewhere between the

1790s and the 1830s. The publication history of Wheatley's poetry demonstrates, however, that the looping, discontinuous "queer temporalities" that Jordan Alexander Stein has traced in the secret lives of Herman Melville's works—temporalities that elude the dominant "sequential" practice of American literary history and instead demand a literary history "organized around slow, recursive, and minor temporalities"—are vital for understanding the writers of the black evangelical Atlantic and their revival (pun intended) by antebellum abolitionists. Like Melville, Wheatley inhabits a world "where readership is not contemporary with publication but at some remove, and where a single author's lifetime straddles different emergent and residual possibilities for voluntary social affiliation."[100] In this sense, what Fanuzzi sees as the "anachronistic" incoherence of the "abolitionist public sphere" might be more usefully interpreted as a reflection of a sacralized mediascape in which the sequential "homogeneous, empty time" and contiguous, bounded space that anchors the "imagined community" of the modern nation-state blends with the non-linear, non-contiguous sacred models of temporality and geography that constitute transatlantic Protestant evangelicalism as a "religious community."[101] Across that fluid, hybrid space, the speakers and subjects of Phillis Wheatley's poems sail until, by book's end, readers might well wonder where exactly to locate her geographically (England, America, or Africa?), spiritually (Christian or "pagan"?), and politically (loyal colonial subject or proto-national patriot?). Wherever she is, one thing seems clear: as if foreshadowing the evacuation of national space by black characters like the Harrises in *Uncle Tom's Cabin*, the author of "A Farewell to America" is no longer on American shores.

The Ethical Horizon: West Indian Emancipation and the Inversion of Evangelical Space

The process of emancipation that began in the British West Indies on August 1, 1834, offered abolitionists a jubilee that could be witnessed and described.[102] Seeking to counter the largely negative accounts that filled American newspapers in the months following, AASS leaders determined to send agents to the islands to create their own report.[103] Ultimately they settled on James Thome and J. Horace Kimball, the editor of an abolitionist newspaper in Concord, New Hampshire. Their tour of Antigua, Barbados, and Jamaica from November 1836 to June 1837 culminated in *Emancipation in the West Indies* (1838), a travelogue that became a staple of AASS antislavery libraries and the most influential single account of West Indian emancipation.[104] In early 1839 Weld, who edited the volume, wrote that "more than any other work published in this Country, [it] has advanced the Anti Slavery cause."[105] More than that, by documenting the outcome of emancipation on the islands, the book challenged the sacred geography promoted by the Benevolent Empire, simultaneously shifting the cosmic drama of redemption history to the Caribbean and refocusing readers' moral maps from the foreign mission field to national space.

Thome and Kimball began on Antigua, one of two islands (along with Bermuda) where emancipation had been immediate, without an intervening period of "apprenticeship."[106] The result, they reported, was a harmonious, racially integrated society where the Sabbath is as reverently observed as "in the retired villages of New England" (*EWI*, 18). Their tour brought them to an annual meeting of Wesleyan missionaries from across the British West Indies, part of an extensive network of some 150 dissenting Protestant missions that had converted nearly 50,000 slaves across the islands by the eve of emancipation.[107] The missionaries recounted a "watch-night" ceremony at a Wesleyan chapel in St. Johns, where hundreds of slaves had gathered to pray and sing hymns as they awaited the arrival of emancipation at the stroke of midnight:[108]

> The missionary then proposed that when the clock on the cathedral should begin to strike, the whole congregation should fall upon their knees and receive the boon of freedom in silence. Accordingly as the loud bell tolled its first note, the crowded assembly prostrated themselves on their knees. All was silence, save the quivering half stifled breath, of the struggling spirit. The slow notes of the clock fell upon the multitude; peal on peal, peal on peal, rolled over the prostrate throng, in tones of angels' voices, thrilling among the desolate chords, and weary heart strings. Scarce had the clock sounded its last note, when the lightning flashed vividly around, and a loud peal of thunder roared along the sky—God's pillar of fire, and his trump of jubilee! (145)

This extraordinary passage, which became a touchstone for August First celebrations held by black churches in the northern United States and appeared in black newspapers as well as in influential addresses by William Ellery Channing and Ralph Waldo Emerson, vividly conveys the millennial lens through which antislavery evangelicals viewed events in the West Indies.[109] Scholars have tended to gloss over the text's religious dimension, emphasizing instead the book's economic analysis of the benefits of wage labor versus slave labor and critiquing the watch-night scene (if they acknowledge it at all) as a covert "form of discipline" that denies agency to the newly emancipated slaves.[110] Yet twenty years after its appearance, Frederick Douglass could still marvel at Thome and Kimball's account as "the most affecting and thrilling I have ever read," recalling how "this vast multitude, as if at the voice of God, the trump of the Archangel, rose from Slavery as from the grave, lifting their scarred and mutilated bodies up as from the jaws of death and hell."[111]

Long before the book was published, the AASS stressed how emancipation had enabled missionaries to bring the Gospel to a vast new audience. Elizur

> THE
> SLAVE'S FRIEND.
>
> Vol. III. No. I.   Whole No. 25.
>
> ST. THOMAS AND ANTIGUA.
>
> In this number will be given extracts of letters from Rev. JAMES A. THOME, written to the editor of the Slave's Friend, from the West Indies.

FIGURE 2.6. "St. Thomas and Antigua." *Slave's Friend* 3, no. 1 (1838): 1. Special Collections Research Center, University of Chicago Library.

Wright Jr. noted that in the wake of emancipation, "Bible, Tract and Missionary Societies at once found ample room for their benevolent labors. Whole cargoes of Bibles and Tracts have been sent to the Islands, and the Missionaries have been received along with these precious presents, with the highest joy" (R 1835, 44). The *Anti-Slavery Record* reported that emancipation meant "LIGHT BREAKING UPON THE WEST INDIES" in the form of "Fifty-nine tons of Bibles ... shipped from England to Antigua and Jamaica, for the use of the emancipated people" (AR 11/35, 131). For evangelical abolitionists, the meaning of August First was inseparable from the expanding religious mediascape of print, missionaries, and benevolent organizations.

As the AASS folded West Indian emancipation into the millennial drama of universal print circulation and mass conversion, illustrations reinforced the glowing accounts. A woodcut accompanying a series of Thome's letters from the West Indies in the *Slave's Friend* depicts a group of black and white children and adults mingling freely in a landscape punctuated by a church tower and a distant cone-shaped mountain (fig. 2.6). Another from the cover of the 1836

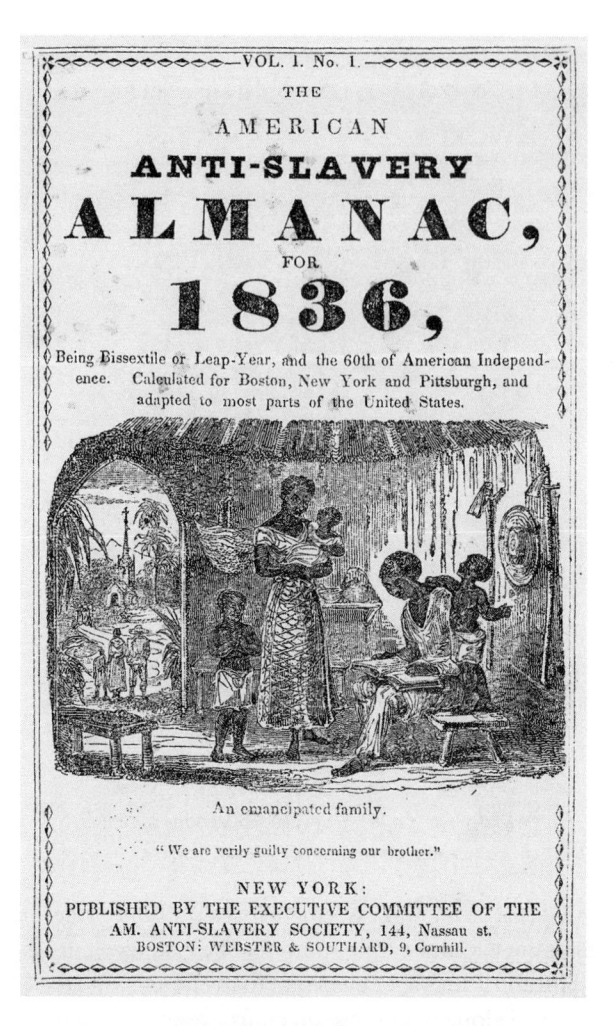

FIGURE 2.7. "An Emancipated Family." *The American Anti-Slavery Almanac, for 1836* (New York: American Anti-Slavery Society, [1835]), 1. Special Collections Research Center, University of Chicago Library.

Anti-Slavery Almanac shows "An emancipated family" (fig. 2.7) gathered around a father who reads a large book (presumably the Bible), echoing the white middle-class family that graced the ATS's *Evangelical Family Library* (see chapter 1, fig. 1.13). But the landscape painting that hangs overhead in the ATS image, as if to signal the expanded spatial awareness produced by reading evangelical print, here pivots and stretches to become an actual landscape framed by the cabin door, through which the emancipated family can advance toward

FIGURE 2.8. Asher B. Durand, *Sunday Morning*, 1839. Oil on canvas, 25¼ × 36¼ in. (64.1 × 92 cm). The New-York Historical Society Museum, Gift of the children of Asher B. Durand, 1903.3, New-York Historical Society. Photography © New-York Historical Society.

a church nestled in a tropical setting. Without the palm trees, the scene could easily belong to one of Asher B. Durand's Sabbath paintings from the same decade (fig. 2.8), highlighting the hope that the "moral landscape" of pious, orderly New England towns could be replicated in the newly emancipated islands.[112] So strong became the association between the West Indies and emancipation that the year after Thome and Kimball published their book, the *Almanac* re-ran its emancipation frontispiece from 1837 (see fig. 2.2) but changed the setting from the United States to the Caribbean, replacing the Capitol in the background with a rising tropical sun (fig. 2.9).[113] By relocating the scene of emancipation, the AASS essentially projected the millennium outward in space rather than forward in time.

That shift highlights the ways West Indian emancipation reshaped evangelical space. Initially the AASS argued that the same biblical passages evangelicals cited to justify missionary work—particularly Christ's Great Commission to "Go ye into all the world, and preach the gospel to every creature" (Mark 16:15)—required them to exert themselves on behalf of slaves. To critics who asked, "What have northern men to do with slavery, and what right have they to interfere with the domestic institutions of the South?" William Jay responded incredulously, "And is this question addressed to the followers of

FIGURE 2.9. "Emancipation, Ruin—Slavery, Salvation!!" *The American Anti-Slavery Almanac, for 1839* (New York: S. W. Benedict [1838]), cover. Photo courtesy of The Newberry Library, Chicago, call no. H 5836.028.

HIM who commanded his disciples to 'go into all the world, and to preach the Gospel to every creature?'" One might as well ask "what right they have to interfere to rescue the widow from the burning pile, or the devotee from the wheels of Juggernaut," he argued, insisting that "Christians are no less bound by the injunction to 'do good unto all men,' to endeavor, by lawful means, to break the fetters of the slave, than to deliver the victim of Pagan superstition."[114] Strengthening the parallel between abolitionism and foreign missionary work was slaveholders' practice of withholding the Gospel from their slaves, who were dubbed the "heathen at home" (R 1836, 74). Whereas Jay argued that Christians had an obligation to free the slaves *and* convert the Hindus, some abolitionists began to place the two projects in tension. As Lydia Maria Child, Grace Douglass, and Angelina Grimké asked in their 1837 *Appeal to the Women of the Nominally Free States*, "Have northern women then nothing to do with this 'NATION OF HEATHEN IN OUR VERY MIDST[?]' Shall we pour our treasures into the funds of the Foreign Missionary Society to send the glad tidings of redeeming love to 'the isles of the Gentiles,' to Russia and Greece, to China and Burmah, and the coast of Africa, and yet sit down in indifference to the perishing souls of *our own countrymen?*"[115]

Such thinking, Thome and Kimball told the Wesleyan Missionary Society of Antigua, had dampened American enthusiasm for foreign missions, for "so long as the cries of these *heathen at home* entered the ears of our young men and young women, they could not, dare not, go abroad. How could they go to Ceylon, to Burmah, or to Hindoostan, with the cry of their *country's heathen* ringing in their ears! How could they tear themselves away from famished millions kneeling at their feet in chains and begging for the bread of life, and roam afar to China or the South Sea Islands!" (*EWI*, 84). White abolitionists weren't the first to argue that missionaries, as David Walker put it, "must learn to do justice at home, before they go into distant lands, to display their charity, Christianity, and benevolence."[116] The difference was that now voices within the Benevolent Empire itself took up that critique and used it to leverage evangelical energies to the abolitionist cause. West Indian emancipation had inverted the evangelical moral geography of Christian center and heathen periphery. When the AASS called on its officers to generate a *"diffusion of light*—such as now beams into our darkness from the West Indies" (*HR* 8/38, 3) by distributing print and setting up meetings in every town, it engaged in a form of countermapping that cast the United States as one of those dark lands, its benevolence overshadowed by another nation, and a monarchy at that.

Grasping the full extent of the abolitionist "project" of "critical remapping," then, means recognizing not only how antislavery activists located national space within "*abolitionism's* hemisphere" but also how they remapped Protestantism's globe.[117] Abolitionists promoted an alternative conception of ethical obligation that imposed a boundary between near and far—what I term an "ethical horizon"—intended to organize the individual's energies. This boundary was flexible and could shrink as circumstances required. When the AASS print campaign had largely retreated northward, Angelina Grimké pulled the ethical horizon closer, emphasizing that the North must recognize "the necessity of her plucking the beam out of her own eye, *before* she goes to the South to rebuke sin there" (*LCB*, 25). But even as she attempted to keep the ethical horizon from inflating too far beyond sectional boundaries, she also worked to keep it from receding back into purely local concern. Readers had to be reminded continually that Southern slavery was not a foreign problem: "*Most persons in the non-slaveholding States, have considered the matter of southern slavery as one in which they were no more called to interfere, than in the abolition of the press-gang system in England, or the tithe-system in Ireland*" (7).

The ethical horizon signals that even as the AASS shared with other benevolent societies the imperative to push ethical obligations beyond local boundaries, it also emphasized a countervailing effort to refocus missionary energies on American slavery. Philadelphia abolitionist Lewis C. Gunn begged Weld to come speak to churchgoers in his city: "They do not look at this subject as they do at foreign missions or domestic missions and other benevolent enterprizes. We wish them to be made to feel that the same argument[s] which lead them to help forward foreign missions, etc., to labor for the conversion of men anywhere, must lead them to become abolitionists."[118] In this sense antislavery print helped shift the evangelical mediascape from its focus on foreign missions to one directed toward domestic reform causes. This does not mean, however, that the abolitionist form of evangelical space simply merged with a national spatial imaginary. The AASS's relationship to the nation remained complex and ambivalent: it drew upon nationalistic feeling to proclaim slavery a "*national* sin" (*LCB*, 7) even as it spread the idea of a stark moral divide between sections that ultimately threatened national unity.[119] It identified "American slavery" as a uniquely evil institution while at the same time situating it and the abolitionist movement within a broad historical and international context that displaced the "United States of Slavery" from the center of the global millennial narrative (fig. 2.10).

So while Trish Loughran is correct that abolitionism in the 1830s "theoriz[ed] a new spatial imaginary" that represented "a geographical critique ... of emerging U.S. nationalism and of federalism's spatial legacy," that critique extended beyond national boundaries and secular political space.[120] The central role of the British West Indies in that countermapping invites us to revisit influential hemispheric formulations of abolitionism and American culture more broadly. Literary abolitionism's Caribbean itineraries, which Martha Schoolman reads in terms of William Lloyd Garrison's spatialized politics of "disunion," should also be situated within the global millennial vision of the movement's evangelical wing, led by the Tappan brothers, Weld, and their acolytes at Lane Seminary and Oberlin.[121] That shift broadens the frame of hemispheric American studies from its focus on political and economic issues to include religion as a salient context for trans-American cultural production. It reveals, for example, how the Caribbean's status as the simultaneous object of British humanitarianism and Anglo-Protestant missionary zeal

MY COUNTRY IS THE WORLD; MY RELIGION IS TO DO GOOD.—*Rights of Man.*

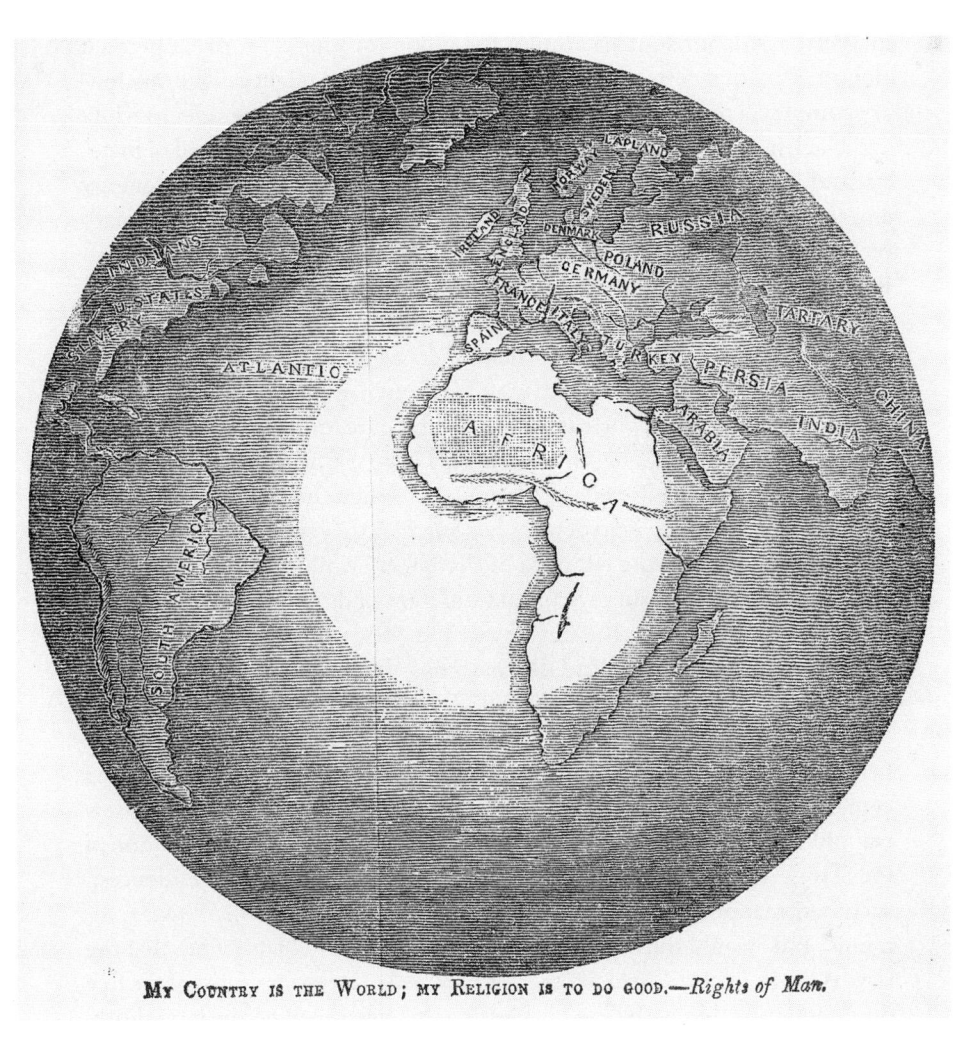

FIGURE 2.10. "My Country is the World; my Religion is to do good." Julius Rubens Ames, *The Legion of Liberty! And Force of Truth, Containing the Thoughts, Words, and Deeds, of Some Prominent Apostles, Champions, and Martyrs* (New York: American Anti-Slavery Society, 1844), frontispiece. Photo courtesy of The Newberry Library, Chicago, call no. H 57.497.

served, in the wake of emancipation in 1834, to undercut the religious imperial fantasies of many American evangelicals, even leading some of them to imagine a reversal of influence running from the islands to the U.S. mainland.

Those fantasies reflected a complex history of missionary involvement with capitalism in general, and slavery and abolition in particular.[122] What Philip Curtin defined as the "plantation complex," an economic and political system that connected New World slave plantations to colonial governments, markets, and labor sources around the globe for four centuries, operated alongside another network of global modernity that we might call the missionary complex, a religioscape that included the transatlantic itineraries of white and black missionaries, slaves, and print.[123] Out of this charged field of material and spiritual relations, a potent source of imaginative and moral energy emerged that fueled the abolitionist mediascape and ultimately left its mark on Anglo-American literary culture. When Emerson asked peevishly in "Self-Reliance," "If an angry bigot assumes this bountiful cause of Abolition, and comes to me with his last news from Barbadoes, why should I not say to him, 'Go love thy infant; love thy wood-chopper: be good-natured and modest: have that grace; and never varnish your hard, uncharitable ambition with this incredible tenderness for black folk a thousand miles off. Thy love afar is spite at home'"; or a decade later, when Charles Dickens (in a novel subsequently reprinted in *Frederick Douglass' Paper*) lampooned the "telescopic philanthropy" of Mrs. Jellyby, who devotes her energies to "educating the natives of Borrioboola-Gha, on the left bank of the Niger" while neglecting her own children, both writers surveyed, from different ends of a global missionary complex routed through the Caribbean and Africa, an ethical horizon that abolitionists had drawn indelibly across the moral map of Western modernity.[124]

In November 1838 the American Anti-Slavery Society mailed out lithographed copies of a letter in Weld's own handwriting requesting contributions to a new pamphlet that would feature "facts and testimony as to the actual condition of the Slaves." Collected from "eye witnesses, with their names and residences," such information would convince skeptics who distrusted "*anonymous* testimony" and "would thrill the land with horror." "The old falsehood, that the slave is *kindly treated*," Weld wrote, "has lullabied to sleep four-fifths of the free north and west; but with God[']s blessing this sleep shall not be unto death. Give facts a voice, and cries of blood shall ring till deaf ears tingle."[125] Pulled between his desire to amplify the facts enough to at last awaken readers' slumbering consciousness and his prophetic threat of the violence that those same horrors would elicit, Weld's missive signaled that after years of concerted efforts to end slavery through media saturation, the AASS's print strategy had reached a breaking point.

The pamphlet Weld described became *American Slavery as It Is*, a 224-page book that was published the following year.[126] In addition to two dozen eyewitness testimonies, it contains hundreds of passages painstakingly culled from stacks of Southern newspapers that Weld salvaged from the New York Commercial Reading Room in New York and lugged home to Fort Lee, New Jersey. There, he would later recall, Sarah Grimké and Angelina Grimké Weld (whom he had married the previous May) worked six hours a day for six months at the kitchen table, combing through more than 20,000 issues. In April 1839 excerpts were printed in the *Emancipator* to drum up publicity, and by May the book was pouring off the presses at the AASS offices in Nassau Street to be sold for 37½ cents.[127]

Abolitionists breathlessly described the book's assault on their sensoriums and braced for its impact on the public. Beriah Green, after reading excerpts in the *Emancipator*, declared the work "thrillingly interesting, powerfully instructive, impulsive enough to get a piece of clay in motion."[128] In May, Lewis Tappan assured delegates gathered in New York for the AASS's anniversary meeting that the book "would make the ears of the inhabitants of this nation, and other nations, tingle" (R 1839, 22). James Thome wrote Weld, "I have waded through the blood and gore of 'Slavery as it is' and have just come out on the other side, all dripping, *dripping*"; he meant it as a compliment.[129] That August, Angelina wrote to British abolitionist Elizabeth Pease that Northern opinion seemed to be "gradually yielding to the heavy strokes of the hammer of truth," but she worried that Southern slaveholders "WILL NOT repent, and that deliverance to the captive will at last come in terrible judgment." It was as if Mrs. Sturges's apocalyptic vision had come true and the nation had arrived at the brink of its awful climax, when the public's failure to heed prophetic warnings ushers in "the dreadful fiat of God's avenging justice." Still, the new book was so raw, so damning, Angelina believed that if anything could change their hearts, this was it: "We are anxious to hear what the South will say to 'Slavery as it is.' The testimonies to her cruelty are so overwhelming and appear to be so incontrovertible, that we cannot imagine how she will defend herself against such bloody accusations."[130]

What promised to give *American Slavery as It Is* such unique power was its ability to transcend the cultural mediation that had enabled critics to dismiss abolitionist texts by likening them to particular aesthetic genres and modes—to "maudlin verses and lying pictures" and "tales" that were "gross exaggerations" if not outright "fabrications."[131] Here, by contrast, was a transparent medium that would drive home the horrors of slavery with the irresistible force of truth. And at first it seemed to be working. Within four months of its release, the book had reportedly sold more than 22,000 copies, a figure that grew to nearly 100,000 copies within a year.[132] It became the most popular work the American Anti-Slavery Society ever produced and remained "the handbook of the antislavery impulse for more than a decade."[133] But while it was widely reviewed in Britain, it didn't receive the attention in the American press that the AASS had hoped for. In fact two modern editors of the text conclude that except for "abolitionist newspapers and a few religious journals, the book was virtually ignored."[134] Massachusetts physician Ebenezer Chaplin gave Weld his diagnosis: "These accounts of cruelty have been so much published and pressed upon the public, that they have in a measure become an old story and the people are becoming, I believe, somewhat weary of them."[135]

A year after the book's release, the American Anti-Slavery Society split over the question of women's membership (among other issues); the Garrisonian faction from Boston took over, and the New York evangelicals limped away to regroup as the American and Foreign Anti-Slavery Society.[136] In the early 1840s Weld and Grimké retreated from the movement to raise their growing family and follow their spiritual lights in new directions, Grimké to the imminent apocalypse of Millerism for a time, Weld away from reformist evangelicalism to a more inward-looking form of Christianity, their paths eventually converging in Spiritualism by decade's end.[137] Their dream of reforming the nation through print had failed.

Or had it? Scholars have long debated the significance of the abolitionist mediascape. Historian Elizabeth B. Clark influentially argued that its graphic portrayals of suffering helped effect "a shift in moral convention" that affirmed an individual human right to "bodily integrity" and freedom from "physical coercion and deliberately inflicted pain." She described that shift as a convergence of two factors: a set of ideas from liberal Protestantism involving the rejection of cruelty and the celebration of the human body; and a distinctive "style of moral reasoning" popularized by evangelical revivalists like Finney, who perfected new modes of pulpit storytelling and other techniques designed to elicit "sympathy and compassion."[138] More recently Loughran has placed abolitionist print at the crux of a transition from early republican fantasies of a unified national culture to the antebellum confrontation with the realities of a regionally differentiated industrial economy and an emerging consumer culture; in the process the AASS leveled a powerful "geopolitical critique of the nation as an integrated space."[139] This chapter confirms aspects of both these conclusions, but it also reveals something else. The contributions of evangelicalism to the rise of the humanitarian sensibility included not only the "affective style" of the revivalists but also a media strategy that sought to disseminate catalytic words and pictures across the nation and beyond.[140] As abolitionists put that model into practice, they not only critiqued the nation but remapped its location in hemispheric and global space, teaching readers to inhabit an eschatological frame that extended to the ends of the earth and the end of days. Drawing energy and ideas from ordinary people like Sturges, former slaves like Ball and Wheatley, and leaders like Weld and Grimké, the abolitionist mediascape mapped sacred geography and history onto a modern nation and an economy built on slavery, and waited for God's judgment to fall.

In 1851, while doing research in the Boston Anti-Slavery Society reading room for her serialized novel that had already begun to appear in the *National*

Era, Harriet Beecher Stowe came across a copy of *American Slavery as It Is*.[141] The text became a vital reference as she wrote *Uncle Tom's Cabin*, providing a basis for key characters and incidents; she cited it twenty-one times in *A Key to Uncle Tom's Cabin* (1853).[142] Supposedly she later told Grimké that while composing the novel she "kept that book in her work basket by day, and slept with it under her pillow by night, till its facts crystallized into Uncle Tom."[143] As *Uncle Tom's Cabin* dethroned *American Slavery as It Is* as the nation's most popular antislavery text, the novel would achieve the national circulation and mass emotional impact that the AASS had dreamed of more than a decade earlier. And as Stowe followed her characters across a national landscape saturated with biblical allusions, sent them back to Africa as missionaries, and concluded with a stern prophecy of imminent doom if the nation failed to free its slaves, she distilled the spatial imaginary of the abolitionist mediascape and animated it with literary techniques she had honed in the evangelical press, creating a single, luminous apocalyptic geography.

3

The Human Medium

HARRIET BEECHER STOWE AND
THE *NEW-YORK EVANGELIST*

EARLY IN *UNCLE TOM'S CABIN*, Aunt Chloe holds a prayer meeting in her cabin that includes Uncle Tom, slaves from the Shelby plantation and other nearby estates, and young George Shelby, the white son of the plantation owner.[1] The hymns and spirituals the group sings are filled with yearning for sacred places: "the golden city," "Jordan's banks," "Canaan's fields," and the "New Jerusalem"—the sacred geography that became central to African American strategies to overcome forced displacement, enslavement, and marginalization in the New World.[2] When an "old gray-headed woman" stands and announces that she is "jest a waitin' for the stage to come along and take me home" (1:51), she evinces a temporal interpretation of the songs' spatial conceit: her arrival in "the land of Canaan" depends not on her physical movement through space but on her faith and patience to await spiritual conveyance there in death. The sung, printed, and spoken words that summon this small religious community into being call its members to hold together in place against the threat of forced dispersal and to orient their utopian desire along the axis of time. This contrasts with the use of language in the next scene, as Mr. Shelby and the slave trader Haley negotiate the bills of sale that will scatter the slave community across space. In an important sense, then, the beginning of Stowe's novel describes a situation in which the language of legislation and economic contracts governs the fate of communities in space, while sacred language guides their passage through time. So when Eliza Harris learns that her son, Harry, has been sold, flees with him under the strength of "the supernatural power that bore her on" (1:80), and arrives at the Ohio River "which lay, like Jordan, between her and the Canaan of liberty on the other side" (1:82–83), her enactment of the prayer meeting's eschatological drama in physical space represents a radical disruption of power.

Eliza's crossing undoubtedly represents the period's most popular fictional instantiation of the spatialization of eschatology—the projection of Christian narratives of sacred history onto the Earth's physical geography—that Protestant evangelicals had developed during the preceding decades. Previous chapters have shown how this "evangelical space" was produced through the combination of religious print and landscape paintings like Thomas Cole's *The Oxbow* and how it spread from the evangelical press into a broader cultural and political sphere through the abolitionist mediascape of the 1830s, which grafted the drama of redemption onto the sectional and transatlantic geographies of slavery. Stowe, who had been steeped in such spatial imagery through her upbringing as the daughter of a renowned evangelical minister (Lyman Beecher), her association with Theodore Dwight Weld and his band of evangelical abolitionists at Cincinnati's Lane Theological Seminary, and her work in the evangelical press since the mid-1830s, could count on her audience to have encountered passages and images that would help them read Eliza's escape within a cosmic framework. Her novel's unprecedented circulation, in turn, undoubtedly inflected the interpretation of other literary and visual texts with little or no explicit religious symbolism, including numerous landscape views looking across the Ohio such as Robert S. Duncanson's *View of Cincinnati, Ohio from Covington, Kentucky* (c. 1851).[3] This chapter explores how Stowe became the medium through which a distinctive form of modern sacred space—one based more on networks of books and pictures than on bricks and mortar—reached a vast reading public and stamped itself indelibly on American culture.

Numerous critics have noted the importance of evangelical Protestantism for understanding Stowe's art, beginning with Jane Tompkins's seminal essay on "sentimental power."[4] More recently Claudia Stokes has shown the how the Second Great Awakening (especially Methodism) shaped Stowe's work, including the encoding of a postmillennial outlook in the "neat matrimonial pairings and newly restored happy families" of her domestic fiction.[5] Kevin Pelletier, by contrast, stresses a darker side to Stowe's eschatological imagination, arguing that critics have tended to overemphasize the role of "sympathetic love" in her work while neglecting the terror of God's wrath that she believed was necessary to provoke social change—a dialectic of love and fear that Pelletier terms "apocalyptic sentimentalism."[6] Others have noted (if only in passing) how Stowe's religious worldview shaped her representation of the novel's geography.[7] At the level of form, Dawn Coleman has explored the novel's deft modulations of "sermonic voice" and Stowe's "democratizing" extension of that voice to a variety of characters in the novel, including blacks and women.[8] But while many scholars have mapped the intersections of Stowe's theology with her literary practice, less attention has been paid to her engagement with religion in a more material sense—as a writer who earned her chops (and a good portion of her household's income) in the evangelical press. That experience shaped the way she represented space in her art as well as her conception of writing as a spatial practice. Producing sacred space for Stowe, in other words, was not simply a matter of imaginatively projecting biblical geography onto the American landscape; it also meant ensuring that one's words circulated widely through a popular mediascape in which print had achieved unprecedented social reach at the same time that it was increasingly being described as a conduit of divine power.[9]

This chapter reconsiders the cultural significance of *Uncle Tom's Cabin* by reframing it as the culmination of Stowe's early writing career in the evangelical press, above all in the *New-York Evangelist*, the influential weekly newspaper where Stowe published more than any other periodical. After a brief glance at Stowe's early use of writing as a religious instrument and an overview of her work for the *Evangelist*, I sketch the paper's emergence in the 1830s and the events that positioned it as an important and controversial evangelical publication when Stowe published her first article there in May 1835. The dozens of articles Stowe published in the *Evangelist* over the next two decades represent a literary apprenticeship in which she taught herself to write entertaining yet salient social commentary that would appeal to the paper's evangelical audience, and then to place that writing strategically in venues where it would circulate widely and engage a broad range of readers. It is no exaggeration to say that without the *Evangelist* there likely would have been no *Uncle Tom's Cabin*, for it was there that Stowe honed what she called her "vocation to preach on paper."[10] After tracing Stowe's work in the *Evangelist* and the ways her temperance tales use characters to dramatize the promise and limits of print's power to reform society, I turn to the novel's apocalyptic imagination. What makes *Uncle Tom's Cabin* such a powerful apocalyptic text, I argue, is not simply its lush counterpoint of millennial and apocalyptic rhetoric but also its enactment of a process of apocalyptic mediation that dramatizes particular ways of interpreting texts and the landscape. Finally, the chapter revisits Stowe's rhetoric of divine mediation—her famous claim that God wrote *Uncle Tom's Cabin*—and argues that such statements deserve to be taken more seriously than they have been, not so much for what they say about Stowe's personal beliefs as for what they reveal about a national mediascape that was simultaneously becoming sacralized and democratized.

In the process, this chapter develops a concept of "mediation" that illuminates three distinct ways in which print functioned in the evangelical public sphere. The first involves print's ability to collapse physical distance by connecting a spatially dispersed evangelical reading public to each other and to the objects of their social concern, resulting in an "imagined spiritual community" distinct from the secular national imaginary defined by Benedict Anderson.[11] The second involves print's capacity to serve as an instrument of moral truth, untrammeled by formal complexity or "merely" aesthetic concerns, and the third involves claims that God participates in the creation of a text and lends it a special social agency. In her work for the *Evangelist*, Stowe engaged each of these forms of mediation—which for convenience might be called spatial, moral, and divine mediation. These pieces do not blend in seamlessly with the textual fabric of the *Evangelist*, however, but stand out like figures in the carpet, dramatizing and recasting the work of mediation carried on there. Above all, they reimagine the print public sphere as a spatially dispersed version of an older, more personal model of moral suasion by figuring the circulation of print as the circulation of characters. The effect was not only to emphasize that a newspaper or a novel could be as convincing and effective a moral instrument as a personal appeal—that print, wielded effectively, could convey the force of a face-to-face encounter. Even as Stowe showed how print could imitate the human, she also revealed an important sense in which people resembled print. Whereas Marshall McLuhan would define media as "extensions" of "our human senses," Stowe reminded her readers that human subjects themselves could be understood as media: as the channels through which information circulates and through which, indeed, God could express himself.[12] By the time Eliza took her courageous leap onto the ice floes of the Ohio, Stowe had worked for nearly two decades to make her character legible as the embodiment of the new forms of mediation reshaping American society.

Preaching on Paper: Stowe and the *Evangelist*

Between May 1835 and the publication of the final installment of *Uncle Tom's Cabin* in the *National Era* in April 1852, Stowe published dozens of pieces in the *New-York Evangelist* (1830–1902), an influential Presbyterian weekly known for its abolitionist views.[13] This body of articles—a generic smorgasbord that includes temperance tales, religious allegories, biblical fiction, and antislavery sketches—represents a substantial portion of Stowe's publications during this period and by far the largest number of her articles published in any single publication. Stowe's work for *Godey's Lady's Book* and the *National Era* are well known to literary historians, but her work for the *Evangelist* has received no sustained critical attention.[14] Recent scholarship exploring the considerable influence of Protestant evangelical print culture on nineteenth-century American literature and culture offers an opportunity to examine Stowe's involvement with the *Evangelist* more closely. What does it mean that the most popular novelist of the nineteenth century received her literary apprenticeship writing for one of the period's most influential evangelical weeklies? And how might that fact put pressure on literary histories that narrate the development of the literary or the aesthetic in terms of the decline or secularization of the religious?[15]

The point is not that Stowe's work for the *Evangelist* necessarily means that she was an evangelical in a theological sense—a Christian who affirms the four doctrinal positions outlined in D. W. Bebbington's classic definition: "conversionism," "crucicentrism," "activism," and "biblicentrism."[16] As scholars have noted, Stowe's shifting religious beliefs and self-identification make it difficult to label her clearly.[17] Nor have I attempted to isolate the role of Stowe's beliefs in her decision to publish in the *Evangelist*. A number of factors undoubtedly influenced her decision, including the fact that the paper paid well.[18] Rather than interpreting Stowe's personal beliefs and motivations, I have chosen to focus on the *Evangelist* pieces themselves and the ways they engage a set of thematic concerns, formal strategies, and assumptions about the role of art in society that were prevalent in the evangelical press. From this perspective, Stowe can be considered an evangelical writer by virtue of her position in a particular mediascape and her rhetorical orientation to an evangelical reading public rather than her personal beliefs.

Given that she was the daughter of one of the nation's foremost evangelical ministers, it is perhaps not surprising that the young Harriet Beecher used her earliest published writing in the service of religious conversion. While still a teenager attending Catharine Beecher's Hartford Female Seminary in the 1820s, she participated in her sister's system of peer-based religious instruction, writing letters to her classmates that monitored their piety and attempted to convert them.[19] These letters reflect Harriet's early grasp of one of the fundamental ideological assumptions motivating evangelical print: the importance of the written word as an instrument to convert others and strengthen the identity of a community of believers.[20] During this time she also served as a contributor and coeditor of the seminary's handwritten *School Gazette*, likely inspired by the example of her father's *Christian Spectator* (1819–38). As her writing career advanced, she explicitly modeled her sense of literary vocation on the ministerial role of her brothers, writing to her brother George in about 1830 that she "was made for a preacher—indeed I can scarcely keep my letters from turning into sermons. . . . Indeed in a certain sense it is as much my vocation to preach on paper as it is that of my brothers to preach viva voce."[21]

Harriet Beecher began to pursue that vocation in the *Evangelist* in 1835. Up to that point she had published several pieces in the Cincinnati-based *Western Monthly Magazine*; but with the exception of a series of Bible lectures by Calvin Stowe (a Lane Seminary professor and her future husband) that she wrote up for the *Cincinnati Journal and Western Luminary* in the winter of 1834–35, her work had not been overtly religious.[22] But with the appearance of her temperance tale "Uncle Enoch" in the *New-York Evangelist* (signed only "E. B.") in May 1835, that began to change.[23] Over the next decade and a half, Stowe published sketches in the paper that promoted the causes of the Benevolent Empire, including temperance, tract distribution, and missions. Other pieces explored the meaning of Christian conduct in everyday life and the nature of religious experience and the inner life. Several fictionalized accounts of Jesus and other biblical figures show Stowe working comfortably within a "homiletic tradition" that mobilized Christian narrative structures in order to encourage readers to rehearse forms of social action.[24] And beginning in 1845, Stowe began to publish abolitionist sketches in the paper. By June 1851, a total of thirty-seven of her pieces had appeared in the *Evangelist*.[25]

Stowe and her family saw her work for the paper not simply as a source of income but as part of their collective ambition to wield moral influence. In May 1842 Calvin encouraged his wife to write more for the *Evangelist* (by then, she had published eight pieces) and similar publications, both for the money it brought in but also "to form the mind of the West for the coming generation"—a goal she pursued in sketches such as "Which Is the Liberal Man" and "What Will the American People Do?"[26] As Stowe's piety deepened in the early 1840s, her work in the *Evangelist* became an important part of her spiritual and artistic development. As she wrote to her brother Charles in 1844,

> I have been considering lately the subject of Christ's *pre*appearances in the Old Testament, and if you see the Evangelist, you will perhaps see some remarks I have written on one of them in your style of descriptive filling out. Also, I have sent to the same paper a piece of poetry on the words, "Now there stood by the cross of Jesus *his mother*," many of the ideas of which were suggested by your lectures, or by the state of feeling consequent on them. I wish you could see them both, because I think you would enter into the strain of feeling in them.[27]

Referring to two of her recent *Evangelist* pieces, "Old Testament Pictures—No. 1" and "Mary at the Cross," Stowe describes adapting her brother's preaching style and ideas to the medium of print and envisions a process of creative synergy in which "feeling" provides a common currency linking spoken and written forms of expression. Her conception of writing as an analog to preaching influenced her literary form as well, perhaps most explicitly in her adaptation of the traditional text-doctrine-application structure of sermonic discourse. Practicing the technique she would later wield so forcefully in *Uncle Tom's Cabin*, Stowe opens "The Unfaithful Steward" with a text from Psalms, relates a parabolic story about a son who squanders his father's estate but is mercifully forgiven, and finally turns to address the reader: "And now, immortal being, whoever thou art, through whose mind this story has passed, has it for thee no meaning?"[28] The fluidity with which ideas, feelings, and style from Stowe's religious milieu circulated through her writing in the *Evangelist* highlights the degree to which that work served as an extension of her family's religious vocation.

Before examining these pieces more closely, it's important to understand what was distinctive about the newspaper where Stowe chose to send so much of her work. Preaching on paper was also the mission of the weekly paper formed in early 1830 by a group of wealthy evangelical New York businessmen— the so-called Association of Gentlemen.[29] Led by the brothers Lewis and Arthur Tappan, the group wanted an organ to promote its form of New School Calvinism (a modified form of Calvinism that afforded a greater role to individual agency) and a range of benevolent causes.[30] The paper's first issue on March 6, 1830, declared it would "promote Revivals of Religion" and "advocate fearlessly, the Bible, Tract, Missionary, Education, Temperance, Sabbath, and Sabbath School Institutions," in the belief that such "efforts [will] be conducive to the enlargement of Christ's Kingdom."[31] The *Evangelist* thus adopted the media strategy and the postmillennial vision of the American Tract Society (ATS) and other benevolent evangelicals discussed in earlier chapters. Every Thursday the paper filled five columns on each of four blanket-folio size pages with an eclectic mix of items, many reprinted from religious periodicals.[32] Its initial roster of some twenty departments, from "Ministers" and "Missionary" to "Ladies," "Parents," and "Youth," indicates its attempts to appeal to a broad middle-class readership that included clergy and lay readers, women and men, and children.[33] The *Evangelist* was not illustrated, which made it relatively cheap to produce compared to other weeklies.[34] According to the "Terms" listed on the front page of each issue, an annual subscription for a single reader cost about $2.50 (depending on the time and method of payment), more expensive than the burgeoning penny press but slightly cheaper than the six-cent papers in the commercial and party presses.[35] The paper advertised to raise revenue, but only for "such matters as are peculiarly interesting to the religious community," including businesses such as temperance hotels and Protestant boarding houses and events like prayer concerts and benevolent society meetings.[36] Although it did not publish subscription lists or circulation figures, a list of its agents in fourteen states and the District of Columbia in 1831 reveal a readership stretching from Maine to North Carolina, and west to Illinois and Kentucky.[37] Its subscription lists topped 10,000 by 1836.[38] Thus the *Evangelist* is representative of the diverse (and sometimes conflicting) functions that evangelical periodicals of the period served: building a denominational identity in a diverse and competitive religious marketplace, promoting benevolent causes intended to foster interdenominational unity, maintaining a sense of distinction from secular publications while simultaneously claiming to wield moral influence in the broader culture, and cultivating a geographically dispersed readership while promoting viewpoints that often exacerbated sectional antagonisms.[39]

The *Evangelist* joined a growing number of religious weeklies in the 1830s and became one of the three most influential Presbyterian weeklies in the United States along with the *New-York Observer* (the *Evangelist*'s Old School Presbyterian rival) and the Philadelphia *Presbyterian*.[40] As a weekly, the *Evangelist* fulfilled specialized functions that distinguished it from quarterlies and monthlies.[41] Weeklies combined the quarterlies' attention to doctrinal matters with a mix of news (both church-related and secular), editorials, and miscellaneous items intended to appeal to a broad lay readership. They served as weapons in contumelious intradenominational battles, but they also performed important integrative functions, mediating between the sacred and mundane worlds and between collective religious narratives and individual lives. As Candy Gunther Brown argues, the frequent publication cycles of the weeklies and their blend of ordinary and "transcendent" subject matter helped spread religious concerns from the Sabbath into the rest of the week and encouraged readers to place their everyday lives within a sacred framework, "infusing sacred influences into everyday times and spaces."[42] The *Evangelist* used this sacralization of everyday life to promote an aggressive reform agenda. It encouraged readers to perform a range of actions—from signing temperance pledges to boycotting businesses that operated on Sunday to circulating antislavery petitions—and to understand them within a collective millennial narrative that Robert H. Abzug terms a "reform cosmology."[43] Such efforts to use print as an instrument of moral suasion and social reform by situating readers within a cosmic drama provided a crucial context in which Stowe developed the literary fusion of political and divine realities in *Uncle Tom's Cabin*.

In addition to the general sense in which the *Evangelist* "preach[ed] on paper" by promoting a particular theological stance and an aggressive social agenda, the most culturally significant moment of the paper's first decade came in the form of a literal act of preaching.[44] When the paper's circulation failed to grow under founding editor Noah C. Saxton, the Tappans replaced him with Congregationalist minister Joshua Leavitt, secretary of the Seaman's Friend Society and author of the popular hymn book *The Christian Lyre*. Leavitt, who had already been helping edit the *Evangelist*, assumed the helm in December 1831, and by the end of 1833 the paper's circulation had doubled to 6,000 subscribers.[45] But following Leavitt's conversion to immediate abolitionism in the summer of 1833, the paper's increasingly vocal abolitionist views began to alienate its readership. In January 1834 Finney warned Leavitt that his abolitionism threatened to destroy the *Evangelist*, but the editor refused to compromise his principles. As antislavery items in the paper multiplied, circulation plummeted: nearly a third of its subscribers canceled their subscriptions in the first half of 1834. That autumn, as the paper hemorrhaged 60 subscribers a day, Leavitt came to Finney distraught, declaring (as Finney later recalled), "I have ruined the Evangelist. I have not been as prudent as you cautioned me to be, and I have gone so far ahead of public intelligence and feeling on the subject [slavery], that my subscription list is rapidly failing; and we shall not be able to continue its publication beyond the first of January, unless you can do something to bring the paper back to public favor again."[46] By November Leavitt and Finney had agreed on a plan to rescue the paper: Finney, by now a nationally renowned revivalist, would deliver a series of weekly lectures to his congregation at the Chatham Street Chapel in New York City, while Leavitt would transcribe the lectures and publish them in the *Evangelist* to boost circulation.

Finney delivered his first Friday-night lecture on December 5, 1834, and Leavitt's transcription appeared in the *Evangelist* the next day.[47] Over the next six months, thousands of readers from Maine to Tennessee and as far west as Illinois and Michigan Territory joined the thousands of listeners who packed the pews to hear Finney's series of twenty-two "Lectures on Revivals."[48] Whether encountered in person or in print, "hearing" was the operative word used to convey the immediacy of Finney's message. As Finney wrote to his wife, Lydia, in November 1834, "You will probably after this hear me preach once a week through the Evangelist as I have consented to preach a course of lectures on revivals & let Br. Leavitt take notes & publish them in order to help the Evangelist as his abolitionism has greatly infused it. & unless something of the kind can sustain it he says it must go down."[49] The following March, Lydia's sister, Susan Andrews, wrote from Michigan Territory, "We have received the revival lectures up to the 31st of Jan. We are very much pleased with them, and I hope we shall profit by the reading of them. I can sometimes when reading them, almost see [Finney] and hear his voice."[50] Some heard the lectures quite literally: in Illinois a minister read Finney's third lecture ("How to Promote a Revival") to a group of forty to fifty people gathered for his monthly prayer concert; in Connecticut at least two ministers sparked revivals by reading the lectures aloud at their weekly prayer meetings; and in Ohio a small prayer group met on Sundays to read them together.[51] In Portsmouth, New Hampshire, "all persons of every congregation in this town" were invited to come to the South Meeting House on Sunday evenings to hear Finney's lectures read aloud from the pulpit.[52] In April an *Evangelist* correspondent from New York wrote, "I have just returned from a tour to the west, passing through this state, Ohio, and Michigan, and I have been highly gratified to observe the almost universally beneficial influence which Mr. Finney's 'Lectures on Revivals' are exerting on the minds of ministers and private Christians, in that section of the country."[53] Evangelical print thus not only provided the occasion for Finney's lectures but amplified them far beyond the immediate setting of their delivery, while an evangelical theory of reading that saw print as a vehicle of immediate presence united Finney and readers of the *Evangelist* within a shared, sacralized mediascape.[54]

Finney's lectures offer a provocative instance of what Lindsay Jones calls "ritual-architectural events," the "ceremonial (and sometime unceremonious) situations that bring people and buildings into active interaction." Reacting against interpretations that claim to identify a stable meaning of sacred architecture in the intentions of architects or in the prescribed ritual uses of the space, Jones takes a hermeneutical perspective in which "the locus of meaning resides neither in the building itself (a physical object) nor in the mind of the beholder (a human subject), but rather in the negotiation or the interactive relation that subsumes both building and beholder." That relation allows Jones to expand what he calls the "architectural situation" to include the landscape outside the building, including "celestial bodies, lakes, trees, mountains, and weather phenomena into the ceremonial context."[55] The architectural situation of Finney's lectures clearly included the Chatham Street Chapel itself and its central role in the transformation of evangelical worship spaces and practices by which, in Jeanne Halgren Kilde's apt phrase, "Church Became Theatre."[56] But that situation clearly extended far beyond its walls, as Finney's words spilled out of the chapel across an expansive web of reading rooms, churches, and homes, inviting audiences to hone their spiritual senses. He placed them alongside the sinner at the brink of Niagara Falls, or beside the "Blessed man" who "used to take the map of the world before him, and pray, and look over the different countries and pray for them, till he absolutely expired in his room, praying."[57] As Finney, Leavitt, and others disseminated such vivid represented spaces through the *Evangelist*'s extensive print network, they contributed to an evangelical mediascape that drew homes and churches, national landscape sites, and the world missionary field into a vast cosmic theater where the millennial drama would unfold.

The promiscuous nature of the antebellum "culture of reprinting" meant that this mediascape encompassed the religious press and secular publications alike.[58] Readers of the *New-Hampshire Morning Star*, the *Ohio Observer*, the *American Presbyterian* in Nashville, and the Baptist *Vermont Telegraph* found entire lectures or lengthy extracts in their papers.[59] A reader from Chesterville, Maine, who read one of the lectures in the *Morning Star* wrote to the paper to relate a personal story that confirmed Finney's idea that God grants knowledge of the future to those who pray; his testimony was in turn reprinted by the *Evangelist*.[60] As far away as Green Bay in Michigan Territory, a missionary to the Stockbridge Indians with the American Board of Commissioners for Foreign Missions reported that Finney's words had reached members of the tribe through the pages of the *Ohio Observer* and declared "the method a very happy one of spreading far and wide, those truths which are of such deep, practical importance as those contained in the Lectures just referred to."[61] Whether the Indians found it so happy is another question, but for the *Evangelist* the strategy had indeed proved effective: subscriptions began to pick up as soon as Leavitt advertised the series, and once the lectures began they drew as many as 200 new subscribers a day.[62] By the time Finney's last lecture ran on May 2, 1835, 2,500 new subscribers had signed up, swelling the paper's circulation to 9,500, bringing it within spitting distance of the rival *New-York Observer* (14,000) but still a far cry from the Methodist *Christian Advocate* (28,000).[63] But Leavitt wasn't done: a week later he announced in the paper that some 2,000 copies of the lectures had been printed in a single five-page extra to offer to each new subscriber.[64] At year's end, Leavitt wrote to readers "to express our thanks for 4,500 new names added to our subscription list during the year 1835."[65] The *Evangelist* was saved. The circulation of Finney's lectures, however, did not stop with the periodical press. Within days of his final lecture, a book version was published under the title *Lectures on Revivals of Religion*.[66] With the publication of a London edition of the *Lectures* in 1837 and their translation into French and Welsh, another wave was unleashed that crossed the Atlantic and sparked a series of revivals in England, Scotland, Wales, and elsewhere.[67]

The widening circuit of Finney's *Lectures* through the *Evangelist*, other newspapers, and commercial publishers provides a striking example of an "evangelical textual community," a network of publishers, authors, and readers whose shared beliefs and reading practices transcend their local religious communities.[68] When Finney and his readers likened the circulation and reception of the lectures to the physical presence of preacher and congregant, they figuratively registered the ability of print to create an extensive "congregation" in which Finney's words, whether performed aloud by ministers and laypeople or read by the fireside, could spark a national revival. Whereas Coleman has contrasted the national reach of Stowe's novel with the constraints of preaching to a particular local audience, arguing that "novels had wings as sermons did not," the impressive mobility of Finney's lectures across space and media formats demonstrates that sermons had wings of their own.[69] His preaching represented a model of moral suasion—spatially mediated yet rhetorically immediate—that Stowe would practice and master over the next two decades as she learned to transmit her writing across the antebellum mediascape. For Stowe, preaching on paper did not simply mean writing moralistic prose; it meant adapting a set of values, ideas, and homiletic conventions—indeed an entire family tradition—to the medium of mass print and then disseminating her words through an array of different publications and literary genres. It meant, in short, harnessing the culture of reprinting for sacred rather than simply national ends.

Eliza's Moving Body: Spatial Mediation and the Circulation of Characters

The stir created by Finney's *Lectures on Revivals* formed the backdrop to Stowe's debut in the *Evangelist*. Her first documented piece in the paper, a temperance tale called "Uncle Enoch," ran on May 30, 1835—four weeks after Finney's final lecture.[70] Temperance had been one of the *Evangelist*'s staple topics since its first issue in 1830, and Leavitt's "radical" temperance views—he not only condemned the liquor traffic but advocated expanding the temperance pledge beyond hard liquor to include beer, cider, and wine—only amplified its message.[71] As the paper published and reprinted pieces detailing temperance efforts in dozens of states from Alabama to Maine and as far west as Michigan, it conveyed the sense of a coordinated movement adequate to tackle a problem that Lyman Beecher and others had labeled a "national" sin since the late 1820s.[72] By conveying to a spatially dispersed readership the sense of a coalescing national movement turning the tide against Demon Rum, the *Evangelist*'s Temperance Department produced a moral geography similar to the one Finney created by "preaching" to readers in several states at once.

"Uncle Enoch" participated in that work of spatial mediation by adding another strand to the expanding network of temperance texts stretching through and beyond the *Evangelist*. But Stowe's tale is significant in part for the way it dramatizes and refigures that process. One of several fictional pieces that began to appear in the paper in late 1834 and 1835—including George Barrell Cheever's "Inquire at Amos Giles' Distillery"—the tale uses dialogue to foreground the process of persuasion, discussion, and debate behind the fledgling temperance movement in the fictional village of Elliston.[73] The local minister's announcement that a visiting temperance preacher will speak that evening precipitates a sequence of conversations and debates that culminate in the formation of a local temperance society. Enoch, a respected village elder, spearheads the effort, securing the support of Elliston's leading families and convincing its principal merchant to stop selling spirits. These encounters allow Stowe to present a variety of arguments against alcohol, such as its contribution to "pauperism and crime, and the cost of drinking,"[74] which her readers could use in conversations with skeptics. The tale thus functions as a kind of instruction manual for replicating a particular model of local activism through its network of readers. Gregg Crane has argued that "Uncle Enoch" captures Stowe's belief in "America's willingness to transform itself by social and legal experiment as a sign of moral health."[75] To the extent that the tale imagines national transformation at all, however, it is not a function of the Constitution or federal law but of a series of intensely local processes of deliberation and consensus-building, a model of social change closer to that envisioned by the period's many utopian communities—what Arthur Bestor called "small-scale experiment indefinitely reduplicated."[76]

Stowe's focus on the interpersonal dynamics of moral suasion seems to obscure the role of print itself. Publications like the *Evangelist* never appear in Elliston: moral authority and influence spread almost entirely through face-to-face interactions. In this sense the tale displays the pastoralism that Paul Boyer and Mark S. Schantz have observed in the publications of evangelical groups like the ATS.[77] In a rapidly industrializing and urbanizing nation characterized by increasing ethnic and religious diversity, such portrayals of bucolic, homogeneous preindustrial villages might be characterized as symptoms of a naïve and misleading conservative ideology incapable of effectively addressing the nation's problems. Yet as scholars more recently have argued, the very evangelical publishing societies that promoted this ideology were skilled at navigating the realities of a complex market society as they used advances in communication, transportation, and organization to pursue religious goals.[78] The *Evangelist* was part of this sophisticated religious communications network of steam presses, urban infrastructure, and interstate distribution networks. In some sense readers of "Uncle Enoch" were meant to be aware of that fact: as they encountered Stowe's tale alongside a host of other items on the page—a poem from the *Journal of Commerce* about Southern slavery, reports of annual temperance society meetings in Boston and New York, a report from the *London Times* about the deaths of two American missionaries in Sumatra, and so on—they were encouraged to think of themselves as part of an extensive evangelical community connected by a network of reform causes, institutions, and publications. But when they turned to "Uncle Enoch" and entered the staid confines of Elliston, they encountered a form of village life at odds with the urban elites and steam presses that produced the *Evangelist*. Stowe's tale effectively pastoralizes its own print network, as if reminding her readers of the original model for a print public. In a sense "Uncle Enoch" presents that public as a technologically expanded version of an older mode of community—or perhaps not so much expanded as serially replicated. In 1835, Stowe is not yet imagining the emphatically national yet intimate reading public she would summon in *Uncle Tom's Cabin* but rather a series of virtuous local communities "indefinitely reduplicated" through the medium of print.

Stowe's subsequent writing in the *Evangelist* continued to negotiate a tension between the long-distance moral suasion enabled by print circulation and that enabled through direct contact between individuals. In her second identified *Evangelist* piece, a temperance tale titled "The Drunkard Reclaimed," a brilliant young socialite named Augusta Elmore complains of "temperance papers—temperance tracts—temperance hotels—temperance this, that, and the other thing, even down to temperance pocket-handkerchiefs for little boys!"[79] But as her lover, the talented Edward Howard, descends into ruin as a result of drink and then is reclaimed through Augusta's devotion and the benevolence of a wealthy philanthropist, personal moral influence appears to be the only viable solution to the problem. The tale nonetheless registers a more complex, less pastoral social world than "Uncle Enoch." From the lifestyle of "elegance and comfort" the couple enjoys in the first installment of the sketch, Edward's drinking lands them in "a small and partly ruinous tenement" in "a city where they were wholly unknown" in the second. Only Augusta's visit to the doorstep of a "princely mansion," where she is recognized by a philanthropist who "in his benevolent ministrations, often passed the dwelling of Edward," sets in motion Edward's reformation and the family's ascent to the "neat little mansion" where they reside at tale's end.[80]

The range of social spaces delineated in "The Drunkard Reclaimed" registers the changes to urban space that accompanied the market revolution in the decades surrounding Stowe's tale.[81] As Paul E. Johnson showed in his account of Finney's revivals in Rochester during the 1820s and 1830s, the economic changes that separated workers from bosses, commercial space from domestic space, and working-class residential neighborhoods from middle-class ones were closely tied to the middle-class perception of drinking as a social threat—a perception that helped fuel the temperance movement.[82] And as Ronald J. Zboray has argued, these same economic changes fostered the national print networks that worked to incorporate local communities into an emerging "national reading public."[83] In other words, the social stratification of urban space and the appearance of Stowe's tale in the *Evangelist* are in some sense complementary developments, for it is precisely when separate neighborhoods of mansions and tenements have appeared that texts purporting to reveal the vices of the slums and the steps necessary to "solve" those vices become a possibility. By following Augusta and Edward through and between cities, "The Drunkard Reclaimed" performs a fictional version of the spatial mediation performed by texts claiming to bridge the divide between mansion and tenement. But instead of the disparaged "temperance papers," it is the philanthropist's benevolent visits to the tenements and Augusta's appearance at his mansion that mediate these vastly different social spaces and ultimately enable the resolution of the tale's central conflict. In a sense, the tale has transformed the circulation of print into the circulation of characters, whose spatial and social mobility figures the supposed ability of print culture to bridge class difference. Through Stowe's re-figuration of the print medium, the characters have themselves become media.

Stowe's temperance tales, in short, encourage us to read her fictional plots at some level as dramas of circulation—as submerged ruminations on the moral influence of print and its limits. The opening of "The Tea Rose" (1842), for example, finds the wealthy heroine Florence L'Estrange reading when her cousin Kate insists that she "put down that wise, good, excellent volume, and talk with a poor little mortal." The tea rose Florence later sends as a gift to brighten the shabby quarters of a local seamstress is not one of Florence's edifying books, but the plant's "white leaves just touched with that creamy tint peculiar to its kind" certainly make it resemble one.[84] In "Which Is the Liberal Man?" (1844), a college valedictorian's decision to forego a promising law career to become a missionary in the West leads him to a land of little print, where he "lived without books, without newspapers" and "exhorted from house to house, labored individually with one after another, till he had, in place after place, brought together the elements of a Christian church."[85] Time and again Stowe evokes the fantasy of a world without print (or at least one where its importance is diminished)—a world in which the mediation of the printed page gives way to the immediacy of personal presence.

One is reminded of the contrast Stowe would draw in *Uncle Tom's Cabin* between Senator Bird's notional understanding of the fugitive slave as "the letters that spell the word,—or, at the most, the image of a little newspaper picture of a man with a stick and bundle," and the powerful effect of Eliza Harris standing in his parlor—what Stowe called "the magic of the real presence of distress" (1:134). Rather than repudiating print in favor of immediate face-to-face appeals, Stowe can be seen as reminding her readership of a differently embodied circulation—one in which the fugitive's distress truly does come through the words on the page, and print fulfills its sympathetic potential as a medium in a way it had not in a work like *American Slavery as It Is* (1839), which (as discussed in the previous chapter) relied largely on newspaper accounts to elicit outrage at the cruelty of slavery. Eliza's flight, which connects characters from diverse places, races, and social positions in a network of sentiment stretching from Mrs. Shelby in Kentucky to Mrs. Smyth in Canada, becomes the novel's fullest incarnation of such a vision. Stowe's sprawling plot enacts the process of reforming social and ethical ties that publications like the *Evangelist* sought to achieve through print circulation. Just as Uncle Tom famously merges with his Bible when Haley declares him "All the moral and Christian virtues bound in black morocco, complete!" (1:216), Eliza's moving body—moving in the sense of both its physical mobility and its ability to compel affect—becomes a figure for evangelical print's aspirations of universal circulation and its power to provoke feeling and action. Whereas Trish Loughran has interpreted the 1850s as marking a transition from print to persons as the most visible mediators of federal consolidation, as "the circulating bodies of fugitive slaves took up the nation-building work once performed by circulating texts," Stowe's characters suggest not so much a shift away from print as a reflection on the twinned relationship of people and print as media.[86]

The semantic richness of Haley's image of being "bound" encapsulates the challenge inherent in Stowe's conflation of people and print: Tom is bound like a book, but also bound as a slave (literally held in bonds) and as a figure representing Africa, which, "for centuries, has lain bound and bleeding at the foot of civilized and Christianized humanity" (*UTC*, 1:vi). Eliza, on the other hand, is unbound (she has thrown off the bonds of slavery) and is now bound in a different sense—like the speaker of the hymn, "bound for the land of Canaan" (1:51). The characters' embodiment of the paradoxical duality of evangelical print—its claims of permanent, fixed, and universal truth, set against its republican promise of uninhibited diffusion and free circulation—hints that while *Uncle Tom's Cabin* in some sense represents a fulfillment of the goal of literary preaching Stowe had long pursued in the *Evangelist*, the novel also probes the contradictions and limits of print's millennial promise.

Reading the Signs with Uncle Tom: Apocalyptic Media

While the northern strand of Stowe's plot enacts an apocalyptic geography based on the postmillennial vision of universal print circulation, affective reading, and social regeneration popularized in the evangelical press, the southern strand has attracted the bulk of critical commentary about the novel's treatment of sacred history and geography. Kevin Pelletier traces Stowe's apocalyptic imagination from Augustine St. Clare's intimations of an impending "*dies irae*" (*UTC*, 2:25) to Simon Legree's terror of the "everlasting fires" of "judgment" (2:218) that await him, concluding that "providential history is Stowe's master narrative, one that subsumes and supersedes all earthly and finite concerns, and the apocalypse is its central figure."[87] Jennifer Rae Greeson, meanwhile, reads Tom's path through the Slave South as a cosmographic journey from the bucolic Shelby plantation through St. Clare's "paradisiacal" estate and into the depths of Legree's "infernal realm," a descent that simultaneously allegorizes the social and economic transformations wrought by the market revolution, "the fall from orderly, patriarchal village life, into the anonymity and brutalization of the industrial city."[88] Yet the apocalyptic contours of Stowe's novel emerge fundamentally, I want to argue, neither from its warnings of God's impending wrath, its intertextual engagement with apocalyptic texts, nor its mapping of contemporary economic and political issues in terms of sacred history and geography but instead from its exploration of the process of mediation between the mundane world and divine realities.

Apocalypse as a literary genre purports to reveal, typically with the help of an angel or other supernatural mediator, "a transcendent world of supernatural powers and an eschatological scenario" through a vision that encompasses the geography and history of the universe.[89] The hero to whom that vision is vouchsafed in turn mediates it for the reader through the apocalyptic text. This process of apocalyptic mediation performs a specifically communal and one might say political function: as Michael E. Vines argues, apocalypse provides "a God's-eye view on human history and activity" that responds to a collective loss of order and meaning. Historically emerging from the travails of the ancient Israelites in exile and bondage, in which the promises of a chosen people's covenant with God have seemingly given way to a world "overrun by those who refuse to acknowledge the one sovereign God and, worse yet, who torment and persecute God's righteous followers," the genre labors to reaffirm a sense of God's order in the face of chaos and evil.[90] Apocalyptic media include the supernatural beings, their human interlocutors, and the written texts that perform this recuperative work.

In this more precise sense, it becomes clear why a pious, enslaved character like Uncle Tom is perfectly positioned to be an apocalyptic hero, one who is "torment[ed]" and "persecute[d]" by men like Legree and whose burden is to achieve an encompassing vision of the universe that restores a sense of divine justice in spite of that treatment. Indeed, Uncle Tom consistently fulfills this orienting function through the words he reads and the scenes he witnesses. He enables Stowe to dramatize the interpretive process of calibrating and reconciling biblical promises of order and justice to a world where evil appears to be in control. "Is God HERE?" Tom asks, Bible in hand, the night after arriving on Legree's plantation, as above him the moon "looked down, calm and silent, as God looks on the scene of misery and oppression" (*UTC*, 2:186). Bridging the gap between Tom's ground's-eye view and the seeming indifference of that divine onlooker becomes the key to resolving his crisis of faith as well as the novel's broader challenge to Christian theodicy (the effort to reconcile the existence of suffering with belief in a good and all-powerful God). As Tom enacts the fraught process of reading the signs of the times on the page and in the world, he becomes the novel's most portentous apocalyptic medium.

Tom's first apocalyptic vision is a panoramic prospect of the Southern plantation system witnessed from the upper deck of a steamboat floating down the Mississippi. Tom is "studying over his Bible" among the cotton bales when he looks up and sees, thanks to the levees that elevate the river twenty feet above the surrounding countryside, "spread out full before him, in plantation after plantation, a map of the life to which he was approaching":

> He saw the distant slaves at their toil; he saw afar their villages of huts gleaming out in long rows on many a plantation, distant from the stately mansions and pleasure-grounds of the master;—and as the moving picture passed on, his poor, foolish heart would be turning backward to the Kentucky farm, with its old shadowy beeches,—to the master's house, with its wide, cool halls, and, near by, the little cabin, overgrown with the multiflora and bignonia. There he seemed to see familiar faces of comrades, who had grown up with him from infancy; he saw his busy wife, bustling in her preparations for his evening meals; he heard the merry laugh of his boys at their play, and the chirrup of the baby at his knee; and then, with a start, all faded, and he saw again the cane-breaks and cypresses and gliding plantations, and heard again the creaking and groaning of the machinery, all telling him too plainly that all that phase of life had gone by forever. (*UTC*, 1:209)

Tom's eerily cinematic experience of this "moving picture" (complete with flashback dissolves and fades) grants readers the literary equivalent of the popular moving panoramas of the Mississippi that transported audiences vicariously down the river using scenes painted on giant rolls of canvas accompanied by travelogue narration and live music.[91] Even as Tom's vision mimics a popular media form—and anticipates the panoramas about slavery exhibited by the famous fugitive Henry Box Brown and the black Cincinnati daguerreotypist James P. Ball a few years later—it describes a geography defined by the absence of media.[92] In contrast to Eliza's ability to forge networks of sympathy across boundaries of race and geography, Tom's view across the expanse of space and time separating him from his Kentucky home only highlights his isolation: "the mail for him had no existence, and the gulf of separation was unbridged by even a friendly word or signal." Here is the nightmare mirror image of Stowe's nostalgic *Evangelist* sketches in which the mass mediation of print has not yet displaced more immediate forms of local community: a place where (to slaves at least) the absence of modern communications networks makes extralocal community all but impossible. In the face of this isolation, Tom's only comfort is to turn to his Bible, where he haltingly "traces out its promises": "Let—not—your—heart—be—troubled. In—my—Father's—house—are—many—mansions. I—go—to—prepare—a—place—for—you" (1:210). In context, this passage from the Gospel of John (14:1–2) promises not simply relief for those who suffer but Christ's imminent return: in response to his Disciples' distress on learning that he would soon leave them, Jesus reassures them, "I go to prepare a place for you. And if I go and prepare a place for you, I will come again, and receive you unto myself; that where I am, *there* ye may be also" (John 14:2–3).

This allusion to the Second Coming might seem a surprising and incongruous shift from the material, economic register of Tom's plantation prospect. But in fact the verse forms a bookend to a biblical passage that precedes Tom's vision. After a romantic paean to the Mississippi comparing the surging waters of the river with the "headlong tide of business which is poured along its wave," Stowe turns to the dark side of that flood of commerce: "Ah! would that they did not also bear along a more fearful freight,—the tears of the oppressed, the sighs of the helpless, the bitter prayers of the poor, ignorant hearts to an unknown God—unknown, unseen and silent, but who will yet 'come out of his place to save all the poor of the earth!'" (*UTC*, 1:207–8). The final quotation, Jean Fagan Yellin notes, is an adaptation of Isaiah 26:21: "For, behold, the Lord cometh out of his place to punish the inhabitants of the earth for their iniquity: the earth also shall disclose her blood, and shall no more cover her slain."[93] Apparently conflated with "the poor of the earth" referenced in Job 24:4, Stowe's allusion references a moment from the so-called Isaiah Apocalypse (Isa. 24–27) when, in response to pleas by the people of Judah for God to swiftly return to punish the wicked and destroy their enemies, the prophet counsels patience and assures them that God will come.[94] Carefully framed between two apocalyptic passages from the Bible, Tom's vision of the Southern landscape clearly is freighted with more than economic significance.

Stowe had evoked such a view once before. In her *Primary Geography for Children* (1833), the popular geography textbook she had authored with her sister Catharine, the lesson on "Western States" invites readers to "stand on the banks of the Mississippi, and see all that goes on": "As far as you can see, up and down the river, from this place, it is covered with flat-bottomed boats, which have come from every part of the valley of the Mississippi, some with flour, and some with corn and meat, and some with cattle and horses and mules." Stowe does not picture plantations or slavery here (she has already done so in the previous lesson on "Southern States"), but the prospect makes visible a vast commercial system uniting a valley that eventually "will have more people in it than all the rest of the United States put together." Yet the political implications of this growth are what most concern her: "Our nation is the first nation of so large a size, that ever set the example of governing itself," she writes. "Now all the other nations in the world are looking at America, to see whether so great a nation will really succeed in governing itself; and if we succeed, then they will feel encouraged to try to be free too." Exporting republicanism around the globe depends on the maintenance of moral and civic order at home, for "if all the people in this country should grow quarrelsome and wicked, and refuse to keep the laws, there would very soon be an end of our government. . . . So you see that if people wish to be free they must be good." This vital link between republican liberty and Christian morality is where benevolent activism comes in:

> This is the reason why it is so very important that bibles and tracts and sabbath schools should be carried every where in this country. They will teach the people to be peaceable and sober, and to obey the laws. You remember how I told you in the article on religion, that there was not a single republican government in those countries where the bible is unknown; and those countries where it is best known, are those in which the people are the most free and happy.[95]

The *Primary Geography* thus lays out a moral geography that connects material prosperity, westward expansion, and the spread of republicanism; but the arrival of this bright millennial future depends on the free circulation of religious print and the institutions that enable it.

In the 1840s as Stowe published pieces in the *Evangelist* arguing for the need to establish "Protestant schools" and Bible-based instruction in the West to safeguard the nation's future, she continued to insist on the need for the religious mediation of American economic and political development.[96] She warned of a region "full of settlers, churchless, schoolless, careless, indifferent to religion, full of superstitious errors or infidel prejudices; *there* must [missionaries] make parishes, make churches, raise schools and build schoolhouses." But she ended her jeremiad with the hope that America would "ris[e] resplendent, like the beautiful city which John saw 'coming down from God out of heaven'" as a result of those labors.[97] Quoting from Revelation 21:2, Stowe signaled that in 1844, more than a decade after her first foray into sacred geography, when she surveyed the Mississippi Valley she still saw mingled there millennial promise and apocalyptic peril.

In light of Stowe's earlier accounts of the Mississippi Valley, her apocalyptic framing of Tom's vision from the steamboat signals that the scene is about more than the exploitation of the market revolution; more, even, than the threat of divine retribution for the cruelties of slavery. It is fundamentally about whether the nation's economic prosperity has become unmoored from republican principles and Christian morals—whether Protestantism has ceased to mediate national development, imperiling the entire millennium. Tom, whom Haley will soon liken to a Bible and who is now shown struggling to master its teachings, embodies that mediation, in terms of both the circulation of the good book through national space and the transmission of Gospel truth among its people. But unlike Eliza's swift passage northward on the wings of sympathy, Tom's restricted movements through the South and the resistance he faces to spreading the Word stand in stark contrast to the *Primary*

Geography's vision of universal circulation, of "bibles and tracts and sabbath schools" being "carried every where in this country." The ability of the Bible and other religious texts to function as transparent conduits of truth, unencumbered by competing interpretive strategies or ideologies of print—what I earlier termed moral mediation—is suddenly thrown into doubt.

In other words, if on one level Stowe's characters dramatize the fate of print's moral mission in antebellum America, Tom represents a scenario not unlike like what the American Anti-Slavery Society had lamented in the 1830s, in which the failure of the Word to circulate freely rendered the South one more "heathen" space on the map, closer to the supposed despotism of Asia than to American democracy. This is precisely how Ophelia St. Clare's New England family, having absorbed their Calvinist moral geography from one of Jedidiah Morse's geography textbooks and Timothy Flint's missionary travelogue, perceives New Orleans: "an awful wicked place" that is "most equal to going to the Sandwich Islands, or anywhere among the heathen" (*UTC*, 1:227).[98] Their preconceptions are confirmed by the "Moorish" aspect of Augustine St. Clare's mansion, which Ophelia judges "rather old and heathenish" (1:236), and by St. Clare himself, whom she considers "very much of a heathen" (1:231). So when St. Clare admits that "Tom is n't a bad hand, now, at explaining Scripture" (1:267) and overhears Tom praying for his conversion, Tom's evangelizing in some sense represents a missionary enterprise that relies on Bible distribution and exegesis to convert the "heathen"—conversion that Stowe presents as a necessary precursor to voluntary emancipation. Two years later, the results are not encouraging: Tom has convinced St. Clare to make a temperance "pledge" (1:294) but has failed to convert him or to convince the sorrow-shattered slave Prue to accept "Lord Jesus" (1:311).

It is against this backdrop of arrested circulation and failed conversion that the novel's most famous apocalyptic scene unfolds, as Tom and Eva read the Bible together in a bower overlooking Lake Pontchartrain. As in the earlier prospect from the steamboat, Stowe signals the scene's apocalyptic content by prefacing it with a scriptural reference, this time alluding to Isaiah 40:7 in the chapter title "The Grass Withereth—The Flower Fadeth" (*UTC*, 2:60). The shift from the Isaiah Apocalypse's threat of divine judgment that framed the steamboat scene to the reassuring promise of Israel's "imminent" return from exile that opens Second Isaiah (chapters 40–55) signals Tom's own state of separation "from all his soul held dear" and his "yearning for what lay beyond" (2:60).[99] His desire is at once geographical (for his family and home in Kentucky) but also eschatological: as Topsy's ingenuous cosmic mapping suggests, when Tom longs for "Kintuck" he both mourns the Edenic "state" from which Adam and Eve "fell" (2:51) and anticipates "what lay beyond," whether that

Pl. 1. Frederic Edwin Church, *Twilight in the Wilderness*, 1860. Oil on canvas, 40 × 64 in. (101.6 × 162.6 cm). The Cleveland Museum of Art, Mr. and Mrs. William H. Marlatt Fund, 1965.233

Pl. 2. Frederic Edwin Church, *The Heart of the Andes*, 1859. Oil on canvas, 66⅛ × 119¼ in. (168 × 302.9 cm). The Metropolitan Museum of Art, bequest of Mrs. David Dows, 1909.95

Pl. 3. Frederic Edwin Church, *Cotopaxi*, 1862. Oil on canvas, 48 × 85 in. (121.9 × 215.9 cm). Detroit Institute of Arts, Founders Society Purchase, 76.89.

Pl. 4. Thomas Cole, *View from Mount Holyoke, Northampton, Massachusetts, after a Thunderstorm—The Oxbow*, 1836. Oil on canvas, 51½ × 76 in (130.8 × 193 cm). The Metropolitan Museum of Art, Gift of Mrs. Russell Sage, 1908, 08.228

Pl. 5. Robert S. Duncanson, *Uncle Tom and Little Eva*, 1853. Oil on canvas, 27¼ × 38¼ in. (69.2 × 97.2 cm). Detroit Institute of Arts, Gift of Mrs. Jefferson Butler and Miss Grace R. Conover, 49.498

Pl. 6. Jasper Francis Cropsey, *Catskill Mountain House*, 1855. Oil on canvas, 29 × 44 in. (73.66 × 111.76 cm). Minneapolis Institute of Art, Bequest of Mrs. Lillian Lawhead Rinderer in memory of her brother, William A. Lawhead, and the William Hood Dunwoody Fund, 31.47. Photo: Minneapolis Institute of Art

Pl. 7. Albert Bierstadt, *Yosemite Valley*, 1868. Oil on canvas, 36 × 54 in. (91.44 × 137.16 cm). Collection of the Oakland Museum of California, Gift of Miss Marguerite Laird in Memory of Mr. and Mrs. P.W. Laird, A64.26

Pl. 8. Albert Bierstadt, *Sunset in the Yosemite Valley*, 1868. Oil on canvas, 36¼ × 52¼ in (92 × 132.75 cm). The Haggin Museum, Stockton, California, 1931.391.11

means a personal reward in the afterlife or the restoration of God's kingdom on Earth.

Tom and Eva themselves are unsure which, for reading "the Revelations and the Prophecies" together, "All that they knew was, that they spoke of a glory to be revealed,—a wondrous something yet to come, wherein their soul rejoiced, yet knew not why." Newly aware of being suspended "between two dim eternities,—the eternal past, the eternal future" (*UTC*, 2:62), Tom and Eva find themselves reading the Bible together in an arbor as the sun sets over Lake Pontchartrain, when John's vision of "a sea of glass, mingled with fire" from Revelation 15:2 suddenly appears manifested in the landscape before them:

> "Tom," said Eva, suddenly stopping, and pointing to the lake, "there 'tis."
> "What, Miss Eva?"
> "Don't you see,—there?" said the child, pointing to the glassy water, which, as it rose and fell, reflected the golden glow of the sky. "There's a 'sea of glass, mingled with fire.'"
> "True enough, Miss Eva," said Tom. (2:63–64)

Eva's rapt recognition of the literal correspondence between the text and the world is met with rather less urgency by Tom, who emphasizes a textual rather than literal correspondence by launching into a hymn that envisions "the new Jerusalem." When Eva asks him, "Where do you suppose new Jerusalem is, Uncle Tom?" he locates it "up in the clouds" (2:64), restoring the dualistic ontology (the strict division between this world and the world to come) that seemed on the verge of dissolving in Eva's vision. Essentially he returns us to Aunt Chloe's prayer meeting and the figurative interpretation of apocalypse represented by the old woman waiting for death to take her "to glory" (1:51).

By arresting the apocalyptic descent to Earth and returning it to its celestial and textual confines, Tom seems to affirm an Augustinian tradition of interpreting Revelation figuratively. In this view, Douglas Robinson explains, "the cosmic battle depicted in the Book of Revelation is no historical prediction, . . . but a spiritual allegory, a narrative metaphor for man's inner ethical growth toward God." This internalization of apocalypse, Robinson claims, is an essentially "conservative" interpretation that suits the interests of those in power by diffusing the "revolutionary" potential of an imminent, literal apocalypse.[100] Tom's Augustinian leanings, a connection Stowe highlights by calling him "respectable enough to be a Bishop of Carthage, as men of his color were, in other ages" (*UTC*, 1:259), links him with the historical St. Augustine's North African milieu just as Tom enters the estate of a character named Augustine. The parallel would seem to confirm Donald G. Mathews's assertion that Tom represents a white conception of Southern "black Christianity" that emphasized its ideals of "love and forbearance" while ignoring the counterbalancing emphasis on "apocalyptic judgment" that saturated slave religion.[101] On Augustine St. Clare's estate, it seems, the City of God and the Earthly City are kept carefully separate.

As a metonymic figure for the Bible, then, Tom appears to represent not just the book itself but a particular way of reading: a distinctive strand of "apocalyptic hermeneutics" that runs counter to the more revolutionary, socially transformational model of textual encounter represented by Eliza.[102] When Eva follows Tom's lead, responding to his suggestion that New Jerusalem is "up in the clouds" with her own description of the "great gates of pearl" (*UTC*, 2:64) she sees there, we observe her in the process of becoming a certain kind of reader—of the Bible, to be sure, but also of the physical world as a text where one might "read the signs of the times" (2:322), as Stowe urges her readers to do. In other words, just as the circulation of characters in Stowe's temperance tales enacts the spatial mediation performed by evangelical print, Eva and Tom's exegetical conversations enact print's moral mediation, the transmission of truth from text to reader upon which evangelical goals of moral suasion depended. But in contrast to the ideal of effortless, transparent transmission assumed by evangelical publishers—what David Paul Nord calls the "'hypodermic needle' theory of 'media effects'"—Stowe highlights the complexities of moral mediation, even in the quintessentially (for Protestants) self-sufficient text of the Bible, as Tom and Eva wrestle with its notoriously opaque apocalyptic books.[103]

For confirmation of this concern with apocalyptic mediation, one need only examine the novel's rich archive of visual representations. In Hammatt Billings's illustration *Little Eva Reading the Bible to Uncle Tom in the Arbor* in the 1852 Jewett edition (fig. 3.1), Eva sits at the center of the composition with Tom seated to her left. She holds Tom's hand with her left hand and points out at the lake with her right, an open Bible resting on her lap. Tom, his profile haloed by the absence of crosshatching, looks not down at the page but out at the sky. Eva's seated posture, the open book, and her gesture all place the scene just as she has stopped reading and pointed to the sunset, suspending readers at the moment when an earthly apocalypse seems most imminent. Billings's emphasis on the textual mediation enacted in Eva's vision of the sunset is typical of illustrations of the arbor scene in the early 1850s. As Peter Betjemann notes, "Eva's body almost always serves as a conduit from print to prospect," "channeling the viewer's gaze from book to sky, from text to image." A telling contrast is Robert Duncanson's 1853 painting *Uncle Tom and Little Eva* (fig. 3.2; see plate 5), which shows a standing Eva pointing and looking skyward. Duncanson has opted to depict a slightly later moment in the scene, when Eva is trying to tell Tom that she is dying: "The child rose, and pointed her little hand

LITTLE EVA READING THE BIBLE TO UNCLE TOM IN THE ARBOR. Page 63.

FIGURE 3.1. Hammatt Billings (illustrator) and Baker and Smith (engraver), *Little Eva Reading the Bible to Uncle Tom in the Arbor* (engraving). In Harriet Beecher Stowe, *Uncle Tom's Cabin*, 2 vols. (Boston: John P. Jewett; Cleveland: Jewett, Proctor & Worthington, 1852), vol. 2, facing p. 63. Photo courtesy of The Newberry Library, Chicago, Special Collections, Case Y 255.S8847.

to the sky; the glow of evening lit her golden hair with a kind of unearthly radiance, and her eyes were bent earnestly on the skies. 'I'm going *there*,' she said, 'to the spirits bright, Tom. *I'm going, before long*'" (*UTC*, 2:64–65). In Duncanson's version Eva no longer holds the Bible (which now sits closed behind Tom) but instead beholds the landscape directly. The effect, Betjemann argues, is to "displace" the novel's "literalist" interpretation of the biblical text in favor of an "unmediated confrontation" with reality: Eva shifts from merely reading the Book of Revelation to receiving an apocalyptic vision herself. In the process, he claims, Duncanson replaces the novel's tepid antislavery politics with a "radical" form of "militant abolitionism."[104]

Even if one accepts Betjemann's characterization of the novel's politics, the fact that Duncanson chose to depict a moment in the novel after the fervor of Eva's initial apocalyptic vision has been defused into a private afterlife in the clouds is surely enough to call into question the radicalism of the painting. But the more basic point at issue here is the notion that Duncanson's painting jettisons the problem of mediation. One might counter that in a sense Eva still *is* holding a Bible—that the position of her hand on Tom's arm echoes the way

FIGURE 3.2. Robert S. Duncanson, *Uncle Tom and Little Eva*, 1853. Oil on canvas, 27¼ × 38¼ in. (69.2 × 97.2 cm). Detroit Institute of Arts, Gift of Mrs. Jefferson Butler and Miss Grace R. Conover, 49.498.

her hand rests on the page in many illustrations (fig. 3.3), visually reinforcing the novel's figuration of Tom as a Bible. Moreover, Eva remains just as much a "conduit" here as she was in the illustrations—perhaps even more so, since without the book on her lap, she herself becomes the medium. Instead of looking over Eva's head at the sky as he does in the Billings illustration, Duncanson's Tom seems to look straight at Eva, her white bosom spread before him like a page. On might say Duncanson cannily visualizes the change Eva undergoes in the novel as her death approaches. When she points to the sunset and becomes transfigured by the glow that "lit her golden hair and flushed cheek with a kind of unearthly radiance" (*UTC*, 2:64), or when her skin grows ever more "transparent" (2:65) until we find her on the veranda with "her Bible half open, her little transparent fingers lying listlessly between the leaves" (2:97), it is as if her body has become a textual and eschatological medium. Just as Eliza functions as the circulating text that links people horizontally across social space, Eva becomes the vertical conduit between this world and the next.

TOM AND EVA IN THE ARBOUR.
"Tom and Eva were seated on a little mossy seat, in an arbour, at the foot of the garden. It was Sunday evening, and Eva's Bible lay open on her knee."—Page 223.

FIGURE 3.3. George Cruikshank (illustrator) and William Measom (engraver), *Tom and Eva in the Arbour* (engraving). In Harriet Beecher Stowe, *Uncle Tom's Cabin* (London: John Cassell, 1852), facing p. 223. Photo courtesy of The Newberry Library, Chicago, Special Collections, Case PS 2954.U5 1852.

It is surely no coincidence, then, that Eva's decline is accompanied by a quickening drumbeat of apocalyptic imagery, beginning with Tom's declaration that "the bridegroom cometh" (an allusion to Christ's Second Coming from Matthew 25:1), continuing with his evocation of "the trumpet sound afore the break o' day" (*UTC*, 2:110) and the narrator's warning that "the veil between the frail present and the eternal future grows thin" (2:111), and culminating with the chapter heading "This Is the Last of Earth" (2:114) that falls like a coffin lid following her death. Tom may have read the sunset in an

Augustinian manner, but by the time Eva dies he has helped teach us to interpret *her* as an apocalyptic text.

The key point is not that Uncle Tom represents a "conservative" reading of Revelation or that Duncanson's painting is less "radical" than the novel but that visual representations of the novel draw attention to its subtle shifts and seams—to the unresolved interpretive dissonance that surfaces between and within the characters as they wrestle with the implications of the apocalyptic text for their lives. It is in this ethical register that Tom begins to converge with Stowe's larger project in the novel. The first hint that he may be able to break out of the failed moral mediation that has dogged his missionary attempts thus far occurs in his deepening relationship to Augustine St. Clare after Eva's death. As St. Clare turns to Eva's Bible for solace, his reading prompts a series of anguished conversations that contrast St. Clare's inability to believe with Tom's faith, here coded as his ability to visualize biblical narrative. When St. Clare marvels, "this is all *real* to you!" after reading the raising of Lazarus, Tom responds, "I can jest fairly *see* it" (*UTC*, 2:123). These exchanges enable Tom to expound his homely form of practical Christianity: "We does for the Lord when we does for his critturs" (2:127). Such lessons culminate in St. Clare's encounter with the "last judgment" (2:136) described in the Book of Matthew (25:31–45), which precipitates his resolve to do "My duty" by emancipating his slaves and eventually, he hopes, to "do something for a whole class" (2:138). Of course Stowe kills St. Clare off before allowing him the opportunity to follow through on his pledge, as if to emphasize that the hermeneutical operation itself—the leap from the apocalyptic text to its ethical imperatives in the world—is her chief concern, not the practical results of acting on those imperatives or the ontological status of apocalyptic prediction.

St. Clare's experience plays on a homology widely accepted by antebellum Protestants between the broad outlines of apocalyptic history and the spiritual lives of individual believers. "Conversion," James H. Moorhead explains, "along with accompanying dreams of the heaven or hell into which death would shortly usher each person, constituted a miniature apocalypse paralleling the historical scenario of the book of Revelation. Just as the Kingdom of God arrived only through overturning and judgment, so, too, believers achieved assurance of salvation only after a season of terror, sometimes prolonged, during which they knew themselves to be destined to hell."[105] This sense of conversion as a terrifying confrontation with the Last Judgment describes well the agony St. Clare experiences following Eva's death, and it clarifies how Tom and Eva function as apocalyptic media by precipitating such spiritual reckonings in others. Even on Simon Legree's Red River plantation, the site in the novel that seems to exist at the furthest remove from any hope of divine intervention, Legree confronts his own Day of Judgment through his terrified encounters with "Damnation!" (*UTC*, 2:216), prompted first by a lock of Eva's hair and then by Tom's warnings of "ETERNITY" (2:229), until on his deathbed he confronts "the lurid shadows of a coming retribution" (2:287–88). Tom's and Eva's ability to provoke this inner apocalypse in their "readers" enacts a model of transparent moral mediation that evangelicals had long sought to achieve through print and that Stowe now made central to the success of her own novel: the idea that words on a page could precipitate a crisis of conscience compelling enough to provoke immediate action.

Critics have long noted Stowe's eschatological preoccupations and debated the precise nature of her millennialism. The general consensus seems to be that she shared and extended the optimistic, Edwardsian postmillennialist theology preached by her father and her husband but that beginning in the 1840s (likely influenced by William Miller's predictions of Christ's imminent return) she was occasionally seized by a sense of impending doom, a dread most famously expressed in her warning of a coming "*day of vengeance*" (2:322) in the "Concluding Remarks" of *Uncle Tom's Cabin*.[106] This oscillation reflects the fact that postmillennialism and premillennialism positions were not necessarily as discrete in the minds of antebellum believers as they now appear: even postmillennialists "betrayed anxieties about a future latent with supernatural judgment and calamity as well as hope."[107] The distinction nonetheless remains significant because it marks divergent understandings of the role of print media in the millennium. As previous chapters have shown, postmillennialists saw print as one of the divinely appointed "instruments" that humans could wield to hasten the gradual unfolding of the millennium within history. Premillennialists like George Duffield, Miller, and Joshua Himes used print to spread their message just as avidly as postmillennialists did, but they saw its role rather differently: not to hasten the Second Coming (which they believed would happen regardless of their actions) but to provide "a sign that the end was near" and to warn the faithful to prepare themselves for Christ's imminent return.[108]

This distinction between print as a human "instrument" and as a "sign" of the end provides a key to understanding *Uncle Tom's Cabin* as an apocalyptic text—not simply as a document that reflects the eschatological stance of its author but as a work that presents itself as integral to the unfolding of God's providential design. So what exactly is the novel's role in that design? If we recognize Stowe's characters as media—both as figures of print circulation and as conduits of words and feeling—the novel's ending seems to affirm their role as millennial instruments. The departure of the Harrises, Topsy, and the other freed slaves for Liberia as missionaries destined to "roll the tide of civilization and Christianity along its shores, and plant there mighty republics" (2:301) dramatizes the prevalent belief among antebellum Protestants (Stowe included) that African colonization and missionary efforts were converging to bring about the millennium, a view reminiscent of the apocalyptic geographies of Jonathan Edwards and Samuel Hopkins, who (as discussed in the previous chapter) placed Africa at the culmination of a global process of evangelization.[109] Uncle Tom too becomes an instrument, as his martyrdom effects the conversion of the "poor, ignorant heathen" (2:278) around him on Legree's plantation and (through his effect on George) the emancipation of the Shelby plantation, converting St. Clare's apocalyptic "*dies irae*" into a joyful "Te Deum" in which the slaves declare, "The year of Jubilee is come" (2:309). But while both strands of the novel's plot thus point toward a millennial dawn that will feature universal Christianization and emancipation, Stowe's "Concluding Remarks" jerk us back from this triumphant account of instrumental media to proclaim the "signs of the times" and warn of "the wrath of Almighty God!" (2:322), suspending readers uneasily between instrument and sign.

The hinge between these alternatives is the reader's own response. In the novel's final chapter, Stowe recalls that after passage of the 1850 Fugitive Slave Act, as some Northerners claimed a duty to assist in the capture and return of fugitives, she thought, "These men and Christians cannot know what slavery is; if they did, such a question could never be open for discussion. And from this arose a desire to exhibit it in a *living dramatic reality*" (*UTC*, 2:314). Once that reality is before readers, she declares, if they still allow slavery to be "passed over in silence" (2:315) and fail to offer "refuge" to fugitives in their churches and schools, and "reparation for the wrongs that the American nation has brought upon them," then "the country will have reason to tremble" (2:318). If readers feel and act rightly, on the other hand, the spread of the novel will have itself confirmed and advanced the millennial narrative through which, as the "Preface" declares, "another and better day is dawning" (1:v). Stowe, in other words, aims to bring the reader to the very brink of inner apocalypse—the same harrowing moment of decision that Finney sought to catalyze in his listeners by placing "the sinner" on the edge of Niagara Falls and that Weld and the Grimké sisters sought to provoke with *American Slavery as It Is*. The difference is that throughout the novel Stowe highlights that moment of reckoning as an act of interpretation—of reading—and not simply of immediate vision. In this sense *Uncle Tom's Cabin* can be thought of not only as a literary apocalypse but a meta-apocalypse—a text that dramatizes the process of hermeneutical engagement with apocalyptic texts and contemplates the dire (indeed, apocalyptic) consequences when moral mediation fails.

"The Humblest of Instruments in His Hand": Stowe's Divine Artistry

Nearly thirty years after the publication of *Uncle Tom's Cabin*, Stowe recounted a vision she had sitting in church in Brunswick, Maine, in February 1851:

> The first part of the book ever committed to writing was the death of Uncle Tom. This scene presented itself almost as a tangible vision to her mind while sitting at the communion-table in the little church in Brunswick. She was perfectly overcome by it, and could scarcely restrain the convulsion of tears and sobbings that shook her frame. She hastened home and wrote it, and her husband being away she read it to her two sons of ten and twelve years of age. The little fellows broke out into convulsions of weeping, one of them saying, through his sobs, "Oh! mamma, slavery is the most cursed thing in the world!" From that time the story can less be said to have been composed by her than imposed upon her. Scenes, incidents, conversations rushed upon her with a vividness and importunity that would not be denied. The book insisted upon getting itself into being, and would take no denial.[110]

Stowe's account of the origin of her novel in a force outside of herself was not an isolated instance. Her son Charles recalled, "As Mrs. Stowe has since repeatedly said, 'I could not control the story; it wrote itself;' or 'I the author of "Uncle Tom's Cabin"? No, indeed. The Lord himself wrote it, and I was but the humblest of instruments in his hand. To Him alone should be given all the praise.'"[111]

Versions of this story have been recounted by Stowe's biographers and critics ever since, with varying degrees of skepticism.[112] An earlier generation of feminist critics tended to dismiss such accounts, recognizing that the myth of Stowe's artless text confirmed a critical tendency to ignore the novel's formal complexity and minimize the talent of its author, who became, in Sandra M. Gustafson's words, "a cosmic dummy inspired by a higher power."[113] But that response elided both the depth of Stowe's investment in the rhetoric of divine mediation and the pervasiveness of women's claims of "prophetic inspiration," which were made by evangelists such as Elleanor Knight and Jarena Lee as early as the 1820s, Spiritualist mediums in the late 1840s and 1850s, and sentimental novelists.[114] Stowe's experimentation with such rhetoric did not originate years after the publication of *Uncle Tom's Cabin*, nor was it the product of "a prolonged spell of religious hysteria" or evidence that Stowe had "confused the details" of the novel's genesis.[115] Far from an aberration, divine mediation figured prominently in the work of influential evangelical leaders and organizations as well as in the *Evangelist* itself. Stowe's claims about her lack of authorial agency should be understood as part of an evangelical rhetoric that emphasized the ability of certain forms of expression to mediate between the divine and the human. Those claims add a crucial new dimension to her effort to reimagine print circulation.

The roots of Stowe's rhetoric of divinely mediated artistry can be traced to the convergence of her literary career with her turn toward evangelical piety in the 1840s. After experiencing a long-awaited "baptism of the spirit" in the winter of 1844, she wrote to her brother Thomas that in that moment, "My *all* changed—Whereas once my heart ran with a strong current to the world, it now runs with a current the other way.... The will of Christ seems to me the steady pulse of my being & I go because I can not help it."[116] Similar accounts of the infusion of divine agency into the human fill the pieces she wrote for the *Evangelist* between her conversion experience and the publication of *Uncle Tom's Cabin*. In "Old Testament Pictures—No. 1," Stowe praised "the old Hebrew Scriptures" for their moving accounts of "the mingling of supernatural influences with the current of human affairs," before presenting an embellished version of the life of the patriarch Jacob, who had "promises, encouragements, visions, and divine manifestations ... showered on him" because of his "fitness" to accomplish the "plan of God."[117] Then in "Earthly Care a Heavenly Discipline," she criticized the tendency to perceive God's providence in the tragedies of life but not its everyday cares, resulting in the Christian's failure to "hear the voice of the Lord God speaking to him" and "to recognize the hand and voice of God through the veil of human agencies."[118] Perhaps she had this sense of agency in mind when she wrote to the Duke and Duchess of Sutherland that the pamphlet she had enclosed (an ATS edition of "Earthly Care a Heavenly Discipline") was "written for my own benefit during a season of heavy trial & deprivation" but "has found without my agency a wide circulation in England."[119] At a time when many women authors felt acutely the risks of public exposure, the letter hinted that the "agency" of others—whether human or divine—provided cover for Stowe's efforts to promote her work.[120]

Stowe's *Evangelist* pieces from the mid-1840s extend her exploration of divine mediation to literary expression. "The Interior Life; or, Primitive Christian Experience" finds a model of divinely mediated literary performance in the epistles of the apostle Paul, who "seems to consider himself as so borne along beyond himself by the power of Christ, that his course of action was more referable to Christ than to himself"; in this state, "the high devotional language of the Bible becomes the spontaneous and habitual language of the soul, more in accordance with its constant and habitual current of feeling than any other."[121] Similarly her poem "Mary at the Cross" envisions the Annunciation in prophetic terms, omitting the presence of the angel Gabriel in order to create a sense of Mary's direct apprehension of the divine plan: "And then it came—that message from the Highest, / . . . / What visions, then, of future glory filled thee!" The next stanza links these prophetic "visions" to a Romantic conception of inspiration, casting Mary as a divinely inspired poet: "Then woke the poet's fire! the prophet's song / Tuned with strange, burning words thy timid voice." By allowing the utterance of Mary's "burning words" to stand for the entire process of conception, gestation, and birth (the next stanza takes us straight to "the lowly manger"), Stowe elevates literary expression to a form of divine incarnation and implies its potential as an agent of God's redemption.[122]

Stowe's sustained attention during the 1840s to what she called the "intercommunion between God and man" and its role in literary expression suggests that her claims of divine involvement in *Uncle Tom's Cabin* did not emerge decades later but rather represented the culmination of years of spiritual reflection.[123] "To the artist is given a divine power likest to that of God," she told a correspondent in September 1852, as publisher John P. Jewett estimated that readers had snatched up more than 75,000 copies of her novel in the seven months since its release.[124] The following year as she pressed forward on her next project, *A Key to Uncle Tom's Cabin*, she continued to use this rhetoric, writing to the Seventh Earl of Carlisle that "I almost tremble when I write it[,] some of it is so dreadful,—but I look on myself as only an instrument in a Higher hand—and I know no one who would do the work with as true a heart of love to those concerned as I shall."[125] Such claims were not restricted to Stowe's personal correspondence: an advertisement for Jewett's cheap 1852 one-volume edition of *Uncle Tom's Cabin* ("An Edition for the Million!") in December 1852 predicted that future generations would "thank the God of Heaven for inspiring a noble woman to utter such glowing, burning truths, for the redemption of the oppressed millions of our race." Another ad Jewett ran in June 1852 quoted a review in the Boston *Congregationalist* that declared, "We look upon the writing of this book as providential, and as the best missionary God has yet sent into the field."[126] Claims about the role of divine agency in Stowe's novel were not the result of an idiosyncratic personal belief that only emerged years later but a strategic appeal to a broadly shared cultural understanding of God's participation in human action, including certain acts of literary expression.

Since at least the 1820s, prominent New School evangelicals had noted the ability of the Spirit to inhabit and propel human expression. Lyman Beecher preached in 1819 that "sermons must be written and preached in demonstration of the Spirit; and the argument of their controversy must be set on fire from heaven, before it will enlighten the dark heart, or melt the heart of stone."[127] Albert Barnes told his congregation in 1829 that they would not be saved by their own exertions alone but "through the special agency of God," who acts "by applying the preached gospel,—by leading the thoughts in a proper manner in the dispensations of his Providence."[128] Finney expressed a similar conception of divine agency when he compared the sinner to the man on the brink of Niagara Falls: "Not only does the preacher cry *Stop*, but, through the living voice of the preacher, the Spirit cries *Stop*. The preacher cries, 'Turn ye, why will ye die.' The Spirit pours the expostulation home with such power, that the sinner turns."[129]

Similar rhetoric peppered the pages of the *Evangelist* in the 1840s. Sermons remained the most common manifestation of divine agency, but preaching was not the only medium of the Spirit.[130] The "religious press, while it is an auxiliary to the ministry," represented "an independent and blessed means of grace and salvation," wrote one correspondent, who urged the coordinated reading of spiritual classics like Baxter's *Call to the Unconverted*: "It would be like concentrating the rays of the sun by a million burning glasses on as many focal points; the fire of repentance, by the Spirit's blessing on one of his most honored instruments, would envelop the land and blend with the light of that glorious millennial morning toward which the eye of the church has been so long gazing with anxious hope and longing desire."[131] Literary authors might even become God's mouthpieces. To one reviewer of William Cowper's *Olney Hymns*, "A preternatural influence hung around him: he felt that the finger of God was upon him; and he humbled himself beneath *His* mighty hand."[132] Another critic declared that Milton's poetry was so powerful that "nothing equal to it ever evolved from the human mind, without special intervention of the Divine Spirit"—leaving ambiguous the question of whether such intervention had actually occurred.[133] And M. E. Doubleday declared Hannah More "as much an instrument raised up, in the language of the Puritans, for the revival and spread of pure evangelical and spiritual religion, in the higher classes of English society, as were Wesley and Whitefield in the lower."[134]

Stowe's meditations in the *Evangelist* on divine agency and human expression, then, circulated alongside similar statements that belonged to a well-established theological discourse—so well established that by 1850 it was familiar enough to be ironized in Hawthorne's account of Arthur Dimmesdale's Election Sermon, "which he wrote with such an impulsive flow of thought and emotion, that he fancied himself inspired; and only wondered that Heaven should see fit to transmit the grand and solemn music of its oracles through so foul an organ-pipe as he."[135] Crucially, Stowe's version of this rhetoric was marked by a flexibility of genre and media that included letters, poetry, and ultimately novels. She was not alone of course: Catharine Maria Sedgwick, Susan Warner, and Elizabeth Prentiss all used similar terms to describe their fiction.[136] But *Uncle Tom's Cabin* did elevate the visibility of such claims, initially through the advertisements and notices that accompanied its publication and ultimately through the origin myth cultivated by Stowe and her nineteenth-century biographers. They helped ensure that when Stowe "preach[ed] on paper," she spoke with a transcendent authority akin to what male preachers had enjoyed for decades.

As Candy Gunther Brown notes, "By disavowing authorship, Stowe marked her novel as a religious work, in a sense inspired by the Holy Spirit; the text did not belong to her, as an author or as a woman, but to the Christian community."[137] In the terms used at the time, the novel was merely an "instrument," a "means"; differently put, Stowe expanded the sense in which her novel, her readers, and she herself could be considered media. Media theorists have recently emphasized that using the word "media" as a singular noun (as opposed to a collection of distinct "mediums") highlights the "fundamental relationality" of the human, the sense that all human experience is inherently mediated—not only by the body and the physical environment but also by evolving technologies, social arrangements, and cultural systems.[138] The antebellum mediascape witnessed major shifts in all of these categories—it changed what it meant to be human. For Stowe, print not only expanded readers' awareness of others and enlarged their network of social ties; it also imbricated them in new systems of information circulation. It sent them from house to house distributing tracts, or running out to buy the latest best seller. Stowe's fiction dramatized the sense that human subjects had themselves become media capable of relaying information across vast expanses of physical and social space. But she combined that "horizontal" model of mediation with a second "vertical" one: the traditional model of divine inspiration. Where they intersected—where a democratic world of mass print met the prophetic fervor of evangelical piety—the antebellum mediascape assumed its most world-shaking, apocalyptic power.

PART II
Geographies of the Secular

4

Pilgrimage to the "Secular Center"

TOURISM AND THE SENTIMENTAL NOVEL

IN OCTOBER 1855 Jasper Francis Cropsey spent three days sketching in the Catskill Mountains, a place he had visited numerous times since his first trip there more than a decade earlier.[1] By year's end the painter had produced at least two views of the Catskill Mountain House, a popular hotel perched on a rocky outcropping overlooking the Hudson River Valley, including one commissioned by James Edgar.[2] *Catskill Mountain House* (fig. 4.1; see also plate 6) joined a sizable body of images of the site produced in the decades following the hotel's 1824 opening, including oil paintings by Thomas Cole (fig. 4.2) and Sanford Robinson Gifford, engravings in guidebooks and periodicals, and even transfer-printed dishes.[3] Cropsey's painting thus seems to fit snugly within a familiar narrative of the interconnected rise of landscape painting, taste, and tourism in the United States in the early nineteenth century.[4] And coming on the heels of Cropsey's overtly religious works including *The Spirit of Peace* (1851) and *The Millennial Age* (1854) (fig. 4.3), it also seems to confirm another standard story of artists' turn from idealizing landscape compositions and moralistic religious allegories to a more naturalistic idiom in the decade following Cole's death in 1848.[5] Like several other American artists who treated apocalyptic themes in their work between 1848 and 1854, by 1855 Cropsey appears to have left those concerns behind, reflecting what many scholars have described as a broader trend toward secularization in American culture at midcentury.[6]

Yet Cropsey's engagement with religious themes did not end in 1854 with *The Millennial Age*. Within days of his trip to the Catskills in October 1855 he proposed a series of paintings to be titled *The Pilgrim of the Cross* to his patron Fletcher Williams, who earlier that year had purchased Cropsey's *The Good Shepherd*, a painting of Jesus tending sheep in a mountain landscape.[7] Moreover, *Catskill Mountain House* portrayed a place whose unique topographical and meteorological features had made it a catalyst for the religious and

FIGURE 4.1. Jasper Francis Cropsey, *Catskill Mountain House*, 1855. Oil on canvas, 29 × 44 in. (73.66 × 111.76 cm). Minneapolis Institute of Art, Bequest of Mrs. Lillian Lawhead Rinderer in memory of her brother, William A. Lawhead, and the William Hood Dunwoody Fund, 31.47. Photo: Minneapolis Institute of Art.

FIGURE 4.2. Thomas Cole, *A View of the Two Lakes and Mountain House, Catskill Mountains, Morning*, 1844. Oil on canvas, 35 13/16 × 53⅞ in. (91 × 136.9 cm). Brooklyn Museum, Dick S. Ramsay Fund, 52.16.

FIGURE 4.3. Jasper Francis Cropsey, *The Millennial Age*, 1854. Oil on canvas, 38¼ × 54 in. (97.2 × 137.2 cm). Collection of the Newington-Cropsey Foundation.

eschatological musings of travelers and fictional characters at least since 1819, when Henry E. Dwight (son of the prominent Congregationalist minister and Yale president) looked out from one of the peaks and saw in the roiling clouds below him "a glowing picture of the general deluge," which gave way before the rising sun to reveal a "landscape [that] unfolds all its beauties, as if it had just sprung into existence at the command of the Creator."[8] Cropsey drew on these associations as he planned *The Pilgrim of the Cross*. In a prospectus for the series, he indicated that the famous prospect would provide a model for the fourth painting in the series, "Land of Beula[h]," which would show "The Celestial City in the distance and angels to & fro"; Cropsey noted, "In the Land of Beu. the cloud scene in the Catskill Mt. upon my visit there in *1853*."[9]

As Cropsey combines a classic Protestant literary allegory (Bunyan's *The Pilgrim's Progress*) with a popular American tourist site to envision a narrative series of religious landscape paintings, we glimpse a convergence of fiction, landscape tourism, and visual culture clearly informed by the evangelical space produced over the previous three decades. As the first part of this book has shown, evangelical preachers, writers, and editors drew upon the work of engravers and landscape painters to visualize the sacred landscapes and geographies that had long structured Protestant narratives of personal and collective redemption. But by the 1850s the mediascape generating such imagined spaces was no longer limited to the Bible, evangelical steady sellers, and illustrated religious tracts and almanacs—the sorts of texts that recast Thomas Cole's view from Mount Holyoke as a narrative of sacred history and geography two decades earlier (see chapter 1). Evangelical space had gone mainstream. By the 1850s, best-selling sentimental novels by the likes of Susan Warner and Maria Cummins used landscape views, including of tourist sites like the Catskill Mountain House, as settings for their young heroines' most significant moments of spiritual vision and moral development. Whereas in the Calvinist fiction of earlier decades, landscape prospects often functioned to remind readers to distance themselves from the world and its pleasures, by midcentury those prospects offered a privileged medium through which characters (particularly women) could gain knowledge of God's unfolding design of redemption history and the providential meaning of their own suffering. Landscape had become an apocalyptic medium. But this fusion of sacred geography with fictional and physical space coincided with the commercialization of American tourism that many observers warned was turning places formerly valued as spiritual retreats into profane spaces devoted to "Mammon" and the display of wealth.[10] At the same time, new developments in the natural sciences (led by figures such as Charles Lyell and Charles Darwin) as well as the influential aesthetic theories of John Ruskin, which stressed the truthful representation of nature based on carefully observed natural facts, called into question the view propagated by Protestant clergy among others of the artist as a spiritual visionary and social prophet who could reveal the sacred meaning manifested in the landscape.[11] In the face of these pressures, what would become of the spatial imaginary that evangelicals had built over the previous three decades to help ordinary people read religious narratives inscribed on the land?

To answer that question, this chapter examines the literary and visual production generated around the Catskill Mountain House and similar tourist sites. That popular mediascape offers a way to rethink standard scholarly accounts that tell the story of antebellum culture as an orderly, linear transition away from the pieties of the Puritan past and toward the spiritual crisis of the Civil War, beyond which the United States advances steadily into a secular, modern future. It unsettles conventional narratives of cultural production built on a modern Western understanding of time as an "irreversible arrow" that grounds the notion of progress and the discrete historical periods that mark, among other things, the emergence of a secular world.[12] This temporal model underlies what could be called the secularization paradigm of nineteenth-century American literary and visual history. On the literary side this paradigm tends to describe a shift from the religious concerns of theological treatises and sermons to the aesthetic and reformist concerns of "secular" literature by the 1850s.[13] In the visual field, the Civil War often serves as the dividing line between a culture in which a widely held religious framework can be assumed, and one in which art reflects an array of psychological, aesthetic, and scientific concerns.[14]

The fascination these tourist sites held for figures like Cropsey and Cummins, however, helps redefine what it means to call antebellum culture secular. In Charles Taylor's terms, it means shifting away from two older definitions of secularity: one that describes the separation of religious institutions from political ones—what in the U.S. context would be called disestablishment—resulting in "public spaces" that are "emptied of God, or of any reference to ultimate reality"; and a second that "consists in the falling off of religious belief and practice, in people turning away from God, and no longer going to Church." What is noteworthy about these definitions is the centrality of space to both of them: we know we are in a secular age when we walk through a public square and no longer see holiday displays or religious processions, and when our weekly itineraries don't include stepping into an ecclesiastical space to worship. But the tourist sites explored in this chapter offer a more complicated story, as a network of public spaces became increasingly invested with sacred presence, and many well-to-do white Protestants turned to them as a new kind of worship space. That reorientation of sacred space, achieved through the efforts of writers, artists, and ministers, points toward Taylor's third definition of secularity, which describes a shift in "the conditions of belief," "a move from a society where belief in God is unchallenged and indeed, unproblematic, to one in which it is understood to be one option among others, and frequently not the easiest to embrace."[15] In this definition space seems to drop out of the picture, as if the clash of religious "options" occurs only in the mind of the individual believer. But as this chapter will show, this contest did indeed play out in space, as places like the Catskill Mountain House became the focus of competing visions of the sacred. This did not simply occur in the physical landscape, however, but across a shifting mediascape of pictures and print. That media environment helps us see the secular not as a sphere from which religion has been evacuated but instead as a condition in which spiritual significance has slipped the strictures of theological utterance to infuse the everyday, and where religious pluralism plays out in the arena of artistic form.

The next section turns to the literary end of things by examining a particularly significant scene that recurred in the popular fiction of the 1850s, in which a young female character reads the landscape as an apocalyptic text. The vision of Revelation that Eva witnesses with Uncle Tom in the arbor (see chapter 3) is no doubt the most famous example, but it was not the first. The first

American "best seller" of the 1850s and one of two works hailed by reviewers as "national" novels in the early part of the decade, Susan Warner's *The Wide, Wide World* (1851) had its own version of that scene that drew upon a long line of Calvinist fiction before it.[16] While Warner's young protagonist looks across an unspecified rural New England landscape, just a few years later another orphaned heroine, this one in Maria Cummins's *The Lamplighter* (1854), would exercise a similar form of spiritual sight at some of the nation's most prominent tourist resorts, including the Catskill Mountain House. These scenes raise fascinating questions about how women came to inhabit the traditionally male-dominated genre of apocalypse by the 1850s and what significance that newfound visionary power had. Moreover, this fusion of apocalyptic vision with the commodified realm of landscape tourism offers an opportunity to interrogate the dynamics of secularization unfolding across antebellum culture. Finally returning to Cropsey's *Catskill Mountain House*, I combine formal analysis of a surprisingly unsettling painting with an excavation of three decades of published accounts of the site to show that by midcentury, evangelicals had succeeded in making the landscape a privileged medium of the sacred even as the stories it told began to escape their control.

Looking Down on Emerson's Farm: Susan Warner and the Theodicy of the Landscape

At a pivotal moment in Susan Warner's *The Wide, Wide World*, as the novel's young heroine, Ellen Montgomery, longs for news of her ailing mother an ocean away, a young Protestant seminarian named John Humphreys who has befriended her uses the winter landscape visible from the window seat of his father's rural New England pastorage as the occasion for a lesson on apocalyptic theology. When asked to describe the scene before her, Ellen notes "the lawn covered with snow, and the trees and bushes; and the sun is shining on everything just as it did the day we came; and there's the long shadow of that hemlock across the snow, and the blue sky."[17] John then directs her attention away from this deceptive surface of things by evoking the apocalyptic imagery of Isaiah and Revelation, telling her, "I know that a day is to come when those heavens shall be wrapped together as a scroll—they shall vanish away like smoke, and the earth shall wax old like a garment;—and it and all the works that are therein shall be burned up" (*WW*, 2:19–20).[18] When at first Ellen is unable "to picture the ruin and desolation of all that stood so fair and seemed to stand so firm before her," John opens his Bible and points her to Isaiah 65:17 and its promise that God will "create new heavens and a new earth, and the former shall not be remembered, neither come into mind." In that new earth, he assures her, separated loved ones will be reunited. If the world Warner evokes is "deeply arbitrary" and "darkly inscrutable" as Wai Chee Dimock argues, the apocalyptic landscape in a sense becomes its chief source of consolation, rendering Ellen's unrelenting suffering bearable within the novel's theocentric Calvinist universe.[19]

David Reynolds has argued that American culture in the 1830s and 1840s witnessed a "convergence of orthodox and liberal fiction in a secular center," a process that culminated in popular novels like *The Wide, Wide World* and *The Lamplighter*. What marks these works as secular for Reynolds is their lack of doctrinal specificity: "it made little difference that the first of these pious best sellers was written by a Presbyterian and the second by a Unitarian."[20] But the apocalyptic lesson John Humphreys teaches Ellen is quite specific; indeed the novel's literalist eschatology might be added to the innate depravity and divine sovereignty that Sharon Kim has argued distinguishes Warner's Calvinist vision from Cummins's emphasis on human goodness and free will. Such distinctions lead Kim to reject Reynolds's claim, arguing that "religious difference has a large effect upon the characters, plot, and formal craft of these works."[21] By revisiting the "secular center," I want to affirm and dilate upon that difference, not primarily by analyzing the novels in relation to their authors' religious backgrounds and beliefs—Warner's evangelical identity as a devout New School Presbyterian, Cummins's more obscure Unitarianism—but by considering how religious spatial narratives structure the novels' physical settings and their protagonists' visual and kinetic movement through space.[22] Those landscapes demonstrate that these works were indeed "secular," though not in the sense Reynolds intended. Popular fiction's construction of sacred space, in other words, helps disrupt what Taylor calls the "subtraction stories" critics have long told about antebellum literary culture—stories in which the literary is what remains when the doctrinal baggage of formal theology is removed—and replaces them with a more nuanced story about literature's role in mediating religious difference in a secularizing age.[23]

The Wide, Wide World follows Ellen's moral and spiritual development through her childhood and adolescence as she copes with the illness and death of her mother and adjusts to a series of relocations that take her from New York City to rural New England and finally to Scotland.[24] In each setting, space functions to literalize the novel's negotiation between human and divine perspectives—what I'll call its ontological dynamics. An early example occurs as Ellen, a girl of about ten years of age who is still traumatized by her recent separation from her mother at the insistence of Ellen's controlling and unloving father, travels from the city to her Aunt Fortune Emerson's farm to await her parents' return from Europe. The rural landscape Ellen glimpses from the coach as she approaches the farm momentarily distracts her from her grief: "Rich fields and meadows lay on all sides, sometimes level, and sometimes with a soft wavy surface, where Ellen thought it must be charming to run up and down. Every now and then these were varied by a little rising ground capped with a piece of woodland; and beautiful trees, many of them, were seen standing alone, especially by the road-side" (*WW*, 1:115). But as darkness falls, Ellen's attention is directed away from the scenery and upward toward more distant realities: "Still looking up at the beautiful quiet stars, she thought of her dear far-off mother,—how long it was already since she had seen her;—faster and faster the tears dropped;—and then she thought of that glorious One who had made the stars, and was above them all, and who could and did see her mother and her, though ever so far apart, and could hear and bless them both" (1:117). As Ellen's interest in this new place gives way to a painful recollection of separation from her mother, the division between earth and sky materializes the gap between a fallen creation and its sovereign creator, and provides a consoling reminder of a divine providence that transcends Ellen's limited understanding. The prospect becomes a manifestation of Christian theodicy, the effort to reconcile the paradoxical coexistence of the declared beauty and goodness of God and his creation with the lived realities of suffering, sin, and evil.[25] Ellen's mother provides the novel's most succinct statement of theodicy when, shortly before her departure, she counsels, "Remember, dear Ellen, God sends no trouble upon his children but in love; and though we cannot see how, he will no doubt make all this work for our good" (1:13). According to what one might call her mother's "educative theodicy"—the belief that "suffering exists . . . because it serves to enrich human experience, to build moral character, or to develop human capacities"—Ellen's conception of a divine perspective that reunites her and her mother within a single field of vision figures spatially this belief that her personal "trouble" and divine "love" can be encompassed within a single providential order.[26]

That elevated viewpoint represents a version of what M. H. Abrams called "the theodicy of the landscape," a Christian theological and literary tradition in which the prospect reflects the coexistence of suffering and goodness in the world and affirms their place in a sacred history of benevolent creation, human sin, just retribution, and, ultimately, divine redemption. Warner's novel deploys this landscape theodicy with remarkable consistency, beginning in the opening pages as Ellen's perspective shifts between the "poor deformed child" she observes in the "ugly city prospect" visible from her bedroom window and the "bright sky above her head," which she cannot see "without thinking of Him who made it" (*WW*, 1:18–19). It persists through Ellen's homesick days in Edinburgh at novel's end, where "the scene of extreme beauty before her seemed rather to increase the confusion and sadness of her mind," until she remembers "that there was One near her who could not change; that Scotland was no remove from him; that his providence as well as his heaven was over her there; that there, not less than in America, she was his child" (2:247). In each case the text's division between land and sky manifests a sharp ontological division between the suffering of this world and the transcendent goodness of God. But whereas Abrams emphasizes Wordsworth's transformation of landscape theodicy into a secular account of the self's interaction with nature, Warner's vision remains resolutely theistic; the redemptive end that her landscape points toward is not Wordsworth's symbolic "apocalypse of nature" but a terrifyingly literal one.[27]

Of course we need not look as far as Wordsworth to demonstrate the contrast between theistic and naturalistic versions of landscape theodicy. As Alan D. Hodder has argued, Ralph Waldo Emerson expressed a theistic apocalypticism akin to Warner's in his early journals of the 1820s (which he titled, oddly enough, the "Wide World"), but his seminal *Nature* (1836) shifted to a "naturalized" apocalyptic rhetoric that recodes the traditional Christian apocalyptic image of the marriage between God and the new Jerusalem as "a marriage between mind and nature." Following Wordsworth's example, the mature Emerson dehistoricizes the apocalypse and moves it "within."[28] But while Emerson invites the application of Abrams's narrative of the internalization of apocalypse to an American context, Warner disrupts the sense of inexorable secularization conveyed in Abrams's account by reminding us that not all literary uses of apocalyptic imagery after Wordsworth were naturalized. Rather than a single tradition running from the Romantics to the Modernists, Warner's theistic landscape theodicy suggests multiple apocalyptic traditions, each with its own ontological dynamics, and raises the question of their relationship to each other. Indeed, *The Wide, Wide World* dramatizes the interaction of those traditions in its own plot. In Jeffrey Stout's terms, the novel stages an encounter between two major "strands" of American religious and ethical thought: an "Augustinian" strand that includes "orthodox Christianity from the Puritanism of Plymouth Rock to the denominational soup of our own day," and an "Emersonian" strand running from Emerson through Whitman and Dewey.[29] The fictional dramatization of this contest between Augustinian and Emersonian "strains of piety" (to adapt Perry Miller's influential phrase) begins appropriately enough when young Ellen and her new Bible—a parting gift from her mother—arrive at Aunt Emerson's farm.[30]

While the namesake of Fortune Emerson might seem to presage a strong, self-reliant presence capable of imparting to Ellen the venerable intellectual and religious traditions of New England—the kind of role model the young Ralph Waldo Emerson enjoyed in his aunt Mary Moody Emerson—events quickly prove otherwise.[31] Aunt Fortune is a cold, joyless spinster incapable of giving Ellen sympathy or affection. She discourages Ellen's fervent desire to study French, music, math, and other "crinkumcrankums," declaring, "I wonder what good they'd ever do you! . . . it doesn't do for women to be bookworms" (*WW*, 1:169). Instead she initiates Ellen's domestic education with a dreary round of housework. Far from a spiritual mentor, Aunt Fortune is what the novel terms a "worldling" (1:290): she never attends church or reads the Bible, she ridicules the idealism of Christian moralists who are "eternally finding out something that isn't as it ought to be among their neighbors" (1:216), and she is so thrifty that she seldom helps others in need, preferring "to gather to herself and heap up of what the world most esteems" (2:51). The clash between these two strong-willed individuals propels the plot for much of the novel, and Ellen's struggle to gracefully submit to her aunt's authority becomes a primary gauge of her character. Paradoxically, only by submitting can Ellen affirm the superiority of the Christian worldview she represents, with its ontological dualism and transcendent goods ("hypergoods," in Charles Taylor's terms), over her aunt's worldview, which denies the possibility of transcendence and rejects the pursuit of higher goods altogether.[32]

The conflict between these worldviews plays out in spatial terms. When a long-awaited letter to Ellen from her mother finally arrives, Aunt Fortune opens and reads it without asking, prompting Ellen to storm from the house and up a path into the nearby mountains. Here the novel's debt to *The Pilgrim's Progress* noted by earlier critics becomes evident.[33] As Ellen ascends the mountain, textual cues activate the spatially inflected narrative pattern that Gregory S. Jackson terms a "homiletic template," specifically the "pilgrimage template" central to Bunyan's allegory.[34] Passing through the "gate," Ellen leaves the main road for a grassy lane that was "not much traveled evidently" and begins to follow "the way," which, as she later learns, leads to the parsonage of Mr. Humphreys, the local Protestant minister whose adult children will become Ellen's spiritual mentors. But for the time being Ellen "forsook the lane" for a "little footpath on the left," a "most lovely wild woodway path; but withal not a little steep and rocky," which she follows until she "began to grow weary" and reaches "a good resting-place" (*WW*, 1:178) on the mountainside. The homiletic cues might seem so subtle as to be unrecognizable until we consider an audience that for decades had vicariously joined Christian at the base of the "hill Difficulty" as he passes through a "gate" and toils up the "narrow way [that] lay right up the Hill" until he finally reaches an "Arbor, made by the Lord of the hill for the refreshment of weary travelers," while his companions Formalist and Hypocrisy turn astray: "one took the way which is called Danger, which led him into a great wood; and the other took directly up the way to Destruction, which led him into a wide field, full of dark mountains, where he stumbled and fell, and rose no more."[35] Given Ellen's love for

The Pilgrim's Progress—she and John and Alice Humphreys later read it aloud for an hour every evening, and the copy John gives her is "her greatest treasure next to her little red Bible" (2:90)—the homiletic context of her movement through space as she struggles to "go straight on in the path of duty" (1:189) is unmistakable. What generates the scene's interest and suspense is its ambiguity in relation to Bunyan's plot, since Ellen's course might plausibly be interpreted as aligning her with Christian following the way up hill Difficulty or with his companion straying on the path of Danger. Warner's intertextual cues, in other words, alert us that Ellen's flight from the farm into the mountains represents an episode of critical importance in her spiritual and ethical development, but the novel creates narrative tension by refusing a straightforward correspondence with its allegorical pretext.

The prospect Ellen discovers at her resting place orients her development in relation to the competing worldviews mentioned above: "For miles and miles, on every side but the west, lay stretched before her a beautifully broken country. Far in the distance a range of low hills showed like a misty cloud; near by, at the mountain's foot, the fields and farm-houses and roads lay [like] a pictured map" (*WW*, 1:179). This view extends the motif identified by Kim, who notes that Ellen's recurring encounters with the landscape activate a biblical allusion to Psalm 121 such that "the act of looking to the hills typologically indicates a looking to God for help."[36] But Ellen's view also suggests another textual parallel: if her flight into the mountains rehearses a Romantic model of consolation in nature derived from Emerson's *Nature* ("In the woods, we return to reason and faith") as Peter Balaam argues, the prospect she encounters from her resting place literalizes one of that text's most famous scenes: that "charming landscape" of "some twenty or thirty farms," in which "Miller owns this field, Locke that, and Manning the woodland beyond. But none of them owns the landscape. There is a property in the horizon which no man has but he whose eye can integrate all the parts, that is, the poet."[37] Whether intentionally or not, Ellen's position above Fortune Emerson's farm performs a kind of wry revision of this passage, such that "Van Brunt owns this field, Emerson that," and so on. In Warner's version, "Emerson" has been displaced from a privileged vantage point into the valley; Aunt Emerson seems to forecast Thoreau's materialistic farmer Flint from *Walden* more than she resembles the transcendent poet of *Nature*.

The difference in elevation between Ellen's perch overlooking the valley and her aunt's farmhouse in the "broken country" below inscribes into space the novel's stark ethical distinction between the Christian benevolence advocated by John and Alice Humphreys and Aunt Emerson's miserly self-absorption. By situating Ellen's prospect in the context of the homiletic path of the "little pilgrim" (*WW*, 2:72) up the mountain, Warner makes the gaze over the landscape less about aesthetic integration (as in Emerson's prospect) than about the young Christian's struggle to achieve a theological and ethical perspective that transcends worldly attachments and self-interest. Warner has taken up the "homiletic landscape" that evangelical illustrated tracts and landscape paintings had for decades used to figure the individual's spiritual progress in spatial terms (see chapter 1) and embellished it with the lushly detailed setting of the "realistic novel."[38] Indeed, given Warner's own work distributing religious tracts in the 1840s, one might say that she has simply scaled up from disseminating the homiletic landscape by hand to reaching a greatly expanded audience through the medium of her own printed words.[39] In that more mimetically robust landscape, characters who had been mere abstractions in Bunyan's allegory—Pliable, Mr. Worldly Wiseman, and the rest—are transformed into a range of social actors and viewpoints competing for influence in antebellum America. Ellen's elevated prospect most directly refutes Fortune Emerson's atheism of course, but it can also be read as a response to the unorthodox spirituality of that other Emerson, the "great schoolmaster" whom Warner met during a trip to Boston in the mid-1840s and about whom she only commented icily, "Mr. Emerson I did n't fancy."[40] Imagining the conversation the two might have had is tantalizing: when the Concord sage declares that only the poet owns the landscape, Warner counters that God alone owns it. Where he rhetorically asks, "What is a farm but a mute gospel?" she retorts that only the Gospel is the Gospel, and too many of our New England farms sorely lack it.[41]

Ellen's ascent brings her closer to the divine perspective she longs for, one that would reunite her and her mother in a single frame of vision and justify the anguish of their separation by showing how God will "make all this work for our good" as her mother had promised. But even her new vantage point is not enough to achieve that perspective: "She felt her own heart sadly out of tune with the peace and loveliness of all she saw. Her eye sought those distant hills,—how very far off they were! and yet all that wide tract of country was but a little piece of what lay between her and her mother. Her eye sought those hills,—but her mind overpassed them and went far beyond, over many such a tract, till it reached the loved one at last. [']But oh! how much between! I cannot reach her!—she cannot reach me!'" (*WW*, 1:179). Only after this admission of utter impotence, so different from the self-sufficient gaze of Emerson's poet, is Ellen granted the help required to integrate the landscape. It comes in the form of a stranger, a young woman named Alice Humphreys who finds Ellen prostrate on the mountainside and comforts her, answering her lament that "Nobody in this world can help me" by assuring her that "there's one in heaven that can" (1:181). Alice guides Ellen farther up the path to another view, this time toward the west:

Both exclaimed at the beauty before them. The view was not so extended as the one they had left. On the north and south the broken wavy outline of mountains closed in the horizon; but far to the west stretched an opening between the hills through which the setting sun sent his long beams, even to their feet. In the distance all was a golden haze; nearer, on the right and left the hills were lit up singularly, and there was a most beautiful mingling of deep hazy shadow and bright glowing mountain sides and ridges. A glory was on the valley.... "Ellen, dear,—he whose hand raised up those mountains and has painted them so gloriously is the very same One who has said, to you and to me, 'Ask and it shall be given you.'" (1:185)

Whereas the earlier prospect evokes a tension between Ellen's awareness of the beauty of the world and her suffering, prompting a recognition of her inability to transcend her embodied condition, this one promises to overcome those conditions through eschatology. The Christological image of the "setting sun" that is able with "his long beams" to effortlessly bridge the physical distance between horizon and the viewer figures spatially the salvation that is available to the sinner so long as she is willing, as Alice says (quoting Christ's words from Matthew 7:7 and Luke 11:9), to ask for it. To this classic typological symbol of Christian death and resurrection, Alice adds a reference to the act of divine creation that "raised up those mountains" and "painted them," and the millennial glow of the "golden haze" and the "glory" enveloping the valley at the day's end. By situating Christian salvation within the temporal bookends of Creation and the millennium, Warner turns the landscape into a text that reveals sacred history.

The spatialization of eschatology enacted in the first meeting between Ellen and Alice converges with the novel's landscape theodicy in the apocalyptic theology lesson Alice's brother John later gives Ellen from the window seat. The lesson is John's attempt to redirect Ellen's longing for an "oracle" that would reveal "what's going to happen" to her mother (*WW*, 2:19) by convincing her how much already *is* known thanks to the Bible's apocalyptic prophecies. They teach, he explains, that "the new heavens and the new earth will be so much more lovely and pleasant that we shall not want to think of these" because "there will be no sin *there*; sorrow and sighing shall flee away; love to each other and love to their blessed King will fill all hearts, and his presence will be with them" (2:20). John's interpretation of the apocalypse consoles Ellen by promising an end to suffering and a reunion with lost loved ones beyond the grave, including John and Alice's own departed mother. As Ellen watches the sunset and listens to her friends talk about the world to come, she begins to relinquish her attachment to the world before her: "It was very, very beautiful;—yet she could think now without sorrow that all this should come to an end; because of that new heaven and new earth wherein righteousness should dwell" (2:21). Just as the landscape had earlier sparked Ellen's awareness of the painful paradoxes of earthly existence and reminded her of her mother's absence, now with the guidance of Alice and John Humphreys it helps her resolve those paradoxes by pointing beyond itself to an existence that transcends earthly space and time. In place of her mother's educative theodicy, Alice and John advance an "eschatological theodicy" that looks beyond history to make sense of suffering, whether to the afterlife or a new millennial age.[42] Apocalyptic eschatology provides answers to the questions posed by theodicy, and that dialogue takes place through the medium of the landscape.

From the Calvinist Novel to the Secular Center

Warner's religious background and her novel's position within a tradition of Calvinist fiction in the United States stretching back more than fifty years shaped the inscription of apocalyptic narrative onto the landscape in *The Wide, Wide World*. In particular, that literary context positioned her to use the landscape as a vehicle for theological instruction. In the eighteenth-century American literary tradition that Reynolds calls the "visionary mode," the protagonist typically experiences a "dream vision" in which an angelic guide "displays the rewards of virtue and the wages of sin either through visions of heaven and hell or through allegorical landscapes." In Reynolds's account, a mode that originated as a vehicle for "rationalists" to critique "religious gloom and determinism" during the revolutionary period had by the 1830s been adopted by liberal Protestant novelists such as Catharine Sedgwick and Lydia Maria Child to attack Calvinist orthodoxy.[43] The prospect that the eponymous heroine of Sedgwick's *Hope Leslie* (1827) surveys from Mount Holyoke (see chapter 1) is a good example of how liberal novelists combined the visionary mode with romantic landscape aesthetics to critique what they perceived as the intolerance and theological narrowness of the Puritan past. During the same period, however, a body of homegrown Calvinist fiction much more sympathetic to that heritage emerged that used the landscape to a very different effect.[44] In addition to the evangelical tracts, abolitionist publications, and religious newspapers discussed in earlier chapters, this fiction established a model upon which Warner and other popular novelists in the 1850s could draw as they fashioned literary landscapes to make religious arguments alongside elements such as dialogue, plot, and direct address. But the Calvinist novel also highlights what is new and significant about those later best sellers: a spatial imaginary in which the landscape operates as a medium that not only tests and reveals moral character but also offers glimpses of the coming Kingdom.

For a sense of that process of development, consider *Justina; or, The Will* (1823), an anonymously authored Calvinist novel (perhaps written by Susan DeWitt) whose only claim to literary fame is that Herman Melville's mother may have read it aloud to him as a child.[45] *Justina* represents an early example of an important shift in spatial representation that occurred when a work that a contemporary review called "completely national, entirely American in its characters, its scenery, and its spirit" combined with what the same reviewer incredulously hailed as "a religious novel!!!"[46] Whereas earlier American works of Calvinist fiction such as Edmund Botsford's *The Spiritual Voyage Performed in the Ship Convert* (1814) feature male protagonists negotiating allegorical landscapes in a Bunyanesque vein, *Justina* inaugurates a Calvinist version of the "orphan's bildungsroman," in which a young American girl must negotiate national and Atlantic geographies as she confronts various trials (her own selfishness and pride above all) and ultimately matures into a pious, moral, and respected young woman who is rewarded with a happy marriage.[47] The protagonist, Justina Melross, is only six when her mother dies and her father, a New York merchant in embarrassed financial straits, decides to take her with him to London to try to rescue his business, leaving her younger sister Augusta with an aunt in a town on the banks of the Hudson. In England Justina receives a thorough education in domestic skills, academic subjects (including geography), her father's Calvinism, and landscape appreciation. Through excursions in the countryside with her father she becomes "an enthusiast in her love for all the scenes of nature," imbibing a version of what D. Bruce Hindmarsh calls the "Calvinist sublime": Justina "felt, indeed, that the Supreme Being was the author of the sublime; for there is not a feeling of the soul, which partakes of the sublime, that does not, by its own impulse, ascend to God. She felt this in every scene in nature, she felt it in every thing that was grand in moral action, or soaring in thought."[48] When her father dies and she returns to America to be reunited with her sister and aunt after nearly a decade, Justina has acquired the cultural equipment to admire the landscape that awaits her as New York harbor emerges into view: "'It is my native land,' cried Justina, as her heart glowed with the thought that she was an American" (*JTW*, 1:39). Indeed she comes to revel in the scenery environing her new home, "a pleasant and healthful town situated on the banks of the Hudson" (1:11), taking excursions with a friend in which "the flowing rivers and verdant landscape excited in each similar feelings of religious adoration" (1:74).

While *Justina* thus participates in the production of the "sanctified landscape" along the Hudson by artists, writers, and tourists in the 1820s, what distinguishes it from the romantic responses of better-known authors like Cooper and Irving is its use of that landscape in the service of a Calvinist ethos of resignation or "weaned affections."[49] Justina's mother expresses this ethos in the novel's opening pages when, grieving at the thought of parting from her children on a transatlantic voyage to regain her health, she exclaims, "Oh! if you knew how I have prayed to be able to resign all my earthly affections; yet it is only for a time; it is only for a few brief years, which will soon pass away, and our reunion will be everlasting in His kingdom, with whom a thousand years 'are but an evening gone'" (*JTW*, 1:3). Such relinquishment of worldly attachments becomes Justina's great test as well: after her sister and aunt wrongly accuse her of trying to steal Augusta's suitor for herself, a heartbroken Justina decides she must leave home, reasoning that "it is our duty to check those idolatrous affections that lead us to place our happiness in a mortal's smile or frown." Expelled from paradise, as it were, she agrees to accompany a cousin to Philadelphia to become a caretaker for an elderly gentleman. Activating the homiletic landscape that had already begun to appear in evangelical tracts by the early 1820s, Justina reasons that life "was but a short, though perhaps thorny journey, through which her Saviour's hand would sustain and lead her; and faith taught her to look forward to a home, where never-ending joys awaited her" (1:100).

Justina's self-imposed exile from New York shifts the meaning of the landscape she observes on her voyage down the Delaware River, its banks "adorned by growing villages, and beautiful country seats" (*JTW*, 1:103). Rather than the invitation to "religious adoration" of God's creation offered by the Hudson, this prosperous landscape ultimately serves as an index of worldliness and pride. In Pennsylvania, Justina's trials at the hands of families who misconstrue her motivations and disdain her Calvinism culminate in her tenure with the Graftons, a Unitarian family that hires her as a governess on their estate outside Philadelphia. Though Justina admires the beauty of the place and often retires to the garden for refuge, she comes to recognize the estate as an accessory to the family's besetting sin: when Mrs. Grafton notices Justina admiring the landscape, "her own form expanded, and her features became inflated with new pride" (2:123). Having divided the national landscape between a medium of divine power in New York and a monument to human pride in Pennsylvania, the novel ultimately allows Justina to return to sacred ground when her aunt and sister realize their mistake and call her home. On the return trip, waking one morning to find herself back on the Hudson, she admires "the magnificent scenery" and returns to a familiar register: "The clouds of mist, which thinly enveloped the mountains, appeared rising like incense to the throne of the Creator. She thought of his grandeur, and her elevated soul silently breathed forth" a hymn addressed "To Him whose temple is all space" (2:225). As it happens, on this very boat rides the suitor who had occasioned Justina's departure in the first place and for whom she has been pining the entire time. With misunderstandings soon cleared up and mutual affection revealed, her virtue and discipline are rewarded with a husband. Apparently that "home, where never-ending joys awaited her," can be found in this life after all.

Despite this happy resolution, *Justina* concludes on a surprisingly ominous note. Echoing an earlier warning by one of Justina's mentors that the spread of heretical (Unitarian) beliefs denying the divinity of Jesus were threatening to derail the millennium, the novel concludes by calling on readers to teach their children true religion, so that "at the last great day, from their graves, they and future generations will rise to call you blessed. And instead of 'calling on the mountains and rocks to fall on you, and hide you from the face of him that sitteth on the throne, and from the wrath of the Lamb,' you will be 'able to stand,' and say with humble confidence, 'Here I am, O Lord! and the children that thou hast given me'" (*JTW*, 2:245). In its direct quotation of a passage from Revelation 6:16–17 announcing that "the great day of his wrath is come," the novel's concluding image evokes an apocalyptic landscape—mountains and rocks literally being torn asunder—that seems to clash with the ontological dualism set up by its repeated evocation of the homiletic landscape: the sense that Justina must simply endure this world in order to ultimately arrive at her heavenly home beyond it. Appearing at the end of a novel in which the individual pursuit of piety far overshadows any sense of collective millennial activism, the passage hints at the path Calvinist fiction would take over the next three decades.

That evolution, though complex and far from linear, led through Sarah Ann Evans's novel *Resignation* (1825), in which the landscape's role in expanding the young orphaned heroine's cognitive map to encompass national and sectional geographies gives way to the spiritual terrain she surveys on her deathbed, where "from the sublime summit of Pisgah, she looked back on all the way through which she had been led, and forward, to a 'better country' than the promised Canaan of the ancient Israelites."[50] It included Anne Tuttle Bullard's *The Wife for a Missionary* (1834), in which an aspiring missionary in search of a suitable helpmeet ascends a knoll near his family's estate to behold "a landscape of singular and diversified beauty" where he can "feast the eye with the works of God" and reflects "that even in *heathen* lands, remote from home, the same works and the same beauties from the same wonder-working hand would attend him still."[51] And it included Joseph Alden's *Alice Gordon* (1847), whose orphaned heroine studies her father's Bible seeking "preparation for a world to come" and finds that it also prepares her to perceive the world around her, "to love the simple and the natural, the beautiful and the sublime. The influence of the Sacred Volume harmonized with, and gave increase of power, to the influence of external nature."[52] While Reynolds encapsulates this evolution as the "secularization of Calvinist fiction"—a process he identifies with a shift from theological "doctrine" to sentimental "plot" as the engine of these texts—the arc from *Justina* to *The Wide, Wide World* suggests that doctrine continues to loom large (indeed, scenes of doctrinal pedagogy are if anything more pronounced in the latter) and that textual elements like setting are as important as plot to the spiritual work the novels seek to perform.[53]

In an effort to broaden our sense of where millennial thought can be found in nineteenth-century fiction, Claudia Stokes has argued that the sentimental marriage plot displayed in Harriet Beecher Stowe's domestic fiction enacts postmillennial eschatology through narrative form: "In their formulaic disentanglement of complex plots into neat matrimonial pairings and newly restored happy families, sentimental novels adapted and modernized religious prophecy to show not only that human beings are indeed marching incrementally toward the predicted new age but also that white, middle-class, North Atlantic Protestant housewives—and not ordained clergy—are chiefly responsible for the fulfillment of scriptural prophecy."[54] Returning to an earlier moment in the history of sentimental fiction, *Justina* previews how eschatology would come to be encoded not only in the novels' tangled love plots but in the varied landscapes and geographies where those plots play out.

Warner's debt to *Justina* (and the orphan bildungsroman more generally) is unmistakable. We see it in Ellen Montgomery's separation from her parents, her transatlantic itineraries, and the use of homiletic space to map her spiritual pilgrimage onto the novel's physical geography. So too, *Justina*'s use of the landscape to materialize religious difference (in particular the heresies of Unitarianism) previews Warner's inscription of moral geography onto the terrain surrounding Emerson's farm. But those continuities belie a substantial difference. The final apocalyptic flourish in *Justina* feels tacked on and inconsequential, and its spatial conceit is never focalized through its heroine: Justina never sees sacred history embodied in the landscape before her. In *The Wide, Wide World*, by contrast, this apocalyptic grace note has been expanded into a sustained motif and transferred from a didactic aside directly into the diegesis, as Ellen repeatedly witnesses and learns to interpret the apocalyptic dimensions of the landscape through the guidance of Alice and John Humphreys.

If that pedagogical project is in some sense haunted by religious difference—the awareness of religious "options" that I'm suggesting marks *The Wide, Wide World* as part of the "secular center"—it also shares common ground with the heterodoxy that Warner's novel playfully invites us to associate with both materialistic atheism and Emersonian idealism. The landscape theodicy Ellen learns from Alice and John is perhaps in a sense not so different from Emerson's, who famously wrote in *Nature* that "there is a kind of contempt of the landscape felt by him who has just lost by death a dear friend" and who later compared the death of his own son to the loss of "a beautiful estate."[55] In *The Conduct of Life* (1860), the work that most closely approximates Warner's concern with the ethics of everyday life, Emerson's confidence that "evil is good in the making," that "whatever lames or paralyzes you, draws in with it the divinity, in some form, to repay," recalls Ellen's mother's faith that God "will no doubt make all this work for our good."[56] The significant difference is not in their faith that suffering will be transformed into good but in the location and the timing of the change. For Warner, ultimately the reconciling vision remains out of the reach of the mortal observer. Christians like Ellen may approach that harmonious prospect as they ascend the road to holiness, but ultimately it remains an article of faith, since true justice occurs not in this world but only at the Last Judgment. Hence the novel's repeated association of the landscape prospect with cosmic dualism and apocalyptic eschatology: the perfect view can only be achieved from a perspective beyond earthly time and space.

For Emerson, by contrast, this process of converting apparent evil to comprehensive good is temporally and spatially compressed so that it is achieved instantaneously within the individual and is instantly perceptible to one whose senses are properly adjusted. Emerson makes this distinction explicit in his 1841 essay "Compensation" by contrasting his position with that of a "preacher . . . esteemed for his orthodoxy, [who] unfolded in the ordinary manner the doctrine of the Last Judgment. He assumed that judgment is not executed in this world; that the wicked are successful; that the good are miserable; and then urged from reason and from Scripture a compensation to be made to both parties in the next life." To this eschatological theodicy, espoused by "the popular religious works of the day" and "literary men" alike, Emerson contrasts his doctrine of "Compensation," the moral "law" that finds in each virtuous act its own immediate reward and in every vice its own punishment.[57] Emerson enacts this compression formally in the orphic, aphoristic style exemplified in *Nature*, which Hodder argues is meant to prompt "the reader's apocalypse" by withholding the means of discursive and narrative modes of reading so as to produce a flash of transcendent perception in the reader, as "revelation breaks in, [and] all distance and duration suddenly dissolve."[58]

Emerson refuses both the systematic, logical argumentation of a theological treatise as well as the narrative continuity of a novel. These alternatives—between "system" and "story" to quote one influential account—correspond to a more recent debate among philosophers between a Kantian ethics that seeks rational, universal principles to prescribe right actions in specific situations (labeled "quandary ethics" by its critics) and "virtue ethics," which emphasizes the role of narrative in developing the set of traits, habits, and dispositions that make up individual character.[59] In this context Warner's novel occupies the latter position as an updated form of the "classic life," a genre that sought to develop virtues by recounting the lives of exemplary (usually male) individuals, whether statesmen and poets in its ancient classical form or pious saints and martyrs in its Christian one. *The Wide, Wide World* provides a fictional, feminized counterpart to Emerson's own foray into the genre in *Representative Men* (1850). But by returning to the essay in *The Conduct of Life*, Emerson resumes a form of ethical discourse developed in the early modern period as a reaction both to the abstraction and rigidity of systematic moral philosophy and to the classic life's lack of particularity and complexity.[60] So while Warner's novel represents a nineteenth-century version of an ethics of character that updates standard Christian "trials of faith" (exemplified by Job and Bunyan's Christian) with modern detail and complexity, Emerson locates ethical reasoning neither in the operations of systematic rationality nor in the process of internalizing exemplary stories but in the individual's direct apprehension of truth: "Forget your books and traditions, and obey your moral perceptions at this hour."[61] The landscape prospects discussed above demonstrate that the forms of ethical work undertaken by Warner and Emerson through their respective genres correspond to distinctive uses of represented space. In Warner's narrative-based ethics, the landscape simultaneously tells the story of Ellen's development and of the unfolding of Christian sacred history. In Emerson's perception-oriented ethics, by contrast, the landscape materializes the poet's epiphanic break with the limits of individual personhood and time.

Warner's narrative landscape represents one of the period's clearest examples of the diffusion of evangelical space into popular fiction. Just as American Tract Society publications and Cole's *Oxbow* used the landscape to calibrate the individual pilgrimage through the world with the approaching millennium, *The Wide, Wide World* uses it to connect Ellen's personal quest for holiness—her climb from the worldliness of the Emerson farm to the pastorage—with the apocalyptic framework expounded by John and Alice. Yet while the novel clearly mobilizes a form of evangelical spatial imagination, it does so differently than the texts discussed in earlier chapters. Those texts promulgated a postmillennial eschatology in which benevolent activism on a national and global scale would help bring about the gradual, progressive dawn of a millennial age within history. John Humphreys's premillennialism, by contrast, envisions the dramatic destruction of the world, when the "heavens shall be wrapped together as a scroll" and the Earth "shall be burned up." He never suggests that human action can hasten or delay its coming, and the spatial and ethical scope of the novel is correspondingly circumscribed. As a contemporary reviewer noted, despite the novel's title Warner's fictional "world" is not "wide" but curiously localized.⁶² With scant reference to the outside world other than the occasional letter from Ellen's mother, the novel remains far from the national and global moral geographies of the evangelical and abolitionist mediascapes. While the growth of Ellen's faith and moral character is central to its plot, the novel never suggests that her development has anything to do with saving the world's heathen or freeing the nation's slaves, or that she has any agency beyond the people she meets face-to-face. The ethical space of *The Wide, Wide World* more closely resembles the linear, pietistic way of Bunyan's Christian pilgrimage through the world than the centrifugally expanding activism of the Benevolent Empire. It would not be until *Uncle Tom's Cabin* began to appear in *The National Era* in June 1851 that the sentimental novel would break free of its personal and local moorings and embrace the global ambitions of evangelical print.

Recognizing the ways a popular novel like *The Wide, Wide World* adapts spatial narratives and tropes from religious media to a fictional setting challenges the way literary critics have tended to understand the relationship of religion and literature. Reynolds emphasizes the "secular" character of Warner's novel because of its lack of doctrinal specificity and its use of everyday events instead of explicit doctrinal statements to convey religious ideas.⁶³ But defining the secular in this way implicitly makes the discursive features of the sermon and the theological treatise the standard of religious literature. Not only does it make novels almost by definition secular (given readers' widely shared emphasis on plot over exposition during this period), but it also ignores entire traditions of writing—from saints' lives to spiritual autobiography to diaries—that privilege narrative and everyday experience as the medium of their religiosity.⁶⁴ As *The Wide, Wide World* draws on a diverse network of such religious texts, from the Bible and devotional classics like *The Pilgrim's Progress* to evangelical tracts and Calvinist novels, it mobilizes their strategies of spatial representation in the service of a set of explicitly religious commitments. Warner's novel is secular only in the specific sense that in its fictional world as well as in the society where it circulated, those commitments could not be assumed to be widely shared.⁶⁵ It is precisely that condition of secularity that generates narrative tension and propels the story: a world in which an orphan girl's growth into a virtuous woman is threatened by the spiritual vacuum left by the crumbling of the established Calvinist order. In Warner's quarrel with both Emersons—the worldly Yankee spinster as well as the heretical Transcendentalist—we begin to glimpse not two separate American Renaissances marked by a division between aesthetic rigor and popular power, or between masculine metaphysics and feminine sentiment, but a single renaissance united by a shared grappling with the secular.⁶⁶

A Sabbath at Catskill Mountain House: Natural Theology and Secularization

Cropsey's *Catskill Mountain House* is a strangely unsettling painting. The viewer stands on a deserted outcropping hemmed in by boulders and a dense stretch of forest punctuated by the skeletal forms of standing, denuded timber. The white hotel perched on its rocky escarpment near the center of the canvas immediately draws the eye into the picture space; its carefully articulated portico and the triangular escarpment to its left emphasize the orientation of the building and the view it was designed to capture, directing our gaze east, down into the hazy golden radiance of the Hudson River Valley on the left side of the painting, where a silver arc of river flashes into the picture space. But the valley floor that so willingly "unfold[ed] its beauties" to Henry Dwight here remains strangely unavailable, confined to a distant edge of the composition. Even as the contrast of light and shadow on the exquisitely modeled pyramidal boulder in the left foreground creates a strong diagonal edge that points down into the valley, our vicarious movement is arrested by a dark, tangled mass of boulders and evergreens that rise up to block the way. The thickly layered paint not only impedes our progress by emphasizing the dense materiality of the forest; it threatens the illusionistic depth of the picture space itself as the landscape hovers on the verge of dissolving back into its medium: globs of paint on a canvas.

Complicating this tension between invitation and refusal on the left half of the picture is the right half. Just below and to the right of the pyramidal boulder pointing into the valley, a smaller boulder, flat and sharp, points with equal insistence to the plateau behind the mountain house. Two dark, slanted tree trunks to the right of the boulder echo its trajectory, and the banked contours of the mountainside funnel the eye across the two lakes and down Kaaterskill Clove toward the pink bank of clouds peeking up behind the mountains to the south. Whereas other views from the same point on North Mountain frame the prospect so as to emphasize the house's relationship to a single visual focus—the lakes (see fig. 4.2) or the Hudson River Valley—Cropsey includes two competing lines of vision, and two very different routes through the picture.[67] As if to highlight this aspect of the painting, the fantastically expressive birch tree in the right foreground writhes its way upward into a Y-shaped fork that suggests the alternative routes into the scene; about halfway to the mountain house is a similar tree just where we might imagine the paths to diverge, standing like a sign at the fork.[68] And in case we thought we could simply stay put and idly contemplate the scene from our perch on North Mountain, Cropsey adds a final unsettling detail to his autumn landscape: signing his name on a leaning, slab-like stone at the foot of the tree, he simultaneously finishes his work and chisels his own "tombstone," a memento mori that signals the fleetingness of life and warns the living to improve the hours.[69]

Thus a work that critics have often described as a rather derivative view of a conventional subject on closer examination presents a complex and challenging split composition that seems to express some deep uncertainty or ambivalence toward the landscape.[70] A glance back at a work by one of Cropsey's major influences, Thomas Cole, helps us begin to interpret the surprising complexity of *Catskill Mountain House*. Earlier I argued that the sacred history referenced iconographically in Cole's *The Oxbow* (1836)—in features such as the anthropomorphic trees that echo the expulsion of Adam and Eve from Eden, the names of Old Testament figures partially inscribed in Hebrew on the mountainside, and the omega (Ω) traced by the river—is also instantiated in the painting's spatial composition: the dramatic compositional break that divides the storm-ravaged mountaintop in the foreground from the radiant valley below inscribes millennial eschatology into the landscape. As we stand in the wilderness of the world contemplating a paradise on the other side of the omega, I argued, the painting's aesthetic problems become eschatological and ethical ones about how viewers negotiate the gap between this world and the next.

In the standard accounts told by art historians, the cultural shift from Cole's quest for a form of "higher landscape" infused with the moralism and narrative power of history painting to the naturalistic aesthetic theory associated with John Ruskin, Asher B. Durand, and Cropsey himself in the 1850s makes the sorts of eschatological questions posed by *The Oxbow* two decades earlier seem irrelevant to a view like Cropsey's *Catskill Mountain House*.[71] Yet the new naturalistic idiom did not preclude artists from treating religious subjects (as the number of Holy Land views produced from the 1850s to the 1870s attests) or from investing naturalistic landscapes with religious narratives and symbols, as Angela Miller has shown.[72] Indeed, the American "manifesto" of Ruskinian naturalism, Durand's "Letters on Landscape Painting" (1855), urges the artist's fidelity to observed nature not in opposition to expressing sacred meaning in the landscape but precisely to ensure that the work of art functions as a faithful medium for the divine truth inscribed there.[73] In this sense Durand sustains Ruskin's insistence that landscape representation testify to the attributes of God and reveal nature itself as the work of "the ultimate artist," a conviction that makes Ruskin "the great theorist of the Protestant aesthetic."[74] Durand writes in his ninth letter that the artist "may displace a tree, for instance, if disagreeable, or render it a more perfect one of its kind if retained, but the elevations and depressions of the earth's surface composing the middle ground and distance ... may not be changed in the least perceptible degree, most especially the mountain and hill forms. On these God has set his signet,

FIGURE 4.4. Detail of Jasper Francis Cropsey, *Catskill Mountain House*, 1855. Oil on canvas, 29 × 44 in. (73.66 × 111.76 cm). Minneapolis Institute of Art, Bequest of Mrs. Lillian Lawhead Rinderer in memory of her brother, William A. Lawhead, and the William Hood Dunwoody Fund, 31.47. Photo: Minneapolis Institute of Art.

and Art may not remove it when the picture professes to represent the scene." Seeking to upend the hierarchy that denigrated "view painting" as a lower, less imaginative form of art than compositions and ideal landscapes, Durand argues that views are in fact the greatest test of "the imaginative artist." The "expression" displayed in a truly imaginative view is less a matter of self-expression than a form of receptivity, a vision that perceives what already exists: "For [the artist's] loftier stature enables him to overlook, without trespass, the enclosure which bounds the view of humbler minds—he comprehends the capabilities of the material presented in all its relations to human sympathy (whether already combined in the actual view, or noted on the tablet of memory), and he reads the historic record which time has written on all things for our instruction, through all the stages of their silent transition, since the period when this verdant earth was a lifeless, molten chaos, 'void and without form.'"[75] Durand's closing phrase tellingly reveals the sort of history the artist "reads" in the view: used in Genesis 1:2 to describe the newly created Earth, and again (with the terms transposed) in Jeremiah 4:23 in a prophetic vision of that Earth's destruction, "void and without form" situates naturalistic views like *Catskill Mountain House* squarely in the realm of apocalyptic eschatology.

Read alongside *The Oxbow* (a view that Cropsey himself drew at least twice in 1853), *Catskill Mountain House* simultaneously evokes and recasts Cole's

FIGURE 4.5. Detail of Jasper Francis Cropsey, *The Millennial Age*, 1854. Oil on canvas, 38¼ × 54 in. (97.2 × 137.2 cm). Collection of the Newington-Cropsey Foundation.

engagement with sacred history.[76] Cropsey's forked birch may not evoke the expulsion from Eden like Cole's blasted trees, but it might be said to reference sacred history in its own way by echoing the rising twin plumes of smoke in Cropsey's *The Millennial Age* (figs. 4.4 and 4.5). Like *The Oxbow*, Cropsey's view depicts a steep drop between the mountaintop and river valley, and the loop of river peeking into the picture space hints that from elsewhere in the scene we could perhaps capture a view of the Hudson similar to Cole's view of the Connecticut. But Cropsey has withheld the vertiginous prospect that gives *The Oxbow* such a palpable sense of cosmic rupture, and if there are any divine characters "written" in the valley, we aren't in a position to read them. Cropsey has placed us at a remove: looking at the house, we look at the place where others have looked; seeing, we can only imagine what they might see. The aesthetic problem remains that of integrating two halves of a landscape, but with the axis between them swiveled to face us like a gun barrel, the eschatological and ethical questions are muddied. We must move into the space, but which way? And what are we even choosing if we move down out of the mountains to the left, or on past the lakes to the right?

To answer these questions, it is helpful to return to the mediascape from which the painting emerged. By the time Cropsey painted *Catskill Mountain House*, visitors had been writing about the site for decades. Dozens of accounts by such eminent writers as James Fenimore Cooper and Harriet Martineau, appearing in popular publications including Nathaniel Parker Willis's *American Scenery* (1840) and *Harper's New Monthly Magazine*, reveal the range of evolving cultural associations the place held for the predominantly genteel and middle-class audience who visited and read about it. These accounts provide a context in which to interpret the choice posed by Cropsey's split composition. Specifically they reveal three cultural conflicts crystallized in the unique geographical and social environment of the Catskills: a tension between religious, typological readings of nature and materialist or scientific ones; divergent appraisals of what economic development meant for the possibilities of experiencing the sacred in the American landscape; and competing accounts of the meaning of suffering and the ethical demands it imposed on others in a society of strangers. In 1854 when the Catskill Mountain House appeared in one of most popular novels of the decade, Maria Cummins's *The Lamplighter*, it highlighted how inextricably connected all of these conflicts had become to questions of aesthetic practice. Issues that had been hashed out in sermons and religious tracts in the 1820s and 1830s, and in abolitionist newspapers and antislavery libraries in the 1830s and 1840s, now were taken up by best-selling novels.

An account of a visit to the Catskill Mountain House by an unidentified author in the annual gift-book *The Atlantic Souvenir* in 1828 displays several of the narrative features that congealed into a fairly standard pattern in the years after the hotel opened in 1824. Boarding a stagecoach in the village of Catskill, the male narrator begins the twelve-mile ascent to the hotel (typically a four- to six-hour trip) with obligatory references to Rip Van Winkle and Leatherstocking. Partway up the mountain he alights from the coach to cover the final two miles on foot, comparing the ascent to life's "journey" and reflecting that it would be "happy for stray-loving mortals, if it were as impossible to leave the way" in life as it is to leave the road, before emerging at the hotel to behold a sublime prospect in which "creation seemed presented in one view." Having encoded the physical terrain as a homiletic landscape, he hikes past the two lakes to Kaaterskill Falls, pausing along the way to contemplate the forest inhabitants ("the children of the mountains" from a nearby log cabin as well as the snakes reputed to live in the area) and to reflect on the "paternal providence" of the "Creator" who provides them food and shelter. The narrator returns to the house in time to see sunset, and an hour later, moonrise. The next morning before departing, he watches the sun rise over a "sea" of clouds shrouding the valley, which burn off to reveal "sunny spots of green fields and sparkling waters" below.[77]

The most telling moment in the *Atlantic Souvenir* account occurs during moonrise, as "an aged minister of the gospel" on the portico points to the sky and says he feels "as if we were in a mighty temple, upon the lofty dome of which is inscribed in characters, that all intelligent beings may read, worship the Creator." A moment later, however, the minister qualifies his enthusiasm, urging his listeners, "Let us not forget that there is another book prepared for the service of this temple, written in characters which none who have the power to know may disregard and be guiltless."[78] His admonition invokes a topos, dating back to the Latin Middle Ages and popularized in the Renaissance, which held that both the Bible and nature were complementary "books" published by the same divine author.[79] Many nineteenth-century evangelicals accepted nature as a legitimate means of knowledge about God, but they insisted that the Bible remained the primary medium of divine truth and was necessary to properly interpret the Book of Nature. In their view, "natural theology" should not be neglected, but it must never be allowed to overshadow the revealed religion of the Bible, as the minister's warning indicates. As Doreen M. Rosman explains, for evangelicals, "reading" nature did not simply provide static evidence of God's attributes; it also corroborated biblical narrative: while the beauty of nature recalled the benevolence of God and the goodness of creation, its beasts of prey and noxious pests provided evidence of nature's corruption as a result of human sin, and its sublime storms and other cataclysmic events recalled and prefigured God's righteous wrath and judgment.[80]

For visitors situated within this sacred history of the creation, fall, and redemption of the world, witnessing the ever-changing landscape prospect from Catskill Mountain House—particularly the thunderstorms that frequently lashed the valley and dramatic sunrises that illuminated thick banks of clouds and mist—afforded a glimpse backward in time to Creation and the Flood in Genesis and forward to the apocalypse. The effect, in the words of one visitor, was "an inward elevation" that facilitated "instructive reflections upon the past, the present, and the future."[81] James Pierce, a charter member of the Catskill Mountain Association, provided an early precedent, writing in 1823 that his dawn prospect from Round Top revealed "a world in miniature" in which the rising sun turned the lakes, streams, and the Hudson below into "crimson floods or lakes of fire," a scene that prompted him to quote an apocalyptic scene from Isaiah 40:4, "The hills were laid low and the valleys exalted."[82] In 1837 Willis Gaylord Clark's "pilgrimage" to the mountain house was rewarded with a vision of the Catskills as they had been "moulded by the hand of the ALMIGHTY." He likened the sunrise the next morning to the prospect the archangel Michael presents to the fallen Adam "from the highest hill of Paradise" in Book 11 of *Paradise Lost*, revealing the entire sweep of human history to come, from Adam's imminent expulsion to the Last Judgment.[83] Harriet

Martineau likewise turned to Milton to help connect the Catskill landscape to sacred history as she ascended to a rocky outcropping that she dubbed the "Devil's Pulpit," likening the prospect to "Satan's glimpses from the Mount of Soliloquy."[84] Later from the mountain house Martineau witnessed "gushes of red lightning" and "sulphurous light" during an evening storm, followed by a predawn fog that dissipated to reveal a radiant Sabbath landscape; that evening the sunset "gave me a vivid idea of the process of creation, from the moment when all was without form and void to that when light was commanded, and there was light."[85] For landscape painter Charles Lanman the novelty of watching a nighttime thunderstorm from the mountain house again drew comparisons to *Paradise Lost*—this time to the "description of hell" in Book 1—but the sunrise he witnessed from nearby South Peak elicited a rapturous millennial vision, beginning with clouds which, like "winged chariots from the city of the living God," heralded the arrival of the sun: "He comes! He comes! The 'king of the bright day!' The crimson and golden clouds are parting, and he bursts on the bewildered sight! One moment more, and the whole earth rejoices in his beams."[86] For Lanman, Martineau, and countless other travelers who read their words and followed in their footsteps, the prospect from the Catskill Mountain House provided a spectacular opportunity to see the sacred narratives they had read about and imagined for years visualized in the landscape before them. Perhaps it comes as no surprise that Cropsey himself read *Paradise Lost* (as well as the *New-York Evangelist*) shortly before making a sketching trip to the Catskills in 1845.[87]

But cracks existed in the seemingly firm interpretive foundation that authorized such readings of sacred history in the landscape. David Murdoch, the editor of a popular anthology of writing about the Catskills first published in 1846, exposed those cracks when he described a disturbing vision that appeared to a group of visitors on the hotel piazza: a ghostly replica of the mountain house floating past in the fog. The apparition elicits competing interpretations: one man explains it to his young daughter, Kate, in terms of "optics": "these effects were produced this afternoon by the rays striking a certain angle of incidence." His explanation prompts a discussion of the visions that "formerly had great effects upon the superstitious mind," including "*second sight*" and battles in the sky. When Kate asks whether "all these appearances in the air are produced by the same causes," his answer is unequivocal: "All by *natural* laws, my child, differently modified." But Kate's uncle, a well-traveled "clergyman," counters with a very different account, one with "a moral to it": "The mysteriously grand temple we have beheld in the cloud has brought to my mind the fleeting nature of all earthly temples," he explains, recalling the Parthenon and other ruins he has visited. "But to-day, as if in mockery of all earthly greatness, we have seen an *airy* Parthenon passing by us like a dream."

As if the point weren't clear enough, the next day a rainbow appears and the same debate plays out between the "*material* husband" and the religious uncle. Murdoch, himself a Dutch Reformed minister, clearly signals where his own sympathies lie, hailing the rainbow as "such a token as Noah saw from Arrarat [*sic*]," a "blessed emblem of hope and immortality." In the end the uncle's position prevails: the approaching sunrise prompts the familiar millennial language from the viewers ("He is coming! he is coming!") as the interplay of clouds and land figures the entire cosmic drama of sacred history, from "the Spirit of God moving on the face of chaos, when he said 'Let there be light, and there was light,'" until the time "when the veil of mystery will be removed, and we shall look no more through a glass darkly."[88]

Though Murdoch's 1846 account concludes by reasserting the moralistic, typological approach to nature characteristic of earlier writing about the mountain house, the "material" man adds a voice absent from the minister's reading of nature in the 1828 *Atlantic Souvenir* discussed earlier. Certainly the contest dramatizes secularization, but in a particular sense: not as a slow leeching away of belief that eventually leaves only aesthetic or ethical concerns—Murdoch's religious rhetoric is just as strong or more so than the earlier accounts—but as the change in "the conditions of belief" that Taylor describes, through which a religious framework becomes simply "one option among others, and frequently not the easiest to embrace." Those options concerned not just how one interpreted nature but the spiritual significance of space more broadly. For Natty Bumppo of Cooper's *The Pioneers* (1823), the climb into the Catskills had represented a withdrawal from the political struggle of the American Revolution to a vantage point where he could "see the carryings on of the world" and survey "all creation."[89] Many genteel visitors to the mountain house expressed variations on this theme, describing the place as a spiritual retreat from sordid realities associated with the city, commerce, politics, or materialism, noting as Martineau did that from up there, "the fields and waters seem . . . no more truly property than the skies which shine down upon them."[90] As Kenneth Myers and John F. Sears have each noted, such claims helped legitimize tourism in the nineteenth century, transforming mere pleasure-seeking into a virtuous "pilgrimage."[91] Like the religious pilgrimages theorized by Victor and Edith Turner, Sears argues, landscape tourism "promise[s] spiritual renewal through contact with a transcendent reality," and this sense of release from "ordinary reality" offered by the tourist site "replicate[s] in significant ways the function of sacred space in archaic societies." The view from the Catskill Mountain House "provided a window on the infinite for those in search of the transcendent elements of tourist experience," a place where "the visitor steps out of the immediate, particular, disordered continuum of life and contemplates the whole from a distance."[92]

At the same time that such sites were being produced as a new form of sacred space, however, they were also "consumer products," raising a dilemma for those who aspired to escape the sordid realities of the market.[93] Some visitors noted with growing alarm that the world's profane tentacles reached even into the Catskills, threatening the possibility of elevating experience. As artists watched tourists invade a place their own work had helped popularize, they retreated to less crowded, cheaper lodgings further down the Clove.[94] Genteel visitors wrinkled their noses at distressing evidence of unwashed America encroaching on their pleasure grounds: the "ugliness" of the cabin-dwelling children near the lakes, the "sprawling shanties" of the "Upper Clove," and the "shabby" village of Palenville, where many locals worked in sawmills and tanneries (and where artists often lodged in inns too rustic for the "comfort-loving tourist").[95] Critics who idealized the region's old order of "honest, industrious and sober" Dutch folk railed against "the late attempts to corrupt them with canals and great state roads; and above all by locating a fashionable hotel in the very centre of their strong hold, the Kaatskill Mountain," exposing them to the "temptation" of "fashion" and the "pestilent novelties" demanded by "rich and idle people."[96] This last accusation touched the heart of the issue: for Protestants whose trip to the mountains enacted a ritual withdrawal from the world, the idea that the resort was in fact the height of worldliness clashed with a deeply ingrained sacred geography. Nathaniel Parker Willis noted the incongruity of finding the "superfluities" of a "luxurious hotel" so high: "It is the more strange, because in climbing a mountain the feeling is natural that you leave such enervating indulgences below. The mountain-top is too near heaven. It should be a monastery to lodge in so high—a St. Gothard, or a Vallambrosa. But here you may choose between Hermitages, 'white' or 'red,' Burgundies, Madeiras, French dishes, and French dances, as if you had descended upon Capua."[97]

Some pious visitors reacted by condemning a litany of vices with the fervor of a seventeenth-century jeremiad. They decried "profanations" like the "monstrous tavern" installed above Kaaterskill Falls at Laurel House—where visitors could sip "brandy-punch" and have chilled bottles of champagne lowered to them at the base of the falls—pleading in verse, "Oh! profane not the place by so low a libation, / While pure from the rock springs the fountain of health!"[98] The 25-cent fee visitors were charged to see the falls was proof the place had been "chained by the cold shackles of the spirit of gain."[99] Worst of all was the possibility that instead of nurturing piety, the resort eroded it by tempting people away from church on the Sabbath.[100] The Reverend Theodore L. Cuyler sought to assuage these worries by describing the "golden Sabbath" he spent at the mountain house, where after watching "the coming of the king of day" at sunrise, he attended three services throughout the day.[101] In

1860 the *New-York Christian Inquirer* calmly assured readers that in the Catskills at least they could enjoy scenery without the taint of worldliness: "We find in the Mountain House not a hotel, but a home, quiet, comfortable and easy. There is none of the stiff finery, and endless promenading, and sensation parties of the lower-world watering places."[102] The claim may have been false, but it indicated a continuing desire among many Protestants to yoke inner piety to outward (and upward) movement through space—to preserve a traditional form of sacred geography in a world that threatened to subject all of nature to the "spirit of gain" and to reduce all religious experience to "optics."

Sleeping through Sunrise: Maria Cummins's *The Lamplighter*

The ability of the Catskill Mountain House to represent the clash between traditional Protestant conceptions of sacred geography and secular currents in antebellum culture reached its greatest visibility in one of the most popular novels of the 1850s, Maria Cummins's *The Lamplighter*.[103] Similar to Warner's *Wide, Wide World*, the novel narrates the hard-won religious and moral development of its heroine, Gertrude Flint, from her early days as an orphaned street-child in a Boston slum through her rescue by a working-class lamplighter, her subsequent adoption and education by a pious middle-class Boston family, and her successful marriage. A crucial episode in this development occurs during a summer trip to the Catskills, when Gertrude has reached the age when suitors begin to call and the worldly temptations of fashionable parties and frivolous gossip threaten to lure her away from piety. Approaching the Catskills by steamboat, Gerty is enraptured by the scenery that "seemed rather a glimpse of Paradise than an actual show of earth." Imagining her mountain destination within a familiar sacred framework, she hopes "to reach the summit of Catskill Mountain before the Sabbath" (*L*, 332), ostensibly to worship where God is nearest. But the spiritual experience she seeks is not exactly what she finds. The first ominous sign occurs on the road to the hotel as Gerty and her chaperone, Dr. Jeremy, exit the coach to continue the ascent on foot. While stopping to admire the widening prospect, they are startled by Mr. Phillips, a melancholy middle-aged man who has repeatedly appeared during the trip and who seems to take a special interest in Gertrude. As the three resume their ascent, Phillips converses impressively on botany and geology; his wealth of knowledge and experience reveals him to have been a "sailor," a "merchant," and a "man of fashion and the world" (340). Gertrude is intrigued and "long[s] to know more of him" (341) but is soon troubled when Mr. Jeremy abruptly announces, "There will be no church for us to-morrow, Gerty."

"No church!" exclaimed Gertrude, gazing about her with a look of reverence; "how *can* you say so?"

Mr. Phillips bestowed upon her a smile of interest and inquiry, and said, in a peculiar tone, "There is no Sunday here, Miss Flint; it does n't come up so high."

He spoke lightly,—too lightly, Gertrude thought,—and she replied with some seriousness, and much sweetness, "I have often rejoiced that the Sabbath had been sent *down* into the *lower* earth; the higher we go, the nearer we come, I trust, to the eternal Sabbath." (341–42)

The exchange dramatizes the confrontation between an urbane conception of religious institutions as corrupt human artifacts whose earthly origins are concealed by a mystifying ideology—what we would today call social constructs—and claims that revealed religion in fact represents transcendent realities handed down from above.[104] In spatial terms, Phillips and Gertrude preview the debate between constructivist or "socio-historical" approaches to sacred space, which tend to take an outsider's perspective, analyzing such spaces as ritually produced by human beings acting within complex social situations; and "substantive" or "ontological" approaches, which emphasize the insider's experience of sacred sites as qualitatively different, as places where sacred power is made manifest, independently of human beings.[105] While Gertrude's reverent gaze signals her sense that she is entering more fully into God's presence as she ascends, Phillips considers himself to be escaping the realm in which the "Sunday" is produced as an authoritative configuration of sacred space and time. With Gertrude's firm response to Phillips's skepticism, the novel lets her win round one—successfully resisting temptation, as it were—only to raise a more sinister situation at the hotel itself.

"Take care, Gerty, and be up in time to see the sun rise," Dr. Jeremy counsels before retiring to his room for the night. By now the apocalyptic double meaning of his warning should be clear, the equivalent of the biblical injunction to vigilance because "the day of the Lord will come as a thief of the night" (2 Peter 3:10). But Gerty does not heed his warning: "She was not up in time, however, nor was the doctor himself; neither of them had calculated upon the sun's being such an early riser" (*L*, 342). Nor has anyone else in the hotel, for by the time Gerty rises to find a "brilliant and glorious dawn" over "a sea of snowy clouds, which wholly overshadowed the lower earth, and hid it from view" (343), the house is still silent. When the party finally emerges to hike up to the "pine gardens" (344), the ominous signs keep coming. Mrs. Jeremy is unimpressed with the view and becomes terrified that her husband will fall to his death; partway up the path, she gets tired, remembers the snakes reported to frequent the area, and demands to be escorted back, leaving

Gertrude to press on alone. Upon reaching an "elevated woody platform" and sitting to rest "at the root of an immense pine tree" (345)—a setting that recalls Martineau's "Devil's Pulpit"—Gertrude hears a nearby rustle and leaps to her feet. But instead of a rattlesnake she finds Mr. Phillips asleep on the ground, in the midst of some terrible dream. "Gertrude was deeply touched. She forgot that he was a stranger; she saw only a sufferer" (346). When a stray tear of "sympathy" falls upon his face and awakens him, he tells her to "never again weep for a stranger; you will have woes enough of your own, if you live to be of my age"; to which Gerty responds, "If I had not sorrows already . . . I should not know how to feel for others; if I had not often wept for myself, I should not weep now for you" (346). The exchange prompts a debate about the meaning of suffering and whether human efforts can relieve it, a question that leads back to the prospect:

> "Do you see," said Mr. Phillips, "this curtain of thick clouds, now overshadowing the world? Even so many a heart is weighed down by thick and impenetrable darkness."
> "But the light shines brightly above the clouds," said Gertrude.
> "Above! well, that may be; but what avails it to those who see it not?"
> "It is sometimes a weary and toilsome road that leads to the mountain-top; but the pilgrim is well repaid for the trouble which brings him *above the clouds*," replied Gertrude, with enthusiasm.
> "Few ever find the road that leads so high," responded her melancholy companion; "and those who do cannot live long in so elevated an atmosphere. They must come down from their height, and again dwell among the common herd; again mingle in the warfare with the mean, the base and the cruel; thicker clouds will gather over their heads, and they will be buried in redoubled darkness."
> "But they have seen the glory; they know that the light is ever burning on high, and will have faith to believe it will pierce the gloom at last. See, see!" said she, her eyes glowing with the fervor with which she spoke,— "even now the heaviest clouds are parting; the sun will soon light up the valley!" (347–48)

With its odd mixture of ominous portents and confident faith, the episode recalls the uneasy blend of millennial expectation and cultural anxiety that characterizes the earlier literary accounts of the mountain house. At the heart of the debate is the question of whether the sort of individual spiritual consolation offered by the homiletic landscape is adequate to the suffering experienced by ordinary people: whether it is accessible to the majority who, Phillips implies, may lack the temperament or spiritual insight to "find the road that leads so high," and even then may find the sense of moral order afforded by the prospect only temporary before they sink back into "redoubled darkness." In other words, Phillips levels a critique of landscape theodicy and implicitly of the fictional project that uses it as a vehicle of moral and religious instruction. Gerty's response, similar to that of John and Alice Humphreys in *The Wide, Wide World*, is to appeal to apocalyptic eschatology, pointing to an imminent millennium in which the "sun" will return to "pierce the gloom at last."

As a crystallization of the decades-long struggle over the meaning of tourist sites like the Catskill Mountain House waged in travel literature and in literary fiction, Cummins's scene in the Catskills helps illuminate the unsettling quality of Cropsey's painting of the following year. Thanks to the worldly commentary of Phillips and Mr. Jeremy, Gerty's experience ascending the road to the mountain house resembles not so much Bunyan's Christian toiling up Hill Difficulty as the genteel ritual depicted in John Rubens Smith's 1830 engraving, *Catskill Mountain-House* (fig. 4.6), in which well-dressed gentlemen and ladies stop to admire the prospect on their way to the "*Celebrated Summer Hotel.*" The perch where Natty Bumppo had gone to distance himself from the vicissitudes of the American Revolution and to reaffirm a sense of "all creation" is in Smith's view occupied by an imposing pillared edifice not unlike the White House itself, with the American flag flying prominently above it. In contrast to this buoyantly nationalistic landscape, Cropsey's view is somber and elegiac: devoid of people, marked by skeletal trees and a crumbling headstone amid autumn colors that presage the coming of winter. The hotel has shrunk to a distant destination with no clear path to reach it, placing the viewer in something like the dilemma faced by Bunyan's Christian (and Ellen Montgomery after him) of choosing between the "narrow way" to the "Arbor, made by the Lord of the hill for the refreshment of weary travelers," and the paths that lead only to "Danger" and "Destruction."

On one level, the choice embedded in Cropsey's painting can be understood in terms of the tensions that had surrounded the mountain house since its construction: competing interpretations of nature and conflicting appraisals of the relationship of landscape tourism to the sacred. On the left half of the canvas, the expansive prospect of earth and sky stretching before the house represents the part of the site that consistently elicited typological and millennial interpretations from its observers, where we might say the religious "option" was most compelling. The right half, containing the path along the lakes to the falls and down into the Clove, leads to many of the "profanations" that disgusted genteel visitors—the log cabins, the tavern, the tourist trap at the falls, the mills and tanneries of Palenville—but also to the less frequented area that one reviewer called "the most charming part of the Catskills" and the part "most preferred by artists for study."[106] Indeed, while staying at a boardinghouse in the Clove in September 1850, Cropsey wrote to his wife, Maria, that

FIGURE 4.6. John Rubens Smith, *Catskill Mountain-House*, ca. 1830. Aquatint engraving, hand-colored. (Philadelphia: Printed by J. Dainty Jr., [1830]). Popular Graphic Arts Collection, Prints & Photographs Division, Library of Congress, LC-DIG-pga-04160.

the gorge "is wild and grand and has almost a soul, so much has the Creator displayed in his handy work in it."[107] In this context the two halves of the composition might be said to speak to divergent conceptions of where the sacred can be found—the elevated prospect or the near-to-hand, the refined or the ordinary.

But *The Lamplighter* highlights another tension that inheres in the view, this one concerning suffering and social ethics. Unlike the intensely internal focus that Warner's landscape theodicy provides Ellen in *The Wide, Wide World*, Cummins presents the millennial landscape glimpsed from the mountain house as linked to an extension of sympathy across physical and social space. Gerty, after all, owes her position—both physically on the mountain and socially in the middle class—to the benevolence of strangers. This is the ethical ideal she defends against Phillips's skepticism in the pine gardens when she argues for an expansive "sympathy" founded in the personal experience of suffering, and for the possibility and duty of the faithful to convey their privileged vision of the divine plan to others—to bring the "light" down from the mountain, as it were. In this context, the two sides of Cropsey's composition might be seen to correspond to two distinct ethical imaginaries and the aesthetic approaches those conceptions imply. On one side is the expansive evangelical ethic of Gerty's eastward prospect, embodied aesthetically in pious literary works like *The Lamplighter* and visually in the broad narrative sweep of Cole's "higher landscape." On the other is a more modest, inward-looking ethic that eschews such grandiose ambitions—one akin to the wry skepticism with which Miles Coverdale views reform projects in Hawthorne's *Blithedale Romance* (1852) or to the intimate, exquisitely observed forest scenes that Asher B. Durand painted in the 1850s (some of the Clove itself) as part of a "therapeutic landscape" that he hoped would offer a morally elevating respite to businessmen mired in the pressures of urban life.[108] What's being dramatized at some level, I'm suggesting, is a conflict over the role art should play in American life: as a moralized instrument of social reform or as a good in its own right that is irreducible to other human goods—what Alasdair MacIntyre would call a "practice," an endeavor defined by its own intrinsic "standards of excellence."[109]

Ultimately, by investing a conventional view of a popular tourist resort with such seemingly unnecessary formal complexity, Cropsey dramatizes the process of antebellum landscape representation coming to a critical awareness of its own prevailing methods and assumptions, particularly as they relate to the sacred meanings of the landscape. That is, *Catskill Mountain House* shows how secularization in the particular sense treated in this chapter—as the condition in which the presence of competing religious "options" is unavoidable—impacted the formal vocabulary used by artists (even deeply devout ones like Cropsey) to address diverse audiences with whom they could not presume a shared set of religious convictions. Broadly speaking, the painting helps us consider how popular artworks of the 1850s that appear to be purely naturalistic at the level of content might have nonetheless continued to speak to religious and ethical concerns through their form. For landscape art in particular, by distilling the theological and epistemological debates encoded in the mediascape that propelled the rise of landscape tourism, Cropsey's painting provocatively reveals how the landscape had come to mediate religious difference in antebellum America. Since the 1820s Protestant evangelicals had sought to use the landscape as a unifying cultural medium, symbolically bridging denominational differences within a united Benevolent Empire and integrating individual journeys of faith within a collective narrative of millennial history. By the 1850s it became clear that even as they had in many ways succeeded in turning the landscape into a religious and moral form of mass media, the messages it conveyed could not be contained by a single master-narrative of sacred history. The landscape told many stories, some of which were not Christian at all but distinctly, gleefully, and wickedly heathen.

5

Cosmic Modernity

HENRY DAVID THOREAU, THE MISSIONARY
MEMOIR, AND THE HEATHEN WITHIN

IN JULY 1852, Henry David Thoreau wrote to his sister Sophia that "Concord is just as idiotic as ever in relation to the spirits and their knockings.... Where *are* the heathen? Was there ever any superstition before? And yet I suppose there may be a vessel this very moment setting sail from the coast of North America to that of Africa with a missionary on board!"[1] The letter's ironic juxtaposition of Spiritualist "superstition" in Concord with evangelical zeal to convert distant "heathen" registers the immense visibility of popular religious cultures in Thoreau's New England and encapsulates one of his most characteristic modes of cultural critique: demanding local reform by inverting discourses typically used to criticize distant others.[2] Even as Thoreau implies that the Protestant foreign missionary impulse is misplaced, his exasperated questions appropriate the terms of missionary discourse, inverting the moral geography that sends missionaries around the globe to redeem the heathen. This ambivalent engagement with evangelical missionary culture structures the literary form of *Walden* (1854), a book that asks, "Under what latitudes reside the heathen to whom we would send light?"[3] In the chapter titled "Economy," Thoreau declares, "Even in our democratic New England towns the accidental possession of wealth, and its manifestation in dress and equipage alone, obtain for the possessor almost universal respect. But they who yield such respect, numerous as they are, are so far heathen, and need to have a missionary sent to them" (*W*, 23). In the midst of a polemic that challenges just such conventional notions of respectability, the speaker assumes the ironic persona of a missionary to New England's white heathen.

This chapter accepts Thoreau's wry invitation to read *Walden* through the lens of Protestant missionary discourse. By attending to a neglected facet of the book's literary ecology, I unsettle familiar understandings of *Walden* as a localist and individualist text, address the neglect of popular religion in recent accounts of the American Renaissance, and revise secular accounts of global modernity by developing a concept of "cosmic modernity." In the process I show how the evangelical mediascape explored in previous chapters shaped parts of antebellum literary culture that on the surface could not be further from the concerns of evangelical authors and readers—in this case the elite, religiously heterodox world of American Transcendentalism. Thoreau's first-person account of his efforts to awaken a group of heathens—"to wake my neighbors up" (*W*, 84)—becomes an ironic retelling of the Protestant missionary memoir, a popular genre circulating on both sides of the Atlantic in the early nineteenth century that portrayed idealistic young men and (especially) women as they searched for callings, left their homes and families to spread the Gospel in foreign lands, and—more often than not—perished there.[4] That retelling involved more than appropriating and subverting a set of generic and rhetorical conventions, though. It meant remapping the global geography of religious, cultural, and racial difference that structured missionary memoirs, the sort of spatial imaginary displayed in William Channing Woodbridge's *Moral and Political Chart of the Inhabited World* (fig. 5.1), a school-atlas map first published in 1826 that classified the world's peoples according to their "State of Civilization," "Government," and "Religion," thus visualizing the "hierarchy of heathenism" that English and American missionary societies used to prioritize their efforts.[5] And it meant replacing the narrative of sacred history implicit in that geography—that religious diversity would give way to a universal Christian community and usher in the millennium.

By exploring Thoreau's engagement with the missionary memoir, the chapter continues a tradition of reading *Walden* as a sophisticated mosaic of literary genres and modes including the georgic, the spiritual autobiography, and the novel.[6] But it extends and reframes that tradition by turning to one of several popular religious genres that have recently drawn critical attention as part of the "evangelical public sphere."[7] My analysis focuses on a group of some sixty Protestant missionary memoirs published in the United States in the four decades between 1814—when Harriet Newell's memoir set the standard for the genre—and 1854, when Ticknor and Fields published the memoir of Henrietta A. L. Hamlin, the same year the firm published *Walden*.[8] Biographical evidence suggests that Thoreau had exposure to Protestant missionary culture through the women in his family, several of whom at one time belonged to the Evangelical Missionary Society of Concord.[9] Given the role such women's groups played in supporting and reading evangelical magazines, Thoreau likely was exposed to evangelical literature at a young age.[10] As late as 1853, Maria Thoreau was urging her nephew to read about the lives of pious evangelicals like the Scottish Presbyterian minister Thomas Chalmers (1780–1847). As

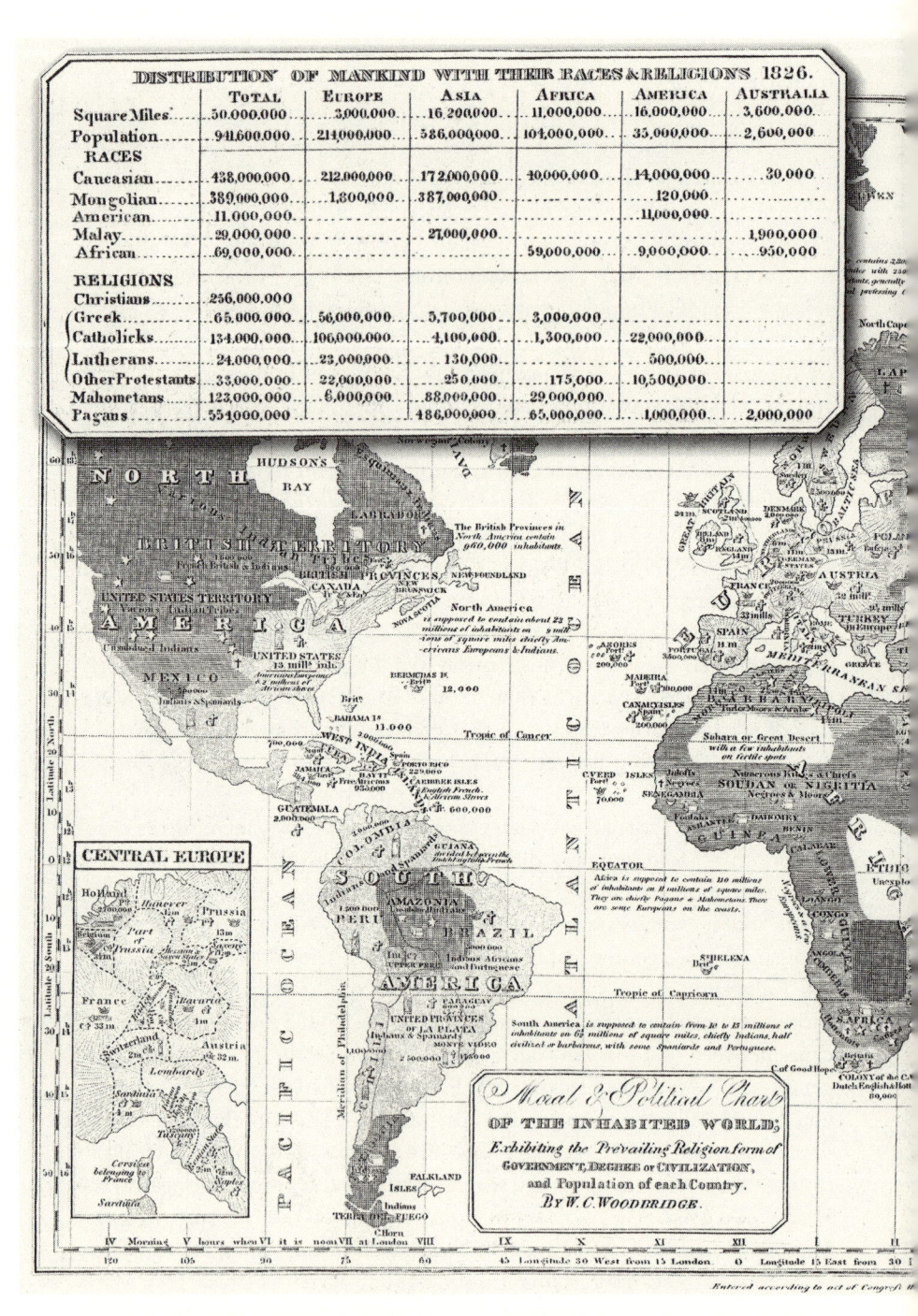

FIGURE 5.1. William Channing Woodbridge, *Moral and Political Chart of the Inhabited World*. In William C[hanning] Woodbridge, *Modern Atlas: On a New Plan, to Accompany the System of Universal Geography*, 6th ed. (Hartford: Beach & Beckwith, 1835). Photo courtesy of The Newberry Library, Chicago, Special Collections, Case folio G 10.979 map [2].

Explanation of Emblems.

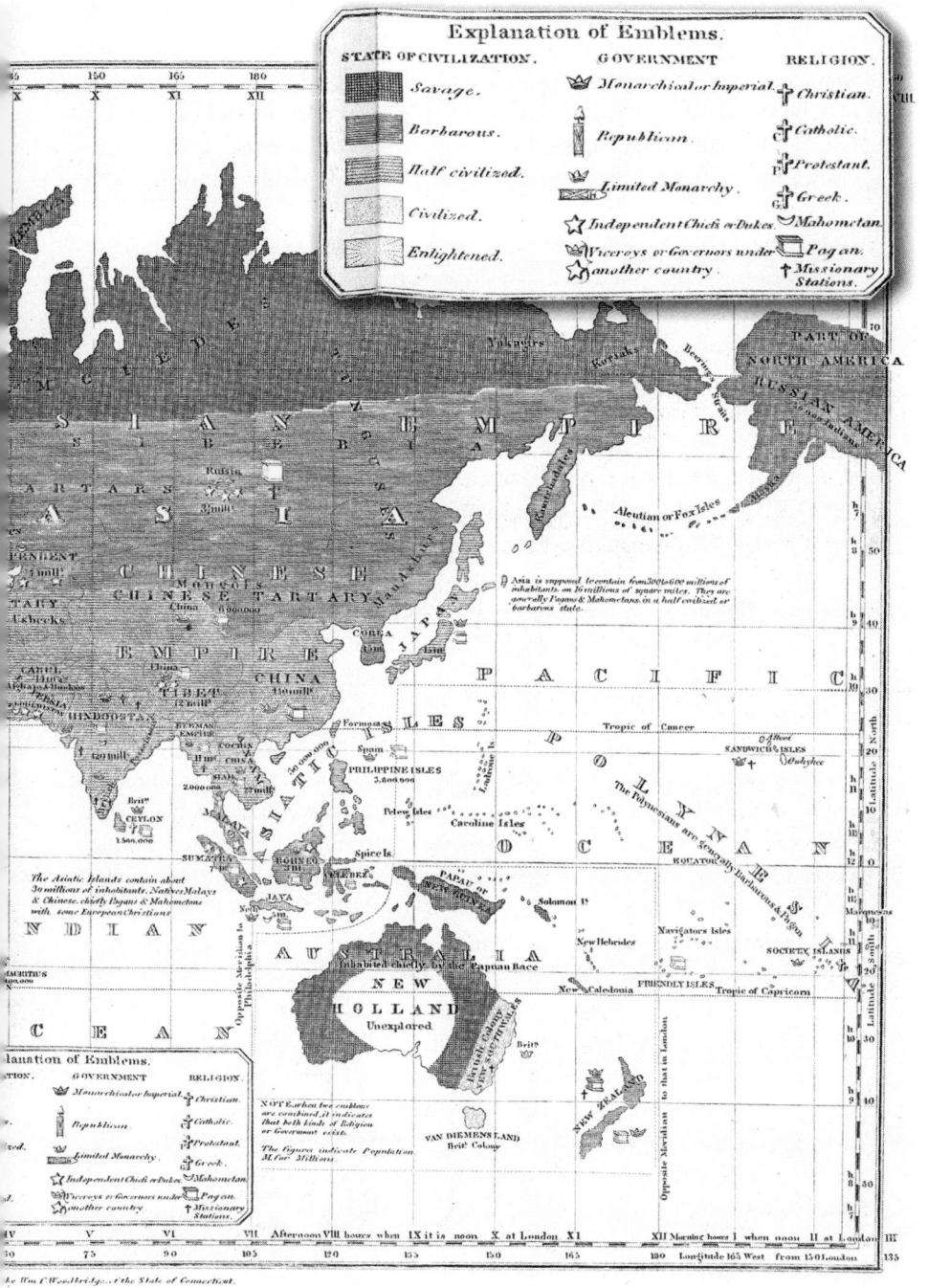

STATE OF CIVILIZATION.	GOVERNMENT.	RELIGION.
Savage.	Monarchical or Imperial.	Christian.
Barbarous.	Republican.	Catholic.
Half civilized.	Limited Monarchy.	Protestant.
Civilized.	Independent Chiefs or Dukes.	Greek.
Enlightened.	Viceroys or Governors under another country.	Mahometan.
		Pagan.
		Missionary Stations.

NOTE. when two emblems are combined, it indicates that both kinds of Religion or Government exist. The figures indicate Population. M. for Million.

Asia is supposed to contain from 300 to 600 millions of inhabitants, on 16 millions of square miles. They are generally Pagans & Mahometans, in a half civilized or barbarous state.

The Asiatic Islands contain about 30 millions of inhabitants. Natives Malays & Chinese, chiefly Pagans & Mahometans, with some European Christians.

The Polynesians are generally barbarous & Pagan.

PART OF NORTH AMERICA
RUSSIAN AMERICA
Aleutian or Fox Isles
CHINESE EMPIRE
CHINESE TARTARY
China
TIBET
HINDOOSTAN
BURMAN EMPIRE
COCHIN CHINA
SIAM
CEYLON
SUMATRA
BORNEO
Spice Is.
CELEBES
JAVA
PAPUA or NEW GUINEA
PHILIPPINE ISLES
Caroline Isles
Pelew Isles
Solomon Is.
New Hebrides
New Caledonia
FRIENDLY ISLES
SANDWICH ISLES
Owhyhee
Navigators Isles
SOCIETY ISLANDS
Marquesas
AUSTRALIA
NEW HOLLAND Unexplored
Inhabited chiefly by the Papuan Race
British Colony of New South Wales
VAN DIEMENS LAND Brit' Colony
NEW ZEALAND

INDIAN OCEAN
PACIFIC OCEAN
POLYNESIA

Tropic of Cancer
Equator
Tropic of Capricorn

by Wm C Woodbridge of the State of Connecticut.

Thoreau recorded in his *Journal*, "My Aunt Maria asked me to read the life of Dr Chalmers—which however I did not promise to do. Yesterday, Sunday, she was heard through the partition shouting to my aunt Jane who is deaf—'Think of it, he stood haf [*sic*] an hour today to hear the frogs croak, and he would'nt [*sic*] read the life of Chalmers.'"[11] Thoreau may not have read the religious works his aunt recommended, but he was undeniably aware of their existence.

In any case, my claim is not that Thoreau read any particular memoir, or even necessarily that he consciously drew on the genre as he crafted *Walden*.[12] Rather, I argue that his writing registers the genre's presence at the level of content and form and that recognizing this can add a new dimension to our understanding of his work and illuminate the far-reaching cultural impact of evangelical mediascapes. Specifically, reading *Walden* as a satirical missionary memoir sharpens our understanding of two familiar aspects of Thoreau's text that often seem to be unrelated or at cross-purposes: the astringent social critique of "Economy," and the book's subsequent focus on individual solitude and self-exploration in nature. Moreover, reading *Walden* in the context of an evangelical print culture noted for its transnational circulation and its spatially dispersed yet affectively intimate textual communities recasts a work typically associated with localism, individualism, and hostility to modernity and reveals important ways in which it is global, communitarian, and modern.[13]

My aim in this chapter, however, goes beyond producing a new interpretation of *Walden* and tracing important but neglected connections between Transcendentalism and evangelicalism. Thoreau's engagement with missionary rhetoric in *Walden* was not unique in U.S. literary culture: between the 1830s and the Civil War, figures as diverse as William Apess, Herman Melville, Harriet Beecher Stowe, and Harriet Jacobs used the figure of the missionary to criticize American society. Addressing readers who "send the Bible to heathen abroad, and neglect the heathen at home," Jacobs declared, "I am glad that missionaries go out to the dark corners of the earth; but I ask them not to overlook the dark corners at home," and urged them to "talk to American slaveholders as you talk to savages in Africa."[14] The prevalence of such statements prompts me to probe a lacuna in the spatial turn in American literary studies when it comes to religion. Influential revisionist studies in the late twentieth century emphasized the popular religious context of the American Renaissance, but the field's more recent turn to hemispheric, transatlantic, and global frameworks has generally not engaged religion in any sustained way.[15] Insofar as this new wave of scholarship is silent on questions of religion, it reproduces the process through which, in Tracy Fessenden's words, "particular forms of Protestantism emerged as an 'unmarked category' in American religious and literary history, . . . [and] a particular strain of post-Protestant secularism, often blind to its own exclusions, became normative for understanding that history."[16] When religion does surface as a category of analysis—when, for example, Wai Chee Dimock traces Emerson's interest in Islam or Thoreau's in Hinduism in order to show how "American literature bursts out of the confines of the nation-state, becoming a thread in the fabric of a world religion"—religion becomes a relatively rarified, scholarly phenomenon that seems quite remote from the vibrant religious atmosphere of revivals, millennial prophecy, and the spirit rappings that so riled Thoreau in Concord.[17] But while scholarly trends might suggest that broadening our scope beyond the nation necessarily means losing sight of the texture of popular religion on the ground, missionary literature tells a different story: here, to read with an eye to popular religion *is* to read globally, and vice versa. *Walden* presents a compelling case study of this textured form of reading—what we might call, following Daniel Hack, close reading at a (cosmic) distance—that illuminates the relationship of nineteenth-century American literature to modernity in all of its dimensions.[18]

In particular, *Walden* dramatizes how, even as flows of goods, people, and information spread "horizontally" across the surface of the globe, compressing physical space and connecting local communities to distant places, those flows catalyzed new "vertical" dynamics of modernity as radically different cosmologies and theologies collided and transformed each other—an "unequal global encounter" that Jared Hickman argues "opened . . . a *metacosmic space*" in which the self-evident authority of competing worldviews was suddenly rendered precarious.[19] Whereas Laura Dassow Walls has shown Thoreau's debt to Alexander von Humboldt's scientific sense of the cosmos as a "harmoniously ordered whole,"[20] this chapter argues that Thoreau was equally captivated by a religious cosmos that stretched beyond the physical phenomena: one that emerged from a diverse matrix of practices, institutions, and forms of knowledge that included Protestant world missions and the comparative study of religion and myth.[21] This is the cosmos *Walden*'s speaker inhabits when he "bathe[s] [his] intellect in the stupendous and cosmogonal philosophy of the Bhagvat Geeta" (298) or compares the arrival of spring to "the creation of Cosmos out of Chaos and the realization of the Golden Age" (313).[22] Thoreau's cosmic imagination, however, will be accessed here not through his well-known reading of Eastern literature but through his polemical engagement with religious cultures closer to home.

Adding the cosmic to the array of Thoreauvian modernities recently explored by scholars might seem to be a contradiction in terms: after all, in Charles Taylor's influential account of secularization, the cosmic is precisely what is lost in the shift from "a limited, ordered and static cosmos to a universe which is immeasurably vast, and in constant evolution." For Taylor, Thoreau emerges as a representative figure of this shift who combines a new sense of a vast, sublime nature that is "other, hostile, indifferent" to humanity (exemplified by his epiphany on Ktaadn) with a new consciousness of "kinship" with nature dramatized in *Walden*. But if no cosmos remains in Taylor's account of the "modern cosmic imaginary," Bruno Latour insists that any viable form of "*cosmopolitics*" must include the "*cosmos*"—that is, it must extend beyond the human to "embrace . . . all the vast numbers of nonhuman entities making humans act," including "divinities and lesser transcendental entities."[23] Latour's recognition of the agency these entities continue to exert in the world suggests that modernity has not meant a "crumbling" cosmos (to quote Robert H. Abzug) so much as a proliferation of cosmic encounters, with effects ranging from the deformation and destruction of religious systems to the emergence of vibrant forms of syncretism, and from the comparative disciplines that culminated in "the pluralist discourse of world religions" to the rise of religious fundamentalisms.[24] From this perspective, the cosmic is not so much eroded within modern secularity as it is energized and elaborated by it— indeed, the cosmic becomes vital as an analytic category precisely when the definitions of the "religious" developed in the West fail to contain the proliferating forms of spirituality unleashed by modernity.[25]

While few would claim that Thoreau was religious in a theistic sense, he does offer a unique window onto this cosmic flowering in the nineteenth century: as an avid reader of the travel literature that exposed many in the West to non-Christian cultures, a practitioner of Romantic "religious universalism," a critic of popular religious culture, a major figure in the history of American "nature religion," and a participant in a Transcendentalist project of asserting the divinity of man, he presents an exquisite miniature image—a microcosm, so to speak—of cosmic modernity.[26] *Walden* shows just how central the evangelical mediascape explored in this book was to the emergence of a vision of the modern world as a religiously pluralistic space—a vision in many ways diametrically opposed to the worldview of evangelicals. It also reveals how that mediascape helped shape the distinct relationship between geographical space and the development of a particular form of modern selfhood. To be sure, Thoreau's efforts to chart the relationship between inner experience and outward nature drew from multiple sources, not least the Renaissance idea of a correspondence between part and whole—microcosm and macrocosm—that he encountered in Sir Thomas Browne, who declared, "We carry with us the wonders we seek without us: there is all Africa and her prodigies in us."[27] But while *Walden*'s concluding command to become "expert in home-cosmography" (320)—to "explore your own higher latitudes" (321)—clearly can be read as an extension of what Browne called "the cosmography of myself," the precise valence of that inward mapping reflected the spatial practices of Thoreau's day, both scientific and religious.[28] If *Walden* stands as a record of the sort of inner "voyage" (320) urged in the "Conclusion," it is not only a Humboldtian voyage of discovery but also a foreign mission determined to convert the heathen within. Charting that voyage reveals not only that popular religion inflected antebellum efforts to imagine how modernity was transforming the globe and local communities alike but also that the modern encounter with religious difference could shape the deepest, most private experiences of the self. Modernity in its cosmic dimensions reaches not only outward around the globe and upward toward the transcendent but inward. That meant that the use of the landscape as a divine medium to envision the coming of the Kingdom turned inward too, setting the stage for a new kind of apocalypse.

The Heathen Next Door: Missionary Literature, Localism, and Cosmic Communities

A curious paradox of *Walden* is that a text so deeply rooted in a specific physical place nonetheless figures the development of its speaker in terms of movement and distance. Culminating in the "home-cosmography" of the "Conclusion," this spatial dynamic is already in full swing on the first page of "Economy." In the emphatically literal space of the opening paragraph ("I lived alone, in the woods, a mile from any neighbor, in a house which I had built myself, on the shore of Walden Pond, in Concord, Massachusetts" [*W*, 3]), each comma becomes the equivalent of clicking the "+" button on Google Maps, zooming in with ever greater specificity. This literal space gives way to a figurative, characterological space in the second paragraph: "Moreover, I, on my side, require of every writer, first or last, a simple and sincere account of his own life, and not merely what he has heard of other men's lives; some such account as he would send to his kindred from a distant land; for if he has lived sincerely, it must have been in a distant land to me" (3–4). As this sentence echoes the clipped cadence of the first, it conveys formally that Thoreau's account of his life at the pond will be just such a "simple and sincere account"—that the act of fixing one's physical location ever more precisely is identical to the act of defining the self, paring away hinterlands and hearsay until only truth remains. At the same time, this condensation of place and self is figured as an extension and expansion into space, as a sincere life carries the writer into a state so distinct from others that he must write to them as if he were far away. For Thoreau, good life-writing thus negotiates a pair of spatial tensions: the writer must evoke a particular place while charting progress through a symbolic inner geography; and he must assert a fundamental difference (distance) from readers while preserving a sense of intimacy with them.

The evangelical missionary memoir was perhaps the contemporary genre that came closest to meeting Thoreau's demands for "a simple and sincere account" of a writer's life. Composed largely of posthumously published correspondence with friends and family relating the hardships of life in foreign lands and the progress of the soul's journey to God, missionary memoirs combine physical distance with emotional intimacy, and observation of specific places with intense scrutiny of spiritual geography. Thoreau himself seems to have recognized the similarity: in an 1849 draft of the second paragraph of "Economy" he explicitly invokes (and disavows) missionary writing as a literary model. The list of things the speaker "require[s] of every writer" continues several sentences beyond its current ending and notes that "he must describe those facts which he knows and loves better than anybody else—*He* must not write on Foreign Missions."[29] This reference to missionary literature preserved in the palimpsest of *Walden*'s manuscript history illuminates the contrast Thoreau draws in the next paragraph: "I would fain say something, not so much concerning the Chinese and Sandwich Islanders as you who read these pages, who are said to live in New England" (*W*, 4). He alludes not to secular travel literature but to the popular lectures and publications about the labors of Protestant missionaries overseas that "constituted most Americans' first significant exposure to non-Western cultures and non-Christian religions" in the nineteenth century.[30]

When Thoreau claims to "have travelled a good deal in Concord," where "the inhabitants have appeared to me to be doing penance in a thousand remarkable ways" that he compares to the ascetic acts of Hindu "Brahmins" (*W*, 4), he plays on his audience's familiarity with a genre of missionary literature marked by its focus on Asia and by its tendency to combine rapt descriptions of exotic places typical of travel narratives with uncomprehending and often hostile portrayals of local religious practices.[31] In turning his critical gaze from Chinese and Sandwich Islanders to New Englanders, Thoreau parodies this pattern, inverting not only its characteristic spatial dynamics—the journey from a supposedly enlightened Christian nation to a distant heathen land—but also its ontological dynamics: he wishes to speak to his audience's outward condition rather than their inward one, their "circumstances in *this* world" (4; emphasis added) rather than in the next. Rather than simply rejecting missionary discourse, Thoreau appropriates it, ironizes it, and turns it inside out.

At least one review suggests his audience got the joke: after Thoreau delivered his lecture titled "Economy—Illustrated by the Life of a Student" on December 20, 1848, the *Gloucester Telegraph* reported that "the lecturer gave a very strange account of the state of affairs at Concord. In the shops and offices were large numbers of human beings suffering tortures to which those of the Brahmins are mere pastimes. We cannot say whether this was in jest or in earnest. If a joke, it was a most excruciating one—if true, the attention of the Home Missionary Society should be directed to that quarter forthwith."[32] By casting his neighbors as the heathen next door, Thoreau reveals the power of missionary encounters a world away to reframe the local.

Thoreau's parody of the missionary memoir might invite any number of readings of *Walden*; here the genre's distinctive use of the protagonist's solitary spiritual ordeal to generate a translocal but affectively intimate community of readers serves to focus attention on the textual communities of *Walden*. Missionary memoirs elude familiar narratives of the secular print-based "imagined communities" of modern nation-states, instead building "imagined spiritual communities" that enabled readers to "imagin[e] themselves in a united spiritual, and generally Protestant, community."[33] *Walden* reproduces the memoir's tension between the text's intimate occasion (as private diaries and letters) and the publicity of their mediation in print. But where traditional memoirs use this tension to evoke an intimate community of Christian readers dispersed across North America and western Europe, Thoreau ultimately deploys it to imagine a textual community standing apart from any particular local or cultural identification—a detachment that marks a key feature of cosmic modernity.

Missionary memoirs mediate individualism and community in part through the interplay of two distinctive spatial imaginaries that parallel the tensions established at the outset of "Economy." Harriet Newell's memoir, which was compiled from her journals and letters after her death and appeared in more than fifty editions by 1840, illustrates how the genre combines a spatialized narrative of its hero's spiritual progress—what Gregory S. Jackson calls a "pilgrimage masterplot"—with an emphatically literal geography that presents the entire globe as an arena for Christian activism.[34] Newell's departure literalizes her spiritual pilgrimage: as she writes her mother after six weeks at sea, "My attachment to the world has greatly lessened since I left my country, and with it all the honors, pleasures, and riches of life. Yes, mama, I feel this morning like a pilgrim and a traveller in a dry and thirsty land, where no water is. Heaven is my home—there I trust my weary soul will sweetly rest, after a tempestuous voyage across the ocean of life" (*HN*, 167). Yet the missionary character of Newell's voyage superimposes that otherworldly pilgrimage onto a global geography with a very different cosmic chiaroscuro, as she asks, "When will the millennial state commence, and the lands which have long lain in darkness, be irradiated by the calm sunshine of the gospel? When will the populous regions of Asia and Africa, unite with this our Christian country in one general song of praise to God!" (143–44). By presenting its protagonist both as a solitary pilgrim fleeing from the "darkness" of "a sinful, stupid world" toward "God's marvellous light" (39) and as an emissary of a radiant "Christian country" charged with redeeming "lands which have long lain in darkness," Newell's memoir dramatizes the "'Christ and culture'" dilemma in which Protestant missionaries "assumed both a deeply affirming and a sharply critical stance toward their own culture."[35]

More broadly, Newell's text illuminates the competing impulses of otherworldliness and activism at the heart of antebellum evangelical culture and their figuration in spatial terms that would later be visualized in illustrated tracts and landscape paintings as what I have described as the homiletic and millennial landscapes (see chapter 1). Indeed, by the 1830s the American Tract Society's tract version of Newell's memoir depicted her gravestone nestled in a peaceful landscape on the Isle de France (Mauritius) (fig. 5.2), where she died in a mud hut seven weeks after giving birth to an infant daughter (who also perished) at sea. The engraving's urn-topped headstone and weeping willow mimic the memorial prints Currier & Ives marketed in the 1830s and 1840s to grieving family members (who would then inscribe the name of the departed loved one on the blank headstone), effectively pulling Newell into the intimate circle of familial mourning rituals.[36] An accompanying elegy penned by her grieving husband, declaring that "Thy weary pilgrimage on earth is o'er, / And thou hast reach'd thy wish'd for home at last," invites readers to interpret the cover illustration as the culmination of Newell's description of herself as "a pilgrim in this barren land" where "I wander from place to place and feel nowhere at home"—to understand the image, in short, as a homiletic landscape. And yet the pastoral scene of her final resting place "in a retired spot beneath the shade of an evergreen" suggests a land less barren than bounteous, simultaneously recalling her rapt description of Serampore as "the most delightful place I ever saw" and anticipating the day when she would "arrive at the destined port of rest" and "unite with the inhabitants of the New-Jerusalem."[37]

The ability of the landscape to figure the missionary's cultivation of otherworldliness while simultaneously projecting hopes of a future Christian paradise onto an exotic landscape found a stunning manifestation in the case of Harriet Ruggles Loomis a few decades later. Whereas Newell's tract begins with an image of her grave in a landscape and concludes by reproducing the stone's inscription, Loomis's gravestone itself depicts an elaborate landscape scene (fig. 5.3). Carved by Connecticut stonecutter James Craig, the marker shows the ship that in 1860 carried the Vermont native and her Presbyterian missionary husband to the West African island of Corisco, where she died of "African fever" in 1861, a month after losing her infant son in childbirth. Even as the marker allows Loomis to continue to speak from the grave, as it were, in phrases culled from correspondence and deathbed testimony demonstrating her pious resignation to the hardships of missionary life—"I never

> **NO. 169.**
>
> MEMOIR
> OF
> **MRS. HARRIET NEWELL,**
> WIFE OF THE
> *REV. SAMUEL NEWELL,*
> MISSIONARY TO INDIA.
>
> *See page 24.*
>
> PUBLISHED BY THE
> AMERICAN TRACT SOCIETY,
> AND SOLD AT THEIR DEPOSITORY, NO. 144 NASSAU-STREET, NEAR
> THE CITY-HALL, NEW-YORK; AND BY AGENTS OF THE
> SOCIETY, ITS BRANCHES, AND AUXILIARIES, IN
> THE PRINCIPAL CITIES AND TOWNS
> IN THE UNITED STATES.
> Vol. 6. E 2

FIGURE 5.2. "Memoir of Mrs. Harriet Newell, Wife of the Rev. Samuel Newell, Missionary to India." Wood engraving. From *Publications of the American Tract Society* (American Tract Society, n.d.), 6:101. Photo courtesy of The Newberry Library, Chicago, call no. C 691.033.

regretted coming to Africa"—the lush tropical landscape and neat rows of huts flanked by two larger framed buildings offer a vision of the moral and spatial order the missionaries sought to impose on the island beginning with the establishment of the Evangasimba Mission Station in 1850. In perhaps the stone's most arresting feature, a two-line inscription in the native language of Benga might suggest either the flowering of a harmonious bicultural Christian society depicted in the landscape or the ability of the natives to speak back to their

FIGURE 5.3. James Craig (carver), gravestone of Harriet Ruggles Loomis, 1861. Newbury, Vermont. Marble. 53 in. (134.6 cm). Farber Gravestone Collection, American Antiquarian Society. Courtesy, American Antiquarian Society.

colonizers; in fact it is a veiled expression of anguish and bitterness toward a missionary organization whose neglect Chauncey Loomis felt had cost him the lives of his wife and son: "I am full of remorse for the evils which you were forced to suffer in that place of sorrow. While today we are parted, in the tomorrow we will be united forever."[38] A missionary memoir in marble, Harriet Loomis's gravestone offers eloquent testimony to the genre's dual spatial narratives while at the same time hinting at the harsh realities and broken lives concealed beneath them.

As missionary memoirs superimpose the allegorical space of Puritan spiritual autobiography onto an exotic space of encounter more akin to the travel narrative, they face in two directions at once: even as the protagonist laments the spiritual state of the non-Christian cultures she observes, the text reflects critically on the spiritual state of her home country. Baptist missionary Ann H. Judson, for example, upon witnessing a traditional wedding procession in Calcutta and "a celebration of the worship of Juggernaut" in Serampore, writes to her sister, "Poor, miserable, deluded beings, they know not what they do. O Mary! the inhabitants of America know nothing of poverty, slavery and wretchedness, compared with the natives of India."[39] But even as Judson recoils at Indian religious practices (and downplays American poverty and slavery by comparison), her memoir ultimately functions to diagnose the spiritual torpor of her fellow Baptists at home. As the editor of Judson's memoir, James D. Knowles, explains in the text's final chapter, "It has been a favorite hope, which has cheered the labor of the Compiler, that this work would assist to invite the attention of our churches to the Burman mission, and to arouse the slumbering energies of the denomination to a degree of zeal and effort, commensurate with their numbers and their increasing power" (*AJ*, 313–14). Knowles highlights the clergy's failure to reap more converts in the United States, asking, "Have not some ministers preached the Gospel in this country, for an equal length of time, with all the advantages of a common language, of Sabbaths, Bibles, tracts, and numberless other auxiliaries to the ministry in a Christian land, without the conversion of a greater number of individuals than Mr. Judson has baptized in Burmah?" (314). The accusation reveals the moral geography typically evoked by the genre to be merely aspirational: the promise of a United States awash in the light of Gospel truth is not yet fulfilled. As Irene Quenzler Brown notes, missionary memoirs "were not so much intended for the missionary ground of the Near East, or the private world of the immediate family, as for the laity of an America facing the challenge of religious pluralism, competition, and disbelief."[40] What has not been adequately emphasized, however, is that memoirs like Judson's taught readers to view these local conditions through the lens of Protestantism's global encounter with religious difference and the eschatological imperatives that motivated it. The result we might call a form of "cosmic localism." It urged readers to adjust their moral appraisal of domestic problems like slavery in relation to the spiritual perils endured by "the perishing heathen of Asia" (*HN*, 160), while at the same time touting the zeal of missionaries abroad in order to galvanize believers at home and to indict them for their failure to promote revivals in their own churches.

Even as the missionary memoir promotes the extension of a fully formed Christian community to new continents, then, its purpose as a text is to build such a community in the first place at home. Similar to the Puritan jeremiad, the memoir functions as a community-building vehicle that sails out into the wilderness in order to constitute a Christian community in its wake that will be united by the image of Christianity's heathen other.[41] But in contrast to the local setting of a traditional jeremiad—a minister preaching to a particular community on a specific occasion—the missionary memoir presents the intimate correspondence between pious friends and relatives as the model for a translocal (and transtemporal) imagined community of believers mediated by print networks that stretch far beyond the nation.[42] Thus the Rev. William Ellis, a prominent English missionary to the South Seas, opened the memoir of his deceased wife, Mary Mercy Ellis, by evoking a community of believers that spans the globe and the ontological gap between worlds: "The disciples of Christ on earth and the redeemed in heaven are all related to one another. They compose but one family, and have one common home, in which all will ultimately meet."[43] The circulation of Mary Ellis's memoir, which was published first in London in 1835 and then a year later in Boston and New York, created a transatlantic community of readers that mirrored the correspondence network Ellis cultivated among her English and American "sisters in Christ" (*ME*, 252) in the South Seas mission. In light of the dialectic the genre establishes between the exemplarity of its pious heroes and the spiritual community they call into being, recognizing *Walden* as an inverted missionary memoir helps us understand the text not only in terms of the solitude and individualism it celebrates but also in terms of the communities it constitutes behind it, as it were. The operative question becomes, if Thoreau styles himself a missionary to New England's heathen, where is he a missionary *from*?

In one sense the speaker of *Walden* is from the village. By going to the woods he recapitulates the missionary's "errand into the wilderness," leaving New England behind and reporting back to his contemporaries as if "from a distant land" (*W*, 3). As Thoreau declares, "it is as solitary where I live as on the prairies. It is as much Asia or Africa as New England" (130). His encounters with the French-Canadian wood-chopper and Irish laborers place these Catholic figures in the position of natives in missionary accounts, and his thwarted efforts to "convert" them to his philosophy parodies the resistance that typically greets missionaries in their memoirs.[44] Thoreau's comic attempt to awaken the wood-chopper, who "had been instructed only in that innocent and ineffectual way in which the Catholic priests teach the aborigines," and in whom "the intellectual and what is called spiritual man . . . were slumbering as in an infant" (147), finally ends in failure: "I never, by any manoeuvring, could get him to take the spiritual view of things" (150). Similarly, long before his failed attempt to get John Field to give up "bogging" (204) and fish instead, Thoreau primes his audience to associate the Irish with Native peoples in North America and the Pacific: "Contrast the physical condition of the Irish with that of the North American Indian, or the South Sea Islander, or any other savage race before it was degraded by contact with the civilized man." Just as the "permanently contracted" bodies and stunted "limbs and faculties" of the Irish laborers recall the contorted bodies of the Hindu "Brahmins" in the opening pages of "Economy," economic development and immigration seem to have transformed the area around Concord into one of the dark "spots on the map" (35). Thoreau's mission to the woods becomes an attempt not simply to convert its Catholic laborers but to redeem nature itself from the commercial forces that have brought them there to chop down the trees, build the railroads, bog the meadows, and yank up the very ice from Walden Pond.

The community being formed behind these encounters, then, would seem to be the audience of well-educated Protestant "neighbors" (W, 4) whom Thoreau calls to awaken from "their present low and primitive condition" and to "rise to a higher and more ethereal life" (41). Unlike Newell's expansive "*christian community*" (HN, 27), the insistently local address that *Walden* retains from its early format as a series of lyceum lectures—its repeated appeals to "my townsmen" (3), "my neighbors" (4), those "here in Concord" (76)—summons a virtuous collective life on a smaller scale, exemplified by Thoreau's proposal for a local system of adult education that would turn New England "villages" into "universities" (109). Whereas the print medium projects the intimate correspondence between Mary Ellis and her "sisters in Christ" (ME, 252) outward into a single universal "family" (25) of believers, Ticknor and Fields's transatlantic print network amplifies *Walden*'s localist rhetoric rather differently, interpellating readers as citizens of many small, cohesive villages that are nonetheless microcosms of the whole—"universities" in the truest sense. In other words, the neglected communitarian element of Thoreau's thought recently explored by Christian Maul emerges not only from Thoreau's words but from their interaction with the material circulation of his texts, yielding a materially grounded politics well suited to the peripatetic author of "Walking."[45]

If in one sense the speaker of *Walden* is from the village, in another he is clearly from elsewhere. Indeed, the opening conceit of "Economy" is that he is a foreign observer of the village's strange rituals. He resembles less a Newell or a Judson than Henry Obookiah ('Ōpūkahaʻia), the Hawaiian Native and Christian convert who spent nearly a decade in New England before his death in 1818 and whose memoir subtly criticizes the spiritual pretensions of his hosts. To be sure, Obookiah's words were used to reinforce the moral geography promoted by the Congregationalist missionary organization that sponsored him, the American Board of Commissioners for Foreign Missions (ABCFM). As he wrote in a letter that was reprinted in an 1816 account of five Sandwich Islanders living in New England that the ABCFM published to raise money for its proposed Foreign Mission School in Cornwall, Connecticut, "I hope the Lord will send the Gospel to the heathen land, where the words of the Saviour never yet had been. Poor people, worship the wood and stone and shark, and almost every thing their gods; the Bible is not there, and heaven and hell they do not know about it." The school would provide "for the education of heathen youth in our country," who (it was hoped) would eventually return to their homelands to aid "in spreading the gospel among the heathen nations" and become "instruments of salvation to their benighted countrymen."[46] When Obookiah died of typhus in February 1818, the loss of the school's star pupil less than a year after opening its doors raised grave doubts about the future of the enterprise. But missionary advocates worked to convert the setback into a providential sign by elevating Obookiah into a kind of martyr, convinced, as Lyman Beecher put it in his funeral sermon, that "his death will give notoriety to this institution—will awaken a tender sympathy for Owhyhee, and give it an interest in the prayers and charities of thousands who otherwise had not heard of this establishment, or been interested in its prosperity."[47] This hope found fulfillment through the *Memoirs of Henry Obookiah* (1818).[48] Compiled by Obookiah's friend and mentor Edwin W. Dwight, the memoir became a sensation in New England and beyond, appearing in about a dozen editions over the next several decades and selling as many as one hundred thousand copies, with the proceeds initially going to the Foreign Mission School.[49] In the words of David W. Forbes, Obookiah's memoir "did more than any other work to interest the general public of New England in supporting a mission to the Hawaiian Islands." The interest (and money) the book generated helped fuel the twelve separate missionary expeditions the ABCFM dispatched to Hawaii between 1820 and 1848.[50]

And yet even as Obookiah's words circulated within a mediascape dedicated to promoting the extension of American missionary networks around the globe, they exerted subtle pressures on the hierarchy of heathenism. His account of his arrival in New York City in 1809 becomes a kind of reverse ethnography in which he marvels at "the curiosity" of watching a play in the theater and "how strange [it was] to see females eat with men" (*HO*, 17) while dining in private homes. After Obookiah experiences difficulty pronouncing certain English sounds and is told "'*Try*, Obookiah, it is *very easy*,'" he explains to his instructor (Dwight) "some of the habits and practices of his own country" (20), including a technique for drinking water out of one's hands; when Dwight is unable to do it and becomes "discouraged," Obookiah turns and "with a very expressive countenance said to him, '*Try, Mr. D., it is very easy*'" (21). This pointed lesson in cultural relativism approaches potentially dangerous territory when instruction turns to religious matters, in particular "the idols of the heathen"; yet here the pattern of imitation and satirical reversal is disrupted, as Dwight declares that Obookiah "was at once very sensibly impressed with the *ludicrous* nature of idol worship" (22). But if Dwight thus suppresses any sense of what "ludicrous" aspects of Christianity might be exposed through colonial encounter, later in the memoir Obookiah levels a different sort of critique at his hosts. Before his admission to church membership in Torringford, Connecticut, in April 1815, Obookiah asks the minister for the opportunity to speak to the congregation; while the minister fails to invite him to speak (claiming to have forgotten), Obookiah later tells him, "I want to ask the people, what they all waiting for? they live in Gospel land—hear all about salvation—God ready—Christ ready—all ready—Why they don't come to follow Christ?" (46). In his subsequent letters, Obookiah expands upon this critique, urging one correspondent not only to pray for "the poor ignorant people at Owhyhee" but to "pray for the poor people in this country as well as the heathen, for their hearts are not with God, and their ears are much deafer than that of the heathen—when they hear the word of God on every Sabbath, and can read the Holy scriptures" (51). Not unlike Phillis Wheatley claiming authority as a Christian convert to preach to white Harvard students through her poetry (see chapter 2), Obookiah uses his celebrity status as an instrument in "the hand of the Divine Providence [that] has brought me here, from that heathenish darkness" (52) to help "thoughtless and stupid sinners, both in this country as well as in other" (77).

Though perhaps not as subversive as Melville's proposal that "four or five Marquesan Islanders [be] sent to the United States as Missionaries," Obookiah's memoir nonetheless blurs the hierarchy of heathenism that placed white Americans at the "apex of both culture and Christianity," and in doing so begins to remap the moral geography of the Anglo-American Protestant missionary enterprise.[51] It demonstrates that the seeds of the countermapping impulse displayed in Thoreau's suggestion that the "heathen" in "our democratic New England towns . . . need to have a missionary sent to them" (*W*, 23) were already present within the missionary memoir itself. Moreover, Obookiah highlights the fact that Thoreau's rhetoric of heathen neighbors instantiated formally a social and religious diversity that already existed on the ground: thanks to commercial networks and religious institutions like the Foreign

Mission School, New England communities had for decades encountered not only Pacific Islanders but people from India, China, and elsewhere.[52] Considered as a figure for one of these foreign visitors, Thoreau's speaker hails not from Concord but from outside of it, and his effort to awaken the heathen in the village functions to constitute a coherent community here in the woods—as Lance Newman puts it, to "claim membership in a community of nature" of the sort Thoreau evokes when he asks, "Why has man just these species of animals for his neighbors . . . ?" (*W*, 225).[53]

Clearly, however, in a more fundamental sense Thoreau's speaker is not simply an observer from a particular place but inhabits a cosmic space that transcends the local altogether: "Both place and time were changed, and I dwelt nearer to those parts of the universe and to those eras in history which had most attracted me. Where I lived was as far off as many a region viewed nightly by astronomers" (*W*, 87–88). From this cosmic perspective, Thoreau's mission to the village seems intended to place his audience at a vantage point from which their own beliefs, customs, and rituals are rendered unfamiliar and strange. The textual community projected behind Thoreau's mission to the village is that of a network of readers who stand apart from any particular local or cultural affiliation, at least temporarily. Such a cosmic community of implied readers is neither the evangelical "priesthood of all believers" nor the hemispheric network of "cosmopolitan ambassadors of culture."[54] While their perspective might indeed be thought of as a form of cosmopolitanism, it lacks the political and secular connotations usually associated with the term. Rather, it resembles that of the practitioners of Romantic religious universalism, the transatlantic network of poets and scholars who combined the insights of German "Higher Criticism" of the Bible with the comparative approaches to Eastern scripture and myth developed in the "Oriental Renaissance."[55] This network included New England contemporaries such as James Freeman Clarke and Theodore Parker, who sought not to debunk religion but to distill the universal truths that lay behind its particular manifestations—believing, as Thoreau wrote, that mythology "contains only enduring and essential truth, the I and you, the here and there, the now and then, being omitted."[56] The readers hailed by such statements might not be world travelers, but as they seek to reconstruct a unified cosmos behind the diversity of religions, they move in the vertical dimension of modernity: they are cosmopolitans, with emphasis on the root *cosmos*.

The question of which way *Walden* faces—the woods or the village—is the key to Thoreau's appropriation of the missionary memoir, replacing the genre's characteristic polarity with an ambiguous circularity. Whereas missionary memoirs call upon readers to affirm a Christian identity in opposition to non-Christian others, Thoreau's readers are placed in the position of both the civilized neighbors left behind by the missionary *and* the heathen being preached to. Positioning his audience simultaneously as observers and observed, Thoreau creates a collective version of the experience of "doubleness" he describes in "Solitude," "by which I can stand as remote from myself as from another." By urging his audience to become its own "spectator," Thoreau seems to offer the possibility of a collective identity grounded upon a community's scrutiny and "criticism" (*W*, 135) of itself rather than on a sense of superiority over distant outsiders. In the process, he undermines the epistemological distinction anchoring evangelical identity—between "true religion," marked by "the essential continuity between thinking subject, object world, and divinity," and the "false religion" of "infidels" who lack this direct knowledge and hence suffer from "a state of being excessively mediated."[57]

While such collective self-scrutiny might seem to offer a localist alternative to a Protestant identity based on global difference, the global remains a powerful presence for Thoreau. When he used the lecture podium to criticize the citizens of Concord for their negative judgment of John Brown in 1859, for example, he again turned his neighbors into foreigners: "We dream of foreign countries, of other times and races of men, placing them at a distance in history or space; but let some significant event like the present occur in our midst, and we discover, often, this distance and this strangeness between us and our nearest neighbors. *They* are our Austrias, and Chinas, and South Sea Islands."[58] Thoreau's use of world geography to figure a local community divided over a pressing national issue captures the complex ways in which antebellum literary culture used the global to frame struggles over local, regional, and national identity. His cosmic localism belongs to a broader cultural enterprise of mapping moral geographies within and beyond the nation. This enterprise constructed the U.S. South, for example, as a site of foreign otherness within the nation, a space where national sins such as slavery and Indian Removal were projected as well as the displaced specter of urban industrialism—what Jennifer Rae Greeson calls "the dark satanic field of U.S. industrial modernity."[59] Whether it was Thoreau comparing his neighbors to Sandwich Islanders or abolitionists pleading for benevolent Protestants to consider the enslaved "heathen at home" (see chapter 2), their engagement with missionary discourse shows not only that reading the global was a condition of constructing domestic space but also that religious difference played a crucial role in that construction. By inscribing the "cosmic drama" of the missionary encounter onto the spaces of modern capitalism, antebellum writers helped produce the numinous, networked spaces of cosmic modernity.[60]

While Thoreau's engagement with the missionary memoir illuminates a widespread cultural practice of imagining the local as a microcosm of global difference, this cosmic localism is balanced by a centrifugal impulse that explodes local forms of community, transcending local affiliations in order to claim membership in a community defined by a shared orientation to truth. These cosmic communities are very different from the "imagined communities" familiar from Benedict Anderson's work on nationalism. To take an example discussed earlier, the evangelical "priesthood of all believers" that unites Christians across vast physical, temporal, and cosmic divides depends on conceptions of language, space, and time that are in many senses closer to those Anderson associates with premodern "sacred communities" than with the forms of print capitalism, bounded territories, and "simultaneity" that he argues ground the modern nation-state.[61] Thoreau's reworking of the missionary memoir helps us see evangelicalism as just one of many nineteenth-century communities connected by what Latour would call "nonmodern" temporalities and spatialities, as well as by a range of what Webb Keane terms "semiotic forms" not limited to printed texts or even to language itself.[62] These communities might include Thoreau's meeting with the "priest of Brahma" (W, 298), Homer, and other historical figures within the frame of nature's seasonal cycles. But they would also include the many bereaved Americans who stepped outside the linear flow of modern time into the sacred time of mourning, and perhaps reunited with departed loved ones through spirit mediums.[63] Above all, they might include the diverse communities of nineteenth-century popular religion, including Mormons, Millerites, and practitioners of obeah as they used gold plates, charts, and obi (bundles of empowered objects) to inhabit a shared cosmos.[64] Such communities complicate Taylor's narrative of modernity as a process of the "Great Disembedding" of individuals from the hierarchical communal structures that link them to the cosmos, to enter into an unmediated, "direct-access society" of nation-states, free markets, and the public sphere.[65] The cosmic communities (or "collectives" in Latour's sense, since they include "humans and nonhumans") evoked by Thoreau and his evangelical interlocutors reveal that beneath the "purification" of disembedding and direct access, modernity has been busily spinning off "hybrids," forms of cosmic belonging mediated by new practices, objects, and institutions; and they suggest that recent theories of religion and secularization might gain from shifting focus from modern individuals to nonmodern collectives.[66]

The Heathen Within: Globalizing Modernity and the Cosmic Self

In the previous section, the missionary memoir served to revise traditional understandings of *Walden* as a localist, individualist manifesto. A neglected facet of *Walden*'s literary ecology revealed how the text recasts local relationships in terms of global encounters and reimagines community based on cosmic detachment rather than local proximity. But in addition to showing how an American literary tradition known for its defense of place and solitude engages with emergent modern forms of space and community, the missionary context enables a richer understanding of the forms of selfhood constructed by that tradition. The present section shifts focus from Thoreau's efforts to reform his neighbors—the heathen next door—to his efforts to purify himself. Given that "a man" is "a microcosm," the rhetorical question posed in "Economy"—"Under what latitudes reside the heathen to whom we would send light?" (W, 77)—implicitly points not simply to New England but also to the reader's own inner latitudes.

The account of the microcosmic self that punctuates "Economy" and the "Conclusion" conveys something of the unity and autonomy that mark what Charles Taylor calls the modern "buffered self," which erects a boundary between itself and the world such that the "self can see itself as invulnerable, as master of the meanings of things for it" and thus as capable "of giving its own autonomous order to its life." As Thoreau puts it, "Every man is the lord of a realm beside which the earthly empire of the Czar is but a petty state, a hummock left by the ice." At the same time, Thoreau's spatialization (and globalization) of the self injects a sense of otherness and multiplicity that is absent from Taylor's formulation. Here the self is figured as both the explorer and the unfamiliar terrain he moves through—"our own interior white on the chart" (W, 321)—or, translated into the cultural terms of Thoreau's missionary persona, as both the Western missionary and the heathen lands he encounters. This doubleness penetrating the heart of the individual represents not so much a return to a premodern "porous self"—one that is "open and porous and vulnerable" to the "spirits, demons, [and] cosmic forces" of an enchanted world—as an alternative form of modern selfhood that is porous in a different way.[67]

A particularly rich facet of Thoreau's engagement with missionary discourse, the conflicted rhetoric of heathenism that he developed in his essays and journals in the 1840s and 1850s, provides a point of entry into the development of this modern cosmic self. Early in his literary career Thoreau displayed both playful identification with and deep respect for the non-Christian systems of ideas and values that he termed "heathen." Writing to Lidian Emerson during his sojourn in Staten Island in 1843, Thoreau asked after her young daughter: "How does the Saxon Edith do? Can you tell yet to which school of philosophy she belongs—whether she will be a fair saint of some Christian order, or a follower of Plato and the heathen?" (C, 144). Earlier that year he had confided to Ralph Waldo Emerson that Lidian "almost persuades me to be a Christian, but I fear I as often lapse into heathenism" (77). But by 1846 Thoreau made clear which he identified with: "Some with whose prejudices or peculiar bias I have no faith—yet inspire me with confidence—and I trust they confide in me also as a religious heathen at least—a good Greek" (*PJ*, 2:239). This "good heathen" persona appears again in *A Week on the Concord and Merrimack Rivers* (1849), where Thoreau repeats his claim to be "a religious heathen at least,—a good Greek" and defends the "heathenish integrity" of a Sunday morning against the dour Christian Sabbath-goers of Billerica.[68] And it appears in the development of *Walden*'s hero, who in the first (1847) draft of the text declares that "the morning is to everyone the season of his ideal life. Then, if ever, we can realize the life of the Greeks—and we are all at some time good heathens enough to acknowledge and worship their Aurora."[69] Walking along the railroad causeway, he could joke that "when the frost had smitten me on one cheek, heathen as I was, I turned to it the other also" (*W*, 266).

The lightness and irony of these moments of professed heathenism should not obscure the serious critique Thoreau leveled against the assumed superiority of Christianity over other faiths. His account of Ossian in an essay published in *The Dial* in 1844 insists that "we cannot but respect the vigorous faith of those heathen, who sternly believed somewhat, and are inclined to say to the critics, who are offended by their superstitious rites, don't interrupt these men's prayers. As if we knew more about human life and a God, than the heathen and ancients."[70] The passage's subtle shift from the past tense (those who "sternly believed") to prayers that seem to be occurring in the present indicates the extension of Thoreau's defense of classical and ancient cultures to contemporary non-Christian ones. As he wrote in his *Journal* in 1850, "I do not prefer one religion or philosophy to another—I have no sympathy with the bigotry & ignorance which make transient & partial & puerile distinctions between one man's faith or form of faith & anothers—as christian & heathen—I pray to be delivered from narrowness partiality exaggeration—bigotry. To the philosopher all sects all nations are alike. I like Brahma—Hare Buddha—the Great spirit as well as God" (*PJ*, 3:62).

Thoreau even envisioned promoting this amalgam of world religions by co-opting evangelical strategies of print dissemination and missionary activity: "It would be a catholic enterprise for this age to print in a series or collectively the Scripture or sacred writings of the several nations the Chinese the Hindoos the Persians the Hebrews or Selections from them—as the written and the recorded truth— ... This would unquestionably be the Bible or book of books. A precious volume which let the missionaries send to the uttermost parts of the earth—what God has revealed of himself to all nations" (*PJ*, 2:259–60). This prospectus for an eclectic competitor to the American Bible Society that would distribute the "world bible" envisioned by some Transcendentalists—a project partially realized in the "Ethnical Scriptures" column that Emerson and Thoreau compiled from Hindu, Confucian, Zoroastrian, Hermetic, and

Buddhist texts and published in *The Dial* from 1842 to 1844—plays on the extraordinary agency Protestant missionaries attributed to the Bible and print more generally and hints that their faith in the print medium amounted to a form of fetishism, "a false imputation of agency" in Webb Keane's words.[71] In each of these instances, Thoreau previews the missionary persona he adopts in *Walden*, emptying out the Christian-heathen binary and positing a fundamental equivalence between belief systems as he promotes a modern conception of religion as a universal category of human knowledge.

Yet even as Thoreau identified with the heathen and defended non-Christian faiths, laying the groundwork for the anti-Christian hero of *Walden* as a "worshipper of Aurora" (*W*, 88) and a student of Hindu scripture, elsewhere he expressed suspicion of heathen "superstition." In an 1852 *Journal* entry he assumes a cosmic vantage point from which all cultures seem equally distant—and equally heathenish:

> It is unsafe to defer so much to mankind & the opinions of society—for these are always & without exception heathenish & barbarous—seen from the heights of philosophy. A wise man sees as clearly the heathenism & barbarity of his own countrymen—as clearly as those of the nations to whom his countrymen send missionaries. The Englishman & American are subject to equally many national superstitions with the Hindoo & Chinese. My countrymen are to me foreigners. I have but little more sympathy with them than with the mob of India or of China. (*PJ*, 4:258)

Just as the equivalence of all faiths to the philosopher enabled Thoreau to find truth in non-Christian traditions in the 1850 *Journal* entry quoted earlier, here a similar perspective—figured spatially as the view from "heights of philosophy"—serves a critical function. In contrast to the "good heathen" who enjoy "vigorous faith" and a direct relationship to nature and the universe, this bad heathenism is at work when Thoreau declares the Gold Rush to be "perfectly heathenish" (*C*, 296) and compares it to "the infatuation of the Hindoos who have cast themselves under the car of Juggernaut";[72] when he dismisses Spiritualism as "superstition" and its participants as "heathen" (*C*, 284); or when he criticizes slavery as "the worship of idols, which at length changes the worshipper into a stone image himself; and the New Englander is just as much an idolater as the Hindoo" (*RP*, 120).

Each of these examples is marked by a corrupting attachment to objects, whether in the form of gold, the wooden medium of spirit rappings, or the human body itself. Similar instances of modern fetishism—of disordered relationships between people and objects—fill the pages of *Walden*: the farmer who is "crushed and smothered" (5) by his barn, the railroad that "rides upon us" (92), the men who "have become the tools of their tools" (37). When

Thoreau likens the "United States Bank" to "an Egyptian temple" and declares that "the religion and civilization which are barbaric and heathenish build splendid temples; but what you might call Christianity does not" (58), he makes explicit this association between modern alienation and the fetishism of non-Christian religions, reproducing the hostility toward those traditions expressed in many missionary texts.[73] Even his admiration for aspects of those religions betrays this Protestant bias as he celebrates written texts over other semiotic forms: "How much more admirable the Bhagvat-Geeta than all the ruins of the East!" (57). In its insistence that readers turn from physical "monuments" (58) to textual and internal ones—perfecting their "abstract thought" rather than their "architecture," and taking "pains . . . to smooth and polish their manners" rather than "hammering stone" (57)—*Walden* dramatizes its project of self-reform as a struggle of Christian spirituality against heathen materialism.

Deployed by turns as a badge of honor and an insult, heathenism becomes the link between Thoreau's critique of New England culture and the drive toward personal purity that emerges most forcefully in the chapter titled "Higher Laws." The dialectic of identification with and revulsion toward heathen alternatives to Protestant Christianity parallels the ambivalence scholars have noted in the speaker's stance toward nature—his conflicted attraction to what he calls the "wild" and the "good" (*W*, 210). As Neill Matheson has shown, Thoreau's exuberant embrace of his own inner animal, epitomized by his impulse to devour the woodchuck in "Higher Laws," collides in that chapter with his drive to purify himself of all traces of animal appetite through vegetarianism and sexual abstinence. Following Giorgio Agamben, Matheson argues that this apparent contradiction reflects a broader disjunction in Western culture between two distinct conceptions of the human: one as a species in opposition to animal species, and another that locates the boundary between the human and the animal *within* the individual person. Although this conflict is not resolved in "Higher Laws," Matheson argues that Thoreau's recognition of "animality within the human" provides the basis for an expanded "ethic of neighborliness" that includes "nonhuman animals as neighbors" in the remainder of *Walden*.[74] The present analysis makes clear that Thoreau's drive for purification in "Higher Laws" is carried out in relation to the inner heathen as well as the inner animal: "Nature is hard to be overcome, but she must be overcome. What avails it that you are Christian, if you are not purer than the heathen, if you deny yourself not more, if you are not more religious?" (221). In other words, the tension between two opposing views of nature that Catherine L. Albanese finds exemplified in "Higher Laws"—between "Nature Real" ("a view of matter as 'really real,' the embodiment of Spirit and the garment of God") and "Nature Illusory" ("a view of matter as illusion and unreality")—corresponds to a tension in Thoreau's attitude toward religion that locates *Walden* within a quite different cultural trajectory. Just as the conflict between what Albanese calls Thoreau's "spiritual paganism" and his "quest for moral purity and purification" reflects the divided legacy of American nature religion and anticipates the contradictions that would bedevil twentieth-century environmentalism, the ambivalence between his professed heathenism and his impulse toward Protestant purity situates him within an equally vexed history of religious encounter reaching from Christian missions to the early twentieth-century discourse of world religions. But whereas some critics see only "confusion" and "vacillation" behind such ambivalence, Matheson's mediation of the animal/human binary raises the possibility that Thoreau's struggle between heathenism and purity opens the way for a more capacious mode of being in which these internalized figures could coexist.[75]

While Thoreau's Protestant imperative to convert the heathen within reproduces the imperial logic of missionary discourse in a sense, recent theorizations of Christian missions suggest that his dramatization of the missionary encounter in the microcosm of the self also evokes an alternative form of modern selfhood that would enable the heathen within to speak. Thoreau's urge to stamp out the inner heathen in "Higher Laws" foregrounds the potentially coercive and destructive aspects of the Romantic "voyage" (320) of self-exploration celebrated in *Walden*. Recognizing that voyage as a missionary enterprise highlights an imperative not merely to discover and chart the vast reaches of the self but to reform and convert them. One imagines the missionary home-cosmographer sailing from one inner continent to the next, preaching here, distributing tracts there, foisting new disciplinary regimes on the natives, saving souls by destroying difference. Yet this caricature does not seem true to the ethos of *Walden*, which repeatedly insists on heeding and honoring the impulses that elude the discipline of the self. As Thoreau counsels in "Higher Laws," "If one listens to the faintest but constant suggestions of his genius, which are certainly true, he sees not to what extremes, or even insanity, it may lead him; and yet that way, as he grows more resolute and faithful, his road lies" (216). If such moments of receptivity and faith are understood to register the voice of Thoreau's inner heathen, his inward missionary voyage begins to look less like the one-sided process of "cultural imperialism" portrayed by an earlier generation of theorists and more like the complex cultural encounters that make the missionary field the epitome of what Ryan Dunch describes as the dual process of "globalizing modernity," in which the "universalizing" thrust of the spread of Western ideas is counterbalanced by "cultural differentiation" as host populations selectively resist and appropriate those ideas.[76] Moreover, as Saba Mahmood suggests, the effects of the missionary encounter were not limited to host cultures but exerted a profound influence on missionaries' home cultures as well.[77] In Latour's terms, the imperative of personal "purification" emphasized in "Higher Laws" can be thought of as concealing the creative forces of "translation" (or "hybridization") unleashed by the missionary encounter.[78] Far from being safely buffered from the outside world, *Walden*'s cosmic self is modern precisely in the way it internalizes the social and cultural encounters of globalizing modernity and recasts them as a compelling psychological and spiritual drama.

As it does so, *Walden* approaches in key respects the form of selfhood nurtured by the tradition of evangelical memoir it parodies. Bruce Hindmarsh has argued that the evangelical conversion narrative that emerged in the eighteenth century represents a modern alternative to the bourgeois narrative identity that privileges individual autonomy and self-fashioning. Whereas texts such as Benjamin Franklin's *Autobiography* narrate a form of identity that "is wholly immanent and springs, as it were, genetically, out of the resources of the subject itself, without reference to external authority," evangelicals like David Brainerd and the English Baptist convert Anne Dutton (1692–1765) speak for a very different form of modern identity, one that emphasizes the self as profoundly shaped by others—by a "community of faith . . . that was as much discovered as it was constructed by human agency"—and ultimately by the transcendent power of God. This "evangelical sense of self [that] involved *both* creativity and discovery, *both* individuation and community," leads Hindmarsh to find in evangelical conversion narratives "an alternative version of Enlightenment individuality" and a corrective to what he describes (following Foucault) as "the 'anthropological sleep' of the modern self"—the myth that that enabled the "self-made man" to "quietly and blissfully elid[e] the contribution that others had made to his identity and the extent to which his autobiography was his own fiction."[79] A version of this alternative individuality appears in nineteenth-century missionary memoirs, where a profound sense of individual responsibility and agency coexists with an all-encompassing providential design and a pious resignation to suffering. But such nonmodern alternatives can also be found outside of evangelical traditions—even within a Romantic literary tradition that is often hastily cited as representative of self-reliant, expressive individualism.[80] Thoreau's experiment inhabiting such a cosmic self in *Walden* is illuminating in part because it reveals surprising "cross-currents" and "cross-pressures" (as Taylor would call them) between the transatlantic evangelical tradition Hindmarsh explores and a Transcendentalist literary culture that would rather, as Thoreau's Aunt Maria complained, "hear the frogs croak" than "read the life of Chalmers."[81]

Such queer collisions of values and belief systems represent part of a much broader "nova effect" that Taylor argues began in the nineteenth century and continues today, "spawning an ever-widening variety of moral/spiritual options."[82] Of particular relevance to the present study is what that process reveals about the influence evangelicals have had on the kinds of stories Americans tell about the land. To suggest that one of the foundational texts of American environmentalism was shaped in profound ways by a popular genre of evangelical memoir is to lend support to the conclusion that historian Mark R. Stoll has reached about the centrality of Protestant Reformed ideas and institutions to the origins of the American environmental movement.[83] But if Thoreau can be considered at some level a practitioner of apocalyptic geography—one who uses the landscape to reveal the nature of ultimate reality and the unfolding of sacred history—it's clear that he did not look toward any kind of immanent, historical millennium. If anything, his inversion of the missionary encounter into an internal drama in *Walden* echoes what Emerson famously called "the apocalypse of the mind," a dialectical process in which expansive moments of vision give way to self-eclipse, which in turn opens onto further revelations in a series of expanding circles.[84] As Alan D. Hodder describes it, "Each stroke of expansion creates a new vision; each stroke of renunciation and contraction abolishes that vision to make way for the new." This "upward spiraling" structure, he argues, recapitulates the pattern of Christian sacred history from the Bible: "Just as in the cosmic apocalypse, where destruction of the world must precede the new creation, so here dissolution of the self precedes the beatific vision of self in God."[85] When Thoreau's "inward apocalypse" is reflected back upon the processes of global modernity that informed it, this dissolution implies a missionary encounter in which the self-evident authority of religious knowledge is ruptured, and heathen words and lands assume a startling agency.[86]

What can a reanimation of the cosmic offer American literary studies? Toni Wall Jaudon has argued that early nineteenth-century literary accounts of obeah religious practices in the Caribbean reveal "a world differently organized" than "the reasonable, objective forms of sense perception that were gaining traction in the Enlightenment," a world she identifies as "a cosmography—a 'totality' within which human life is understood to unfold."[87] Paying greater attention to the traces of such worlds in the literary archive, she argues, can counter the long-standing tendency to conflate religion and Protestant Christianity in American literary studies, as well as the implicit secular bias in the field's more recent transnational turn. While Jaudon's analysis suggests a neat divide between the cosmic imagination of creole religions and the rationality of Enlightenment and Protestant secularism, Thoreau's engagement with the missionary memoir demonstrates that nonmodern epistemologies, collectives, and subjectivities emerge not only from the spatial and social margins but from the Protestant center. Cosmic localism suggests that the erasure of non-Protestant religious difference that Tracy Fessenden notes has enabled "equating American Protestantism with American culture" was countered by cultural practices that reinscribed global religious difference within the microcosm of the local.[88] Cosmic communities capture the ways modern imagined communities extend not just beyond the nation-state but beyond the human itself. And the cosmic self reveals how modern individuals, far from simply becoming buffered selves, the sole source of agency and value in a disenchanted world, may remain "responsive to callings from some source outside ourselves," whether transcendent or immanent, and come to define "human flourishing" in terms of "*harmony* with the demands of external callings"—a responsiveness Akeel Bilgrami calls a form of "reenchantment in a secular age."[89] To return to Latour one final time, the accounts of modernity critiqued here remain largely narratives of purification; what is needed now is a literary history of translation. Such an account might reveal that literature all along has been a space where the modern illusion that we "all inhabit the same world," "*the one* cosmos," has been challenged by the fact of cosmic multiplicity—by the reality that a shared cosmos is not given but must be negotiated—and that as such, literature was and remains a vital resource for building a truly common world.[90]

In a *Journal* entry dated January 1857, Thoreau returned to a theme that had occupied him for more than a decade:

> I wish to get the Concord, the Massachusetts, the America, out of my head and be sane a part of every day. If there are missionaries for the heathen, why not send them to me? I wish to know something; I wish to be made better. I wish to forget, a considerable part of every day, all mean, narrow, trivial men (and this requires usually to forego and forget all personal relations so long), and therefore I come out to these solitudes, where the problem of existence is simplified. I get away a mile or two from the town into the stillness and solitude of nature, with rocks, trees, weeds, snow about me. I enter some glade in the woods, perchance, where a few weeds and dry leaves alone lift themselves above the surface of the snow, and it is as if I had come to an open window. I see out and around myself. (*J*, 9:208–9)

In this quietly searching passage we glimpse a persona very different from the abrasive, outspoken critic of "Economy." Instead of insisting that his heathen neighbors "need to have a missionary sent to them," here Thoreau evinces uncertainty, an acknowledgment of his own incompleteness and insufficiency. Rather than a "good heathen," *Walden*'s healthy "worshipper of Aurora," here he stands as one genuinely in need of light. Here it is not confident knowledge but the experience of *not* knowing that proves decisive, precipitating reciprocal forms of porousness as "the Concord, the Massachusetts, the America," are enabled to pass "out of my head," while he himself passes out of town and into the woods. But these liberating passages are only preparatory to the most freeing passage of all, as the speaker becomes porous to himself, emerging from himself like the objects that "lift themselves" from the field of snow—or like that "strong and beautiful bug" that hatches from the "dry leaf" of a New England table to a "beautiful and winged life" (*W*, 333). Is not *Walden*'s final image of the dawn an awakening from a kind of anthropological sleep? As a moment of humility gives way to a new clarity of vision beyond the self, Thoreau intimates not simply a passage out of society to solitude but out of one form of selfhood into another, and into a new way of being with others.

6

The Sensational Republic

CATHOLIC CONSPIRACY AND THE BATTLE
FOR THE GREAT WEST

AS THOREAU AND HIS FELLOW Transcendentalists searched for a cosmic perspective from which the world's religious diversity would coalesce into a universalistic form of spirituality, other Americans who surveyed the religious landscape at midcentury saw vast armies massing for an impending holy war. Many Protestants expected the decisive battle of this apocalyptic struggle to occur in the Mississippi Valley, the very terrain long believed to guarantee the cheap land and free labor necessary to preserve republican liberty from the corruption and despotism they saw embodied in the Roman Catholic Church.[1] While this stark apocalyptic geography drew deeply from the words of evangelical preachers and publications in northeastern cities, its dark conspiratorial energy rippled across the antebellum mediascape and fed a spatial imaginary in the West with its own cosmic contours.[2] There, in cities including Cincinnati, St. Louis, Pittsburgh, Louisville, and Detroit, a set of vibrant regional literary cultures emerged that used popular genres of sensational fiction (along with their vivid anti-Catholic imagery) to challenge the claims of eastern elites to cultural, political, economic, and spiritual authority—and ultimately to expose deep fissures in American secularity itself.

A striking example of how the landscape mediated these regional and cosmic conflicts appears in a neglected city-mysteries novel by Emil Klauprecht, a prominent German American journalist and editor in Cincinnati's German-language press during the 1840s and 1850s.[3] In the culminating scene of Klauprecht's *Cincinnati, oder Geheimnisse des Westens* (*Cincinnati; or, The Mysteries of the West*; 1854–55), the Anglo-American protagonist, Washington Filson, stands on Mount Adams and surveys a "perfect panorama of the city of Cincinnati and its surroundings," where "the fabulous history of this region, with its sudden transition from the savage isolation of the primeval forest to the noisy bustle of a populous metropolis is displayed before him." Filson's eye

FIGURE 6.1. Asher B. Durand, *Progress (The Advance of Civilization)*, 1853. Oil on canvas, 58 7/16 × 82¼ in. (framed) (148.43 × 208.92 cm). Virginia Museum of Fine Arts, Richmond. Gift of an anonymous donor. Photo: Travis Fullerton. © Virginia Museum of Fine Arts.

traces a path from the horizon, where "the forest heights of Kentucky yet wave, as lonely and dense as in the days of Boone and Kenton," through "log cabins and fences and clearings," to the nearer "commodious frame houses built of boards or brick and shaded by orchards," and finally across the Ohio River to the city itself, the "daughter of free labor," spangled "with railroads and canals, with her hundreds of steamers, factories and shops."[4] Under Filson's gaze the landscape materializes a progressive narrative of frontier history, as if he stands in the radiant industrial future depicted in Asher B. Durand's *Progress (The Advance of Civilization)* (1853) (fig. 6.1) looking back over the technological and economic changes that have unfolded across the picture space.[5] But in contrast to the "confidently nationalistic message" Durand conveys as (in Angela Miller's words) he "telescope[s] the discrete stages of America's movement from wilderness to civilization into one image," Klauprecht celebrates regional identity in a manner analogous to the boosterish views frequently featured in the local press, including views by Klauprecht's own lithography firm (fig. 6.2).[6]

Looming over this prosperous scene, however, is a sight that signals the region's grave peril, for in "the middle of this broad, rich panorama was the cathedral, which was still being built" (*CMW*, 624). The rising spire of a Catholic church recalls the shadowy Jesuits who have hounded Filson for the entire

FIGURE 6.2. Klauprecht & Menzel (lithographers), *Cincinnati in 1841*, 1841. Color lithograph, 5½ × 9 1/3 in. (13.9 × 23.7 cm). I. N. Phelps Stokes Collection of American Historical Prints. New York Public Library, Stokes 1841-F-37.

novel. As he stands contemplating this "fortress against Protestantism" (624) he is approached by former U.S. senator Thomas Hart Benton of Missouri, who reveals that thanks to an old legal dispute, Filson is the legitimate owner of the entire city. Warning that "a dark time is coming for our republic" (629), Benton reveals a Jesuit plot to seize Cincinnati and ultimately to overthrow republican governments in America and Europe. He urges Filson to sell the city to a group of New York real estate agents in order to fund a national print campaign to mobilize public opinion against the Jesuits. But Filson, who has fought for the republican cause in Mexico and in Europe, recognizes this plan as a plot to capture the city for eastern elites. He makes his own appeal to republican values by again turning to the prospect:

> This productive city lies at our feet, and thousands of brave craftsmen have erected a homestead for their children with the sweat of their brows; thousands of widows and orphans have nothing save a few feet of land, and I am supposed to send the usurers of New York to them to drive them from their well-earned possessions to instill them with increased dislike for the laws of the land and its officers, which are unfortunately so often ready to build the palace of a rich man on the ruins of the hovels of the poor? (630)

Speaking in the accents of republican "producer ideology," Filson tears up the original document of sale and declares that "this beautiful valley does not belong to the heirs of [his grandfather] John Filson. The men of craftsmen's ability and commercial daring, the factory owners and the merchants, the artists and the mechanics, in a word, the people has made this ground their own, has crowned the daughter of the wilderness as Queen of the West" (632).[7]

The scene at Mount Adams combines two distinct traditions of spatial imagination. In the first, originating in eighteenth-century republican political theory, the elevated prospect embodies the white male viewer's status as an independent citizen whose virtue enables him to transcend political faction and economic self-interest to govern in the name of the common good.[8] In the second, a form of Protestant sacred geography reaching back to the earliest English colonization of the Americas, the continental interior represents Catholic space—traversed by Jesuit missionaries, occupied by French and Spanish forces, and inhabited by crypto-Catholic Indians.[9] By combining the republican prospect with this image of the West as Catholic space, Klauprecht pits a prosperous regional landscape against a centralized papal order that many antebellum Protestants saw ominously embodied in the cathedrals, seminaries, and other Catholic buildings sprouting up in cities throughout the United States.[10] Catholicism becomes a symbol of a host of external forces that threaten to dominate the region, including the distant, powerful institutions that Benton himself represents: New York banks, the U.S. government, even evangelical benevolent organizations.[11] And crucially, Filson's ability to recognize these threats depends not on arguments or reasoned debate but on his immediate perception of the landscape.

The spatial mode of political pedagogy on display in Klauprecht's novel and other works of sensational fiction produced in the region known as the "Great West" is the subject of this chapter. That pedagogy used the landscape to help western readers grasp the perilous nature of their geopolitical and cosmic situation and to rehearse the virtues and actions necessary to salvage it. In tales of virtuous working girls and mechanics, greedy bankers and Jesuits, and bloodthirsty outlaws and Indian renegades that were serialized in weekly story papers and reprinted in cheap pamphlet novels, this regional corner of what David Anthony calls the "sensational public sphere" evoked a set of alluring but dangerous spaces that helped readers cognitively map an expanding federal republic and an emerging market society in a manner analogous to the evangelical mediascape explored in earlier chapters of this book.[12] But just as Thoreau parodied the sacred geography of Protestant world missions, regional authors and editors undertook a form of cosmic countermapping, constructing alternative geographies that revised Protestant calls to wage holy war in the West. While at times echoing evangelicals' nativist rhetoric, regional literati translated those warnings of apocalyptic doom into republican jeremiads that urged readers to resist the creeping specter of civic corruption, cultural colonization, economic exploitation, and political domination.

By tracing that regionalist project, this chapter undertakes its own form of countermapping to expand the geographical contours of nineteenth-century sensational fiction. Standard accounts have failed to engage this literary terrain in part because the Great West is simply not part of a critical mental map that remains fixated on northeastern publishing centers and imperial peripheries. Compounding the problem, an overly narrow focus on the city itself—on the labyrinthine, dungeon-like spaces of George Lippard, George Thompson, and other sensational authors—has led critics to interpret city-mysteries fiction primarily in terms of the rise of crime, prostitution, and other aspects of urban history at the expense of a broader set of political issues including the relations of cities to their hinterlands, and regional and sectional rivalries.[13] Finally, while critics have carefully analyzed the dynamics of class, race, and gender in sensational fiction, they have largely neglected the role of religion in the sensational imagination, an omission that is particularly problematic given the field's emphasis on works set in Catholic borderlands.[14] Correcting these biases makes possible a more textured literary history that reclaims a rich patchwork of regional literary and print cultures, expands our sense of the political stakes of "sensation," and illuminates how colonial sacred geographies shaped the production of modern secular space in antebellum America.

This chapter also aims to trouble our understanding of republicanism in antebellum political culture. Regional literary production provides a window into the "regional and class-based variations in the evolution and uses of republican ideology" that Steven J. Ross has argued must be distinguished from the elite national voices privileged by the historians who forged the "republican synthesis" of the 1960s and 1970s.[15] Considering cheap pamphlet novels and regional story papers as expressions of "alternative republicanism" developed by slaves and other "subaltern peoples" connects sensational literature to the elite body of orations, essays, sermons, and novels that Sandra M. Gustafson associates with "modern republicanism" in the early nineteenth century.[16] But in contrast to the "deliberative fictions" of Lydia Maria Child and James Fenimore Cooper, which place reasoned argument and public debate at the center of republican practice, the works examined in this chapter cast civic virtue in terms of immediate perception—the sort that enables Filson to grasp the falsity of Benton's arguments as clearly as he sees the city before him.[17] In what I call "perceptual fictions," republican self-government is more like looking at a painting than weighing arguments on the Senate floor. By shifting focus from deliberation to perception, sensational fiction goes beyond a critique of public discourse to diagnose the process of political mediation that makes deliberation possible in the first place. It suggests that what causes democratic institutions to break down is not simply a failure of deliberation but a problem rooted in the very structure of modern liberal democracies.

As Talal Asad has argued, that structure is marked by problems of mediation that bedevil the fiction of "direct access" in modern secular societies—the idea that all individuals enjoy equal, unmediated access to the rights of citizenship, debate in the public sphere, and participation in the free market.[18] Noting a widening gap between citizens and their elected representatives, the growing influence of lobbyists and pressure groups on politics, and increasing corporate control of media outlets, Asad argues not only that "in crucial ways this is not at all a direct-access society" but that the modern nation is "always mediated"—by images in the mass media, by political symbols, and above all by a notion of citizenship that subsumes individual affiliations such as "class, gender, and religion" (and I would add region and race) within a national identity. This process of "transcendent mediation," Asad argues, is the essence of modern secularism.[19] The nation's growing inability to mediate the diverse identities of its people and the increasingly apparent failures of the fiction of direct access are precisely the problems that sensational fiction exposes with such lurid panache. And it is under this rubric of mediation that the elevation of Catholic conspiracy to such startling and seemingly bizarre proportions in countless sensational novels begins to make sense: not as a religious mystification of "real" underlying conflicts in society (immigration, economic competition, shifting gender roles, racial conflict, etc.) as many critics have argued but as a symptom of a secularism in which mediation has gone haywire—of a society that has paradoxically become excessively mediated and not mediated enough.[20]

In what follows, I first use Klauprecht's novel to reframe critical accounts of the period's "exhibitionary" culture—its avid consumption of museums, galleries, and other visually oriented public exhibits—by showing that the spectacles antebellum Americans encountered in public spaces as well as in sensational fiction taught them a kind of double vision, simultaneously viewing themselves as citizens and as apocalyptic observers. Turning next to a classic city-mystery, George Lippard's *New York: Its Upper Ten and Lower Million* (1853), I reconsider what defines a work as regional. Originally published in Cincinnati, Lippard's novel used Catholic conspiracy to offer western readers a view of themselves from the imperial center; that perspective enables a remapping of the geography of sensational fiction and a reconsideration of the model of "frontier" space famously articulated by Frederick Jackson Turner. The issues Lippard raised found their fullest articulation in the *Columbian & Great West*, a neglected regional story paper that probed the West's relationship to political, economic, and religious power, culminating in its serialization of a city-mystery set in Cincinnati. As the paper's editors and contributors debated whether the West could mediate the nation's economic and religious conflicts—a possibility I term a "sacred spatial fix"—they exposed contradictions in American secularism that presaged the most apocalyptic geography of all: a nation torn apart by civil war.

The Cosmic Exhibitionary Complex

Landscape representation played a crucial role in eighteenth-century republican ideology. In a range of cultural forms from prospect poems to picaresque novels and panoramas to architectural views, writers and artists on both sides of the Atlantic used the prospect to grapple with the problems raised by the emergence of modern market societies.[21] They asked, for example, whether the classical ideal of civic virtue—the citizen's ability to discern the public good and act in its behalf—was still necessary or even possible in a society characterized by a complex division of labor and new economic theories that argued for the social utility of self-interest. In James Thomson's poem *The Seasons* (1744–46), the scene the landed gentleman surveys from his estate materializes the contest of public virtue and corruption, contrasting the social harmony embodied in the pastoral "happy World" with "these iron Times" when "Love" has "sunk to sordid Interest," a condition that urgently requires him to intervene and reform the social order.[22] This use of the prospect as a symbol of republican disinterest was translated to the American context in poems like Timothy Dwight's *Greenfield Hill* (1794), but it also figured prominently in the ratification debates on the U.S. Constitution. Federalists repeatedly urged Americans to transcend the "narrow," "contracted," and "local views" assumed by state officials under the Articles of Confederation and instead to take the "enlightened," "enlarged," and "comprehensive view[s]" that would enable representatives to transcend local, particular interests and legislate in favor of the common good.[23] A Federalist writing in the New York *Daily Advertiser* distilled this spatial imagery when he compared those who opposed the Constitution to "insects and worms [who] are only seen on their own dunghill. There are minds whose narrow vision can look over the concerns of a State or Town, but cannot extend their short vision to Continental concerns."[24] This use of the prospect as a metaphor for political mediation in an extended republic was literalized in the circular panorama of Annapolis that Charles Willson Peale undertook in 1788, a project that Wendy Bellion has argued represented an attempt to construct "a pictorial analogue for the American republic" in which the view of the city from the Maryland State House and an external view of the state house itself would combine to capture "the dialectical agency of the new American citizen—namely, a practice of citizenship in which one was expected at once to participate actively in government and to step outside its operations to assess its performance objectively."[25]

One could productively situate the republican prospect within what Tony Bennett has termed "the exhibitionary complex," the transatlantic network of museums, world's fairs, art exhibitions, and other public institutions emerging in the late eighteenth and early nineteenth centuries that taught people to regard themselves as "the subjects rather than the objects of knowledge." The experience of being a spectator in these public spaces, Bennett argues, helped produce "a voluntarily self-regulating citizenry" capable of "seeing themselves from the side of power" rather than only being seen *by* power and thus ultimately becoming "both the subjects and the objects of knowledge" simultaneously.[26]

In *Cincinnati*, Filson's view from Mount Adams extends this pedagogical project, but it departs in key respects from earlier versions. Traditionally, private property ownership made possible the gentleman's elevated perspective and the independence and civic virtue it symbolized—virtues deemed unavailable to "professional men, tradesmen, merchants, and ... artisans and laborers," who "were assumed to be concerned solely or largely with the immediate ends of that occupation."[27] Filson, however, stands on public property, and his virtue depends on giving up his estate: on *not* owning landed property to ensure that the "thousands of brave craftsmen" retain title to their "homestead[s]" (*CMW*, 630).[28] In contrast to the agrarian bias of both the English country Whig tradition and Jeffersonian republicanism, participation in a modern industrial economy here becomes the foundation of a prosperous and independent republican society rather than a threat to it. In fact, Filson's view of a city that "emerged from the forehead of the giant of the primeval forest, armed at the outset with railroads and canals, with her hundreds of steamers, factories and shops" (624), elides the agrarian empire altogether, revealing instead a pattern of land and resource use typical of emerging western centers such as Cincinnati, St. Louis, and Chicago, where industrial capitalism unleashed explosive urban growth and created a vast regional hinterland that supplied the metropolis with raw materials and provided new markets for the consumer goods it produced.[29]

Benton, a former U.S. senator who wields a broad knowledge of the domestic and international scene and who claims to speak for the interests of the entire nation, represents the 1850s equivalent of the Federalist "comprehensive view." Indeed, during the 1840s the Cincinnati Observatory became a controversial symbol of what some saw as a "Federalist" effort to impose a national system of scientific institutions on the nation—an effort led by none other than former president John Quincy Adams, the great champion of federally funded internal improvements.[30] In light of such fears of federal encroachment, Benton's presence at an observatory that Adams himself had helped dedicate (on a hill that was renamed Mount Adams in his honor) re-enacts the Federalist mode of vision of the late 1780s and the highly mediated form of political representation it sought to naturalize, only to unmask it as a threat to regional autonomy. The prospect functions as precisely the sort of exhibitionary space Bennett describes, teaching readers to "se[e] themselves from the side of power," to be both "subjects" of knowledge—republican citizens—and "objects" of the power wielded by national elites.

If Filson in some sense is a surrogate viewer who teaches readers to see Cincinnati (and themselves) from the dual perspective of republican and federal power, the cathedral introduces a new dimension to the sensational exhibitionary complex. Watched over by the distant and shadowy power of Rome, the citizen is reduced to an object of power of a different sort, returned to a colonial geography divided by warring imperial and cosmic forces.

From the earliest days of European colonization, the Americas represented an apocalyptic geography where Catholics and Protestants expected God's providential plot to be fulfilled. While for Franciscans and Jesuits in Spanish America that plot hinged upon converting natives to Christianity, for the English colonies to the north it centered on an internal struggle to form holy communities of the elect by rooting out the corrupt vestiges of Catholicism. As J. H. Elliott explains, for colonial authorities in Virginia and New England, "America thereby assumed its position as a new battleground in the unrelenting struggle between the forces of light, represented by the Protestant Reformation, and the satanic forces of darkness, which had their seat in Rome."[31] English colonists frequently projected that threat onto wilderness and frontier spaces, a practice reinforced by the presence of Catholic empires to the north, west, and south.[32] In colonial New England, Indian captivity narratives described colonists' forced removal to Canada as a harrowing descent into a Catholic space where white Protestant women endured the persecution of native "*Idolaters*" (who in some cases had actually been converted to Catholicism by their French Canadian allies) and sometimes faced forced conversion and the Catholic baptism of their children after being redeemed by the French.[33] This conception of the North American "frontier" as Catholic space persisted in the early republic. Elizabeth Fenton notes that in novels by Charles Brockden Brown and Catharine Sedgwick published from the 1790s to the 1820s, "the West does not appear as the hopeful site of democratic exchange" but rather as "a site of Catholic despotism threatening the nation's Protestant unity."[34] Histories of North America by Protestants and Catholics alike confirmed this fraught sacred geography, tracing its roots not just to the Spanish presence that left territories from Florida to New Mexico "stamped with a Catholic character" (in the words of Catholic historian Thomas D'Arcy

McGee) but back further still to what Jenny Franchot describes as "a pre-Columbian Catholicism . . . carried in the minds and cultures of North American and Mesoamerican Indians, whose faintly understood cultures seemed to resemble Romanism in sufficiently astonishing ways that at points they simply merged as twinned images of popery."[35]

The influx of Catholic immigrants and institutions into the trans-Appalachian West beginning in the 1820s reanimated this Protestant sacred geography. Franchot describes a distinctive bifurcation within antebellum Protestant conceptions of history and geography: "history—as the study of change—was a Protestant possession; the stagnant terrain of the past belonged to Catholics. The New Testament, Protestant history, and America's Manifest Destiny moved jointly forward; Catholicism, divorced from time and Scripture, stood still."[36] Yet the long-standing image of the Mississippi Valley as Catholic space meant that Manifest Destiny moved not just away from Old World stagnation but toward it, setting up an inevitable confrontation. Catholicism fit neatly into the existing paranoid structure of republican ideology: the specter of Catholic "stasis or even regression" in the interior amplified perennial republican fears of imperial overextension and decline that dogged U.S. expansionists well into the nineteenth century.[37] By the 1830s, as Frederick Marryat predicted that "all America west of the Alleghenies will eventually be a Catholic country," prominent evangelical nativists such as Samuel F. B. Morse and Lyman Beecher pointed to the activities of Catholic missionary associations as evidence of a conspiracy whereby, in Bryan Le Beau's words, "the Pope, in concert with the despotic nations of Europe, intended to extend his dominion into the heart of the American republic—the Mississippi River Valley—from which he would defeat republicanism in the United States and stem its tide worldwide."[38] "This cause is the cause of the *West*," the *Home Missionary* magazine proclaimed in 1839, "for there the great battle is to be fought between truth and error, between law and anarchy—between Christianity, with her Sabbaths, her ministry and her schools, on the one hand, and the combined forces of Infidelity and Popery on the other."[39] A decade later, influential New School Presbyterian minister Albert Barnes was still arguing that "the West may now be regarded as the great battle-field of the world—the place where probably, more than any where else, the destinies of the world are to be decided."[40]

The built landscape furnished palpable evidence of that cosmic struggle. Observers noted that Catholics were transforming the nation's urban landscape as parishes erected convents, schools, universities, and especially churches. According to one estimate, the number of Catholic churches in the United States swelled from just over 120 in 1820 to more than 2,500 in 1860—an increase that far outstripped any other denomination.[41] Protestant elites in the Northeast were among the earliest and most vocal critics of this Catholic construction boom. Morse, in a text that has been called "the manifesto of the early nineteenth-century anti-Catholic movement," warned readers in 1834 that misguided liberal tolerance toward Catholics was hastening the day when "we will build for them their fortresses on our own soil, to attack our own strong holds, and then we will trust to their mercy." He pointed to the new Catholic cathedral in St. Louis as "another step forward in the march against our freedom."[42] Residents of western cities were quick to echo his rhetoric. "In this place, the Roman Catholics are prosperous," a St. Louis man wrote to his brother in Vermont in 1843: "They are now building two new churches here, one of which is expected to cost over $70,000. That denomination is now very active and successful in its labors throughout the Union. They are erecting a splendid cathedral in Cincinnati, where they already have a very large and good one, besides several churches; a new and very large German Catholic church in Pittsburgh, two new ones in Boston, one in New York, and a college at Worcester, Mass." Noting the "political dangers of Popery, its anti-republican tendencies, the allegiance of its clergy to a foreign potentate, their close and sympathetic union by which they act throughout the length and breadth of the land as one man," the correspondent urged vigilance to prevent Catholicism from overspreading the nation.[43]

While for some observers this construction wave confirmed the fears propagated by evangelical elites, for others it furnished evidence of the growing architectural stature and refinement of western cities and bolstered their claims to be cultural centers of the region or even the nation. In Cincinnati, which Jon Butler notes "exemplified the explosion of urban church construction in antebellum America," a correspondent to the *Scioto Gazette* boasted in September 1844 that "the architecture of this city will vie with that of any other city in the Union" and pointed to the unfinished cathedral as proof:

> The new Roman Catholic Cathedral, in the north-western part of the city, is a massive pile, which for solid masonry and chasteness of design and architecture, stands unrivalled in the West. It is built of hewn stone, quarried near Portsmouth, and appears as if intended that its existence was to parallel the rock of ages. The interior is yet to be finished, and will be done on a scale of magnificence, and decorated in a style comporting with the exterior, and the peculiar taste of that denomination. It is also to be furnished with a chime of bells. In the Court the Bishop's residence is in progress. All is surrounded by a high stone wall and iron railing, encompassing half a square. This is the fourth religious edifice that the Catholics have in Cincinnati; and all are among the largest of the city. The foundation of the *fifth* is to be started this Fall.[44]

As the passage unfolds, regional pride for this specimen of architectural progress slides into observations that hint at the fears of anti-Catholic commentators (the presence of powerful church officials, the property's concealment from public view, the proliferation of Catholic buildings in the city); yet the correspondent does not expand on the threat Catholicism may pose but instead moves on to other features of the cityscape. To be sure, the passage reflects the "ambivalence" that characterized Protestant attitudes toward Catholicism during the period, as ministers across the country condemned Catholicism while appropriating elements of Catholic architecture and worship.[45] But what is significant in this instance is how the Protestant attraction to Catholic cultural forms bolsters a sense of regional cultural distinction and civic pride.

Similar cultural aspirations accompanied the construction of cathedrals in other western cities, sometimes without any hint of ambivalence at all. In Cleveland, where by 1848 the Catholic population had grown to more than four thousand, spurring plans to build a new cathedral, the editors of the *Cleveland Herald* wrote that "we have seen a drawing of the proposed edifice, which will add very much to the good taste and inviting appearance of our beautiful young city." They encouraged all who were "interested in the growth and prosperity of the city" to contribute money to support its construction.[46] Similarly in 1853 the *Milwaukee Daily Sentinel* pronounced the lavish interior of the nearly completed St. John's Cathedral (featuring stained glass from Pittsburgh, paintings from Munich and Milan, a carved wooden altar from Belgium, a pipe organ from Cincinnati, and a gas chandelier from Philadelphia) to be "in excellent taste." Noting that "all the work has been done upon it by Milwaukee artisans, and they have been employed throughout without distinction of nation or religion," the paper predicted that the cathedral complex would be "one of the most striking ornaments of our city."[47] At the cathedral's consecration two weeks later a reporter, though clearly not Catholic, predicted that "when this beautiful city of Milwaukee will have grown perhaps to fifty times its present size—when our children's children will have been forgotten—its then inhabitants looking on this building—may say, 'this was the flood-mark here, of the Religion of Jesus Christ in 1853.'"[48] The combination of cosmopolitan refinement, civic boosterism, and even a kind of ecumenical Christian millennialism in these press accounts nicely captures how locals repurposed the trope of the West as Catholic space to nourish a vision of regional cultural and economic autonomy.

The sense of regional identity that led non-Catholic commentators to celebrate Catholic buildings for their refinement and good taste also provoked clashes over the political import of the Catholic presence. In 1835 the Cincinnati-based *Western Monthly Magazine* published a scathing review of

Lyman Beecher's *A Plea for the West* that called his views "pernicious and absurd . . . because they drew a broad line of distinction between the east and the west, assigning a degree of moral purity and elevation to the one, and of darkness and degradation to the other, not justified by the actual condition of either." Though Beecher was the rare elite anti-Catholic writer who had actually lived in the West, the reviewer (likely the magazine's editor, James Hall) charged that "Dr. Beecher's dreams about Rome, and Vienna, and Metternich, have unsettled the usually steady balance of his mind" and distorted his perception of Catholics in the region. Beecher's account of a "conspiracy against our liberties," the reviewer continued,

> is a charge made without the support of a single tittle of testimony—without the production of a single overt act of hostility, towards our government, on the part of the Roman Catholics. It is a charge made against a body, in which were numbered many of the patriots of the revolution, and of those who, at a later period, have participated in the counsels of the nation, or have bared their breasts in battle to the enemies of our country, and among whom are found thousands of reputable, industrious citizens, whose integrity is above suspicion, and whose love of country is too pure and elevated to be tainted by the breath of a calumny so gratuitous and unfounded.

Turning next to Beecher's fears that Catholic clergy would control the votes of their flocks and use them to secure "copious appropriations of land for the endowment of their institutions," the reviewer confronted the central role of the built environment in Beecher's conspiracy theory and revised the entire Protestant historical geography upon which it rested. Catholics, the reviewer argued, "were the first settlers of all that is now Louisiana, Mississippi, and Missouri. They first introduced education into our valley, and their schools and colleges were, for a series of years, the only nurseries of learning, west of the mountains." This history gives Catholics just as much right as Protestants (more, even) to receive public endowments of land for educational institutions, but up to now their smaller numbers have prevented it: "Why should not the catholics share the munificence of congress with other sects? . . . In all the western states, land has been given largely for education; the college lands, under the fair operation of that rule of republics which gives power to the majority, have fallen solely into the hands of protestants."[49] But as the Catholic population grows, the reviewer implied, the nature of federal political representation would mean more endowments to Catholic institutions, and thus more Catholic buildings. From the perspective of a regional literary magazine devoted to ameliorating the "difference in the degree of cultivation" between eastern and western states, the ability of Catholic institutions to compete for public money was not cause for alarm but a vital resource for the cultural development of the region.[50]

This is not to suggest that the reviewer's stance was a popular one—indeed, public backlash against the piece was so strong that it prompted Hall to step down as the magazine's editor.[51] But the review does reveal how resentment toward the cultural imperialism of eastern elites could provoke revisionist narratives of regional progress that grant Catholicism a startling centrality. And it makes clear that Catholic buildings did not simply represent accumulations of cultural and physical capital but that they materialized the workings of republican political mediation. Where the *Western Monthly* reviewer interpreted those buildings as a sign that representative democracy was working properly, for critics like Beecher they offered troubling reminders of government's failure to adequately mediate Catholic identity—the failure (in Asad's formulation) to achieve secularism's defining function of "transcendent" political mediation that "redefines and transcends particular and differentiating practices of the self that are articulated through class, gender, and religion" and replaces them with the unifying identity of national citizenship.[52] While Beecher and Morse lament the failure of American-style secularism—a secularism that Tracy Fessenden reminds us has historically been Protestant—the regional countermappings of Hall and Klauprecht, despite their starkly different appraisals of the Catholic presence in the West, resist the secular demand for transcendent mediation.[53] Instead, they use the built landscape to envision alternative models of republican political mediation in which categories of identity such as religion, region, and class remain operative.

While Catholic buildings provided a resonant figure for political mediation across an expanding federal republic, they represented mediation on a "vertical" axis as well, embodying an alternative view of the role of materiality and the senses in spiritual life. As Martin Spalding, the archbishop of Louisville, explained to an interfaith group of visitors to the city's newly opened Cathedral of the Assumption in 1852, for Catholics the "Sanctity" of a church meant that it was a qualitatively different form of space: God was literally present in a way he was not in ordinary profane space, a presence epitomized by the sacrament of the Eucharist, in which bread and wine became the actual body and blood of Jesus. Spalding noted that the difference between this conception of divine immanence and the Protestant understanding of sacred space, in which a church interior was no more inherently sacred than any other, was reflected in the many sensuous elements of Catholic worship, in "churches decorated with all the ornaments of the fine arts, and filled with beautiful and appropriate symbols that raise the heart to heavenly things and to God."[54] Protestant critics made a similar distinction but cast it in starkly different terms. After observing a Catholic Mass in Cincinnati's St. Peter in Chains

Cathedral in 1847, Methodist clergyman Benjamin F. Tefft described the ceremony as calculated "to make a bold impression on the imagination, and to captivate the sense": "With real skill have they united architecture, painting, sculpture, and music, together with several of the less prominent of the fine arts, to make a combined and uniform effect." Noting that the Mass had been "apparently abridged, so as to suit the characteristic haste of the American public," Tefft groused that "every thing, from first to last, is nicely adapted to the prevailing prejudices of the people on whom they desire to act."[55] Whereas in the conspiracy theories of Beecher and Morse, Catholics pose a threat because they are insufficiently mediated (their religious identity is inadequately subsumed into national identity), here the problem with Catholic ritual is that the divine presence is excessively mediated—by the senses, by objects, by priests—rather than directly encountered by the individual through the Word.[56] Critics might try to defuse the "common Catholic assumption that art, as perceived through the senses, could offer legitimate avenues to God."[57] Rapt Protestant ministers and artists might even tell themselves that they could savor the aesthetics of Catholic interiors while denying their status as divine media.[58] But the popular consumption of Catholic sensation in antebellum America, whether by viewing images of Catholic spaces, visiting those spaces in person, or incorporating Catholic elements into Protestant worship, points to an increasing willingness to broaden the bandwidth, so to speak, of spiritual media in antebellum America: to accept buildings, paintings, and other art objects as conduits of religious truth.

The complex layering of republican, regional, and sacred geographies that coalesce in the view from Mount Adams complicates our understanding of the relations of landscape and power in antebellum America. Recognizing literary and visual prospects as nodes within the exhibitionary complex counterbalances the critical tendency to interpret panoramas and other visual technologies of the period in terms of the totalizing power of Foucault's "sovereign gaze."[59] They were instruments of democratic self-governance and regional autonomy as well as imperial domination. More fundamentally, attending to the cosmic dramas enacted in those landscapes unsettles the implicit theory of secularization that informs both Foucault's "carceral archipelago" and Bennett's exhibitionary complex—the assumption that the state has colonized the omnipresent gaze of God and usurped the disciplinary functions of the Church.[60] Antebellum America was replete with exhibitionary spaces in which transcendent forms of knowledge and power took center stage. The Catholic churches where Americans of all theological stripes converged to witness sacramental spectacles represent particularly prominent sites within a vast network of such numinous spaces. Similarly, when Americans and travelers attended the "Infernal Regions" exhibit at Cincinnati's Western Museum, when they flocked to see sacred dioramas and apocalyptic paintings, and when they entered the gaudy gallery of scenes that make up the sensational novel they entered a cosmic exhibitionary complex in which being subjects and objects of knowledge meant more than being national citizens: it meant contemplating the structure of the cosmos and the design of history.[61] It meant attempting to discern apocalyptic signs of the times alongside threats to republican liberty and being surveilled by a powerful network of Catholic conspirators as well as "Federalist" statesmen. It meant occupying civic space and sacred space simultaneously: inhabiting a thriving but vulnerable western republic *and* an embattled Protestant outpost in a continental Catholic geography with roots stretching deep into the colonial past.

Mapping the Middle Ground: George Lippard and Turnerian Space

In the closing chapters of George Lippard's *New York: Its Upper Ten and Lower Million*, the virtuous mechanic hero, Arthur Dermoyne, finds himself dispossessed. As one of seven provisional heirs (along with a banker, a clergyman, a statesman, a Southern slaveholder, a merchant, and a wealthy libertine) of a fabulous estate worth $100 million, Dermoyne and his fellow heirs represent the diverse interests that comprise antebellum U.S. society. The question that propels this typical sensational "inheritance plot"—Who will inherit the Van Huyden estate and, by extension, control the future of the republic?—has been settled.[62] The future does not belong to the laborer, at least not in the East. The final scene finds Dermoyne far from New York, on the "vast prairies, which stretch between the Mississippi and the Rocky Mountains," leading a group of "emigrants, mechanics, their wives and little ones, who have left the savage civilization of the Atlantic cities, for a free home beyond the Rocky Mountains." Turning back to survey the wagon train winding over the plains, he declares, "'Thus far toward freedom! Here they come,—three hundred serfs of the Atlantic cities, rescued from poverty, from wages-slavery, from the war of competition, from the grip of the landlord! Thus far toward a soil which they can call their own; thus far toward a free home.'" Lippard declines to ironize this vision but instead ends the novel echoing Dermoyne's Christian "Socialist" vision, appealing to Jesus to "go with the People" in their "exodus" to "the Promised Land" in the West.[63]

In one sense this fantasy of escape from eastern industrialism into the "free" lands of the West is utterly familiar, an expression of the agrarian mythology that underwrote U.S. westward expansion and achieved its apotheosis in Frederick Jackson Turner's "frontier thesis," the idea that "the existence of an area of free land, its continuous recession, and the advance of American settlement westward, explain American development."[64] But Lippard's story reveals a wrinkle in that narrative that centers on the shifting meaning of republicanism. By the 1850s artisans, newspaper editors, and others had argued for decades that the urban "mechanic" was a citizen every bit as important to the health of the republic as the yeoman farmer; this ideology of "artisan republicanism" has provided scholars with an important perspective through which to interpret working-class culture, city-mysteries fiction, and Lippard's work in particular.[65] But Lippard's description of the emigrants as "serfs" fleeing "the grip of the landlord" to "a soil which they can call their own" erases that ideological labor and transforms an urban, skilled labor force back into agrarian folk. The binary he establishes between eastern urban "wages-slavery" and western agrarian free labor seems to foreclose any possibility of artisan free labor in the West. The mechanics can only take possession of "free" soil at the cost of being dispossessed of the very thing that American workers had long fought to establish as their property: their labor.[66]

This absence of an ideological middle ground between agrarian and mechanic strands of republican ideology finds physical manifestation in the scene's elision of continental geography. Lippard initially suggests that "the New World" is to be found on the "vast prairies, which stretch between the Mississippi and the Rocky Mountains"; yet when he describes the emigrants as fleeing the "savage civilization of the Atlantic cities" for "a free home beyond the Rocky Mountains," those prairies vanish, and the logical structure of the sentence consigns everything east of the Rockies to the domain of the "Atlantic cities." What happened to the Mississippi Valley? The invisibility of the continental interior presents a geographical absence corresponding to the novel's ideological lacuna. Dwelling on those twin absences and their persistence in recent accounts of antebellum popular fiction can help revise our sense of the period's literary geography. In an influential interpretation developed by Shelley Streeby and Jesse Alemán, sensational fiction was largely produced and consumed in northeastern cities, but its settings occupy imperial theaters in Texas, California, Mexico, and the Caribbean, enabling metropolitan readers to fantasize about empire from afar.[67] This approach, which we might call the center-periphery model of popular fiction, largely ignores the vast territory between eastern centers and the imperial periphery, flattening a diverse literary landscape of regions and ignoring the republican geographies they produced. Like Lippard's novel, these critics leave blank the space that Richard White called "the middle ground."[68]

The obscure publication history of Lippard's *New York*, which initially appeared not in New York but in Cincinnati, meant that it circulated in the very region where its spatial and ideological lacunae were most likely to be grasped.

The novel participated in a process of regional self-construction led by a group of western "men of letters" who labored to define a regional identity in relation to the supposedly corrupt and aristocratic societies of eastern cities and southern plantations.[69] The result, which took shape in the regional press and ultimately in a body of local sensational fiction, was a regional variant of republican ideology that privileged the ideological and geographical middle ground: the promise of western cities nurturing a form of truly free urban labor, protected from the twin perils of "wages-slavery" and chattel slavery. But crucially, this project of regional self-fashioning had to grapple with questions of religious identity in a place where Catholic, Protestant, and Native American religious traditions had long mingled and competed. The precarious nature of the republican vision that emerged from this regional literary sphere—its vulnerability to corruption within and exploitation from without—frequently found expression in terms of this religious difference. In *New York*, a global Catholic conspiracy serves to expose the contours and contradictions of America's fractured republican geography. That conspiracy provides a mediating link between inner and outer processes of U.S. settler colonialism, exposing the "political 'doubleness'" that historian Bethel Saler defines as a shared legacy of settler nations, their "ambivalent double history as both colonized and colonizers."[70] By dramatizing a system of western development that forecasts Turner's frontier, Lippard helps us begin to fill in the blank spaces in the center-periphery models of literary history; but the novel's ultimate displacement of religious conflict locates it in Turnerian space in another sense as well, one that exposes fissures in the secular foundations of American empire.

In the early 1850s George Lippard made three extended visits to Ohio from his home in Philadelphia to recover from personal tragedy, lecture, visit friends, and sightsee.[71] The first two trips occurred while Lippard was writing *New York*, and the third occurred shortly after he finished the manuscript.[72] While the details of Lippard's publishing arrangements remain obscure, by September 1853 Ohio newspapers were reporting that a new work by Lippard would be published in Cincinnati.[73] That fall two local publishing houses specializing in popular fiction, H. M. Rulison and E. Mendenhall, published editions of *New York*.[74] Ads began appearing in Ohio in November and outside the state in December, tracing a widening orbit of publicity that reached Philadelphia, New York, and Baltimore by year's end.[75] When news of Lippard's death reached Cincinnati in February 1854, the *Columbian & Great West* noted that "his last work, 'Upper Ten and Lower Million,' published in our city, is having a great sale."[76] That spring, rising demand led Mendenhall to place ads announcing, "TWO-HUNDRED AGENTS WANTED TO SELL NEW YORK, ITS UPPER TEN AND LOWER MILLION" and claiming "20,000 COPIES SOLD IN THREE MONTHS."[77] By the end of 1854, booksellers from

Wisconsin to upstate New York and up and down the East Coast from New York to Charleston were advertising that they had copies of the novel on hand.[78]

Mendenhall's ads presented an ambivalent sense of New York City's uniqueness, filtering Lippard's account of the city through a western regional sensibility. A typical ad explained, "It has been the object of the author of the present work to picture New York as it is. Its terrible contrasts of wealth and poverty, luxury and misery, virtue and crime, velvet and rags; its bankers and mechanics, stock speculotors [sic] and watch stuffers, grave men of business, and men who have neither business, work or bread.... These are hard contrasts, but these contrasts are New York." The city's "contrasts" stemmed in part from the confluence of people from many geographical regions and nations: "as New York is the great reservoir, into which perpetually flow, the luxury and misery, the virtues and the crimes, both of the old world and the new, so the author... has pictured not only its permanent but also its floating population, and grouped together characters from the old world, and from all parts of the Union."[79] New York transcended particular "parts of the Union" in implicit contrast to regional cities that merely belonged to them. Subsequent versions of Mendenhall's ad supplemented this account with enthusiastic regional press commentary that stressed the absorbing quality of Lippard's novel: the *Cincinnati Enquirer* wrote that it furnished "one continued scene of excitement from the commencement to the end" and compared it to the fiction of Alexandre Dumas and Eugène Sue, the *Cleveland Daily Plain Dealer* hailed it as "a novel of most thrilling interest—such an [sic] one as having been commenced, you will set [sic] up all night to finish," and the *Louisville Courier* claimed that "it will be impossible for any person who commences this work, to leave it off until he has turned over its last page."[80] The combination of a rhetoric of "absorptive reading" with the portrayal of New York as a fascinating but potentially overwhelming spectacle conveyed the challenge city-mysteries fiction posed: Could western cities eager to demonstrate their cultural influence produce their own "thrilling" popular literature while still affirming their republican image as places that had avoided the corrupting extremes of wealth and urban disorder associated with New York?[81]

Readers in Cincinnati, Cleveland, or Louisville were thus primed to find in Lippard's novel a view of New York from the hinterlands, an ambivalent spectacle against which to compare their home cities. But at key moments in the novel that perspective was reversed, and western readers encountered a view of themselves from the metropolitan center—of a valuable continental interior coveted by the imperial gaze of eastern elites. Crucially, that gaze is inseparable from Catholic designs. Early in the novel a shadowy legate (papal ambassador) named Gaspar Manuel, newly arrived in New York from Cuba, meets with Ezekiel Bogart, the general agent who manages the Van Huyden estate. Bogart catalogues the breadth of the estate's assets, including "lands in the western country—lands purchased for fifty thousand dollars, at a time when Ohio was a thinly settled colony and all the region further west a wilderness—but lands which are now distributed through five states, and which, dotted with villages, rich in mines and tenanted by thousands, return an annual rent of,——" (*NY*, 63). With a few swift strokes, Lippard traces a colonial history of settlement, state formation, and economic development resulting in a system of rent-based exploitation of western people and lands.

But simply describing the capture of western resources is insufficient to convey the scope of the crisis. The next scene finds Manuel in the New York home of a prelate (a local Catholic official) hovering over "a map of the American Continent" (*NY*, 67). Predicting that "the north, that is the Republic of the United States, will finally absorb and rule over all the nations of the Continent," the prelate reveals a papal conspiracy to infiltrate the seat of power:

> New York is in reality, the metropolis of the Continent; from New York as from a common center, therefore all our efforts must radiate. From New York we will control the Republic, shape it year by year to our purposes; as it adds nation after nation to its Union, we will make our grasp of its secret spring of action, the more certain and secure; and at last the hour will come, when this Continent apparently one united republic, will in fact, be the richest altar, the strongest abiding-place, the most valuable property of the Church. Yes, the hour will come, when the flimsy scaffolding of Republicanism will fall, and as it falls, our Church will stand revealed, her foundation in the heart of the American Republic; her shadow upon every hill and valley of the Continent. (68)

This plot ranges from securing the riches of California's gold fields to promoting nativist parties in northeastern cities that will polarize the populace and prevent Catholic immigrants from assimilating. As church officials scheme to use U.S. imperial expansion to extend their power, Manuel becomes a mediating figure connecting the nation's internal process of exploiting territory that has already been absorbed into its federal structure to its external process of expansion into Mexican California and other lands. He straddles the divide between "postcolonial republic" and "settler empire" that Saler argues defines "the United States as a settler nation"—"its struggle to broker its postcolonial republican commitments with its federal, colonial administration over its variegated territorial populations."[82]

Lippard essentially undertakes a version of what Fredric Jameson influentially described as a geopolitical form of "*cognitive mapping*," an effort to image "the great global multinational and decentred communicational network in which we find ourselves caught as individual subjects."[83] Jameson subsequently argued that postmodern film genres like the conspiracy thriller embodied "a geopolitical unconscious," "an attempt to think the world system as such." But the forerunners of those thrillers, popular sensational novels like Lippard's, anticipated those efforts to map the complex dynamics of modern empire. What distinguishes Lippard's geopolitical unconscious from its postmodern counterpart, however, is his use of the Catholic Church and other global religious networks as media enabling the individual to "think the world system." Whereas Jameson assumes a secular world—he's concerned with "what a global or world system might look like after the end of cosmology"—Lippard shows us what that system looks like from a perspective of a religious cosmology that remains very much alive, in effect animating a form of cosmic cognitive mapping.[84]

Lippard's cognitive mapping is colonial as well as cosmic, training western readers to use maps and landscape prospects to see the Great West as what Bernard DeVoto famously called a "plundered province."[85] In a sense Lippard anticipates Jack P. Greene's critique of historians' tendency to privilege the national over the colonial—to read early American history as the prelude to the main event that begins with U.S. independence. Greene argues for "a massive extension of the colonial perspective into the national era" that would recognize the states added to the union after 1776 as "the products of an ongoing colonizing process"—as "settler republic[s]" that produced "an astonishing variety of distinctive and largely self-governing polities and their relationships to the weak federal state."[86] This perspective destabilizes the standard periodization of eighteenth-century colonies and nineteenth-century nations and disrupts the familiar story of the rise of republicanism in the revolutionary period and its eclipse by liberalism.[87] But it also enables revision of the dominant critical literary geography of antebellum sensation by mapping regional Republics of Sensation in the middle ground.

Of course in Lippard's *New York* all the familiar nodes of the center-periphery model remain in play, as a Cuban legate bargains with a New York banker over land in California still claimed by the Mexican government. But his survey of exploited miners and millworkers in New York, Pennsylvania, and Ohio, culminating in the mechanics' exodus across the western prairies at novel's end, supplements that model with a layered, developmental spatial model closer to the one outlined by Turner in his 1893 essay "The Significance of the Frontier in American History" and elaborated in his subsequent writings on regions in American political life.[88] Turner's "frontier thesis" has long been debated, critiqued, and refuted, but in recent decades scholars in a variety of disciplines have argued for its continued relevance for understanding the colonial past.[89] Affirming Turner's claim that "American history has been in a large degree the history of the colonization of the Great West," William Cronon, George Miles, and Jay Gitlin argue that despite the well-known "contradictions and errors of his scholarship, Turner was surely right to see the long European (and African and Asian) invasion of North America—and the resistance to it by the continent's existing inhabitants—as the pivotal event in American history."[90] More recently, scholars seeking to better understand the dynamics of settler colonialism have adopted a modified Turnerian framework to gain insights into colonial encounters around the globe.[91]

These efforts to update Turnerian space to highlight connections between regions and empire suggest parallel possibilities in literary studies. Popular works of sensational fiction by Lippard and others, much of it distributed through regional print networks, can provide key insights into the historical process of regional "self-shaping" and its relationship to U.S. imperialism.[92] Where Streeby locates Lippard's life and work along a "double axis of city and empire" that juxtaposes his participation in national labor and land reform movements with his support for the Mexican War—city-mysteries like *The Empire City* (1850) and *New York* with international race romances like *Legends of Mexico* (1847) and *'Bel of Prairie Eden* (1848)—mapping him in Turnerian space reveals a different constellation of places, concerns, and texts.[93] It foregrounds the Lippard who traveled to western cities and angrily condemned politicians who "have made their fortunes for years, by robbing the Indians of the West."[94] It helps us look beyond the controversy *The Quaker City* (1845) stirred up in Philadelphia to consider its reception in Cincinnati or St. Louis and how that influence might have dovetailed with Lippard's labor organization, the Brotherhood of Union, which beginning in 1849 established dozens of "circles," in western states, including thirty-seven in Ohio alone.[95] And it reminds us that as we parse the imperial politics of Lippard's *Legends of Mexico*, we should also consider the republican politics of *Washington and His Generals; or, Legends of the Revolution* (1847), which was often the first work associated with Lippard's name in the early 1850s and remained so popular at the time of his death in 1854 that one writer declared that "though all else should fail, [it] will ensure perpetuity to the author's name."[96] Each of these perspectives invites a fresh examination of Lippard's city-mysteries and Mexican War fiction with an eye to literary geographies that exceed and complicate the "double axis of city and empire."

Adopting a modified Turnerian literary geography can help fill gaps in prevailing critical mental maps, but how does it relate to the cosmic cognitive mapping on display in works like *New York*? How do we make sense of the tales of Catholic conspiracy or, on the other side of the colonial divide, the native prophecy and pan-tribal revivalism that appear in regional frontier biographies of figures such as Tecumseh and Black Hawk?[97] In a word, is Turnerian literary space secular?

Religion certainly is not a major focus of Turner's. While his first published essay, "The Significance of History" (1891), affirmed that "even the religious life needs to be studied in conjunction with the political and economic life, and vice versa," his seminal exposition of the frontier two years later hardly mentions religion.[98] When we are directed, in one of the indelible scenes of "The Significance of the Frontier in American History," to "Stand at Cumberland Gap and watch the procession of civilization, marching single file—the buffalo following the trail to the salt springs, the Indian, the fur-trader and hunter, the cattle-raiser, the pioneer farmer—and the frontier has passed by," the missionary is conspicuously absent from Turner's train of trailblazers. Only in the essay's closing paragraphs does religion briefly appear in the guise of Beecher's *Plea for the West*, which Turner cites as evidence of the "efforts of the East to regulate the frontier" through "educational and religious activity." But the anti-Catholicism of Beecher's *Plea* is not even mentioned, and when Turner turns to the subsequent scramble to establish "home missions" and "Western colleges" on the frontier, it is solely a Protestant affair: "the real struggle was between sects." Turner concludes blandly that "the religious aspects of the frontier make a chapter in our history which needs study," implicitly acknowledging that he himself has not undertaken such a project.[99]

While Turner's frontier is a largely secular space in the older sense of a sphere free of religion, his assumption of Protestant primacy and his erasure of non-Protestant populations mark it as secular in the sense described by Tracy Fessenden, who has shown "how particular forms of Protestantism emerged as an 'unmarked category' in American religious and literary history." This "post-Protestant secularism" explains how public schools in the United States could be considered secular even though the King James Bible was part of the curriculum: because they did not favor any particular Protestant sect.[100] So naturalized is this strain of secularism in Turner's thought that one might say it has been absorbed into the continent itself, as his famous image of the United States as a "continental page" that we "read" to discover "the record of social evolution" incarnates a kind of Protestant textualism.[101] In other words, Turnerian space is secular not because it is a space free of religion but rather because it is so saturated with Protestantism that its sectarian character is rendered invisible.

It is in this sense that Turnerian space offers analytical purchase for understanding Catholic conspiracy in sensational fiction. Turner's definition of the frontier as "the line of most rapid and effective Americanization" provides the mechanism by which the national, sectional, and ethnic differences of white settlers are sublimated into "a composite nationality": the frontier provides the "crucible" in which local, particular identities are melted into a common national identity. In other words, it is a site of the transcendent political mediation that Asad describes as characteristic of modern liberal democracies. Recognizing religion as one of the key features of identity that must be transcended for secularism to be successful enables the reinscription of the religious difference that has been erased from Turner's frontier scene of national mediation. When that happens, the Turnerian frontier clash of "savagery and civilization" metamorphoses into a Manichean struggle between Protestants and Catholics. In other words, the sensational imagination takes up what Turner would later describe as the inexorable, progressive frontier process of Americanization and probes the incomplete work of political mediation left in its wake, essentially rewinding history and reanimating the apocalyptic geographies of the colonial past. In place of Turner's confident teleology from frontier colony to settled nation, sensation portrays a process in which political mediation is disrupted, arrested, and reversed, a continent where the frontier "wave" of Americanization doesn't roll placidly on to the Pacific but breaks against conflicting identities and non-national communities that retain the potential to pursue other political and cultural futures.[102]

Streeby may be right that Lippard "placed his hopes in another version of (Turnerian) exceptionalism," but not simply because he believed that "'free' Western lands might serve as a safety valve for such domestic social and economic antagonisms and that U.S. expansion would mean the extension of the area of freedom rather than the violent conquest of other nations." When Lippard elides the continental interior and converts the "battle" (NY, 282) he has predicted between Catholics and Protestants into an orderly westward exodus through a landscape devoid of religious conflict, he inhabits another dimension of Turnerian space: a post-Protestant secular landscape of transcendent political mediation that displaces religious difference to the margins. By the same token, when Streeby writes that Lippard supported war with "Catholic Mexico" to guarantee "freedom and democracy" for the (Protestant) United States, she reveals the extent to which she and other literary geographers of the "Empire of Sensation" inhabit Turnerian secular space as well.[103] Or perhaps it might be more accurate to call it Lippardian space, the geography of corrupt eastern industrial cities and vacant hinterlands elaborated in the antebellum sensational literary imagination. Meanwhile, on those supposedly empty "vast prairies," a group of regional writers, editors, and publishers began to fill in the blank spaces on the literary map.

The Great West and the Sacred Spatial Fix

The clash between the West's political identity and its cultural ambitions reflected in the marketing of Lippard's *New York* played out in one of the region's premier literary weeklies, the *Columbian & Great West*, and culminated in its publication of a western city-mystery novel that responded directly to Lippard. The story of how this came about reveals how regional culture grappled with the spatial problems of capitalism analyzed by nineteenth-century social theorists and, more recently, by human geographers; moreover, that culture connected those material conflicts over land use to religious conflict in a way that challenges and revises standard mappings of the antebellum political landscape.

Proudly proclaiming itself "Devoted to Western Literature and Western Interests," the Cincinnati-based weekly story paper (which began in 1848 simply as the *Great West*) was launched by Cincinnati publisher Robinson and Jones.[104] It featured original pioneer tales and border legends by popular regional authors such as Emerson Bennett and Charles Summerfield—the same sort of fare the firm published in its cheap 25-cent pamphlet novels—as well as reprinted fiction by luminaries such as Charles Dickens, Alexandre Dumas, and George Lippard. Printed in nine columns across four "mammoth size" pages, the *Great West* was as big and cheap as eastern story papers, its editors boasted, but it was "thoroughly western in its character," and "WESTERN PEOPLE SHOULD SUSTAIN IT, in preference to the flood of trash emanating east of the mountains."[105] Beyond advancing a regional literary agenda, the paper's editors promoted a geographically expansive conception of the West that stressed its urban character: "We do not design the '*Great* West' for a merely local sheet, but shall endeavor to present in its columns a picture of the whole Mississippi valley. Especial effort will be made to keep well advised of the most prominent facts of interest in all the great western cities," which meant providing "the news of each important point from Pittsburgh to New Orleans."[106] Over the next two years the paper opened offices in Pittsburgh, Louisville, St. Louis, and (briefly) Detroit; news items were initially divided between these "Western Cities" and "Eastern Cities" including New York, Philadelphia, and Baltimore.[107] Its coverage reflected the agenda of cultural, economic, and political autonomy that the editors announced in the very first issue: "Depending on western patronage it will endeavor to promote western interests, encourage western literature and art, sustain western effort in every branch of industry, and in every mode in the power of its conductors assume an independent position."[108]

The political and economic aspects of that agenda found expression in a regional republican rhetoric that stressed the West's promise of shared prosperity and its ability (thanks to its abundant land) to avoid the disparities in wealth that afflicted eastern and European societies. In a series of articles titled "The West: Its History and Resources," editor L. A. Hine confidently predicted that "after the battle of the present is fought, none of this vast population are to know the pains of poverty, but all are to have every want abundantly supplied. True, we cannot now, in our infancy, with more than a thousand millions of unsold acres, boast of freedom from extremes of wealth on the one hand, and extremes of poverty on the other. But to-day pure and mighty influences are at work, which will fraternize the race, and secure to all an abundance from the common bounties of heaven."[109] Complementing this sense of regional exceptionalism, the paper regularly reported on crime, labor strife, and anti-Catholic violence in eastern cities.[110] In articulating a version of the "safety-valve" theory that had shaped Anglo-American attitudes and policy toward western lands for a century—the theory that "free land will constantly attract laborers from the cities and thus keep wages high"—the paper promoted a version of what David Harvey calls "the spatial fix," the idea that the "internal contradictions" that afflict societies under market capitalism can be resolved by "an *outer* transformation through imperialism, colonialism and geographical expansion." Nineteenth-century theorists who first noted this dynamic pointed to the North American "frontier" as an example of the spatial fix in action, but the pressing question for Johann von Thünen, Hegel, and Marx (as well as for Turner decades later) was whether it represented a permanent "solution" to the conditions of capitalism or only a temporary reprieve that would ultimately reproduce those conditions in new lands.[111]

If the editors of the *Great West* initially expressed the optimistic view, by the early 1850s, as troubling signs of economic inequality and urban disorder in western cities crept into the paper's coverage, the second possibility seemed increasingly likely. In February 1850 editors warned that migration from "the overcrowded east to the broad and productive west" was bringing not only "the hardy son of toil" but also "the enervated child of wealth"—ministers and other members of "learned or aristocratic professions."[112] Meanwhile the labor unrest that had typically filled the "Eastern Cities" column began to appear closer to home.[113] "Our Firemen had a row on Tuesday night of last week, in imitation of their Philadelphia brethren," the paper reported. "We hope they are not going to re-enact here the scenes that have so thoroughly disgraced that city."[114] But "re-enact" they did, and the riots continued into the summer.[115] In April 1850 a piece titled "The Laboring Poor" contrasted the desperate conditions of London workers with those in Cincinnati, where wages were supposedly 50 percent higher; but it also cited a report of the Cincinnati Relief Union as evidence of poverty in that city and predicted that as the population of the West increased, "the independence of the laborer will diminish, from his inability to become a land-holder, and he must be thrown into the market of labor."[116] Perhaps most tellingly, urban slums had appeared in the Queen City. In 1853 the editors reported the existence of "poor people in Cincinnati, living in crazy, rickety old buildings, in damp cellars, beneath noisome yards, by the very circumstances surrounding them, being made quarrelsome, intemperate, vulgar and vicious"; they called for "a thorough investigation into the condition of these people" that "would lead to the recommendation of practical plans for their elevation and improvement."[117] Thus when Lippard's *New York* appeared in the city in late 1853, it entered an anxious discussion already underway in the regional press about urban disorder in the West and its relation to that found in other industrial cities in Europe and the northeastern United States.

The central role of immigration in that discussion, whether the arrival of "aristocratic" Protestant ministers or poor Catholic workers, hints at the religious dimensions of the region's social and economic conflicts. The *Great West* complicates its own mapping of the region as a safety valve with a hemispheric account of embattled republicanism in the Catholic Americas. Its inaugural issue contained the first of an original series titled "Sketches of Travel in Central America" by regional author F. Lindo. Though a far cry from the sensational pyrotechnics of Lindo's novel *Revenge; or, The Robber of Guatemala* (published in pamphlet form by Robinson and Jones the same year), "Sketches" begins with a history of revolution and republican instability: "Like the numerous other Republics scattered over the continent of South America, Central America has from time to time, since her Declaration of Independence, been the scene of numerous revolutions and counter revolutions, which have laid waste her country, cramped her commerce, impoverished her inhabitants, rent asunder all the ties of kindred, and caused many dreadful scenes of carnage and bloodshed." While noting these states' overthrow of Spanish rule and their efforts to build republics modeled upon the United States, Lindo describes a descent into political chaos fueled by religious conflict. The threat initially appears in the form of anti-Catholic violence by Honduran general Francisco Morazán, who, having seized power in four of the five young Central American republics in 1828, invaded Guatemala the following year and immediately coordinated an "attack . . . against the religion and the religious institutions of the place," ransacking and occupying churches, emptying convents, and banishing many of the friars and monks. The kind of violent attacks against Catholic institutions that nativists had stoked in the Northeast in the name of moral order here emerge as symptoms of moral depravity and despotism; yet Lindo goes on to relate how Rafael Carrera, the young Guatemalan leader who quickly emerged to lead the resistance against Morazán, received support from the local Catholic clergy, who encouraged a native population still "emerg[ing] from the darkness of idolatry" to see Carrera as a divine figure. As Carrera revealed himself to be just as cruel and brutal as Morazán, a protracted civil war ensued. The sketch closes with a scene of post-republican anarchy, in which "numberless bands of marauders of either party roved about the country robbing and murdering passengers": "The Federal Government might now be said to have been entirely dissolved, and every state to constitute a small and distinct Republic, there being no acknowledged President."[118]

From one perspective Lindo's history simply rehearses racist Anglo-American beliefs about the unfitness of non-white Catholics for republican self-governance. But as it projects the specter of political disorder and disunion outward onto non-Protestant locales in Central America, the sketch also displays the dynamic Susan Griffin has described in nineteenth-century British fiction in which the dangers posed by a "foreign" Catholicism sublimate the internal anxieties and conflicts generated by colonialism, shoring up the construction of an "emphatically Protestant" national identity that is "acutely threatened from without and within."[119] This effort to ease internal pressures through appeals to global geographies of religious difference parallels the economic displacement represented by the spatial fix. In other words, Lindo's account of the failure of Central American republicanism shows how Protestant secular modernity attempts to exorcise its own political and economic conflicts and to cast them out into the Catholic wilderness: a sacred spatial fix.

Of course the Mississippi Valley *was* the Catholic wilderness, or at least it had been historically. The *Great West* acknowledged as much in an account of the history of the Catholic presence in North America and its role in the region's economic and political development. The same article by Hine that opens by explicitly elaborating the spatial fix, explaining how the region's free land will guarantee an escape from economic inequality, abruptly shifts to a history of European settlement of North America in which Spain "claimed the whole as a free gift from Pope Alexander the sixth." This papal land-grab becomes the opening act in an unfolding continental drama of murder and colonial exploitation by gold-grubbing Spanish "adventurers." Hine presents these men not as medieval throwbacks but as forerunners of modern *homo economicus* driven by "motives of temporary gain," so that "the most covetous as well as the most unscrupulous were the first to hail the lakes and rivers, the hills and the mountains, as also the broad rolling prairie and the stately forests of the western continent." Here the Black Legend, the myth that contrasted the horrors of Spanish colonization of the New World with the supposedly benign process overseen by Protestant Europeans, converges with an economic myth about the Catholic origins of the capitalist exploitation of the Americas. Unfortunately the next several installments of Hine's series do not survive, so it's unclear how the Catholic presence in the West has shaped the "battle of the present" that will guarantee "abundance" to the "almost innumerable millions who are to live from [the West's] exuberant soil."[120] But to the extent that Marx's predictions prove correct—that the spatial fix is merely a temporary remedy for the structural contradictions of capitalism—Hine implies that the failure of the West to escape the pattern set by Atlantic cities would mean a reversion to the region's original Catholic economic geography—a fall back into Catholic space.

For Lindo and Hine, the colonial history of the Americas tempers the proto-Turnerian progress narrative characteristic of the paper's frontier tales. Here the East-West axis of a work like Emerson Bennett's *Mike Fink: A Legend of the Ohio* (which began in the same issue as Hine's series on the West) meets a South-North axis that locates the Mississippi Valley within a fractious hemispheric postcolonial geography where a secular, nationalist teleology can never be assumed. This was the geography readers found in "The Mystic Clan," a chapter from Emerson Bennett's novel *The Traitor; or, The Fate of Ambition* (1850) that the paper published as a front-page "Historical Romance" on April 27, 1850. The chapter introduces an Italian Jesuit priest named Father Anselmo who, following a failed conspiracy attempt to "effect the disunion of the [U.S.] Republic," has moved to New Orleans and formed a secret order of "men of all professions . . . scattered all over the States and throughout Spanish America." Summoning a secret meeting of this Mystic Clan, Anselmo describes Aaron Burr's conspiracy to lead an army down the Ohio and Mississippi rivers, seize New Orleans, and march into Mexico to "establish an empire, extending southward to the Isthmus of Darien, westward to the Pacific, northward to the lakes, and eastward to the Alleghany mountains," with New Orleans as its capital. After the clan's members enthusiastically vote to support the plot, they remove their cowls and masks to reveal a who's who of the city's political and military leaders. While Bennett's Catholic conspiracy plot comes straight out of Lippard's sensational playbook, his geographical framing gives that plot a distinctive regional twist, blending hemispheric Catholic space with a tradition of republican political thought that had long warned of the danger of western territories escaping the national orbit and following other political destinies.[121]

While the *Great West*'s nonfictional and fictional accounts of the past warned of the threat Catholic space posed to republican ideals, its coverage of the contemporary Catholic presence was more circumspect. "Recently our city was agitated by a passionate and prejudiced excitement, growing out of stimulated religious and political hates and prejudices," the editors declared in a report titled "The Catholic Element in America" in April 1854. Noting that Catholics made up about two million out of a total U.S. population of twenty-six million, the editors argued that "the aggregate force of Methodists, Baptists and Presbyterians is amply sufficient to preserve, yet awhile, the Protestant integrity of the nation" and that therefore "the zeal of those persons, who stand up in market places, and proclaim great danger of the subversion of our Government from Catholic influence, is rather distempered."[122] But if Catholic immigrants were not the immediate political threat that some nativists claimed, were they nonetheless an economic threat? In March 1850 the paper excerpted an item from the Cincinnati *Catholic Telegraph* that urged Irish laborers to stay home: "If the unfortunate people of the old country who emigrate to this, only knew the hardships endured by those who, from want of means, are forced to wander about New York, Boston, Philadelphia, Cincinnati and New Orleans, begging from door to door for the means of supporting life, they would prefer *to remain at home*, sooner than come to America *without the means* of getting into the interior and western States. A strong, active, and industrious Irish workman might as well commence digging his own grave, as to shut himself up in one of our large cities," where they will find only "misery, poverty, wretchedness, and starvation." Here the *Great West* editor breaks in to object:

> But whither shall the penniless poor go to escape the miseries of poverty? They are generally unacquainted with the agricultural system of this country, and cannot obtain a living as hired laborers on the farm. They have no money to go west, and settle themselves—what can they do! They get from seventy-five cents to one dollar a day in cities, and can live on a trifle; while they could not obtain eight dollars a month in the country, unless they found employment on some public works.

It is a startling exchange: a secular (and hence tacitly Protestant) paper rejecting a Catholic paper's claim that Irish workers should stay in Ireland and arguing that they should become urban wage laborers, at least temporarily. Urban employment, the piece makes clear, is not a permanent solution but a transitional state to agricultural settlement through land reform: "Were the wilderness free to actual settlers in limited quantities there would be some encouragement for poor foreigners, and the poor natives also to clear our cities and settle in their own homes, where they could obtain abundance, and live in quietude and virtue."[123] So firm is the editor's belief in the agrarian safety valve that Catholic immigrants pose no real threat to republican order so long as they eventually can pass through the cities and disperse into the hinterlands where, like Turner's frontier settlers, they will undergo seamless mediation into virtuous republican citizens.

Indeed, within the paper's producerist worldview, Catholic immigrant laborers were far preferable to Protestant missionaries, teachers, and other eastern "non-producers" who the editors warned were being sent westward from New England by "organizations, which, by combined influence, hope to get rid of an unproductive and idle population of young *gentlemen and ladies.*" The prospect of an "eastern aristocracy... endeavor[ing] to get rid of its surplus progeny" through benevolent efforts highlights the religious dynamics of the safety valve theory as interpreted by western boosters. Surveying the continent from the Mississippi Valley, they beheld a prospect starkly different than the benighted backwater described by northeastern evangelicals—a place in desperate need of efforts (in the sarcastic words of the *Great West*'s editors) "to improve western morals and educate our *heathen* youth."[124] Here, as the influx of "surplus progeny" from New England that threatens the region's economic prosperity merges with the religious imperialism threatening its cultural autonomy, the *Great West*'s economic and cultural agendas become one. We witness the spatial fix from the outside, as it were: a resentful view from the periphery that grasps how the Protestant center has constructed the West as "*heathen*" space in order to provide a safety valve for eastern economic and social pressures.

Thus, even as regional boosters promoted their own spatial fix in order to relieve Cincinnati and other western centers of their growing populations of poor workers, they resisted the region's positioning as a spatial fix for larger metropolitan centers to the east. This bifurcation recalls Saler's sense of the "political 'doubleness'" of the states of the Old Northwest and highlights the religious dimensions of that doubleness. The *Great West* promoted its own version of the sacred spatial fix when it chronicled political chaos in Central America or envisioned land reform transforming urban Catholic workers into virtuous republican yeomen. Yet its defense of Catholic immigration and its rejection of the cultural imperialism of northeastern evangelicals suggest an alternative spatial logic: rather than a Protestant center projecting internal conflicts outward onto Catholic space, here a distant metropole that is coded as Catholic—whether the European source of Catholic immigrants or an eastern evangelical establishment whose sinister scheming seems downright Romish—is mediated by the secular (Protestant) republican periphery.

From the Empire City to the Queen City: City-Mysteries and the Vision of the Secular

These anxious debates about the nature of western development formed the backdrop to the homegrown urban literature that began to appear in the *Columbian & Great West*. The first efforts were tame, a far cry from the gritty urban mysteries set in eastern and European cities.[125] This reflected the genteel aspirations of a paper that criticized works by Eugène Sue and Edward Bulwer-Lytton as part of "that noxious flood that, under the general name of 'Cheap Literature,' has within the past eight or ten years submerged so much of classic literature, and drowned out so much of good taste and wholesome sentiment."[126] City-mysteries fiction was on the radar, but its reputation for low subject matter and stylistic license made it an object of satire more than emulation: as one headline quipped, "Mysteries and Miseries. Of the Life of a City Editor. From the Yankee Blade—By One of 'Em."[127] Nonetheless, by the early 1850s the paper's literary content was shifting: its long-time staples—frontier tales, excerpts of popular works by the likes of Dickens and Dumas, and high-toned literary notices—began to give way to samples of city-mysteries fiction from abroad, urban sketches from Cincinnati and other cities, and news reports of horrific explosions and murders beneath headlines bristling with exclamation points.[128] The paper had brought together all the ingredients for a homegrown city-mystery—but it had not yet produced an actual specimen.

That was about to change. In February 1855, the paper's editors announced that starting in March the paper would publish "The Queen City—Its Mysteries and Miseries," a "thrilling novelette, by C. P. Bickley, Esq., which will run through six or seven numbers in our paper."[129] Noting that Bickley was "one of the most popular of Western authors," the paper promised that "the scenes are natural and life-like—and the characters drawn with a bold and fearless pen. We feel no hesitation in saying that it is one of the most thrilling stories we have ever read."[130] The novel's prologue telegraphed its intertextual engagement with Lippard's *New York*, stating the author's "resolution of giving in novel form a true picture of life in the Queen City, including its 'upper ten and lower million.'"[131] In a pamphlet edition of the novel published later that year as *The Mock Marriage*, publisher E. Mendenhall amplified the connection by placing a full-page ad for *New York* on the back cover.[132]

Despite the suggestion that the novel would present Cincinnati as a western rival to New York, threatened by similar disparities of wealth, *The Mock Marriage* opens with a literary prospect that seems closer to Klauprecht than Lippard. The reader surveys the site of Cincinnati as it existed sixty years earlier, a small military fort "on the border of a beaver pond, in the middle of a dense forest of beech trees." Jumping forward to the present, "the dense forest has been leveled and extirpated; the beaver pond has been filled up, and in lieu thereof has arisen a mighty city—the 'Queen of the West.'" Instead of "towering beech, elm, and sycamore," the eye finds "lofty steeples, whose spires pierce the sky, while from river to hill-side and summit, covering all the space, are churches, colleges, public edifices, and private mansions, standing on well-bowldered streets and avenues" (*MM*, 9). A scene that draws attention to the city's thriving religious and civic institutions and its balance of private wealth and public infrastructure seems an inauspicious start to a novel promising to unveil the city's "Mysteries and Miseries." Unlike Klauprecht's view from Mount Adams, here the built environment is studiedly non-sectarian, registering the city's prosperity without revealing signs of religious conspiracy or economic inequality that might undermine it.

Almost immediately, however, social disorder appears. "The composition of Cincinnati is truly fragmentary, and the population presents many varieties," Bickley notes, describing a "foreign population" of some sixty thousand Europeans made up largely of Germans and Irish, as well as "a large colored population, consisting chiefly of emancipated slaves and their children." Each of these groups, he claims, has failed to fully integrate into the life of the city in some way, whether economically or culturally. The free black community's "many fruitless attempts to elevate itself" have failed in part because the abolitionist community is more interested in helping runaway slaves and distributing tracts than "establishing schools and educating 'the dear colored people'" (*MM*, 10). The Germans have refused to assimilate, settling in a quarter "where they have German churches, German schools, German theaters, German papers" and where they indulge their "pernicious" habits of "drinking, theatergoing," and other "amusements" on the Sabbath, while the rest of the week they pursue "the 'almighty dollar'" at the expense of "every public good" (11). The Irish, though they have the potential to become "valuable citizens," hail "from a priest-ridden land" and so tend to "clan together, and keep up their distinctive Irish peculiarities," acting "as though every person they met, who was not an Irishman, was their enemy" (11–12). In Bickley's view, racial, ethnic, and religious difference poses a clear threat to the city's progress, defined in terms of open markets, republican virtue, and Protestant moral order. Nonetheless, this opening chapter concludes with the confident assertion that "the relative position of Cincinnati is highly favorable to its growth and permanent prosperity" (12). Bickley means "position" literally: "Situated at the base of the valley of the Miamis, one of the most fertile of all vallies [*sic*], abounding in agricultural products of every variety, . . . and commanding by its lines of communication an area of two hundred thousand square miles, it is destined, at no distant day, by the centralization of internal commerce, and the development of its own resources, to rival New York itself" (12). Zooming out to situate Cincinnati within its vast hinterland, Bickley provides a perspective from which the city's social conflicts can be resolved into a unified and productive whole, essentially visualizing the spatial fix in the pastoral landscape. In what might be called a panoramic social aesthetic, issues such as ethnic particularity, religious difference, and racial inequality pose no real threat to a prospect whose unity is grounded in the providential circumstances of geography itself.[133]

Yet this initial sense of assurance quickly crumbles. The real danger, it turns out, is not these heterogeneous social elements but a sinister combination of a "sporting culture" of sexually aggressive young men and the city's wealthy elites.[134] Bickley introduces two well-born libertines who will drive that staple of city-mysteries fiction, the seduction plot: Charles Pembroke, a handsome and talented son of an elite Virginia family who has moved to Cincinnati after the death of his parents only to fall into "dissipation" (*MM*, 12) and gamble away his inheritance; and his friend Gus Williams, a gambler and rake of obscure origins who is a clear nod to Gus Lorrimer, the villain of Lippard's *Quaker City*. When they encounter a pretty, virtuous seamstress named Adelaide Wilson hurrying home to her sick mother one night and Pembroke accompanies her home intending to seduce her, they reveal a form of social disorder resembling that of New York and Philadelphia, undermining the panoramic social aesthetic Bickley has used to frame the city and its hinterland.

Adelaide's vulnerability is a sign of emerging social stratification in the Queen City. As the child of a middle-class widow who has slipped into poverty after being cheated by the executor of her husband's estate, Adelaide retains both the "neatness by which persons of the middle class are generally distinguished" (*MM*, 14) and her mother's Protestant piety. Her brother, Tom Wilson, has taken a job as a fireman and dreams of marrying his sweetheart but has begun to drift into a rowdy working-class bar culture where he can indulge his love for whiskey, or "'craythur' as an Irishman would say" (31). Despite clinging precariously to middle-class Protestant values against a rising tide of urban disorder, the Wilsons find themselves sucked into an urban underworld that churns into life every night while the "respectable portion of the city's population" (18) sleeps, epitomized by an organized crime ring called the "Mystic League" that recalls Bennett's Jesuit-led "Mystic Clan" five years earlier.

As the Wilsons struggle against disorder from below, Cincinnati's republican order is also threatened from above. The "thieving land sharks" who have preyed on the Wilsons are commonly viewed as "shrewd business men"; many are "prominent members of [the] church, and profess (!) to be pious and devout Christians" who regularly observe the Sabbath and "contribute freely for missionary purposes from their hoarded wealth" (*MM*, 32). Just as Bickley codes Cincinnati's underworld as Catholic, he tars the city's wealthy elites as hypocritical Protestants, borrowing a trope from the pages of Lippard and Thompson.[135] Bickley's central example of someone who "swindles his fellow man in a commercial way during the week, worships God in a twenty dollar pew on the Sabbath, and spends his nights in a brothel" (53) is Jonathan Snobson, "a model of American aristocracy" who "represent[s] a class found in all our principal American cities" (26). A farm boy who rose from nothing to become a successful businessman, Snobson has retired with his fortune to a lavish mansion on Fourth Street to indulge his aristocratic pretensions. When he learns that a European nobleman is to visit Cincinnati, he exclaims, "A real Baronet! ... I must try to find out where he is sojourning, and introduce him into OUR circle. He must be shown that there is an 'upper ten' in America, notwithstanding all their talk about democracy and equality" (27). Snobson is especially excited by the idea of being immortalized as "one of the representatives of 'upper-tendom' in the United States" (29) once the Baronet publishes an account of his travels. The presence of men like Snobson pulls Bickley's exceptionalist regional account back within a national framework of fading republican ideals. Cincinnati's ability to represent "America" here signals not the city's prosperous expansion but its infiltration by aristocratic social distinctions, abetted by a self-serving commercial elite that masks its exploitative behavior behind a veneer of Protestant piety.

Yet even as Snobson suggests that Cincinnati has become as corrupt as any other American city, Bickley quickly equivocates: "The Queen City, in some respects, is widely different from any other American city; and we do not know that we can with propriety say that it has an 'upper ten.' It certainly has its wealth, and must in its necessity have its nabobs, but the most of them are engaged in the active cares of life." Cincinnati may suffer from extremes of wealth, but what distinguishes it is the fact that most of its wealthy citizens have not retired to idly enjoy their wealth. Bickley appeals, in short, to a form of producer ideology that posits a harmony of social interests among mechanics and businessmen so long as they continue to work. His portrait of Snobson, while accurate, "is only drawn to represent a certain portion" of the city's elites, "the moneyed aristocracy"; the task of the novel remains to represent the rest of the social landscape in order to reveal what distinguishes Cincinnati "from any other American city" (*MM*, 29). The panoramic social aesthetic encapsulated in Bickley's opening chapter—an initial unity that is challenged by the appearance of social diversity but is ultimately transcended by a unity that inheres in geography itself—here is recapitulated and projected across the entire novel.

This structure can be traced through the novel on two levels: in the plot itself, as the fate of the Wilsons, the seduction schemes of Williams and Pembroke, and Snobson's social ambitions enact an allegory of Cincinnati's development; and in a series of urban sketches that interrupt the action to provide local color and an opportunity for Bickley to hold forth on the city's problems. In one of these sketches, a crowd in front of the National Theater becomes "a panorama of real life": "Here is a scene for contemplation: a picture of life as it is. Let us walk through the crowd, and observe its composition"

(*MM*, 15–16). The ensuing parade of urban types includes the "dandy," the "country merchant," and the "market-man." The sketch soon pivots, however, from aestheticized "contemplation" of social diversity to alarm at the threat it poses: quoting Unitarian minister William Ellery Channing, Bickley laments how the theater "has nourished intemperance, and all vice" and calls for a form of theater that would be a "means of refining the taste and elevating the character of a people" (16). With this moralistic pirouette, the idea conveyed in the novel's opening prospect—that social variety naturally produces a mutually beneficial economic order that becomes visible once we achieve a perspective broad enough to encompass the whole of society—is suddenly undercut. In place of an aesthetic mode that materializes and naturalizes laissez-faire capitalism, Bickley offers one that is not content to "contemplate[e] social diversity and represent it "in a life-like manner" (36) but must manage and reform it through the agency not of "the clergy" but of "the press" (17). Here the novel's use of the prospect as a metaphor for the comprehension of a specialized regional economy gives way to a civic discourse that links elevated vision with the moral discipline imparted by print.

While the jarring inconsistencies in Bickley's novel might be attributed to hasty composition or poor craftsmanship, the effect is to destabilize his initial account of Cincinnati as a prosperous republican society in which wealth is equitably shared. Can the threat of social stratification and moral disorder enacted in the plot and in the intercalary sketches ultimately be contained and overcome? The verdict must await the novel's conclusion. Bickley's final sketch offers a potential source of stability, placing "a free press" in the position of an independent observer responsible for surveying the whole of society and keeping competing elements in check: "In a republican government, like the one under which we live, all sources and levers of power should be carefully watched, and every step beyond the proper limits, that may be assumed by either an individual or a clique of individuals, should be instantly held up to public scrutiny. The press is certainly a most important power in this, as it necessarily must be in all republican governments." Yet Bickley warns of "a servility in the press of the United States . . . which is neither American nor Christian" (*MM*, 83). He unleashes a blistering critique of the fiction of the public sphere as it is conceived in modern secular democracies—in Charles Taylor's formulation, "a public sphere, in which people conceive themselves as participating directly in a nationwide (sometimes even international) discussion" rather than being "mediated" by hierarchies of social rank, local authorities, and other modes of "belonging."[136] For Taylor, that older, hierarchical social imaginary is rooted in the ancient political institutions of Europe, above all in the monarchy and the Catholic Church. These are precisely the institutions to which Bickley turns for comparison, describing how in "the despotic governments of Europe," monarchs who wish to go to war use the press to manipulate "public opinion" (83). Bickley dismisses such a possibility in the United States, where "there can never be a concentration of power in a single individual," and he rejects allegations that "foreign governments ha[ve] a paid press in this country" with the exception of "the Pope of Rome" (84). Even the pope does not pose a real threat, for "the Roman Catholic press dare not utter political sentiments anti-American in character, since public opinion would root them out as the vilest foes to human happiness" (84).

Ultimately the trouble with the American press, in Bickley's view, is that it is mediated not by kings or the pope but by the market economy. Declaring that "speculation reigns supreme in America" and that "the all-absorbing object of exertion now, and here, is money," he reasons that it is "no wonder, then, that newspaper editors and companies sell the right of private judgment, and cater to popular sentiment. A, B, or C, though known villains, by a few dollars can command the columns of newspapers, and thus force themselves on the community as paragons of virtue and excellence." Having earlier presented an example of this sort of corruption in the figure of newspaper editor Q. Quintum Quilldriver (whose copy is entirely driven by advertising revenue), Bickley laments that "for twenty cents a line, groggeries, gambling saloons, oyster cellars, theaters, etc., can be puffed to their heart's content. This is the degradation of the press. Many newspapers have mottoes or declarations setting forth their object to be, the diffusion of useful and Christian knowledge, and political information; but which, in reality, are mere mercantile bulletins." In place of this commercialized press, Bickley urges "the three thousand papers now published in the United States" to "devote, each week, one of their papers to conveying to the people the rudiments of popular education": "Let any competent editor, for one year, devote even one column to the geography of the United States, and, in less than half the time, he will find himself surrounded with a far more enlightened community than is usually found" (*MM*, 85). To recall the terms of the republican prospect, the newspaper editor has replaced the landed gentleman as the figure with a comprehensive view of society. He has the power to convey the knowledge afforded by that perspective (including, literally, his grasp of "geography") to the public to create an "enlightened community" around him. But Bickley concludes emphatically that such an "independent" (86) press does not currently exist in Cincinnati any more than it does in the nation as a whole, foreclosing the novel's last hope for unifying and managing the city's diversity.

At the level of plot, the result is equally pessimistic. Gus Williams convinces Agnes Merton, the beautiful sister of a young clerk he knows, to marry him and then abandons her; ruined, she descends into prostitution and insanity. Pembroke likewise succeeds in luring Adelaide Wilson to a brothel, where he drugs her, imprisons her in a secret cell, and rapes her; she later commits suicide. Williams and Pembroke are not allowed wholly to escape justice (or at least vengeance), for in the novel's climactic scene, as Williams participates in yet another mock-marriage ceremony, the city police arrive accompanied by Tom Wilson, who strangles Pembroke to death while the police arrest Williams. But the wealthy father of the intended victim, eager to avoid scandal, declines to press charges as long as Gus leaves town. (Whether he actually does remains uncertain, leaving occasion, Bickley hints, for a sequel.) The "infamous Madam E.," the brothel owner who conspired with Pembroke to seduce Adelaide, flees for New York, "where a wider field was probably offered for the exercise of her peculiar talents" (*MM*, 102). Tom marries his sweetheart and they move to a "little cottage ... some thirty or forty miles from the city" to start a family. He "has left the city—the scene of his many trials and triumphs, joys and sorrows—has given up 'der machine,' and become one of 'nature's noblemen'" (102). His fate marks a striking parallel with that of Lippard's Dermoyne and with the protagonists of Klauprecht's *Cincinnati*, who all abandon the city for farms in Iowa. In all three novels, the characters' ability to escape the conditions of industrial capitalism for "free land" outside the cities might be interpreted as evidence of the spatial fix in action, except that none of the novels indicate that this mobility guarantees fair working conditions in the cities the workers have left behind. Despite the efforts of regional authors and editors to portray the western city's escape from a descent into corruption and to articulate a regionally specific, urban form of republicanism that would make industrialism compatible with independence and virtue, their concluding scenes of exile and pastoral refuge ultimately reveal the region being pulled back into the orbit of national history and an agrarian myth that could only imagine the Great West as rural space.

The regionalists' choice of genre likely contributed to the failure of their literary project. That is, "the apparent contradiction between narrative and ideology" that Michael Denning has argued accounts for the absence of a genuine "mechanic hero" in city-mysteries fiction also prevented the representation of a western city that could be reformed rather than abandoned.[137] Yet I want to suggest that the problem was not simply formal. Rather, these authors grasped contradictions in what Taylor terms "horizontal, direct-access societies"—those characterized by "a public sphere," "the development of market economies, in which all economic agents are seen as entering into contractual relations with others on an equal footing; and; of course, the rise of the modern citizenship state."[138] By exposing how these fictions of direct access break down in practice into various layers of mediation, sensational authors anticipated Asad's critique of secular liberal democracies: that secularism promises individuals direct access to the nation while concealing the extent to which access remains limited by their particular positions in social and physical space—if they are non-white, for example, or poor, or Muslim, or if they live far from metropolitan centers. In antebellum America, writers working outside the national literary establishment were well positioned to grasp this reality. By adopting spatial and visual metaphors that had been used to figure political mediation since the American Revolution, they probed the limits of direct access in an expanding, diverse, and economically stratified society. In the process they articulated a potent literary critique of the secular.

Catholicism served as an especially powerful symbol in that critique. In one sense it represented the historical alternative to direct access, the "hierarchical, mediated-access societies" of premodern Europe where, Taylor writes, "belonging to a larger whole, like a kingdom, or a universal church, was through the imbrication of more immediate, understandable units of belonging, [such as the] parish, manor, town, cloister, into the greater entity."[139] The similarities between this account of nested affiliation and American federalism point to another, seemingly contradictory image of Catholicism as the harbinger of modern bureaucracy. This is the image that led Francis Parkman to cast the Society of Jesus as (in Jenny Franchot's words) a "hierarchical, finally totalitarian organization" and the Jesuits as "representatives of the modern state out to cultivate and systematize the savage remnants of the globe."[140] Simultaneously hinting at the persistence of local affiliations from the premodern past and the seeds of a bureaucratic morass in the postmodern future, Catholicism served to expose the fiction that a modern, direct-access society had flowered in antebellum United States, revealing instead the sensational spectacle of mediation gone haywire: of a society at once too mediated (insofar as many Americans still enjoyed no real access to the springs of political and economic power) and not mediated enough, in the sense that national power increasingly reached directly into the lives of citizens without the mediation of state and local governments.[141]

Then as now, "deliberation" alone was not enough to solve the problem. While Gustafson is surely correct to note "the importance of moderate, thoughtful consideration of public issues" to modern republican practice, focusing exclusively on "deliberative processes" risks neglecting the conditions of representation that make deliberation possible in the first place—the very conditions that were contested so passionately in the ratification debates of the U.S. Constitution.[142] Who was authorized to speak for whom, how should they be chosen, and how could they be kept accountable to the public? To get at those conditions, what was needed was not more deliberation but perception: the ability to see who was doing the deliberating on whose behalf and who got left out. Sensational fiction offered readers training in this form of civic scrutiny, whether it was aimed at New York, a regional hub in the West, or one of the many smaller cities and towns where city-mysteries appeared in the 1840s and 1850s. Novels that emerged from outside northeastern power centers, including Klauprecht's *Cincinnati*, Bickley's *Queen City*, and (in a different way) Lippard's *New York*, make the geographical dimensions of political mediation—the ways physical distance from the centers of power tends to equal political distance, reproducing a colonial relation—uniquely visible.

Yet the modes of perception these novels cultivate are not limited to the purely this-worldly register that Taylor calls "the immanent frame."[143] Rather, by training readers to recognize the failures of secular mediation in all of its dimensions—religious as well as social and political—these works connect the political and economic dilemmas of the extended republic to a cosmic frame of reference. They warn of a society in which workers have no safety valve through which to escape, where corrupt politicians operate without fear of accountability, Catholic immigrants fail to absorb republican values, and Protestant natives betray the spirit of their faith. Klauprecht closes his novel by quoting a Catholic newspaper from New York that reveals that the Jesuit threat is undiminished and that the Church continues "to gather the means to make the soil of Washington and Jefferson into a place for a baleful conflict for which it has prepared through so many hundred years" (*CMW*, 657). The renewed specter of holy war suggests that the sacred spatial fix is no more permanent than its economic counterpart. Rather, the failure of secular mediation—the failure to forge a national identity that transcends religious difference—ushers in the return of a repressed colonial apocalyptic geography. On this sensational terrain, an embattled Protestant empire wages holy war against the infidels lurking without its borders and within, who plot to turn the continent back into the Catholic space it always has been.

Epilogue

IN MARCH 1861 a steamboat pilot named Samuel Clemens wrote to his brother Orion from St. Louis. Responding to some piece of religious news in Orion's last letter, Clemens wrote sardonically, "You have paid the preacher! Well, that is good, also. What a man wants with religion in these breadless times, surpasses my comprehension." He then turned immediately to an extraordinary art exhibition he had just attended with his sister, Pamela, where they witnessed "the most wonderfully beautiful painting which this city has ever seen":

> I have seen it several times, but it is always a new picture—*totally* new—you seem to see nothing the second time which you saw the first. We took the opera glass, and examined its beauties minutely, for the naked eye cannot discern the little wayside flowers, and soft shadows and patches of sunshine, and half-hidden bunches of grass and jets of water which form some of its most enchanting features. There is no slurring of perspective effect about it—the most distant—the minutest object in it has a marked and distinct *personality*—so that you may count the very leaves on the trees. When you first see the tame, ordinary-looking picture, your first impulse is to turn your back upon it, and say "Humbug"—but your third visit will find your brain *gasping* and straining with futile efforts to take all the wonder in—and appreciate it in its fullness—and understand how such a miracle could have been conceived and executed by human brain and human hands. You will never get tired of looking at the picture, but your reflections—your efforts to grasp an intelligible Something—you hardly know what—will grow so painful that you will have to go away from the thing, in order to obtain relief. You may find relief, but you cannot banish the picture—it remains with you still. It is in my mind now—and the smallest feature could not be removed without my detecting it. So much for the "Heart of the Andes."[1]

Coming on the heels of his exasperated dismissal of religion, Clemens's awestruck response to Frederic Church's *The Heart of the Andes* (see Plate 2) raises questions about what exactly this "miracle" of a picture meant to him. Did his account of it mark an extension of his discussion of religion, a recognition of the way the painting had been presented as a spiritual aid by reviewers and clergymen as it toured the country? Did it represent a tacit answer to the question of "what a man wants with religion in these breadless times," or did it rather signal the abandonment of religious questions in favor of a more secular domain of aesthetic judgment and optical phenomena? And what are we to make of the tension between the tenacious hold of the painting on Clemens's mind—an object that "you cannot banish"—with his pat dismissal of it?

This incident encapsulates the tension between two scholarly versions of Mark Twain: an older account of the religious vandal personified in the gleeful, irreverent narrator of *The Innocents Abroad*—the arch realist who declared the task of the humorist to be "the deriding of shams, the exposure of pretentious falsities, the laughing of stupid superstitions out of existence"; and a more recent account that sees Twain as a conflicted, one might say Melvillean, figure who raged against the religious platitudes of his age yet refused to abandon the search for spiritual truth—a tortured soul who could affirm in the same breath "that Christianity is the very invention of Hell itself" and "that Christianity is the most precious and elevating and ennobling boon ever vouchsafed to the world."[2] As Tracy Fessenden notes, this latter account registers the difficulty of neatly mapping Twain's career onto an Enlightenment "binary between belief and unbelief," complicating the "comic and emancipatory view of secularization" that celebrates "the emancipatory power of unbelief." But if Twain represents in microcosm the contradictions and limitations of the new secular synthesis emerging in the post–Civil War United States, a "Protestant-secular continuum" that "accommodates varying (though not all) degrees of Protestant Christian commitment while rendering alternative religious worlds un-American or invisible," his ambivalent response to *The Heart of the Andes* signals equally seismic shifts in the national mediascape.[3] Those developments would ultimately lead to the eclipse of evangelicals' use of the landscape as a spiritual medium but also to the persistence and transformation of their distinctive mode of apocalyptic vision.

As this book has shown, that mode was the product of several cultural forces that converged beginning in the 1820s: the rise of a popular national landscape aesthetic embodied in a network of public galleries, exhibitions, and tourist sites, the spiritual dimensions of which were explored in the words of evangelical ministers and authors; the ascendance of a reform-oriented strain of Protestant evangelicalism that saw human actions as decisive factors in bringing about the millennium; and the development of a modern system of mass media capable of disseminating words and images to millions of people simultaneously. Together these factors created a sacralized mediascape in which the landscape was the central image, one capable of revealing the contours of sacred history and geography and locating the individual believer within that cosmic drama.

After the Civil War that synthesis began to fray. In the visual realm, already in the 1850s and 1860s the atmospheric luminism of painters like Sanford Robinson Gifford and John Frederick Kensett signaled a turn away from "the narrative or plot-based approach to landscape painting" pursued by Cole, Church, and other Hudson River School painters in favor of "a visual universe purged of time, progress, and history." As Angela Miller explains, by the last quarter of the century "the literary mediation of the Sister Arts had given way to a greater reliance on the intrinsic qualities of the image and its ability to mimic the sensations and aesthetic perceptions encountered in nature itself. One no longer required an interpretive text; the image *was* the text."[4] Meanwhile by the 1860s critics had begun to question the Ruskinian pursuit of carefully observed natural detail that Church had wrought to such perfection, and artists increasingly turned away from Anglo-American aesthetic models toward European ones. George Inness epitomized this turn to a more "cosmopolitan" mode of vision that drew from French contemporaries like Jean-François Millet, Théodore Rousseau, and other Barbizon school artists, leading critics to hail him as the quintessentially "modern" American artist after the Civil War.[5] At the same time, an emerging split between "high" and "low" culture increasingly hampered the ability of Great Pictures like Church's to both please the critics and wow the crowds who flocked to panoramas and other visual spectacles.[6] When Albert Bierstadt's *The Last of the Buffalo* (1888) was rejected by the American selection committee for the 1889 Exposition Universelle in Paris, the gigantic canvas unwittingly memorialized not just the decimation of the bison but, as Tim Barringer puts it, "the impending extinction of a cultural aesthetic—the nineteenth-century American Sublime."[7]

The strain of postmillennial evangelicalism that had played such a vital role in shaping that aesthetic underwent significant changes itself in the decades following the Civil War. In the short term, the Union victory energized many Northern evangelicals, confirming their belief in the United States as God's chosen people, rekindling a sense of reformist activism, and raising hopes of a dawning millennial age.[8] The war seemed to confirm the ascendance of evangelical culture and its success in molding middle-class culture in its own image. As George Marsden puts it, "In 1870 almost all American Protestants thought of America as a Christian nation.... The Civil war, widely interpreted as 'a true Apocalyptic contest,' had been the greatest test of American evangelical civilization." Yet that order, premised on "the interrelationship of faith, science, the Bible, morality, and civilization," faced a multipronged crisis that ranged from the intellectual challenges posed by German "higher criticism" (which had begun to percolate through American thought in the 1830s) and Darwinian evolution to a new set of social conditions including immigration, urbanization, industrialization, and labor strife.[9]

As a result, in the 1870s evangelicalism splintered into a number of competing "subcultures" defined by distinct moral concerns and eschatological visions.[10] Among these was the liberal Protestant theology of Henry Ward Beecher, who sought to reconcile Christianity to modern culture in part by identifying morality as the essence of religion and denying any sense of the supernatural apart from natural processes.[11] For liberals like Beecher, millennialism ceased to be "an article of literal belief" and became instead "a theological metaphor for social progress."[12] The opposite tack was taken by the emerging strain of evangelicalism that united Wheaton College president Charles Blanchard with the popular Chicago revivalist Dwight L. Moody in urging Christians to separate from a corrupt world (largely by renouncing "worldly pleasures"). Corresponding to this conflict between Christianity and modern culture that would define twentieth-century fundamentalism was a premillennialism that required not benevolent action to bring about God's Kingdom (as antebellum revivalists like Finney had preached) but simply converting individual sinners. As Moody famously declared in tones that would become increasingly familiar to twentieth-century evangelicalism, "I look upon this world as a wrecked vessel. God has given me a lifeboat and said to me, 'Moody, save all you can.'"[13] This pessimistic outlook was elaborated by the dispensational prophecies of Irish theologian John Nelson Darby, a member of the evangelical Plymouth Brethren sect who narrated sacred history as a series of seven historical eras or "dispensations" he found described in the Bible. To Darby, "the world was not getting better, but instead growing increasingly wicked. Men and women could do nothing to forestall God's imminent judgment."[14] Introduced to North America by several personal trips Darby made between 1862 and 1877 and popularized through a series of conferences and publications that began in the late 1870s and culminated with the *Scofield Reference Bible* (1909), dispensationalism ensured that twentieth-century evangelicalism would continue to be captivated by the apocalypse.[15] But it was a premillennial apocalypse in which the Earth was merely a husk to be discarded, not a sacred medium through which believers could read the signs of the times as it had been for Jonathan Edwards and his followers.

Finally, the Civil War dramatically reshaped America's religious mediascape. Deepening sectional divides over slavery in the 1850s decimated the membership rolls and contributions of the major evangelical publishing societies (the American Bible Society, American Tract Society, and American Sunday School Union) and undermined their claims to be truly national organizations. Meanwhile the schisms that had split the Presbyterians, Methodists, and Baptists over the slavery issue in the 1830s and 1840s fueled denominational publishing efforts that increasingly competed with the interdenominational societies. In response to these sectional and denominational pressures, after the Civil War the evangelical societies turned to foreign missionary work, efforts to convert Native Americans, and specialty publications, but the decline was unmistakable: once part of a vast media empire fueled by grandiose ambitions of converting the entire world, they had been reduced to "niche publisher[s]." "In every sense—doctrinal, denominational, technological, and organizational," David Paul Nord notes, "the religious landscape of late nineteenth-century America was too rich and pluralistic for any one national agency to dominate."[16] The mediascape that accompanied this emerging religious landscape was equally diverse. It included dispensationalist organs such as the Zion's Tower Tract Society and the Moody Press, which unlike the antebellum national societies viewed print media not as an "instrument" for hastening the millennium but as "a sign that the end was near."[17] Liberal Protestants continued to promote a kind of secularized, reform-oriented postmillennialism, but their use of visual images shifted from the "didactic" mode of antebellum evangelicals to a "devotional conception of images" that stressed the formation of individual character through engagement with refined works of art. With that shift, David Morgan explains, the goal became "no longer to teach students to decipher the visual texts . . . but to create in the aesthetic space of contemplation a devotional mood of reverence and pure ideals." Viewed through this new Protestant visual aesthetic, which flourished well into the twentieth century, "images . . . were not illustrations, not avenues for transmitting information, not bound to texts but were the product of genius and therefore, although informed by texts like the Bible, were independent works of creative imagination."[18] For liberals, in other words, pictures had ceased to function as sacred media: they had become works of art. As the postwar mediascape split into proto-fundamentalist and liberal media spheres, it was further segmented into elite and low camps, as biblical scholars trained in the German higher criticism increasingly rejected forms of apocalyptic prophecy, even going so far as to call the Book of Revelation "a millennial mirage."[19]

Overall, then, the postbellum years witnessed a proliferation and fragmentation of religious media culture akin to the phenomena described by Trish Loughran between the Revolution and the Civil War, in which the explosion of print media led not to national consensus but to discord and division. In the case of the religious press, however, the result was not only political conflict but the collision of competing cosmic visions, the sort of "metacosm" that Jared Hickman describes as one of globalizing modernity's most distinctive products.[20] The irony, as James H. Moorhead sees it, is that while the engineers of the evangelical mediascape "expected to use the technological revolution in communications to create a consensus of views," in the end "the religious press of the antebellum period did not achieve a single mass culture but rather spawned a variety of religious subcultures, each with its own vision of the millennium."[21]

Thus within a decade after the Civil War ended, the constellation of landscape aesthetics, postmillennial Protestant culture, and mass print media that had converged to produce evangelical space had unraveled. Yet the cultural edifice it had helped to create remained. Several of the figures discussed here produced their most enduring work after prolonged, direct contact with the evangelical mediascape: Cole and Church through their evangelical patrons and friends; Finney and Theodore Dwight Weld through their revivalism; Stowe through the evangelical press; Angelina Grimké and Susan Warner through their tract distribution efforts; even Thoreau and Lippard had intimate knowledge of evangelical culture through their families and educational experiences. Many others in the period, however, would have encountered evangelical space only through its mediation in popular culture—by reading about Uncle Tom and Eva in the arbor, say, or gazing at a painting in a gallery. Rebecca Harding Davis likely absorbed the apocalyptic sensibility that infused "Life in the Iron-Mills" as much from her reading of Stowe as from any personal experience with evangelical religion; likewise the glimpse of the "Celestial City" that the March sisters and Laurie observe in the sunset over Boston in *Little Women* (1868–69) undoubtedly owes more to Louisa May Alcott's immersion in novels than to tracts or revival sermons.[22] Once the underlying evangelical mediascape was gone and only its most luminous cultural fruits remained—novels, paintings, mountain hotels—what became the legacy of its unique form of apocalyptic vision in American culture?

For one thing, it lived on as a subject of satire. Within months of seeing *The Heart of the Andes* in St. Louis, in August 1861 Samuel Clemens embarked for Nevada Territory, the first of several journeys over the next decade that would make Mark Twain the nation's most trenchant observer of sacred geography at home (in *Roughing It*) and overseas (in *The Innocents Abroad*). The latter is of course well known for its comic unmasking of the "Holy Land mania" that drew thousands of American artists, historians, missionaries, and tourists to the Middle East in the decades following the Civil War.[23] After participating in the first organized American tourist excursion to Palestine in 1867, Twain unleashed "an unprecedentedly savage satire of the pious pilgrimage, ridiculing himself and his companions in the process."[24] As Hilton Obenzinger notes, *The Innocents Abroad; or, The New Pilgrim's Progress* (1869) "mark[ed] the transition of the American in the Holy Land from pilgrim, adventurer, or scholar to tourist" and in the process "transformed the sacred site into a modern tourist attraction." At the heart of this shift lies a distinctive state of modern mediation: "The value of the touristic sight is not determined by an aura of authenticity alone but by the site's capacity to frame the touristic imagination through multiple images of itself, through its narrativization by local guides, and through its textualization by guide-books, travel books, and other sources, so that it could be re-collected in—and transformed by—memory."[25] In contrast to the evangelical mediascape explored in this book, in which sacred space is generated precisely through the proliferation of spatial images across multiple textual and visual formats, Twain by this account considers modern mediation (in its textual and visual as well as its economic forms) as a secularizing force that can only dissolve aura and render all formerly sacred spaces profane.

Twain's experiences in the American West become a recurrent counterpoint and antidote to the hypermediated character of Old World sites in *The Innocents Abroad*. In one memorable example, Twain jumps from the "tedious" nature of European train travel to a reminiscence of his exhilarating stagecoach ride from Missouri to California, "two thousand miles of ceaseless rush and rattle and clatter, by night and by day, and never a weary moment, never a lapse of interest!" Later, the storied waters of Lake Como pale "compared with the wonderful transparence of Lake Tahoe ... where one can count the scales on a trout at a depth of a hundred and eighty feet."[26] Tahoe's crystalline water is an apt emblem of the unmediated experience that promises to turn the jaded tourist back into a genuine adventurer and pilgrim, even as Twain's hyperbolic claims (180 feet!?) cannily draw attention to the prior mediation of western space through the tall tale. Twain's ability in such moments to simultaneously evoke an uncorrupted space of pure, immediate experience—a kind of western Eden—and hint at the cultural forces already working to colonize and commodify that space generates much of the pathos of his account but also articulates a key dilemma of modern sacred space.

If to draw attention to mediation is by definition to deflate and unmask sacred space for Twain, apocalyptic vision becomes a point of special tension. After all, the apocalyptic mode is both inherently mediated by texts and itself performs the supreme unmasking—the unveiling of truth behind the illusion of the material world. The apocalyptic visionary is in a sense the ultimate realist. Yet at key points Twain critiques the fusion of apocalyptic vision with physical geography that antebellum Protestants had developed into such a powerful spiritual medium. Twain relates the story of a group of Millerites (followers of the premillennialist prophet William Miller) in Smyrna who, after "much buzzing and preparation" for the end of the world, "ascended the citadel hill early in the morning, to get out of the way of the general destruction" (*IA*, 416).[27] As they waited, a ferocious thunderstorm storm blew in and

AN APPARENT SUCCESS.

FIGURE 7.1. "An Apparent Success." Mark Twain, *The Innocents Abroad; or, The New Pilgrim's Progress* (Hartford, CT: American Publishing Company, 1869), 416. Courtesy, American Antiquarian Society.

deluged the city. "When the storm finished and left every body drenched through and through, and melancholy and half-drowned, the ascensionists came down from the mountain as dry as so many charity-sermons! They had been looking down upon the fearful storm going on below, and really believed that their proposed destruction of the world was proving a grand success" (417). In a scene that recalls tourists' use of storms and other meteorological phenomena from the Catskill Mountain House to visualize sacred history, the credulous Millerites highlight the dangers of conflating physical geography with the prophecies revealed in scripture. The accompanying illustration (fig. 7.1), with its swirling storm clouds, dramatic chiaroscuro, and zigzag lightning bolts, plays on the visual formula British painter John Martin had made famous in apocalyptic scenes like *The Deluge* (1834), *The Destruction of Sodom and Gomorrah* (1852), and *The Great Day of His Wrath* (1853), while its deadpan caption, "An Apparent Success," punctuates the entire incident with withering irony.[28] The equation of apocalyptic vision with illusion is reinforced when Twain later describes a landscape prospect glimpsed from the window of an

Italian "temple" that initially strikes the viewer as "the faintest, softest, richest picture that ever graced the dream of a dying Saint, since John saw the New Jerusalem glimmering above the clouds of Heaven"; but a moment's reflection reveals the impression to be a trick, for "without the yellow glass, and the carefully contrived accident of a framework that cast it into enchanted distance and shut out from it all unattractive features, it was not a picture to fall into ecstacies over" (IA, 522–23).

So when the narrator of *Roughing It* (1872) describes his joy at being offered "the sublime position of private secretary" to his brother, the newly appointed secretary of Nevada Territory, and declares that "it appeared to me that the heavens and the earth passed away, and the firmament was rolled together as a scroll," the hyperbolic image not only pokes fun at the breathless naiveté of his younger self but signals a resumption of the quest that had propelled *The Innocents Abroad*: the search for sacred space in a mediated age.[29] If a space that has not been profaned exists anywhere, it would seem to be at Lake Tahoe, where Twain's narrator and his friend Johnny find "the fairest picture the whole earth affords" (RI, 169), a place where the air "is the same the angels breathe" (170). But the friends' wilderness idyll in this paradise is interrupted when their unattended campfire ignites a forest fire while "we stood helpless and watched the devastation":

> Within half an hour all before us was a tossing, blinding tempest of flame! It went surging up adjacent ridges—surmounted them and disappeared in the cañons beyond—burst into view upon higher and farther ridges, presently—shed a grander illumination abroad, and dove again—flamed out again, directly, higher and still higher up the mountain-side—threw out skirmishing parties of fire here and there, and sent them trailing their crimson spirals away among remote ramparts and ribs and gorges, till as far as the eye could reach the lofty mountain-fronts were webbed as it were with a tangled network of red lava streams. Away across the water the crags and domes were lit with a ruddy glare, and the firmament above was a reflected hell! (176)

As in the apocalyptic landscapes in *The Innocents Abroad*, Twain is captivated by the mediated nature of the scene: "Every feature of the spectacle was repeated in the glowing mirror of the lake! Both pictures were sublime, both were beautiful; but that in the lake had a bewildering richness about it that enchanted the eye and held it with the stronger fascination" (RI, 176). As horror gives way to sheer sensory pleasure, the power of the reflected image to absorb the viewer's attention away from the real thing suggests the tendency of such sublime visions to become reified as aesthetic objects instead of windows onto the realities they represent—to become art rather than media.

That tendency is particularly relevant to the western setting of *Roughing It*. Just as Davis's characters in "Life in the Iron-Mills" bring a cultural tradition of apocalyptic vision to bear on the spaces of industrial capitalism, Twain's narrator finds apocalypse vividly enacted before him in the despoliation of a natural landscape through human negligence. Whereas Davis anticipates one legacy of evangelical space in the "homiletic realism" of Jacob Riis's *How the Other Half Lives* (1890) and other Progressive Era texts that documented (and spiritualized) the social consequences of urban industrialism, Twain points toward another cultural trajectory that used words and images to train the public's "spiritual sight" on natural landscapes like the mountains that John Muir would famously declare "the Range of Light, surely the brightest and best of all the Lord has built"—places "where one might hope to see God."[30]

As the examples of Twain and Muir suggest, in the aftermath of the Civil War, the West became an arena where antebellum traditions of sacred geography lived on in a number of cultural registers. They persisted, for example, in the saga of the "Exodusters," freedpeople who struck out for all-black towns like Nicodemus, Kansas, in the late 1870s or (a decade later) to Langston City, Oklahoma, encouraged by black promoters' promises of a "Negro Canaan." Not unlike the Old Testament narratives it was based on, such rhetoric concealed the fact that these "Promised Land[s]" belonged to someone else, carved out of Indian reservations whose occupants had of course already been previously dispossessed and removed there.[31] Partly in response to the traumas of settler colonialism, in the late 1880s another apocalyptic geography emerged in Ghost Dance Religion, a pan-tribal revival movement that combined indigenous prophetic traditions with elements of Protestant Christianity (as well as Catholic and perhaps Mormon influences). It originated with the visions of a Northern Paiute holy man named Jack Wilson (also known as Wovoka), who by some accounts predicted an imminent millennium that would sweep whites from the land, restoring game animals and the indigenous communities that had long depended on them; interpretations of Wovoka's message spread from Nevada's Walker Valley to Indian reservations across the West, carried by dozens of tribal delegations and amplified by a modern mediascape that included railroads, newspapers, and the U.S. mail, leading one historian to declare that the movement "functioned in many ways like evangelical Christianity."[32] But perhaps the most direct and consequential legacy of evangelical space occurred in the preservation movement that remapped the ancestral homelands of those native peoples as "wilderness" areas, sacred geographies where dramas of personal redemption and social regeneration could be enacted on a national scale.[33]

In 1863, while Twain was still roughing it in Nevada Territory and writing for the Virginia City *Territorial Enterprise*, German-born American painter

FIGURE 7.2. Albert Bierstadt, *Yosemite Valley*, 1868. Oil on canvas, 36 × 54 in. (91.44 × 137.16 cm). Collection of the Oakland Museum of California, Gift of Miss Marguerite Laird in Memory of Mr. and Mrs. P. W. Laird, A64.26.

Albert Bierstadt spent seven weeks in the Yosemite Valley camping with travel writer Fitz Hugh Ludlow. In the account of the trip Ludlow published in the *Atlantic Monthly* the following June (the same month Abraham Lincoln signed the Yosemite Grant Act setting aside the area as a park), he at first noted skeptically reports of the valley as "the original site of the Garden of Eden," only to find himself overwhelmed by the vista that opened before him at Inspiration Point, a "vision" of "a new heaven and a new earth into which the creative spirit had just been breathed."[34] Bierstadt, who had recently cemented his reputation as the nation's foremost painter of the Far West, was similarly enraptured, declaring Yosemite to be "the garden of Eden," "the most magnificent place I was ever in."[35] Over the next five years Bierstadt produced several large canvases of Yosemite, including *Yosemite Valley* (1868) (fig. 7.2; see plate 7) and *Sunset in the Yosemite Valley* (1868) (fig. 7.3; see plate 8).[36] Presenting the same view with dramatically different light effects and moods, the pair becomes a kind of narrative diptych. The allusion to Cole's *Expulsion from the Garden of Eden* (see fig. 1.3) that critics have found in the exaggerated shape of Sentinel Rock on the left side of both Yosemite pictures signals Bierstadt's transposition of an antebellum tradition of representing sacred history in the landscape to a Western locale that had recently captured the public imagination.[37] In the shift from the topos of Yosemite-as-Eden in *Yosemite Valley* to the strangely sinister

FIGURE 7.3. Albert Bierstadt, *Sunset in the Yosemite Valley*, 1868. Oil on canvas, 36¼ × 52¼ in. (92 × 132.75 cm). The Haggin Museum, Stockton, California, 1931.391.11.

sunset that Andrew Wilton calls "an apocalyptic vision," Bierstadt conveys an unspecified sense of foreboding in an ostensibly pristine landscape that foreshadows Twain's literary account of his own "expulsion from Eden" at Tahoe the following year.[38]

In a commercial sense, Bierstadt's enormous paintings of the Sierras and the Rockies were attempts to capitalize on the popularity of Church's Great Pictures by expanding into the newly opened territories of the Far West.[39] On this score their success was mixed: "We have seen few landscapes since the 'Heart of the Andes' that will compare with this," the San Francisco *Golden Era* marveled upon seeing Bierstadt's *Looking Down Yosemite Valley, California* (1865) at the National Academy of Design; Ambrose Bierce, meanwhile, declared the painting to be the "parent of ten thousand abominations" and celebrated the (false) reports that the painting had been destroyed in a fire.[40] The unveiling of *The Domes of the Yosemite* (1867) in a New York exhibition space specially designed to give visitors the sensation of standing on the canyon rim gazing down into the valley prompted more critical sniping: the *New-York Tribune* declared the picture "destitute of grandeur," but Mark Twain disagreed.[41] Writing as a correspondent for the San Francisco *Daily Alta California*, he quipped that the painting was "very beautiful—considerably more beautiful than the original." The peaks, the valley, and the trees were all "correct" and "look just as they ought to look, and they all belong to California," but "the atmosphere" was off: it must have been "imported ... from some foreign country, because nothing like it was ever seen in California. . . . It is more the atmosphere of Kingdom-Come than of California." Twain dilated on the point: "Some of Mr. Bierstadt's mountains swim in a lustrous, pearly mist, which is so enchantingly beautiful that I am sorry the Creator hadn't made it instead of him, so that it would always remain there. In the morning, the outlines of mountains in California, even though they be leagues away, are painfully bold and sharp, because the atmosphere is so pure and clear—but the outlines of Mr. Bierstadt's mountains are soft and rounded and velvety, which is a great improvement on nature."[42] By wryly placing the painter and "the Creator" at odds, Twain punctured the "Protestant aesthetic" that had long dominated American landscape painting, an aesthetic premised on the claim that the painter, like the preacher of the Puritan plain-style, was simply a transparent medium who enabled the perfection of God's creation to shine through his works.[43] And by emphasizing the discrepancy between "Kingdom-Come" and "California," Twain disrupted the elision of physical geography and sacred history that was the hallmark of antebellum evangelical space. To a realist sensibility that placed a premium on verisimilitude, the fusion of earthly and sacred that was once the gold standard of antebellum painting now seemed bankrupt.

Even if critical acclaim from the art establishment was no longer assured for such pictures, they served another role as part of a campaign to generate public support for preserving Yosemite and other scenic areas. Bierstadt's paintings joined a host of images of the valley circulating in the national mediascape in the 1860s, including photographs by Charles Leander Weed and Carleton E. Watkins (the latter of which may have inspired Bierstadt's own trip when they were exhibited at Goupil's Gallery in New York in 1862) and woodcut illustrations that accompanied newspaper and magazine articles.[44] Because of their size and luminous quality, Bierstadt's paintings were ideally suited to this latest extension of sacred geography, providing visualizations of the glowing prose of preservation advocates like Ludlow (the son of a Presbyterian minister) and Unitarian minister Thomas Starr King, whose travels in Yosemite in 1860 inspired a popular series of letters that ran in the *Boston Evening Transcript* as well as several sermons to his San Francisco congregation.[45] Critics and historians disagree about how much impact Bierstadt actually had on the preservation campaign. While his role in efforts to strengthen protections for wildlife in Yellowstone National Park in the 1880s and 1890s is well documented, evidence in the case of Yosemite is more circumstantial: a recent study concludes that "given Bierstadt's lofty reputation in 1864, his works must have had some influence in the establishment of the park."[46] No doubt

Bierstadt's impact would have been greater if the *Atlantic Monthly* had illustrated Ludlow's series of articles about Yosemite and other California sites with his friend's pictures, but the magazine's policy was not to run illustrations.[47]

What seems clear is that the shifting contours of the national mediascape made it less and less likely that such landscape paintings would function as the sort of sacralized media they had as recently as the late 1850s when *The Heart of the Andes* absorbed the attention of critics, ministers, and ordinary viewers alike. Bierstadt's Yosemite pictures were not widely exhibited: the year after appearing in the 1865 National Academy of Design exhibition in New York, *Looking Down Yosemite Valley, California* was exhibited in Philadelphia, Milwaukee, and Cincinnati, an itinerary dwarfed by the transatlantic routes of Church's paintings. *The Domes of the Yosemite* did only slightly better, appearing in New York, Philadelphia, Boston, and London; the apocalyptic *Sunset in the Yosemite Valley* was exhibited in London but apparently never in the United States.[48] When they were exhibited, the paintings tended to become battlegrounds for critical debates over accuracy, not arenas for enacting spiritual dramas. Bierstadt attempted to hitch his star to other media forms, authorizing engravings of his work for magazines and books as well as chromolithographs for the print market.[49] But in the age of photography, this could only take a painter so far. By the 1870s, Bierstadt's paintings were out of style as works of art, and as media they were obsolete.

Another medium with its own roots in antebellum spiritual perception had stepped into the breach: photography.[50] In 1890, as Riis created a sensation with his riveting images of the living conditions of the urban poor, Muir published two articles in the *Century Illustrated Magazine* detailing the natural splendor of the Yosemite with lavish descriptions, maps, and photographs.[51] Muir wrote the articles at the urging of Robert Underwood Johnson, an associate editor at the *Century*, to enlist public support for a bill being debated in Congress to establish Yosemite National Park.[52] The first article, "The Treasures of the Yosemite," opens with an account of Muir's first journey on foot into the Yosemite Valley to encounter a "landscape" that he declared "the most divinely beautiful and sublime I have ever beheld." He described the Sierra Nevada as "so gloriously colored and so radiant that it seemed not clothed with light, but wholly composed of it, like the wall of some celestial city." Spending a decade in this "Range of Light," "rejoicing and wondering, seeing the glorious floods of light that fill it," had confirmed that initial impression, yet also revealed its fragility: "But no terrestrial beauty may endure forever," Muir warned. "The glory of wildness has already departed from the great central plain. Its bloom is shed, and so in part is the bloom of the mountains. In Yosemite, even under the protection of the [state] Government, all that is perishable is vanishing apace."[53] With its counterpoint of millennial promise and apocalyptic warning worthy of a Puritan jeremiad, Muir's rapturous vision of divine immanence in the landscape coexists with a sense of something beyond its "terrestrial beauty." This ontological dualism recalls the spatial dynamic displayed in Cole's *Oxbow*, in which the viewer stands in the wilderness of the world gazing at a greater world to come.[54] But Muir's apocalyptic geography reverses Cole's: rather than equating the world with the mountain and paradise with the valley floor below, his ecological recasting of *The Pilgrim's Progress* places Christian's goal of the "celestial city" high in the Sierras and implicitly locates the City of Destruction in Oakland where he began. Whereas Riis leads readers down into the hellish depths of the city, Muir guides them up into ever more remote reaches of the Yosemite and away from the rising tide of development. The photographs and process reproductions embedded in Muir's text visualize this sacred geography, as readers witness the "destructive work" of agricultural plowing that has already penetrated the valley's meadows and then press on further up the valley past landmarks like "El Capitan" and "Cathedral Rocks." The pilgrimage culminates with a vision of an early winter flood that Muir had witnessed nearly twenty years before:

> The warm, copious rain falling on the snow was at first absorbed and held back, and so also was that portion of the snow that the rain melted, and all that was melted by the warm wind, until the whole mass of snow was saturated and became sludgy, and at length slipped and rushed simultaneously from a thousand slopes into the channels in wild extravagance, heaping and swelling flood over flood, and plunging into the valley in one stupendous avalanche.
>
> The mountain waters, suddenly liberated, seemed to be holding a grand jubilee. The two Sentinel cascades rivaled the great falls at ordinary stages, and across the valley by the Three Brothers I caught glimpses of more falls than I could readily count; while the whole valley throbbed and trembled, and was filed with an awful, massive, solemn, sea-like roar.[55]

Combining the eruptions of Thoreau's famous thawing railroad bank in *Walden* with millennial imagery reminiscent of the post-emancipation jubilee envisioned by antislavery reformers, Muir conveyed his ecstatic experience in the Sierra to the *Century*'s national readership in the hope of moving them to action. As he later explained in a published collection of his magazine articles, "I have done the best I could to show forth the beauty, grandeur, and all-embracing usefulness of our wild mountain forest reservations and parks, with a view to inciting the people to come and enjoy them, and get them into their hearts, [so that] at length their preservation and right use might be made sure."[56] On September 30, 1890, Congress voted to establish Yosemite National

Park across an area that closely followed the boundaries Muir advocated in the *Century*, an area far larger than California congressman William Vandever had proposed in the original Yosemite bill in March 1890; President Benjamin Harrison signed the bill into law the next day, creating the United States' third national park.[57]

In a major new interpretation of the history of American environmentalism, Mark R. Stoll has argued that it was not Transcendentalists like Emerson and Thoreau but nineteenth-century Presbyterians and Congregationalists from New England who provided the major impetus for the environmental movement in the United States, combining a distinctive Reformed theological tradition of perceiving God's presence in the natural world with a civic tradition of protecting forests and parkland for public use.[58] This book has shown that in addition to these elements, Protestant evangelicals contributed a formal strategy for spreading their ideas: a way of using words and images, print and preaching—media, broadly conceived—to sacralize space. For much of the century, preachers, writers, artists, and reformers had used apocalyptic visions of the landscape to persuade audiences to transcend mundane, particular concerns in order to achieve a comprehensive view of society and the universe. They urged individuals to change their lives to reflect the true extent of their obligations—to journey through that enlarged ethical landscape toward distant others and a better world waiting on the horizon. Now on the threshold of a new century, Muir and others adapted that spiritualized mediascape to convince Americans of their obligations to the land itself. Twain would no doubt appreciate the irony that the effort to regain paradise may in fact destroy it, as recent reports of national parks being "loved to death" attest.[59] But there is a deeper irony here: that as even as they succeeded in sacralizing the American landscape, evangelicals themselves would increasingly turn away from the vision of environmental stewardship they had helped build.

The second half of the twentieth century witnessed an upsurge of "environmental apocalypticism" inaugurated by Rachel Carson's *Silent Spring* (1962) and fed by mounting concerns over human-caused climate change and the global mass-extinction it has set in motion.[60] In an age of climate crisis, modes of apocalyptic imagination have proliferated across literary genres and media, propelling best-selling nonfiction works like Bill McKibben's *The End of Nature* (1989) and Elizabeth Kolbert's *The Sixth Extinction: An Unnatural History* (2014), fiction from Leslie Marmon Silko's *Almanac of the Dead* (1991) to the proliferation of climate fiction (or "cli-fi"), and films including Al Gore's *An Inconvenient Truth* (2006) and Benh Zeitlin's *Beasts of the Southern Wild* (2012). Perhaps not since the threat of nuclear Armageddon during the Cold War has apocalypticism so gripped the popular imagination. Conservative evangelical culture, meanwhile, experienced its own "revival of apocalypticism" during the postwar period that encompassed Billy Graham's stark warnings of impending judgment in his revivals beginning in the late 1940s, Hal Lindsey's popular exposition of dispensationalist prophecy *The Late Great Planet Earth* (1970) (supposedly "the best-selling nonfiction book of the 1970s"), and Tim LaHaye and Jerry B. Jenkins's best-selling *Left Behind* novels (1995–2007) and their various film and video game spinoffs chronicling the seven-year period known as the "Tribulation," in which those who have not yet accepted Jesus (and who are therefore "left behind" on Earth while true believers are spirited away in the Rapture) remain to battle the Antichrist until Jesus returns one final time.[61] The system of dispensational premillennialism elaborated in these works keyed biblical prophecy to current political events ranging from the Middle East and Vietnam to feminism and the civil rights movement, giving apocalyptic speculation a new influence and urgency in American culture that ultimately reached all the way to the White House.[62]

Among the striking facts about these parallel mediascapes is their mutual estrangement, both from each other and from their historical roots. Whereas antebellum evangelicals not only welcomed new media as instruments of divine will but helped lay the foundations of contemporary "network culture" through their pioneering role in developing mass media, the *Left Behind* novels capture the profound ambivalence with which many contemporary evangelicals regard modern media technologies and modernity in general, which are cast as part of a global "Beast system" that is the Antichrist's chief weapon in the impending apocalyptic battle.[63] Perhaps even more striking is conservative evangelicals' abandonment of environmental concerns since the late 1970s and 1980s, even as the specter of climate apocalypse has galvanized the broader public.[64] Lisa Vox has written that evangelical climate denialism is the result of several factors, including the belief that only God has the power to change the climate and that only he can fix it: as Republican representative Tim Walberg of Michigan told constituents at a 2017 town hall meeting, "As a Christian, I believe that there is a creator in God who is much bigger than us. And I'm confident that, if there's a real problem, he can take care of it." Moreover, evangelicals' fear of globalism (and globalization) as a tool of the Antichrist means that they tend to see international climate accords like the 2016 Paris Agreement as conspiracies designed to scare people into creating a "One World Government" ruled by the Antichrist himself.[65] Some even go so far as to welcome climate catastrophe as a vehicle of divine judgment, believing that "God is going to use climate change to enact his wrath on the world."[66] The supreme irony, then, is that after all antebellum evangelicals did to popularize apocalyptic thinking in America and harness it for social reform, conservative evangelicals today adamantly refuse to confront the mounting signs of environmental crisis and indeed actively resist efforts to ameliorate it, partly as a result of their premillennialist worldview.

Environmentalists, meanwhile, have sought to distance their climate predictions from the alarmism often associated with apocalypticism, whether of the religious or scientific varieties. Despite being described by the *New York Times Book Review* as "a man preaching apocalypse," McKibben warned in *The End of Nature* that global warming and the "political unrest" it threatened to unleash provided "a perfect culture for the fungus of fanaticism and unreasoning religion"—exhibit A being a dispensationalist "tract" he had recently been handed "explaining that climate change was a signal of the coming 'rapture.'"[67] More recently David Wallace-Wells has expressed a similar discomfort with apocalyptic rhetoric in climate change discourse, sarcastically referring to the "bee rapture" and other forms of "ecological Armageddon" and noting that people's images of "climate crisis" are "often pieced together from perennial eschatological imagery inherited from existing apocalyptic texts like the Book of Revelation" and other such "ravings." Yet he also implies that such apocalyptic traditions represent a potential cultural resource for recognizing that crisis for what it is: "You'd think that a culture woven through with intimations of apocalypse would know how to receive news of environmental alarm," Wallace-Wells writes, but "we have not yet developed anything close to a religion of meaning around climate change that might comfort us, or give us purpose, in the face of possible annihilation." Considering the worst-case scenarios of civilizational collapse and human extinction, he admits, "It takes an apocalyptic imagination to picture that happening just a decade from now, to be sure. But, given the basic trend lines, it also raises the question of why the rest of us aren't imagining things more apocalyptically ourselves."[68] Torn between disdain of apocalypticism and appeals to it, such accounts seem to bolster Vox's point that "scientific apocalyptists" historically lacked "a language of crisis of their own" and therefore frequently borrowed from religious discourse.[69] But just as conservative evangelicals seem to have willfully forgotten the legacy of their postmillennial forebears, McKibben and Wallace-Wells have allowed dispensational premillennialism to stand for the whole of apocalyptic thought in America, distorting that broader tradition, obscuring its foundational role in modern environmentalism, and ceding a powerful rhetorical tool to the forces of denialism.

And yet, whether knowingly or not, these environmental works remain subtly but unmistakably informed by the religious tradition of apocalyptic imagination this book has explored. We see it most clearly in their inevitable turn to moments of cosmic geography, whether McKibben's final scene witnessing the Perseid meteor shower from a "rocky summit" where a "vast nature" beyond human control can once more be apprehended (a revelation he likens to the prospect the archangel Raphael shows Adam in *Paradise Lost*) or Wallace-Wells's closing image of the *Pale Blue Dot*, the photo captured by the *Voyager 1* space probe in 1990 that shows Earth as a shining speck in an endless sea of stars, revealing "the inescapable smallness, and fragility, of the entire experiment we're engaged in, together, whether we like it or not."[70] In perhaps the most spectacular example, Al Gore's *An Inconvenient Truth* begins with the 1968 *Earthrise* photo taken from the Moon, interweaves landscape photographs of disappearing glaciers from Kilimanjaro to the Himalayas with a computer-generated globe that dramatizes the past and future effects of climate change, leads his audience on a tour through a series of "catastrophes like a nature-hike through the Book of Revelations," and finally zooms back out to *Earthrise* and *Pale Blue Dot* as Gore declares climate change a "moral issue" and that "it is our time to rise again to secure our future."[71] Though absent any explicit theistic message or religious eschatology, the film uses satellite imagery and digital technology to achieve a perspective that is fundamentally apocalyptic: one that attempts to transcend finite human conceptions of space and time through an all-encompassing vision of the universe that seeks to restore a sense of cosmic order in the face of chaos, injustice, and suffering. Climate change, Wallace-Wells notes (borrowing a term from Timothy Morton), is a "hyperobject," "a conceptual fact so large and complex that, like the internet, it can never be properly comprehended."[72] As Gore toggles back and forth between particular landscapes and global and cosmic geographies, he recalls antebellum Americans' encounter with a similarly bewildering hyperobject: globalization. And he reminds us that the apocalyptic imagination might yet help chart a course through this emerging new Earth where a grave sense of human responsibility confronts the fearsome reality of vast, punishing forces beyond our control.

NOTES

Introduction

1. Rebecca Harding Davis, "Life in the Iron-Mills," *Atlantic Monthly*, April 1861, 430 (hereafter cited in the text as *LIM*).

2. Rebecca Harding Davis to James T. Fields, January 26, 1861, Richard Davis Papers, 1863–1916, Accession #6109 through 6109-e, Special Collections, University of Virginia Library, Charlottesville.

3. For "Life in the Iron-Mills" as a repudiation of antebellum romanticism and religion, see Sharon M. Harris, *Rebecca Harding Davis and American Realism* (Philadelphia: University of Pennsylvania Press, 1991), 27–33, 36–39, 48–56. For the shift from romanticism to realism more broadly, see Louis J. Budd, "The American Background," in Donald Pizer, ed., *The Cambridge Companion to American Realism and Naturalism* (Cambridge: Cambridge University Press, 1995), 21–46.

4. Janice Milner Lasseter, "The Censored and Uncensored Literary Lives of *Life in the Iron-Mills*," *Legacy* 20 (2003): 175–90.

5. Lasseter, "Censored and Uncensored"; Beth Maclay Doriani, "New England Calvinism and the Problem of the Poor in Rebecca Harding Davis's 'Life in the Iron-Mills,'" in *Literary Calvinism and Nineteenth-Century Women Authors*, ed. Michael Schuldiner (Lewiston, NY: Edwin Mellen, 1997), 179–224; William H. Shurr, "Life in the Iron-Mills: A Nineteenth-Century Conversion Narrative," *American Transcendental Quarterly* 5.4 (1991): 245–57.

6. Norman Cohn, *Cosmos, Chaos, and the World to Come: The Ancient Roots of Apocalyptic Faith* (New Haven: Yale University Press, 1993), 163.

7. Collins, "Apocalypse," 409.

8. See, for example, Alexander Smyth, *An Explanation of the Apocalypse, or Revelation of St. John* (Washington City: Way & Gideon, 1825).

9. Vines, "Apocalyptic Chronotope," 113.

10. Robinson, *American Apocalypses*, 2–3.

11. Brückner, *Geographic Revolution*, 4.

12. Cohn, *Cosmos*, 162.

13. Stowe, *Uncle Tom's Cabin*, 2:63–64, 1:204.

14. George Barrell Cheever, "Inquire at Amos Giles' Distillery," *Liberator*, February 21, 1835, 32.

15. See Reynolds, *Faith in Fiction*, 9–15.

16. Seth L. Sanders, "The First Tour of Hell: From Neo-Assyrian Propaganda to Early Jewish Revelation," *Journal of Ancient Near Eastern Religions* 9.2 (2009): 151.

17. Jackson, *Word and Its Witness*, 64, 264.

18. Dimock, *Through Other Continents*, 3.

19. Anderson, *Imagined Communities*, 24; Elizabeth Maddock Dillon, "Religion and Geopolitics in the New World," *Early American Literature* 45.1 (2010): 194.

20. King, *Imagined Spiritual Communities*, 7.

21. For the "visual form" of traditional apocalyptic revelations, see Cohn, *Cosmos*, 164. For the American visual tradition, see Husch, *Something Coming*.

22. See "Sacred Dioramas," *New-York Evangelist*, August 31, 1848, 139; Davis, *Landscape of Belief*, 57; and Huhtamo, *Illusions in Motion*, 155–57.

23. "Western Artists: Hiram Powers," *Western Monthly Magazine*, April 1835, 246; Rebecca A. G. Reynolds, "'Almost a Buckeye': Hiram Powers and Cincinnati, His Adopted Hometown," in *Hiram Powers: Genius in Marble*, ed. Lynne D. Ambrosini and Rebecca A. G. Reynolds (Cincinnati: Taft Museum of Art, 2007), 31–32; for the exhibition's relation to "Life in the Iron-Mills," see Bill Brown, "The Origin of the American Work of Art," *American Literary History* 25.4 (Winter 2013): 785.

24. For Puritans, see P. Miller, *Errand into the Wilderness*, 1–15; for Leatherstocking, see H. Smith, *Virgin Land*, chap. 6; for *letrados*, see Gruesz, *Ambassadors of Culture*, 16–17; for the black Atlantic, see Gilroy, *Black Atlantic*.

25. See Lloyd Pratt, *Archives of American Time: Literature and Modernity in the Nineteenth Century* (Philadelphia: University of Pennsylvania Press, 2010), 11–12, 187–91.

26. Martin Brückner and Hsuan L. Hsu, eds., *American Literary Geographies: Spatial Practice and Cultural Production, 1500–1900* (Newark: University of Delaware Press, 2007). For moral geography, see *A Dictionary of Human Geography*, ed. Alisdair Rogers, Noel Castree, and Rob Kitchin (Oxford: Oxford University Press, 2013), s.v. "moral geographies"; and David M. Smith, *Moral Geographies: Ethics in a World of Difference* (Edinburgh: Edinburgh University Press, 2000), 48–53.

27. A. Miller, *Empire of the Eye*.

28. "The Printing Business, &c, Fifty Years Ago," *Daily Evening Transcript* (Boston), March 3, 1851, 2.

29. For the postsecular, see the December 2014 issue of *American Literature* (86.4) devoted to the topic; and Tracy Fessenden, "The Problem of the Postsecular," *American Literary History* 26.1 (Spring 2014): 154–67. Taylor, *Secular Age*, 22.

30. See Davis, *Landscape of Belief*; and Morgan, *Protestants and Pictures*.

31. Sedgwick, *Atlantic Monthly*, 39–41, 81. For Church's "Great Pictures," see Gerald L. Carr, *Frederic Edwin Church: The Icebergs* (Dallas: Dallas Museum of Fine Arts, 1980), 23–30; and Raab, *Frederic Church*, 7. Reviews include "Art. The Heart of the Andes," *Atlantic Monthly*, May 1859, 128–29.

32. Carr, *Frederic Edwin Church*, 27.

33. Quoted in David C. Huntington, *The Landscapes of Frederic Edwin Church: Vision of an American Era* (New York: George Braziller, 1966), 82.

34. Bunyan, *Pilgrim's Progress*, 29, 114, 59.

35. Reprinted as [Theodore Ledyard Cuyler,] "Church's 'Heart of the Andes,'" *Littel's Living Age*, July 1, 1859, 64.

36. The paintings are *Christian on the Borders of the "Valley of the Shadow of Death," Pilgrim's Progress* (1847), and *The River of the Water of Life* (1848). See Kelly, *Frederic Edwin Church*, 18, 31; and Huhtamo, *Illusions in Motion*, 184.

37. Bedell, *Anatomy of Nature*, 78.

38. The cities were New York, Boston, Philadelphia, Baltimore, Cincinnati, Chicago, St. Louis, and Brooklyn. See Kevin J. Avery, *Church's Great Picture: The Heart of the Andes* (New York: Metropolitan Museum of Art, 1993), 40–44.

39. Manuscript sermon by Rev. Z. M. Humphrey, Olana State Historic Site, Hudson, NY, New York State Office of Parks, Recreation, and Historic Preservation, OL.2000.1021.1–.2.

40. The sermon is quoted in a letter from Richard T. Miller to Frederic Edwin Church, dated March 15, 1860, Olana State Historic Site, Hudson, NY, New York State Office of Parks, Recreation, and Historic Preservation, OL.1998.1.42.1.A–.B. See also Raab, *Frederic Church*, 63.

41. Quoted in Raab, *Frederic Church*, 63.

42. For the print, see Avery, *Church's Great Picture*, 40; and John K. Howat, *Frederic Church* (New Haven: Yale University Press, 2005), 90.

43. John Bunyan, *The Pilgrim's Progress, by John Bunyan in the Dakota Language*, trans. Stephen R. Riggs (New York: American Tract Society, [1858]).

44. Isabel Hofmeyr, *The Portable Bunyan: A Transnational History of* The Pilgrim's Progress (Princeton: Princeton University Press, 2004), 1, 32.

45. Jennifer L. Roberts, *Transporting Visions: The Movement of Images in Early America* (Berkeley: University of California Press, 2014), 1, 3.

46. For Church's painting as a composite view inspired by Humboldt, see Gould, "Church, Humboldt, and Darwin"; for controversy over the painting's detail, see Raab, *Frederic Church*, 1, 59, 66–67, 69–72, 75.

47. Appadurai, *Modernity at Large*, 35.

48. See Kilde, "Approaching Religious Space," 197–98.

49. Tweed, *Crossing and Dwelling*, 61, 123, 158.

50. Charles Hirschkind, *The Ethical Soundscape: Cassette Sermons and Islamic Counterpublics* (New York: Columbia University Press, 2006), 6, 2.

51. Morgan, *Visual Piety*, 1–3; for the modern "scopic regime," see Leigh Eric Schmidt, *Hearing Things: Religion, Illusion, and the American Enlightenment* (Cambridge, MA: Harvard University Press, 2000), 7, 15–17, 20 (quotes on 17).

52. Schmidt, *Hearing Things*, 54.

53. Michael Leja, "Issues in Early Mass Visual Culture," in *A Companion to American Art*, ed. John Davis, Jennifer Greenhill, and Jason D. LaFountain (Malden, MA: Wiley Blackwell, 2015), 1305. For Edwardsian "spiritual sight," see Jackson, *Word and Its Witness*, 68.

54. Mitchell, "Imperial Landscape," 5.

55. Robert M. Kitchin, "Cognitive Maps: What Are They and Why Study Them?" *Journal of Environmental Psychology* 14.1 (1994): 1–19.

56. Butler, *Awash*, 54.

57. See Dell Upton, *Holy Things and Profane: Anglican Parish Churches in Colonial Virginia* (New York: Cambridge, MA: MIT Press, 1986); Gretchen Buggeln, *Temples of Grace: The*

Material Transformation of Connecticut's Churches, 1790–1840 (Hanover, NH: University Press of New England, 2002); R. Smith, *Gothic Arches*; Kilde, *When Church Became Theatre*.

58. See David Chidester and Edward T. Linenthal, eds., *American Sacred Space* (Bloomington: Indiana University Press, 1995); Louis P. Nelson, ed., *American Sanctuary: Understanding Sacred Spaces* (Bloomington: Indiana University Press, 2006); and Margaret M. Grubiak, *Monumental Jesus: Landscapes of Faith and Doubt in Modern America* (Charlottesville: University of Virginia Press, 2020).

59. For influential accounts of this tradition, see Tuveson, *Redeemer Nation*; Bercovitch, *American Jeremiad*; and Davis, *Landscape of Belief*.

60. Louis P. Nelson, "The Rediscovery of American Sacred Spaces," *Religious Studies Review* 30.4 (October 2004): 257; Peter W. Williams, "Sacred Space in North America," *Journal of the American Academy of Religion* 70.3 (September 2002): 606.

61. Harvey, "Space as a Keyword," 272.

62. Harvey, *Cosmopolitanism*, 135, 139.

63. Beecher, *Plea for the West*, 33–34, 7, 10, 9, 12.

64. For the concept of "cosmic drama," see Abzug, *Cosmos Crumbling*, 5, 30–31.

65. Noll, *America's God*, 564–65.

66. Noll, *America's God*, 165–66, 175–76 (quotes), 182–83. The literature on the Benevolent Empire is vast, but the term was first coined by Barnes, *Antislavery Impulse*, 18.

67. See Nord, *Faith in Reading*; and Morgan, *Protestants and Pictures*.

68. For topoi, see Erkki Huhtamo, "Dismantling the Fairy Engine: Media Archaeology as Topos Study," in *Media Archaeology: Approaches, Applications, and Implications*, ed. Erkki Huhtamo and Jussi Parikka (Berkeley: University of California Press, 2011), 27–47.

69. Huhtamo, *Illusions in Motion*, 364–66.

70. Lefebvre, *Production of Space*, 26, 33, 38–39. For the sake of clarity I have adopted the term "material space" used by Harvey instead of Lefebvre's "perceived" space, since visual representations of space are also perceived. Harvey, "Space as a Keyword," 279. Harvey proposes a framework for thinking about space that combines his own triad of "absolute, relative, and relational space" with Lefebvre's triad and argues that both are necessary to understand modern space and time. Harvey, *Cosmopolitanism*, 133–34.

71. Lefebvre, *Production of Space*, 34, 48, 254, 256.

72. Kim Knott, "Spatial Theory and Method for the Study of Religion," *Temenos* 41.2 (2005): 159. See also Knott, *Location of Religion*, chap. 2.

73. Kilde, "Approaching Religious Space," 184, 188, 185, 194, 199.

74. Lane, *Landscapes of the Sacred*, 43–44.

75. Quoted in Obenzinger, *American Palestine*, 24.

76. Lawrence Buell, "Religion on the American Mind," *American Literary History* 19.1 (Spring 2007): 32.

77. Warner, "Evangelical Public Sphere."

78. Reynolds, *Faith in Fiction*, 5; Taylor, *Secular Age*, 3.

79. Asad, *Formations*, 2.

80. Warner, "The Evangelical Public Sphere," Lecture 3. See also Brooks, *American Lazarus*; and May, *Evangelism and Resistance*.

81. De Certeau, *Practice of Everyday Life*, xix.

82. Frederick Douglass, "The American Apocalypse: An Address Delivered in Rochester, New York, on 16 June 1861," in *Frederick Douglass Papers*, 3:438–39.

83. David C. Huntington, "Church and Luminism: Light for America's Elect," in *American Light: The Luminist Movement, 1850–1875*, ed. John Wilmerding (New York: Harper & Row with the National Gallery of Art, 1980), 179–82 (quote on 182); Eleanor Jones Harvey, *The Civil War and American Art* (Washington, DC: Smithsonian American Art Museum with Yale University Press, 2012), 43–45; Harvey notes the resonance between Douglass's address and *Cotopaxi* on p. 43.

84. Douglass, "American Apocalypse," 437–38.

Chapter One: Thomas Cole and the Landscape of Evangelical Print

1. An earlier version of this chapter appeared as Jerome Tharaud, "Evangelical Space: *The Oxbow*, Religious Print, and the Moral Landscape in America," *American Art* 28.3 (Fall 2014): 52–75, https://doi.org/10.1086/679708, © 2014 Smithsonian Institution. "Mr. Finney's Lectures on Revivals: Lecture XII," *New-York Evangelist*, February 21, 1835, 30. Throughout this book, emphasis is in the original unless otherwise indicated. For Finney's lectures, see William G. McLoughlin, introduction to Charles Grandison Finney, *Lectures on Revivals of Religion*, ed. William G. McLoughlin (Cambridge, MA: Belknap Press of Harvard University Press, 1960), vii–lix. The audience figure is based on seating estimates of the chapel and Finney's reports of capacity crowds at his evening services in late 1834. See Hardman, *Charles Grandison Finney*, 251–52; and Hambrick-Stowe, *Charles G. Finney*, 150–51.

2. For the demographic makeup of the church, see Hardman, *Charles Grandison Finney*, 260–62; and Kilde, *When Church Became Theatre*, 31, 37. Black attendees were required to sit in a separate section. For the *Evangelist*, see chapter 3. For Finney's views of conversion, see Hardman, *Charles Grandison Finney*, 85–86.

3. Beth, [No title], *New-York Evangelist*, July 25, 1835, 208.

4. Mary Bartlett Cowdrey, ed., *National Academy of Design Exhibition Record, 1826–1860*, 2 vols. (New York: New-York Historical Society, 1943), 1:31, 162, 214; 2:14, 53.

5. The *Evangelist* articles cited are Isaac Bird, "Jerusalem," August 18, 1838, 129; A Visitor in New York, [No title], September 15, 1838, 146; "Public Taste," April 4, 1844, 54; and "National Academy of Design," April 20, 1848, 62.

6. For more on this group of evangelicals, see the introduction. Morgan, *Visual Piety*, 1–3. For the Protestant moralization of art, see Harris, *Artist in American Society*, chap. 12.

7. For bourgeois patronage, see Wallach, "Thomas Cole," 38–42.

8. For free churches, see Hardman, *Charles Grandison Finney*, 178–91, 259–61.

9. Erskine Mason, "Resisting the Spirit," in *A Pastor's Legacy: Being Sermons on Practical Subjects* (New York: Charles Scribner, 1853), 361–62.

10. For Talbot's purchase of *The Oxbow* and his religious background, see David Bjelajac, "Thomas Cole's *Oxbow* and the American Zion Divided," *American Art* 20.1 (Spring 2006): 60–83.

11. Thomas Cole to Luman Reed, March 2, 1836, Thomas Cole Papers 1821–1863, from the collections of the New York State Library, Manuscripts and Special Collections, Albany, New York, Box 1, folder 2 (microfilm copy, reel 1).

12. Noll, *America's God*, 161.

13. For the communication and transportation "revolutions," see Howe, *What Hath God Wrought*, 211–35 (quote on 225). The Second Great Awakening remains a contested term; overviews of the historiography include Joseph Conforti, "The Invention of the Great Awakening, 1795–1842," *Early American Literature* 26.2 (1991): 99–118; Hatch, *Democratization*, 220–26; and Howe, *What Hath God Wrought*, 171–195.

14. Lefebvre, *Production of Space*, 26, 33, 38–40. For the sake of clarity I have adopted David Harvey's phrasing to explain Lefebvre's spatial triad. Harvey, "Space as a Keyword," 279. See also the introduction.

15. For influential accounts of what W. J. T. Mitchell terms the "imperial landscape," see Albert Boime, *The Magisterial Gaze: Manifest Destiny and American Landscape Painting* (Washington, DC: Smithsonian Institution Press, 1991); A. Miller, *Empire of the Eye*; and Mitchell, "Imperial Landscape."

16. For Edwards's influence and its expression in evangelical print culture, see Joseph A. Conforti, *Jonathan Edwards, Religious Tradition, & American Culture* (Chapel Hill: University of North Carolina Press, 1995), xi, 5, 33, 37, 41, 46–49, 70.

17. For a recent rehearsal of these themes, see Tim Barringer, "Thomas Cole's Atlantic Crossings," in *Thomas Cole's Journey: Atlantic Crossings*, ed. Elizabeth Mankin Kornhauser and Tim Barringer (New York: Metropolitan Museum of Art, 2018), 20, 57, 59–61; and Elizabeth Mankin Kornhauser, "Manifesto for an American Sublime: Thomas Cole's *The Oxbow*," in *Thomas Cole's Journey*, 64, 66, 73, 76–82, 89.

18. Alan Wallach, "The Ideal American Artist and the Dissenting Tradition: A Study of Thomas Cole's Popular Reputation" (Ph.D. diss., Columbia University, 1973); Alan Wallach, "The Voyage of Life as Popular Art," *Art Bulletin* 59.2 (June 1977): 234–41; Michael Gaudio, "At the Mouth of the Cave: Listening to Thomas Cole's *Kaaterskill Falls*," *Art History* 33.3 (June 2010): 458–64.

19. Stoll, *Inherit the Holy Mountain*, 12; Bjelajac, "American Zion," 62.

20. Thomas Cole, "Essay on American Scenery," in *American Art, 1700–1960: Sources and Documents*, ed. John W. McCoubrey (Englewood Cliffs, NJ: Prentice-Hall, 1965), 100.

21. Morgan, *Protestants and Pictures*, 130.

22. For overviews of Cole's career, see Louis Legrand Noble, *The Life and Works of Thomas Cole* (1853; Cambridge, MA: Belknap Press of Harvard University Press, 1964); and Ellwood C. Parry III, *The Art of Thomas Cole: Ambition and Imagination* (Newark: University of Delaware Press, 1988). Cole's description of "The Future Course of Empire" is in the Cole Papers, NYSL, Box 5, folder 3 (reel 3).

23. For Cole and allegory, see Wallach, "Ideal American Artist," 148–57; and Wallach, "Voyage of Life." For the Bunyan illustrations see Bjelajac, "American Zion," 81.

24. In addition to the accounts by Bjelajac and Stoll cited above, these accounts include Edward S. Casey, *Representing Place: Landscape Painting and Maps* (Minneapolis: University of Minnesota Press, 2002), chap. 4; Ellwood C. Parry III, "Overlooking the Oxbow: Thomas Cole's *View from Mount Holyoke* Revisited," *American Art Journal* 34–35 (2003–4): 7–61; Oswaldo Rodriguez Roque, "*The Oxbow* by Thomas Cole: Iconography of an American Landscape Painting," *Metropolitan Museum Journal* 17 (1982): 63–73; and Wallach, "Making a Picture."

25. For the popularization of landscape, see Nancy Siegel, *Along the Juniata: Thomas Cole and the Dissemination of American Landscape Imagery* (Huntington, PA: Juniata College

Museum of Art with University of Washington Press, 2003). Eliot Candee Clark calculated that attendance at the National Academy's exhibitions in the 1830s peaked in 1838 at about eighteen thousand, a figure that pales beside the five million tracts that David Paul Nord estimates the American Tract Society produced each year from 1829 to 1831. Clark, *History of the National Academy of Design, 1825–1953* (New York: Columbia University Press, 1954), 63–64; Nord, *Faith in Reading*, 86.

26. Michael Baxandall, *Painting and Experience in Fifteenth-Century Italy: A Primer in the Social History of Pictorial Style* (Oxford: Oxford University Press, 1972), 29–40.

27. A. Miller, *Empire of the Eye*, 40, 48.

28. Wallach, "Thomas Cole," 79. Cole used the phrase to describe *The Garden of Eden* and *Expulsion from the Garden of Eden* in an 1828 letter to his patron Robert Gilmor.

29. Cowdrey, *National Academy*, 1:87–88.

30. Luman Reed to Cole, February 26, 1836, Cole Papers, NYSL, Box 2, folder 5 (reel 1).

31. A. Miller, *Empire of the Eye*, 49.

32. For charges of plagiarism, see Parry, *Art of Thomas Cole*, 73–75.

33. "Excursion to Mount Holyoke," *New-York Morning Herald*, August 5, 1830, 2.

34. "Mount Holyoke," *Masonic Mirror: and Mechanics' Intelligencer*, July 9, 1825, 3.

35. R. Claggett, *The American Expositor; or, Intellectual Definer: Designed for the Use of Schools*, 2nd ed. (Boston: Gould, Kendall & Lincoln, 1836), 70.

36. Edward Hitchcock, *Report on the Geology, Mineralogy, and Zoology of Massachusetts* (Amherst, MA: J. S. and C. Adams, 1833), 141, 150. Hitchcock's claims were widely circulated in the press. See, for example, "Traces of the Deluge in Massachusetts," *Zion's Herald* (Boston), September 21, 1836, 152.

37. Bedell, *Anatomy of Nature*, 29–33 (quotes on 29).

38. See Davis, *Landscape of Belief*, 13–15.

39. For Bible illustration, see Gutjahr, *American Bible*, 36–37, 47–76 (quote on 74, figures on 71). The first 50,000 copies were sold in 54 separate installments that readers could bind themselves.

40. See Nord, *Faith in Reading*, 22–23, 133; and David D. Hall, *Worlds of Wonder, Days of Judgment: Popular Religious Belief in Early New England* (New York: Knopf, 1989), 24–31, 39.

41. Jacob Abbott, *The Young Christian; or, A Familiar Illustration of the Principles of Christian Duty*, rev. ed. (New York: American Tract Society, 1832), 229–31.

42. Morgan, *Visual Piety*, 1.

43. Jackson, *Word and Its Witness*, 68, 102–3.

44. Abbott, *Young Christian*, 227.

45. Matthew Baigell and Allen Kaufman, "Thomas Cole's 'The Oxbow': A Critique of American Civilization," *Arts Magazine* 55.5 (January 1981): 136–39.

46. *Holy Bible*, King James Version. Subsequent biblical quotations refer to this edition.

47. Edwards, *History*, 516. Edwards's *History*, a series of posthumously published sermons originally delivered from his Northampton pulpit in 1739, appeared in dozens of editions in the nineteenth century and was "as influential as any other single book in fixing the cultural parameters of nineteenth-century American Protestant culture." Wilson, introduction to *History*, 82. See also Conforti, *Jonathan Edwards*, 47–49.

48. David Bjelajac, *Millennial Desire and the Apocalyptic Vision of Washington Allston* (Washington, DC: Smithsonian Institution Press, 1988), 8, 11.

49. Thomas H. Luxon, *Literal Figures: Puritan Allegory and the Reformation Crisis in Representation* (Chicago: University of Chicago Press, 1995), 4, 46.

50. H., "A Journey in New-England," *Evangelical and Literary Magazine*, January 1823, 11.

51. Edwards later denied making the claim. See Jonathan Edwards, *The Great Awakening*, ed. C. G. Goen (New Haven: Yale University Press, 1972), 71, 560.

52. Conforti, *Jonathan Edwards*, 38. For Edwards's influence on evangelicals during the Second Great Awakening more generally, see Conforti, "Invention"; Conforti, *Jonathan Edwards*, 4–6, chaps. 1–2; Holifield, *Theology in America*, 341–77; David W. Kling, "Edwards in the Second Great Awakening: The New Divinity Contributions of Edward Dorr Griffin and Asahel Nettleton," in *After Jonathan Edwards: The Courses of the New England Theology*, ed. Oliver D. Crisp and Douglas A. Sweeney (New York: Oxford University Press, 2012), 130–41; Noll, *America's God*, 258–59.

53. Conforti, *Jonathan Edwards*, chap. 4.

54. Boyer, *Urban Masses*, 15–17.

55. Bjelajac, "American Zion," 76, 65–66.

56. James Stuart, "Northampton," *Rural Repository*, June 22, 1833, 13. Others include H., "A Journey in New-England," 12; *The Traveller's Guide, in New England* (New York: A. T. Goodrich, 1823), 41; E., "Mount Holyoke," *Christian Watchman*, October 12, 1838, 162; and J. W., "Mount Holyoke," *Christian Watchman*, June 28, 1839, 101.

57. Conforti, *Jonathan Edwards*, 62–63. The memoir was *An Account of the Life of the Late Reverend Mr. David Brainerd* (1749).

58. Jonathan Edwards, "Conversion of President Edwards. From an Account Written by Himself," in ATS, *Publications of the American Tract Society*, 5:252–53, 262, 259–60. Hereafter citations from the *Publications* will be cited *PATS* with volume and page number.

59. David Morgan, "The Emotional Technology of Evangelicalism," *American Art* 25.3 (Fall 2011): 14.

60. See Gatta, *Making Nature Sacred*.

61. Edwards, "Conversion," 257.

62. For Edwards's millennialism, see Ruth Bloch, *Visionary Republic: Millennial Themes in American Thought, 1756–1800* (New York: Cambridge University Press, 1985), 16–18; and Wilson, introduction to Edwards, *History*, 90–94.

63. Edwards, *History*, 483–84.

64. Bloch, *Visionary Republic*, 229–30; Moorhead, "Between Progress."

65. See Moorhead, "Millennium and the Media"; and Nord, *Faith in Reading*, 27–40, 62–71, 76–97.

66. Nord, *Faith in Reading*, 82–86.

67. Justin Edwards, "Usefulness of Tracts," in *PATS*, 4:111.

68. Morgan, *Lure of Images*, 14.

69. *Circulation and Character of the Volumes of the American Tract Society* ([New York]: American Tract Society, 1848), 63.

70. "Great System of Benevolence for Evangelizing the World," in *The Christian Almanack, for the Year of Our Lord and Saviour Jesus Christ, 1822* (Boston: Lincoln & Edmands for the

New-England Tract Society, [1821]), 20. Subsequent citations of the *Almanack* reflect variations in the spelling and title.

71. For the *Almanack*, see Morgan, *Protestants and Pictures*, 44–46, 49–74.

72. For the Connecticut Missionary Society and the moral geography it promoted, see DeRogatis, *Moral Geography*; for Edwards's influence on home missions specifically, see pp. 38–40.

73. "The Conversion of the World the *Business* of Christians," in *The Christian Almanac, for New-England, for the Year of Our Lord and Savior Jesus Christ, 1836* (Boston: Gould, Kendall, & Lincoln for the American Tract Society, [1835]), 32.

74. Demos, *Heathen School*, 74; for agricultural education, see pp. 22, 72.

75. "A Letter," in *The Christian Almanack, for the Year of Our Lord and Saviour Jesus Christ, 1825* (Boston: Lincoln & Edmands for the American Tract Society, [1824]), 41–42.

76. For a similar account of this dual impulse, see C. Brown, *Word in the World*, 169.

77. "The Church Safe," in *PATS*, 5:131–32.

78. "The Benevolence of God," in *PATS*, 1:328, 331.

79. Jackson, *Word and Its Witness*, 23.

80. For the *peregrinatio*, see Abrams, *Natural Supernaturalism*, 164–69.

81. See David E. Smith, *John Bunyan in America* (Bloomington: Indiana University Press, 1966), chap. 2.

82. Bunyan, *Pilgrim's Progress*, 113, 116, 43.

83. Luxon, *Literal Figures*, 31.

84. For examples of the latter two, see Abbott, *Young Christian*, 294–98, 308, 311–13; and "Advice to the Keeper of a Turnpike Gate," in *PATS*, 6:29–35.

85. "The Warning Voice," in *PATS*, 1:79.

86. Daniel Tyerman, "The Life and Conversion of the Dairyman," in *PATS*, 3:362.

87. Edward Payson, "The Seaman's Chart: An Address to Seamen, Delivered before the Portland Marine Bible Society," in *PATS*, 5:180.

88. Matthew P. Brown, *The Pilgrim and the Bee: Reading Rituals and Book Culture in Early New England* (Philadelphia: University of Pennsylvania Press, 2007), 70.

89. Finney, *Lectures on Revivals*, 450–53, 456; see also Hardman, *Charles Grandison Finney*, 254–56.

90. Sweeney, "Advantages of Genius," 119–23, 127.

91. C. Brown, *Word in the World*, 28.

92. Parry, "Overlooking the Oxbow," 44. For *The Oxbow* as a synthesis of the beautiful and the sublime, see also Casey, *Representing Place*, 67–69; and Rodriguez Roque, "Iconography," 71–72.

93. [Catharine Maria Sedgwick,] *Hope Leslie; or, Early Times in the Massachusetts*, 2 vols. (New York: White, Gallaher, and White, 1827), 1:164–65. The passage is anachronistic, since Northampton was not settled until 1654.

94. [Sedgwick,] *Hope Leslie*, 1:167–68.

95. Reynolds, *Faith in Fiction*, 5.

96. See, for example, *Traveller's Guide*, 44–47; and E. Hoyt, *Antiquarian Researches: Comprising a History of the Indian Wars in the Country Bordering Connecticut River and Parts Adjacent, and Other Interesting Events . . .* (Greenfield, MA: Ansel Phelps, 1824), 124–25 (quote on 124).

97. For "countermapping," see Kevin St. Martin, "Toward a Cartography of the Commons: Constituting the Political and Economic Possibilities of Place," *The Professional Geographer* 61.4 (November 2009): 493–94; Lisa Brooks, *The Common Pot: The Recovery of Native Space in the Northeast* (Minneapolis: University of Minnesota Press, 2008), chap. 5.

98. For Apess's childhood and religious awakening, see Philip F. Gura, *The Life of William Apess, Pequot* (Chapel Hill: University of North Carolina Press, 2015), 6–43; for his use of print, see 39, 44.

99. Barry O'Connell, introduction to Apess, *On Our Own Ground*, xxxvi (quote); Gura, *Life of William Apess*, 87, 89, 98–99.

100. Brooks, *Common Pot*, 163; Apess, *Indian Nullification of the Unconstitutional Laws of Massachusetts Relative to the Mashpee Tribe; or, The Pretended Riot Explained*, in *On Our Own Ground*, 170 (hereafter cited in the text as *IN*).

101. DeRogatis, *Moral Geography*, 6.

102. Noll, *America's God*, 176.

103. For Apess's *Eulogy* as a "direct challenge" to the accounts of Everett and others, see Gura, *Life of William Apess*, 108–9 (quote on 108).

104. Edward Everett, *Orations and Speeches, on Various Occasions* (Boston: American Stationers' Company, 1836), 594, 593, 591.

105. Apess, *Eulogy on King Philip, as Pronounced at the Odeon, in Federal Street, Boston*, in *On Our Own Ground*, 278 (hereafter cited in the text as *KP*).

106. The original piece (which Apess slightly misquotes) was "Illinois," *New-York Evangelist*, August 1, 1835, 213.

107. Clayton Zuba, "Apess's *Eulogy on King Philip* and the Politics of Native Visualcy," in *Early American Literature* 52.3 (2017): 651–77.

108. Renato Rosaldo, "Imperialist Nostalgia," *Representations* 26 (Spring 1989): 107–22.

109. Ambrose Serle, "The Happy Negro," in *PATS* 1:77–80. See also Legh Richmond, "The African Servant," in *PATS*, 2:213–28; and (for a more critical account of slavery) "The Forgiving African," in *PATS*, 3:381–84. See also Schantz, "Religious Tracts," 439–40.

Chapter Two: Abolitionist Mediascapes: The American Anti-Slavery Society and the Sacred Geography of Emancipation

1. [Mrs. Sturges] to Theodore Dwight Weld, March 19, 1835, Weld-Grimké Family Papers, William L. Clements Library, University of Michigan. See also Robert H. Abzug, *Passionate Liberator: Theodore Dwight Weld and the Dilemma of Reform* (New York: Oxford University Press, 1980), 130–31.

2. Tuveson, *Redeemer Nation*.

3. For the visionary mode, see Reynolds, *Faith in Fiction*, 10; Nat Turner, *The Confessions of Nat Turner*, ed. Thomas R. Gray, in *Slave Narratives*, ed. William L. Andrews and Henry Louis Gates Jr. (New York: Library of America, 2000), 253.

4. Weld quoted in Hardman, *Charles Grandison Finney*, 87. For Weld's career, see Abzug, *Passionate Liberator*, 47–50, 57, 70, 86; and Gilbert H. Barnes and Dwight L. Dumond, introduction to *Letters of Theodore Dwight Weld, Angelina Grimké Weld and Sarah Grimké, 1822–1844*, ed.

Gilbert H. Barnes and Dwight L. Dumond (Gloucester, MA: Peter Smith, 1965), xxi–xxii, 9 ("holy band" on xxi, 9).

5. [Angelina Grimké, Sarah Grimké, and Theodore Dwight Weld], *American Slavery as It Is: Testimony of a Thousand Witnesses* (New York: American Anti-Slavery Society, 1839).

6. Weld was appointed editor of the society's non-periodical publications in May 1838. See the Minutes of the Executive Committee of the American Anti-slavery Society, vol. 1 (1837–1841), 62, Manuscript in the Anti-Slavery Collection, Rare Books & Manuscripts Department, Boston Public Library, call no. Ms.fa.33. This resource is available online at https://archive.org/details/minutesofexecutio1amer. He also edited the society's *Anti-Slavery Almanac* from 1838 to 1841. See Benjamin P. Thomas, *Theodore Weld: Crusader for Freedom* (New Brunswick, NJ: Rutgers University Press, 1950), 167–68.

7. For the campaign, see Barnes, *Antislavery Impulse*, 100–104; Bertram Wyatt-Brown, "The Abolitionists' Postal Campaign of 1835," *Journal of Negro History* 50.4 (October 1965): 227–38; Bertram Wyatt-Brown, *Lewis Tappan and the Evangelical War against Slavery* (Cleveland, OH: Press of Case Western Reserve University, 1969), 149–66; Richard R. John, *Spreading the News: The American Postal System from Franklin to Morse* (Cambridge, MA: Harvard University Press, 1995), chap. 7.

8. Ryan Cordell, "Reprinting, Circulation, and the Network Author in Antebellum Newspapers," *American Literary History* 27.3 (Fall 2015): 418. The parallel is not precise, since the AASS was initially quite centralized, though it became less so by the end of the decade as its state societies and local auxiliaries assumed more autonomy.

9. Robert Fanuzzi, *Abolition's Public Sphere* (Minneapolis: University of Minnesota Press, 2003), 11.

10. Appadurai, *Modernity at Large*, 35.

11. See Elizabeth B. Clark, "'The Sacred Rights of the Weak': Pain, Sympathy, and the Culture of Individual Rights in Antebellum America," *Journal of American History* 82.2 (September 1995): 463–93. Clark opens her essay with Sturges's letter but identifies its "fundamental trope" as "the story of the suffering slave" (463) rather than its elaborate apocalyptic geography.

12. Gilroy, *Black Atlantic*; for the plantation zone, see Monique Allewaert, *Ariel's Ecology: Plantations, Personhood, and Colonialism in the American Tropics* (Minneapolis: University of Minnesota Press, 2013), 30; for the Slave South, see Greeson, *Our South*, 13–14, 118–19; for provision grounds, see Simon Gikandi, *Slavery and the Culture of Taste* (Princeton: Princeton University Press, 2011), 239–45. For an overview, see Leigh Anne Duck, "Plantation Cartographies and Chronologies," *American Literary History* 24.4 (Winter 2012): 842–52.

13. Amy Clukey, "Plantation Modernity: *Gone with the Wind* and Irish-Southern Culture," *American Literature* 85.3 (September 2013): 506. For the neglect of religion in standard analyses of global modernity, see Hickman, "Globalization and the Gods."

14. Martha Schoolman, *Abolitionist Geographies* (Minneapolis: University of Minnesota Press, 2014), 5.

15. Kilde, "Approaching Religious Space," 198.

16. James H. Moorhead, *American Apocalypse: Northern Protestants and National Issues, 1860–1869* (New Haven: Yale University Press, 1978).

17. See Paul Goodman, *Of One Blood: Abolitionism and the Origins of Racial Equality* (Berkeley: University of California Press, 1998); Julie Roy Jeffrey, *The Great Silent Army of Abolitionism:*

Ordinary Women in the Antislavery Movement (Chapel Hill: University of North Carolina Press, 1998); Bruce Laurie, *Beyond Garrison: Antislavery and Social Reform* (New York: Cambridge University Press, 2005); Timothy Patrick McCarthy and John Stauffer, eds., *Prophets of Protest: Reconsidering the History of American Abolitionism* (New York: New Press, 2006); and Manisha Sinha, *The Slave's Cause: A History of Abolition* (New Haven: Yale University Press, 2016).

18. Sinha, *Slave's Cause*, 253–54.

19. McCarthy and Stauffer, introduction to *Prophets of Protest*, xx–xi.

20. Sinha, *Slave's Cause*, 5, 1.

21. Michael Warner, "The Evangelical Black Atlantic: Wheatley and Marrant," Lecture 3 of "The Evangelical Public Sphere."

22. David Brion Davis, "The Emergence of Immediatism in British and American Antislavery Thought," *Mississippi Valley Historical Review* 49.2 (September 1962): 209–30.

23. These were the American Board of Commissioners for Foreign Missions (1810), the American Education Society (1815), the American Bible Society (1816), the American Colonization Society (1816), the American Sunday School Union (1824), the American Tract Society (1825), the American Temperance Society (1826), and the American Home Missionary Society (1826). Their self-designation as national organizations reflected aspiration rather than reality, as reflected by the significant suspicion of and resistance to their activities, particularly in the South. See Bertram Wyatt-Brown, "The Antimission Movement in the Jacksonian South: A Study in Regional Folk Culture," *Journal of Southern History* 36.4 (November 1970): 501–29; and John W. Kuykendall, *Southern Enterprize: The Work of National Evangelical Societies in the Antebellum South* (Westport, CT: Greenwood, 1982).

24. For the role of evangelicals in the group, see Carwardine, *Evangelicals and Politics*, 134–35; James Brewer Stewart, *Holy Warriors: The Abolitionists and American Slavery* (New York: Hill and Wang, 1976), 50–51.

25. Loughran, *Republic in Print*, 305.

26. *The Declaration of Sentiments and Constitution of the American Anti-Slavery Society* (New York: American Anti-Slavery Society, 1835), 6. For the campaigns, see Nord, *Faith in Reading*, 83–86.

27. *First Annual Report of the American Anti-Slavery Society* (New York: Dorr & Butterfield, 1834), 11 (annual reports hereafter cited in the text as *R* followed by the year).

28. Quoted in Wyatt-Brown, *Lewis Tappan*, 143. These periodicals will be cited parenthetically as *E, HR, AR,* and *SF* with the dates in numerical form, except for the *Slave's Friend*, which will be cited by volume and number.

29. Barnes and Dumond, *Letters*, 225.

30. Wyatt-Brown, "Abolitionists' Postal Campaign," 229.

31. Charles F. Irons, *The Origins of Proslavery Christianity: White and Black Evangelicals in Colonial and Antebellum Virginia* (Chapel Hill: University of North Carolina Press, 2008), 171–74; Leonard L. Richards, *Gentlemen of Property and Standing: Anti-Abolition Mobs in Jacksonian America* (New York: Oxford University Press, 1970), 15–18, 48–62, 73–77; Sinha, *Slave's Cause*, 250–51; Larry E. Tise, *Proslavery: A History of the Defense of Slavery in America, 1701–1840* (Athens: University of Georgia Press, 1987), 263–66, 316, 319–22; Wyatt-Brown, "Abolitionists' Postal Campaign," 230–35.

32. See, for example, Angelina Grimké, *Letters to Catherine* [sic] *E. Beecher* (Boston: Isaac Knapp, 1838), 89 (hereafter cited in text as *LCB*).

33. The libraries are briefly mentioned in Barnes, *Antislavery Impulse*, 139–40, 264n21. The following account is gleaned almost entirely from AASS materials.

34. The AASS claimed to have published 5,000 bound volumes and 8,500 pamphlets in 1836 (*R* 1836, 35); by 1839 this grew to 19,958 bound volumes and 304,514 tracts and pamphlets (*R* 1839, 52). Periodical numbers over the same period are as follows: *Anti-Slavery Record* (385,000 in 1836; 103,000 in 1837; 40,000 in 1838; last issue published December 1837); *Emancipator* (210,000 in 1836; 217,000 in 1837; 193,800 in 1838; 213,120 in 1839; 211,600 in 1840); *Human Rights* (240,000 in 1836; 189,400 in 1837; 187,316 in 1838; 148,800 in 1839; 6,000 in 1840); *Slave's Friend* (205,000 in 1836; 130,150 in 1837; 97,600 in 1838; no figures for 1839; last issue published February 1839). These figures are from the following: *R* 1836, 35; *R* 1837, 32; *R* 1838, 46; *R* 1839, 52. Figures refer to the period between the annual May meetings.

35. Minutes of the Executive Committee, 31.

36. Minutes of the Executive Committee, 76.

37. Massachusetts (*Philanthropist* [New Richmond, OH], April 3, 1838, 1; *E* 6/21/38, 30); Maine (*E* 3/15/38, 178); Vermont (*E* 5/10/38, 7); New Hampshire (*L* 6/15/38, 95); Ohio (*Philanthropist*, July 3, 1838, 1; *E* 10/3/39, 91); New Jersey (*E* 9/5/39, 74); Illinois (*Philanthropist*, November 26, 1839, 1).

38. Ohio (*E* 2/13/38, 3; *E* 10/3/39, 91); Massachusetts (*E* 5/31/38, 19); Connecticut (*E* 9/27/38, 89; *E* 12/6/38, 127); Indiana (*Philanthropist*, February 12, 1839, 1); Iowa (*E* 4/8/41, 199).

39. *Friend of Man* (Utica, NY), March 14, 1838, 1; an identical list was printed in *HR* 9/38, 1.

40. For a similar handwritten list of libraries attributed to Elizur Wright Jr., see "E. Wright Jr's selection for libraries," in Memorandum, Manuscript in the Anti-Slavery Collection, Rare Books & Manuscripts Department, Boston Public Library, call no. Ms.A.9.2, vol. 11, no. 13.

41. For the Evangelical Family Library, see C. Brown, *Word in the World*, 86–87.

42. Barnes claimed the libraries were distributed "by the thousands." *Antislavery Impulse*, 139.

43. For Lundy's request, see Minutes of the Executive Committee, 72.

44. "Sketch of the American Anti-Slavery Society, No. 11," *Emancipator and Free American* (Boston), October 9, 1844, 95.

45. "Second Annual Report of the American and Foreign Anti-Slavery Society," *Emancipator and Free American* (Boston), May 26, 1842, 15.

46. For the shift from centralized to local control, see Barnes, *Antislavery Impulse*, chap. 14.

47. See Barnes, *Antislavery Impulse*, 100, 104; Wyatt-Brown, "Abolitionists' Postal Campaign," 228, 237; Stewart, *Holy Warriors*, 70, 73; John, *Spreading the News*, 278; Irons, *Origins of Proslavery Christianity*, 173; Fanuzzi, *Abolition's Public Sphere*, xv. For a rare positive assessment of the campaign, see Stephanie M. H. Camp, *Closer to Freedom: Enslaved Women and Everyday Resistance in the Plantation South* (Chapel Hill: University of North Carolina Press, 2004), 101–2.

48. Harvey, *Cosmopolitanism*, 134–37; Butler, *Awash*, 270.

49. C. Brown, *Word in the World*, 9.

50. "Horrors of Heathenism," in *PATS*, 10:29.

51. A. E. Grimké, *Appeal to the Christian Women of the South* (New York: American Anti-Slavery Society, 1836), 2, 27, 31.

52. Greeson, *Our South*, 118, 139–40.

53. Camp, *Closer to Freedom*, 6–7, 108.

54. De Certeau, *Practice of Everyday Life*, xix.

55. Angelina Grimké, *Walking by Faith: The Diary of Angelina Grimké, 1828–1835*, ed. Charles Wilbanks (Columbia: University of South Carolina Press, 2003), 3–4. For tract distribution, see pp. 9–10, 108.

56. See also "A Prostituted Press" (*E* 2/15/38, 164); and Maria Weston Chapman, *The Liberty Bell* (Boston: American Anti-Slavery Society, 1839), 69.

57. See J. R. Kerr-Ritchie, *Rites of August First: Emancipation Day in the Black Atlantic World* (Baton Rouge: Louisiana State University Press, 2007), 49, 89–90, 235. The biblical source text is Leviticus 25:8–17. For a period discussion of the term, see [Theodore Dwight Weld], *The Bible Against Slavery*, 3rd ed. (New York: American Anti-Slavery Society, 1838), 23, 35, 54–55, 57, 61–62, 66.

58. My use of these terms follows Jackson, *Word and Its Witness*, 23.

59. Ian Frederick Finseth, *Shades of Green: Visions of Nature in the Literature of American Slavery, 1770–1860* (Athens: University of Georgia Press, 2009), 154.

60. *The American Anti-Slavery Almanac, for 1837* (Boston: N. Southard & D. K. Hitchcock, [1836]), 31 (hereafter cited in the text as *A* followed by the year).

61. Finseth, *Shades of Green*, 154–55; D. Miller, *Dark Eden*, 56–57; A. Miller, *Empire of the Eye*, 183, 186–87, 231, 238.

62. Charles Ball, *Slavery in the United States: A Narrative of the Life and Adventures of Charles Ball, A Black Man* (1836; New York: John S. Taylor, 1837), 46–47 (hereafter cited in the text as *CB*).

63. Joseph D. Ketner, *The Emergence of the African-American Artist: Robert S. Duncanson, 1821–1872* (Columbia: University of Missouri Press, 1993), 74–76.

64. For the critique of plantation agriculture, see John R. Stilgoe, *Common Landscape of America, 1580 to 1845* (New Haven: Yale University Press, 1982), 74–77; and John Michael Vlach, *The Planter's Prospect: Privilege and Slavery in Plantation Paintings* (Chapel Hill: University of North Carolina Press, 2002), 24–25.

65. John Greenleaf Whittier, "The Abolitionists," in *The Works of John Greenleaf Whittier*, vol. 3 (Boston: Houghton Mifflin, 1892), 84.

66. For the controversy surrounding the text's composition and publication, see Hank Trent's introduction to James Williams, *Narrative of James Williams, An American Slave*, annotated ed., ed. Hank Trent (Baton Rouge: Louisiana State University Press, 2013), x–xxiv.

67. James Williams, *Narrative of James Williams, An American Slave* (New York: American Anti-Slavery Society, 1838), 26–27 (hereafter cited in the text as *JW*).

68. Eddie S. Glaude Jr., *Exodus! Religion, Race, and Nation in Early Nineteenth-Century Black America* (Chicago: University of Chicago Press, 2000), 56.

69. See chapter 1.

70. Stowe, *Uncle Tom's Cabin*, 1:110.

71. R. J. M. Blackett, *The Captive's Quest for Freedom: Fugitive Slaves, the 1850 Fugitive Slave Law, and the Politics of Slavery* (New York: Cambridge University Press, 2018), 359, 375–76.

72. Camp, *Closer to Freedom*, 109, 98.

73. Phillis Wheatley [and George Moses Horton], *Memoir and Poems of Phillis Wheatley, A Native African and a Slave; Also, Poems by a Slave*, 3rd ed. (1833; Boston, Isaac Knapp, 1838), t.p., 48 (hereafter cited in the text as *PW*).

74. Sylvia R. Frey and Betty Wood, *Come Shouting to Zion: African American Protestantism in the American South and British Caribbean to 1830* (Chapel Hill: University of North Carolina Press, 1998), 28–29.

75. Thomas Thompson, *An Account of Two Missionary Voyages by the Appointment of the Society for the Propagation of the Gospel in Foreign Parts* (London: for Benj. Dod, 1758), 83, 86–87. For SPG activities in America, see Butler, *Awash*, 34, 104, 127.

76. Edwards, *History*, 472.

77. Quoted in Gerald R. McDermott, *One Holy and Happy Society: The Public Theology of Jonathan Edwards* (University Park: Pennsylvania State University Press, 1992), 78.

78. Joseph A. Conforti, *Samuel Hopkins and the New Divinity Movement: Calvinism, the Congregational Ministry, and Reform in New England between the Great Awakenings* (Grand Rapids, MI: Christian University Press, 1981), 143–48.

79. Phillis Wheatley, *Complete Writings*, ed. Vincent Carretta (New York: Penguin, 2001), 152.

80. For the failure of Hopkins's colonization efforts, see Catherine A. Brekus, *Sarah Osborn's World: The Rise of Evangelical Christianity in Early America* (New Haven: Yale University Press, 2013), 294, 313; Brooks, *American Lazarus*, 30; and Conforti, *Samuel Hopkins*, 148–57. For the millennial views of Wheatley and Hopkins, see Brekus, *Sarah Osborn's World*, 312–14; and May, *Evangelism and Resistance*, 60–61.

81. For early colonization efforts in Liberia, see C. P. Groves, *The Planting of Christianity in Africa: Volume One to 1840* (1948; London: Lutterworth, 1964), 290–94.

82. Kilde, *When Church Became Theatre*, 38–39.

83. *Examination of Mr. Thomas C. Brown, a Free Colored Citizen of S. Carolina, as to the Actual State of Things in Liberia in the Years 1833 and 1834, at the Chatham Street Chapel, May 9th & 10th, 1834* (New York: S. W. Benedict, 1834), 28.

84. F. Freeman, *A Plea for Africa, Being Familiar Conversations on the Subject of Slavery and Colonization*, 2nd ed. (Philadelphia: J. Whetham, 1837), 111, 172.

85. Lydia Maria Child, *An Appeal in Favor of that Class of Americans Called Africans* (New York: John S. Taylor, 1836 [1833]), 148–49, 170.

86. Olaudah Equiano, *The Life of Olaudah Equiano, or Gustavus Vassa, the African* (Boston: I. Knapp, 1837), chaps. 1–2; A Lady of Boston [Mary Webb], *Memoir of Mrs. Chloe Spear, A Native of Africa, who was Enslaved in Childhood, and Died in Boston, January 3, 1815 . . . Aged 65 Years* (Boston: James Loring, 1832), 9–15. Margaretta Odell's "Memoir" of Wheatley was first printed in Boston publisher George W. Light's 1834 edition of Wheatley's poems, was reprinted in 1835, and was included in Isaac Knapp's 1838 edition of Wheatley's *Memoir and Poems*.

87. [Webb], *Chloe Spear*, 17.

88. See Albert J. Raboteau, *Slave Religion: The "Invisible Institution" in the Antebellum South* (New York: Oxford University Press, 1978), chap. 2; Frey and Wood, *Come Shouting*, chap. 2.

89. For Odell, see Jennifer Rene Young, "Marketing a Sable Muse: Phillis Wheatley and the Antebellum Press," in *New Essays on Phillis Wheatley*, ed. John C. Shields and Eric D. Lamore (Knoxville: University of Tennessee Press, 2011), 219–21, 238n10; and Julian D. Mason Jr., introduction to *The Poems of Phillis Wheatley*, revised and enlarged ed., ed. Julian D. Mason Jr. (Chapel Hill: University of North Carolina Press, 1989 [1966]), 39n4.

90. All three editions of Wheatley's poems published in the 1830s arrange the poems in this order; I have consulted numerous editions of Wheatley's poems published in the 1770s and 1780s and between 1802 and 1816 (when the last edition was published before the 1834 edition) and have not found another edition with this order.

91. "A Farewell to America" is the third poem from the end (just before "A Rebus" and "Answer to the Rebus"), mirroring the position of "On being brought from Africa to America." For the 1772 Somerset case and its relation to Wheatley, see Vincent Carretta, introduction to Wheatley, *Complete Writings*, xiii–xxxi.

92. Conevery Bolton Valencius, *The Health of the Country: How American Settlers Understood Themselves and Their Land* (New York: Basic Books, 2002), 3.

93. Schoolman, *Abolitionist Geographies*, 25, 60.

94. Howe, *What Hath God Wrought*, 312; Kerr-Ritchie, *Rites of August*, 49–50.

95. Carretta, introduction to Wheatley, *Complete Writings*, xxix.

96. Raboteau, *Slave Religion*, 97–98; Brooks, *American Lazarus*, 29–30; Blackett, *Captive's Quest*, 91–92, 104, 113–14, 132–33.

97. See Max Cavitch, *American Elegy: The Poetry of Mourning from the Puritans to Whitman* (Minneapolis: University of Minnesota Press, 2007), 193–94.

98. Ironically, Wheatley had herself rejected similar proposals to send her back to Africa as a missionary in the 1770s. See Mason, *Poems of Phillis Wheatley*, 10, 18, 203–4n17, 211.

99. Gilroy, *Black Atlantic*, 12, 17, 79, 152.

100. Jordan Alexander Stein, "American Literary History and Queer Temporalities," *American Literary History* 25.4 (Winter 2013): 855, 857, 863. For a sense of the complexity of Wheatley's publication history, see William H. Robinson, *Phillis Wheatley: A Bio-Bibliography* (Boston: G. K. Hall, 1981); and Young, "Marketing a Sable Muse."

101. Fanuzzi, *Abolition's Public Sphere*, xv, 11; Anderson, *Imagined Communities*, 24, 25, 12.

102. For its significance for U.S. abolitionists, see Kerr-Ritchie, *Rites of August*, chap. 2; and Edward Bartlett Rugemer, *The Problem of Emancipation: The Caribbean Roots of the American Civil War* (Baton Rouge: Louisiana State University Press, 2008), chap. 5.

103. Rugemer, *Problem of Emancipation*, 156–60.

104. James A. Thome and J. Horace Kimball, *Emancipation in the West Indies: A Six Months' Tour in Antigua, Barbadoes, and Jamaica, in the Year 1837* (New York: American Anti-Slavery Society, 1838) (hereafter cited in the text as *EWI*). For the journey and the book, see Rugemer, *Problem of Emancipation*, 165–70.

105. Theodore Dwight Weld and Angelina Weld, "An Appeal to the Philanthropists of Great Britain on Behalf of Oberlin College," in Barnes and Dumond, *Letters*, 742.

106. For apprenticeship, see Kerr-Ritchie, *Rites of August*, 16–17, 26–28, 53–54; Rugemer, *Problem of Emancipation*, 3, 157–59, 164–69, 232; and Schoolman, *Abolitionist Geographies*, 15–16, 54, 71.

107. Kerr-Ritchie, *Rites of August*, 18.

108. Watch nights were the Methodist form of the ceremonies that colonial officials had ordered to be held at chapels and churches across the islands on the night of July 31 in an attempt to ensure social order. Kerr-Ritchie, *Rites of August*, 18–20.

109. For the black community, see Kerr-Ritchie, *Rites of August*, 89–90, 220. William E. Channing, *An Address Delivered at Lenox, on the First of August, 1842, the Anniversary of*

Emancipation in the British West Indies (Lenox, MA: J. G. Stanly, 1842), 18; R. W. Emerson, *An Address Delivered in the Court-House in Concord, Massachusetts, on 1st August, 1844, on the Anniversary of the Emancipation of the Negroes in the British West Indies* (Boston: James Munroe, 1844), 13.

110. Schoolman, *Abolitionist Geographies*, 75. For a less critical reading that nonetheless emphasizes the way the scene downplays human agency, see Rugemer, *Problem of Emancipation*, 167.

111. Frederick Douglass, "Freedom in the West Indies: An Address Delivered in Poughkeepsie, New York, on 2 August 1858," in *Frederick Douglass Papers*, 3:216.

112. DeRogatis, *Moral Geography*, 46.

113. Such visual parallels between emancipation in the British West Indies and American emancipation also appeared on the banners that decorated August First celebrations in Northern cities. See Kerr-Ritchie, *Rites of August*, 56, 63.

114. William Jay, *An Inquiry into the Character and Tendency of the American Colonization, and American Anti-Slavery Societies*, 2nd ed. (New York: Leavitt, Lord & Co., 1835), 202.

115. *Proceedings of the Anti-Slavery Convention of American Women* (New York: William S. Dorr, 1837), 18.

116. David Walker, *Walker's Appeal, in Four Articles; Together with a Preamble, to the Coloured Citizens of the World, but in Particular, and Very Expressly, to those of the United States of America, Written in Boston, Massachusetts, September 29, 1829*. 3rd ed. (Boston: David Walker, 1830 [1829]), 21.

117. Schoolman, *Abolitionist Geographies*, 6, 22.

118. Lewis C. Gunn to Weld, July 22, 1839, in Barnes and Dumond, *Letters*, 691.

119. See also Ronald G. Walters, *The Antislavery Appeal: American Abolitionism after 1830* (Baltimore: Johns Hopkins University Press, 1976), 135.

120. Loughran, *Republic in Print*, 305–6.

121. Schoolman, *Abolitionist Geographies*, 25, 65; for one outgrowth of that vision, see Gale L. Kenny, *Contentious Liberties: American Abolitionists in Post-emancipation Jamaica, 1834–1866* (Athens: University of Georgia Press, 2010).

122. For connections between commerce and missions, see Conroy-Krutz, *Christian Imperialism*, 25–30; for slavery, abolition, and missions, see Frey and Wood, *Come Shouting*, xiii–xiv, 27, 130–32; Kenny, *Contentious Liberties*, 4–5, 7–9; Kerr-Ritchie, *Rites of August*, 17–18, 29–30; and Rugemer, *Problem of Emancipation*, 26–27, 29.

123. Philip D. Curtin, *The Rise and Fall of the Plantation Complex: Essays in Atlantic History* (Cambridge: Cambridge University Press, 1990), ix–x, 11–13.

124. Ralph Waldo Emerson, "Self-Reliance," in *Collected Works*, 2:30; Charles Dickens, *Bleak House* (New York: Penguin, 1996), 49, 53. For the reprinting of *Bleak House*, see Hack, "Close Reading."

125. Weld to Gerrit Smith, November 28, 1838, in Barnes and Dumond, *Letters*, 717.

126. In addition to the letters cited, the following account of *American Slavery as It Is* draws from Abzug, *Passionate Liberator*, 210–14; Barnes, *Antislavery Impulse*, 139, 163, 263n20; Catherine H. Birney, *The Grimké Sisters: Sarah and Angelina Grimké* (Boston: Lee and Shepard, 1885), 256–59; and Loughran, *Republic in Print*, 355–59.

127. Barnes and Dumond, *Letters*, 755, 761, 777.

128. Beriah Green to Weld, April 14, 1839, in Barnes and Dumond, *Letters*, 755.

129. Thome to Weld, November 22, 1839, in Barnes and Dumond, *Letters*, 817.

130. Angelina G. Weld to Elizabeth Pease, August 14, 1839, in Barnes and Dumond, *Letters*, 784–85.

131. [William Henry Drayton?], *The South Vindicated from the Treason and Fanaticism of the Northern Abolitionists* (Philadelphia: H. Manly, 1836), 17, quoted in Tise, *Proslavery*, 344. The comparison to "tales" is from Southern newspaper publisher Duff Green (quoted in *HR*, 9/35, 3).

132. Barnes, *Antislavery Impulse*, 276n5; Richard O. Curry and Joanna Dunlap Cowden, introduction to *Slavery in America: Theodore Weld's* American Slavery as It Is, ed. Richard O. Curry and Joanna Dunlap Cowden (Itasca, IL: Peacock, 1972), xxii; Loughran, *Republic in Print*, 357.

133. Barnes, *Antislavery Impulse*, 139.

134. Curry and Cowden, *Slavery in America*, xxi.

135. Ebenezer Chaplin to Weld, October 1[?] 1839, in Barnes and Dumond, *Letters*, 799.

136. For details, see Sinha, *Slave's Cause*, 256–65.

137. Abzug, *Passionate Liberator*, 229, 233–34, 237–40, 246–53.

138. Clark, "Sacred Rights," 464, 463, 476.

139. Loughran, *Republic in Print*, 309.

140. Clark, "Sacred Rights," 476.

141. Fields, *Life and Letters*, 147.

142. Thomas, *Crusader for Freedom*, 223; Kirkham, *Building*, 102.

143. Quoted in Barnes, *Antislavery Impulse*, 231n21.

Chapter Three: The Human Medium: Harriet Beecher Stowe and the *New-York Evangelist*

1. An earlier version of this chapter appeared as Jerome Tharaud, "The Evangelical Press, Harriet Beecher Stowe, and the Human Medium," *Arizona Quarterly* 69.2 (Summer 2013): 25–54. In this chapter Harriet Beecher Stowe will be abbreviated as HBS in the notes for book titles that use her full name, manuscript letters written by her, and articles by her published under the byline Harriet Beecher Stowe. Pieces by Stowe that identify the author only by a set of initials will be indicated in the notes.

2. Stowe, *Uncle Tom's Cabin*, 1:51 (hereafter cited in the text as *UTC*); Melvin Dixon, *Ride Out the Wilderness: Geography and Identity in Afro-American Literature* (Urbana: University of Illinois Press, 1987), 2–3, 11–20.

3. For Duncanson's painting, see David M. Lubin, *Picturing a Nation: Art and Social Change in Nineteenth-Century America* (New Haven: Yale University Press, 1994), 119; for similar views, see Katz, *Regionalism and Reform*, chap. 3.

4. Tompkins, *Sensational Designs*, 122–46.

5. Stokes, *Altar at Home*, 23, 106–7.

6. Kevin Pelletier, *Apocalyptic Sentimentalism: Love and Fear in U.S. Antebellum Literature* (Athens: University of Georgia Press, 2015), 26–27.

7. Greeson, *Our South*, chap. 7; Joan D. Hedrick, *Harriet Beecher Stowe: A Life* (New York: Oxford University Press, 1994), 214–15 (hereafter cited as *HBS*); Loughran, *Republic in Print*, 386; Tompkins, *Sensational Designs*, 137–38.

8. Coleman, *Preaching*, 157, 168.

9. For the sacralization of print, see Hatch, *Democratization*, 11, 141–46; Morgan, *Lure of Images*, chap. 1; and Nord, *Faith in Reading*.

10. Quoted in Hedrick, *HBS*, 64.

11. King, *Imagined Spiritual Communities*, 7; Anderson, *Imagined Communities*, 6–7.

12. Marshall McLuhan, *Understanding Media: The Extension of Man* (New York: McGraw-Hill, 1964), 21.

13. For the *Evangelist*, see Gaylord P. Albaugh, *History and Annotated Bibliography of American Religious Periodicals and Newspapers Established from 1730 through 1830*, vol. 1 (Worcester, MA: American Antiquarian Society, 1994), 377–79; and Frank Luther Mott, *A History of American Magazines, 1741–1930*, 5 vols. (Cambridge, MA: Belknap Press of Harvard University Press, 1958–68), 1:373, 2:63, 140, 3:74.

14. For *Godey's* and the *National Era*, see Hedrick, *HBS*, 133, 135–37; Susan Belasco Smith, "Serialization and the Nature of *Uncle Tom's Cabin*," in *Periodical Literature in Nineteenth-Century America*, ed. Kenneth M. Price and Susan Belasco Smith (Charlottesville: University Press of Virginia, 1995), 69–89; Barbara Hochman, *Uncle Tom's Cabin and the Reading Revolution: Race, Literacy, Childhood, and Fiction, 1851–1911* (Amherst: University of Massachusetts Press, 2011), chap. 1. Hedrick has given the most attention to Stowe's *Evangelist* pieces to date, discussing several of them in *HBS*, 133–35, 141, 149–50, 156–57, 170–72, 200. See also David S. Reynolds, *Mightier than the Sword:* Uncle Tom's Cabin *and the Battle for America* (New York: Norton, 2011), 21–23, 27–28, 30.

15. See, for example, Douglas, *Feminization*, 85, 108–9, 113–15, 168, 228–34; Reynolds, *Beneath*, 7, 37–38, 89–90.

16. D. W. Bebbington, *Evangelicalism in Modern Britain: A History from the 1730s to the 1980s* (London: Routledge, 1989), 3.

17. C. Brown, *Word in the World*, 18.

18. In an 1842 letter to her husband, Stowe recounted a meeting with the Rev. Nathaniel Emmons Johnson, the paper's coeditor: "I have seen Johnson of the 'Evangelist.' He is very liberally disposed, and I may safely reckon on being paid for all I do there." She made sure that was the case, urging Calvin in subsequent letters to go to the *Evangelist* office in person to collect the money owed her. Quoted in Charles Edward Stowe, *Life of Harriet Beecher Stowe, Compiled from Her Letters and Journals* (Boston: Riverside-Houghton, Mifflin, 1890), 103 (hereafter cited as *Life of HBS*). For subsequent letters, see HBS to Calvin Stowe dated May 23–27, 1844, and HBS to Calvin E. Stowe, Before September 1–2, 1844, E. Bruce Kirkham Collection, Harriet Beecher Stowe Center, Hartford, CT.

19. Hedrick, *HBS*, 39–40; Coleman, *Preaching*, 158–59.

20. See C. Brown, *Word in the World*, 9–10; Nord, *Faith in Reading*, 25, 30–31, 113–14; Warner, "The Evangelical Public Sphere," lecture 1: "Printing and Preaching: What Is a Sermon?"

21. Quoted in Hedrick, *HBS*, 64.

22. For the lecture series, see Forrest Wilson, *Crusader in Crinoline: The Life of Harriet Beecher Stowe* (Philadelphia: Lippincott, 1941), 151–52. Wilson notes that the *Journal* was "the leading Presbyterian newspaper of the West" (116).

23. E. B., "Uncle Enoch," *New-York Evangelist*, May 30, 1835, 88. Subsequent citations to items from the *Evangelist* will be abbreviated *NYE* with the date in numerical form.

24. Jackson, *Word and Its Witness*, 4–5 (quote on 4).

25. This figure was calculated by searching the *New-York Evangelist* on the ProQuest *American Periodicals Series II* online database, supplemented with the lists in Hedrick, *HBS*, 476–77; Margaret Holbrook Hildreth, *Harriet Beecher Stowe: A Bibliography* (Hamden, CT: Archon, 1976), 112–38; and Kirkham, *Building*, 246–49. I counted each part of multiple-part series as a separate article.

26. Quoted in Hedrick, *HBS*, 140. Beecher's comment on the West was referring to another publication, but in the same letter he encourages her to write more for the *Evangelist*. HBS, "Which Is the Liberal Man? A Sketch of Western Missionary Life" [part 1], *NYE* 1/25/1844: 13; HBS, "Which Is the Liberal Man? A Sketch of Western Missionary Life" [part 2], *NYE*, 2/1/1844: 17; HBS, "What Will the American People Do?" [part 1], *NYE*, 1/29/1846: 17; and HBS, "What Will the American People Do?" [part 2], *NYE*, 2/5/1846: 21.

27. Quoted in Lyman Beecher, *Autobiography*, ed. Barbara M. Cross, vol. 2 (Cambridge, MA: Belknap Press of Harvard University Press, 1961), 361–62.

28. HBS, "The Unfaithful Steward," *NYE*, 4/7/1842: 53.

29. For the founding of the *Evangelist*, see H. Davis, *Joshua Leavitt*, 67–68.

30. For New School Calvinism, see Holifield, *Theology in America*, 374–77; and Marsden, *Evangelical Mind*.

31. "New York Evangelist," *NYE*, 3/6/1830: 1.

32. In 1856 the format expanded to eight pages.

33. Albaugh, *American Religious Periodicals*, 378.

34. Mott, *History of American Magazines*, 2:18.

35. Michael Schudson, *Discovering the News: A Social History of American Newspapers* (New York: Basic Books, 1978), 17.

36. "Terms," *NYE*, 4/13/1839: 57.

37. "Agents for the New York Evangelist," *NYE*, 8/20/1831: 289.

38. H. Davis, *Joshua Leavitt*, 112–13, 130.

39. See Albaugh, *American Religious Periodicals*, xvi–xxi; C. Brown, *Word in the World*, chaps. 5–6; and Candy Gunther Brown, "Religious Periodicals and Their Textual Communities," in *The Industrial Book, 1840–1880*, ed. Scott E. Casper, Jeffrey D. Groves, Stephen W. Nissenbaum, and Michael Winship (Chapel Hill: University of North Carolina Press with the American Antiquarian Society, 2007), 270–78.

40. Mott, *History of American Magazines*, 2:63; H. Davis, *Joshua Leavitt*, 69.

41. For religious weeklies, see Albaugh, *American Religious Periodicals*, xii; C. Brown, *Word in the World*, 173–74; Howard Eikenberry Jensen, "The Rise of Religious Journalism in the United States" (PhD diss., University of Chicago, 1920), 157–63; Mott, *History of American Magazines*, 1:136–38.

42. C. Brown, *Word in the World*, 173.

43. Abzug, *Cosmos Crumbling*, 7.

44. The following account of Finney's "Lectures on Revivals" draws from H. Davis, *Joshua Leavitt*, 112–14; Charles Grandison Finney, *Memoirs of Charles G. Finney* (New York: Fleming H. Revell, 1876), 328–31; Hambrick-Stowe, *Charles G. Finney*, 145, 149–56; and Hardman, *Charles Grandison Finney*, 276–78.

45. H. Davis, *Joshua Leavitt*, 112.

46. Finney, *Memoirs*, 330, 329.

47. "Mr. Finney's Lectures on Revivals," *NYE*, 12/6/1834: 194.

48. Maine: John Chaney Jr., "Miscellaneous," *NYE*, 7/25/1835: 201; Tennessee: [No title,] *NYE*, 10/17/1835: 258; Illinois: "From a Correspondent in Illinois," *NYE*, 2/21/1835: 31; Michigan: "Finney's Lectures," *NYE*, 11/28/1835: 273.

49. Charles G. Finney to Lydia Andrews Finney, November 24, 1834, Charles Grandison Finney Papers, 1782–1875, Oberlin College Library, Oberlin, Ohio, reel 3. Original letter held by the Oberlin College Archives.

50. Susan Andrews to Lydia Andrews Finney, March 17, 1835, Finney Papers, reel 3. Original letter held by the Oberlin College Archives.

51. "From a Correspondent in Illinois"; "Killingworth, Conn.," *NYE*, 3/21/1835: 47; "Westfield, Conn.," *NYE*, 3/28/1835: 51; "Use of the Evangelist," *NYE*, 3/28/1835: 51.

52. [No title,] *Portsmouth Journal of Literature and Politics* (Portsmouth, NH), May 30, 1835: 4.

53. Candor, [No title,] *NYE*, 4/25/1835: 65.

54. See Nord, *Faith in Reading*, 114, 133.

55. Lindsay Jones, *The Hermeneutics of Sacred Architecture: Experience, Interpretation, Comparison*, vol. 1: *Monumental Occasions: Reflections on the Eventfulness of Religious Architecture* (Cambridge, MA: Harvard University Press, 2000), xxviii, 41, 49–50.

56. Kilde, *When Church Became Theatre*, 27–37.

57. For the Niagara scene, see chapter 1; for the map scene, see "Mr. Finney's Lectures on Revivals: Lecture V," *NYE*, 1/3/1835: 2.

58. McGill, *Culture of Reprinting*, 4–5.

59. [No title,] *NYE*, 10/17/1835: 258. Other excerpts include [No title,] *New-Hampshire Sentinel* (Keene, NH), March 26, 1835: 1; "Mr. Finney's Lectures," *New-Hampshire Sentinel* (Keene, NH), April 23, 1835: 1; "From Finney's Lectures," *Farmers' Cabinet* (Amherst, MA), April 24, 1835: 1.

60. Chaney, "Miscellaneous"; the original letter was dated May 15, 1835.

61. "Finney's Lectures," *NYE*, 11/28/1835: 273.

62. H. Davis, *Joshua Leavitt*, 114.

63. The 2,500 figure is from "Evangelical Record," *NYE*, 1/9/1836: 7; the other figures are from "American Periodicals," *NYE*, 5/9/1835: 75.

64. "The Lectures," *NYE*, 5/9/1835: 74.

65. "Another Year," *NYE*, 1/2/1836: 2.

66. Charles G. Finney, *Lectures on Revivals of Religion* (New York: Leavitt, Lord & Co., 1835).

67. Hardman, *Charles Grandison Finney*, 277, 398–99; Finney, *Memoirs*, 330–31.

68. C. Brown, *Word in the World*, 9–13.

69. Coleman, *Preaching*, 172.

70. E. B., "Uncle Enoch."

71. H. Davis, *Joshua Leavitt*, 90–92.

72. Noll, *America's God*, 297.

73. George Barrell Cheever, "Inquire at Amos Giles' Distillery," *NYE*, 2/14/1835: 28. Other examples include "Effects of Rum," *NYE*, 11/29/1834: 192; "A Change Indeed," *NYE*, 1/3/1835: 4; and "The New Store," *NYE*, 3/7/1835: 40.

74. E. B., "Uncle Enoch."

75. Gregg Crane, "Stowe and the Law," in *The Cambridge Companion to Harriet Beecher Stowe*, ed. Cindy Weinstein (Cambridge: Cambridge University Press, 2004), 166.

76. Arthur Bestor, *Backwoods Utopias: The Sectarian Origins and the Owenite Phase of Communitarian Socialism in America, 166–1829*, 2nd enlarged ed. (1950: Philadelphia: University of Pennsylvania Press, 1970), 231.

77. Boyer, *Urban Masses*, 27–33; Schantz, "Religious Tracts," 432–33.

78. C. Brown, *Word in the World*, 14–15, 19–20; Gutjahr, *American Bible*, 29–36; Nord, *Faith in Reading*, 6–7.

79. HBS, "The Drunkard Reclaimed" [part 1], *NYE*, 11/30/1839: 189.

80. HBS, "The Drunkard Reclaimed" [part 1]; HBS, "The Drunkard Reclaimed" [part 2], *NYE*, 12/7/1839: 193–94.

81. Larson, *Market Revolution*, 31–32, 80–83, 98; Boyer, *Urban Masses*, 3–4; Upton, *Another City*, 22–31.

82. Paul E. Johnson, *A Shopkeeper's Millennium: Society and Revivals in Rochester, New York, 1815–1837* (New York: Hill & Wang, 1978), 43–61.

83. Ronald J. Zboray, *A Fictive People: Antebellum Economic Development and the American Reading Public* (New York: Oxford University Press, 1993), 13.

84. HBS, "The Tea Rose," *NYE*, 3/17/1842: 41.

85. HBS, "Which Is the Liberal Man?" [part 1].

86. Loughran, *Republic in Print*, 380.

87. Pelletier, *Apocalyptic Sentimentalism*, 118.

88. Greeson, *Our South*, 174, 179.

89. Collins, "Apocalypse," 409.

90. Vines, "Apocalyptic Chronotope," 113.

91. See Huhtamo, *Illusions in Motion*, 176–80, 186–90, 251–59; and John Francis McDermott, *The Lost Panoramas of the Mississippi* (Chicago: University of Chicago Press, 1958).

92. Brown's *Grand Panorama of American Slavery* and Ball's *Splendid Mammoth Pictorial Tour of the United States* debuted in 1854 and 1855, respectively. Huhtamo, *Illusions in Motion*, 185.

93. Harriet Beecher Stowe, *Uncle Tom's Cabin*, ed. Jean Fagan Yellin (New York: Oxford University Press, 1998), 526.

94. J. J. M. Roberts, introduction to "Isaiah," in *The HarperCollins Study Bible*, New Revised Standard Version, ed. Wayne A. Meeks (New York: HarperCollins, 1993), 1012, 1047–48.

95. C. and H. Beecher, *Primary Geography for Children, on an Improved Plan* (Cincinnati: Corey & Fairbank, 1833), 104, 108–9.

96. "What Will the American People Do?" [part 1].

97. "Which Is the Liberal Man?" [part 2].

98. For Morse as a moral geographer, see DeRogatis, *Moral Geography*, 130–35.

99. Roberts, "Isaiah," 1012.

100. Robinson, *American Apocalypses*, 14, 17.

101. Donald G. Mathews, *Religion in the Old South* (Chicago: University of Chicago Press, 1977), 229–31.

102. Robinson, *American Apocalypses*, 10.

103. Nord, *Faith in Reading*, 133.

104. Peter Betjemann, "The Ends of Time: Abolition, Apocalypse, and Narrativity in Robert S. Duncanson's Literary Paintings," *American Art* 31.3 (Fall 2017): 101–3, 84.

105. Moorhead, "Between Progress," 538–39.

106. See especially Stokes, *Altar at Home*, 103–41; Helen Petter Westra, "Confronting Antichrist: The Influence of Jonathan Edwards' Millennial Vision," in *The Stowe Debate: Rhetorical Strategies in* Uncle Tom's Cabin, ed. Mason I. Lowance Jr., Ellen E. Westbrook, and R. C. De Prospo (Amherst: University of Massachusetts Press, 1994), 141–58; and Joshua D. Bellin, "Up to Heaven's Gate, Down in Earth's Dust: The Politics of Judgment in *Uncle Tom's Cabin*," in *Harriet Beecher Stowe's* Uncle Tom's Cabin*: A Casebook*, ed. Elizabeth Ammons (New York: Oxford University Press, 2007), 215, 218–19.

107. Moorhead, "Between Progress," 534; see also Ben Wright and Zachary W. Dresser, introduction to *Apocalypse and the Millennium in the American Civil War Era*, ed. Ben Wright and Zachary W. Dresser (Baton Rouge: Louisiana State University Press, 2013), 2–3.

108. Moorhead, "Millennium and the Media," 223–24.

109. See George M. Fredrickson, *The Black Image in the White Mind: The Debate on Afro-American Character and Destiny, 1817–1914* (1971; Middletown, CT: Wesleyan University Press, 1987), 105, 108, 110–11, 115–16; and Joseph Moore, "Colonization and the Limits of Antislavery in Upcountry South Carolina," in Wright and Dresser, *Apocalypse and the Millennium*, 95–98.

110. Harriet Beecher Stowe, *Uncle Tom's Cabin; or, Life among the Lowly* (1852; Boston: Houghton, Osgood, 1879), xi.

111. C. Stowe, *Life of HBS*, 156.

112. Coleman, *Preaching*, 159; Fields, *Life and Letters*, 146–47, 163–66, 377; Thomas F. Gossett, *Uncle Tom's Cabin and American Culture* (Dallas: Southern Methodist University Press, 1985), 88, 91–97; Hedrick, *HBS*, 155–56; Kirkham, *Building*, 72–75; Reynolds, *Mightier than the Sword*, xiii–xiv, 1, 33–34; C. Stowe, *Life of HBS*, 148–49; Lyman Beecher Stowe, *Saints, Sinners and Beechers* (Indianapolis: Bobbs-Merrill, 1934), 181–82; Wilson, *Crusader in Crinoline*, 255–60.

113. Sandra M. Gustafson, "Choosing a Medium: Margaret Fuller and the Forms of Sentiment," *American Quarterly* 47.1 (March 1995): 42. See also Tompkins, *Sensational Designs*, 126; and Ann D. Wood, "The 'Scribbling Women' and Fanny Fern: Why Women Wrote," *American Quarterly* 23.1 (Spring 1971): 3–24.

114. Catherine A. Brekus, *Strangers and Pilgrims: Female Preaching in America, 1740–1845* (Chapel Hill: University of North Carolina Press, 1998), 160, 162–74, 179–86, 192–93, 201, 260, 280, 321 (quote on 170); for Spiritualist mediums, see Jeffrey Sconce, *Haunted Media: Electronic Presence from Telegraphy to Television* (Durham, NC: Duke University Press, 2000), 44–50; and Reynolds, *Mightier than the Sword*, 35; for the sentimental tradition, see Stokes, *Altar at Home*, 31–32.

115. Gossett, *Uncle Tom's Cabin*, 96, 93 ("hysteria"); Kirkham, *Building*, 75 ("confused").

116. Quoted in Hedrick, *HBS*, 149, 155.

117. HBS, "Old Testament Pictures—No. 1," *NYE*, 11/14/1844: 181.

118. HBS, "Earthly Care a Heavenly Discipline," *NYE*, 8/1/1850: 121.

119. Quoted in Hedrick, *HBS*, 428n55.

120. For risks of public exposure, see Gustafson, "Choosing a Medium," 40–44; Mary Kelley, *Private Woman, Public Stage: Literary Domesticity in Nineteenth-Century America* (New York: Oxford University Press, 1984), 28–29; and Wood, "'Scribbling Women,'" 6–8.

121. HBS, "The Interior Life; or, Primitive Christian Experience," *NYE*, 6/19/1845: 97.

122. HBS, "Mary at the Cross," *NYE*, 11/28/1844: 192.

123. HBS, "Heinrich Stilling," *NYE*, 2/6/1851: 21.

124. HBS to Edward Brooks Hall, September 25, 1852, Kirkham Collection. Original manuscript held in the Stowe Collection, courtesy of the George J. Mitchell Department of Special Collections & Archives, Bowdoin College Library, Brunswick, Maine. Michael Winship, "'The Greatest Book of Its Kind': A Publishing History of 'Uncle Tom's Cabin,'" *Proceedings of the American Antiquarian Society* 109.2 (2002): 314.

125. HBS to George William Frederick Howard, Seventh Earl of Carlisle, January 7, 1853, Kirkham Collection. Original manuscript held in the Papers of Harriet Beecher Stowe, Accession #6318-c, Series 2, Box 1, Folder 28, Albert and Shirley Small Special Collections Library, University of Virginia Library, Charlottesville.

126. Ads quoted/reprinted in Claire Parfait, *The Publishing History of Uncle Tom's Cabin, 1852–2002* (2007; London: Routledge, 2016), 79, 55.

127. Lyman Beecher, *Sermons Delivered on Various Occasions* (Boston: T. R. Marvin, 1828), 216.

128. Albert Barnes, *The Way of Salvation; a Sermon Delivered at Morris-Town, New Jersey, February 8, 1829* (Morristown, NJ: Jacob Mann, 1830), 17.

129. "Mr. Finney's Lectures on Revivals: Lecture XII," *NYE*, 2/21/1835: 30.

130. For sermons, see W. G., "Revival in Williams College," *NYE*, 4/11/1840: 58; "Dr. Chalmers," *NYE*, 4/27/1843: 65; "The Ways of God's Spirit," *NYE*, 1/4/1844: 1; A Student, "Revival in Hamilton College," *NYE*, 4/10/1845: 57; "The Word of God in the Heart," *NYE*, 11/6/1845: 178; Rev. Dr. Humphrey, "Letter from a Father to His Son in the Seminary of A.," *NYE*, 7/5/1849: 105.

131. C., "Simultaneous Reading," *NYE*, 3/10/1842: 37.

132. C., "The Thinker. No. XLIII," *NYE*, 1/11/1840: 8.

133. "Elements of Prose and Poetry," *NYE*, 4/7/1842: 56.

134. Mrs. M. E. Doubleday, "Life and Writings of Hannah More," *NYE*, 4/25/1844: 65.

135. Nathaniel Hawthorne, *The Scarlet Letter* (1850; New York: Penguin, 1994), 192.

136. Wood, "'Scribbling Women,'" 8; C. Brown, *Word in the World*, 130, 135.

137. C. Brown, *Word in the World*, 98.

138. W. J. T. Mitchell and Mark B. N. Hansen, introduction to *Critical Terms for Media Studies*, ed. W. J. T. Mitchell and Mark B. N. Hansen (Chicago: University of Chicago Press, 2010), xii.

Chapter Four: Pilgrimage to the "Secular Center": Tourism and the Sentimental Novel

1. Cropsey's journal recounts that he arrived in the mountains on the afternoon of Monday, October 16, spent the next three days gathering sketches and other materials, and returned to the village of Catskill on the evening of Thursday, October 19. The trip is recorded in a notebook inscribed "J. F. Cropsey[,] New York 1855" in the Jasper Francis Cropsey Papers, 1845–1868, Newington-Cropsey Foundation, Hastings-on-Hudson, NY. Reproductions obtained from the Archives of American Art, Smithsonian Institution (microfilm, reel 4086) and cited with

permission of the Newington-Cropsey Foundation. For a chronology of Cropsey's visits to the Catskills, see Kenneth Myers, *The Catskills: Painters, Writers, and Tourists in the Mountains, 1820–1895* (Yonkers, NY: Hudson River Museum of Westchester, 1987), 120–21.

2. Of the five paintings of Catskill Mountain House that Cropsey is known to have produced during his lifetime, two were completed in 1855, and a third around the same time. See Anthony M. Speiser, ed., *Jasper Francis Cropsey: Catalogue Raisonné, Works in Oil, Volume One: 1842–1863* (Hastings-on-Hudson, NY: Newington-Cropsey Foundation, 2013), 192–97, 380–81. While several scholars have written that the version of *Catskill Mountain House* discussed in this chapter (now owned by the Minneapolis Institute of Art) was completed by December 1855 (when Cropsey recorded the third and final payment from Edgar in his account book), Anthony M. Speiser maintains that based on Cropsey's typical payment arrangements, the painting was likely "completed or almost completed" during the summer of 1855, when the second payment was recorded (email message to author, September 3, 2019). But based on similarities between a sketch Cropsey inscribed "Pine on South Mt Catskill, Oct. 16, 1855," an undated drawing of the same tree beneath the Catskill Mountain House in Cropsey's sketchbook, and the details of the painting itself, it seems likely that Cropsey did not complete the painting until after his October 1855 trip. For earlier accounts, see Myers, *Catskills*, 121; Carrie Rebora's catalogue entry in John K. Howat, ed., *American Paradise: The World of the Hudson River School* (New York: Metropolitan Museum of Art, 1987), 204; and Andrew Wilton's catalogue entry in Wilton and Barringer, *American Sublime*, 84. For the sketches, see the sketchbook labeled "Sketches by Jasper Francis Cropsey," p. 59 and unnumbered pages between 111 and 111A, Cropsey Papers, reel 337. "Pine on South Mt Catskill" is reproduced in Kenneth W. Maddox, *An Unprejudiced Eye: The Drawings of Jasper F. Cropsey* (Yonkers, NY: Hudson River Museum, 1979), 47. Several scholars have identified Edgar as a resident of Chicago, but Rebora notes that "research in city directories has not located Edgar in Chicago" (Howat, *American Paradise*, 204). Evidence suggests rather James A. Edgar of New York City, a merchant who was a member of the American Art-Union in the late 1840s and who purchased Cropsey's *Cottage Girl* in 1852. City directories list Edgar as a resident of New York in 1855–56. See Speiser, *Jasper Francis Cropsey*, 116; *Transactions of the American Art-Union, for the Year 1849* (New York: George F. Nesbitt, 1850), 92; H. Wilson, comp., *Trow's New York City Directory, for the Year Ending May 1, 1856* (New York: John F. Trow, 1855), 258.

3. For the history of the hotel and its literary and visual representation, see Myers, *Catskills*, 36–38, 49–76; David Schuyler, *Sanctified Landscape: Writers, Artists, and the Hudson River Valley, 1820–1909* (Ithaca, NY: Cornell University Press, 2012), 9, 20–25; John F. Sears, *Sacred Places: American Tourist Attractions in the Nineteenth Century* (New York: Oxford University Press, 1989), 66–71; and Roland Van Zandt, *The Catskill Mountain House* (New Brunswick, NJ: Rutgers University Press, 1966).

4. For versions of this account, see Myers, *Catskills*; Schuyler, *Sanctified Landscape*; Sears, *Sacred Places*; Wallach, "Thomas Cole," 28–31; and Andrew Wilton, "The Sublime in the Old World and the New," in Wilton and Barringer, *American Sublime*, 44–48.

5. See, for example, Peter Bermingham, *Jasper F. Cropsey, 1823–1900: A Retrospective View of America's Painter of Autumn* (College Park: University of Maryland Art Gallery, 1968), 20–21. For the shift toward naturalism in landscape painting more generally, see A. Miller, *Empire of*

the Eye, 66–68; Roger B. Stein, *John Ruskin and Aesthetic Thought in America, 1840–1900* (Cambridge, MA: Harvard University Press, 1967), 112–13, 194; Sweeney, "Advantages of Genius"; and Wilton, "Sublime in the Old World," 27–31.

6. Husch, *Something Coming*, 208.

7. J. F. Cropsey to Fletcher Williams, October 29, 1855, Cropsey Papers, reel 336. The letter was the first of two that Cropsey sent to Williams containing thumbnail sketches of the proposed series, which was never executed. See Maddox, *Unprejudiced Eye*, 49. For *The Good Shepherd*, see Mishoe Brennecke, ed., *Jasper F. Cropsey: Artist and Architect* (New York: New-York Historical Society, 1987), 72–73.

8. Henry E. Dwight, "Account of the Kaatskill Mountains," *American Journal of Science and Arts* 2.1 (April 1820): 20.

9. "The Pilgrim of the Cross," Cropsey Papers, reel 336.

10. Schuyler, *Sanctified Landscape*, 25–26, 37 (quote on 26).

11. Recent accounts of this shift include Bedell, *Anatomy of Nature*; Gould, "Church, Humboldt, and Darwin"; Linda S. Ferber, "Asher B. Durand, American Landscape Painter," in *Kindred Spirits: Asher B. Durand and the American Landscape*, ed. Linda S. Ferber (New York: Brooklyn Museum, 2007), 161; and Raab, *Frederic Church*, 15–16, 59–60, 62–63, 144–45. For Ruskin's influence, see Stein, *John Ruskin*; for Protestant clergy, see Harris, *Artist in American Society*, 311–16.

12. Latour, *We Have Never*, 10.

13. See Douglas, *Feminization*; Reynolds, *Faith in Fiction*; and Reynolds, *Beneath*. This shift may be described in positive terms (Reynolds) or negatively (Douglas).

14. For an especially clear example of this periodizing interpretation of visual culture, see D. Miller, *Dark Eden*. Even Angela Miller's sensitive account implicitly confirms this paradigm when she writes of the "fundamentally new context" after the Civil War, when "the terms of collective redemption that had shaped the rhetoric of prewar landscape gave way to a more personal engagement with nature." *Empire of the Eye*, 136.

15. Taylor, *Secular Age*, 2–3.

16. Frank Luther Mott, *Golden Multitudes: The Story of Best Sellers in the United States* (New York: R. R. Bowker, 1947), 122–24, 307. For "national" novels, see Nina Baym, *Novels, Readers, and Reviewers: Responses to Fiction in Antebellum America* (Ithaca, NY: Cornell University Press, 1984), 245–46. The other novel was *Uncle Tom's Cabin*.

17. Elizabeth Wetherell [Susan Warner], *The Wide, Wide World*, 2 vols. (New York: George P. Putnam, 1851), 2:19 (hereafter cited in the text as *WW*).

18. The biblical sources for the scroll imagery are Isaiah 34:4 and Revelation 6:14. The rest of the sentence is drawn from Isaiah 51:6.

19. Wai Chee Dimock, *Residues of Justice: Literature, Law, Philosophy* (Berkeley: University of California Press, 1996), 135. For Warner's novel as a Calvinist text, see Sharon Kim, "Puritan Realism: *The Wide, Wide World* and *Robinson Crusoe*," *American Literature* 75.4 (December 2003): 783–811. For the centrality of Ellen's suffering to the novel's Calvinist theology, see Marianne Noble, *The Masochistic Pleasures of Sentimental Literature* (Princeton: Princeton University Press, 2000), 95–98.

20. Reynolds, *Faith in Fiction*, 5.

21. Kim, "Puritan Realism," 786.

22. For Warner's religious background, see Edward Halsey Foster, *Susan and Anna Warner* (Boston: Twayne, 1978), 22, 27–31; and Peter Balaam, *Misery's Mathematics: Mourning, Compensation, and Reality in Antebellum American Literature* (New York: Routledge, 2009), 75–78, 80–90; for Cummins's, see Kim, "Puritan Realism," 787–89; and Claudia Stokes, "'Sinful Creature, Full of Weakness': The Theology of Disability in Cummins's *The Lamplighter*," *Studies in American Fiction* 43.2 (Fall 2016): 142–43, 153–56.

23. Taylor, *Secular Age*, 22.

24. My characterization of the setting as New England requires some clarification. The novel never explicitly identifies the precise setting of the fictional town of Thirlwall, which is described merely as a "remote country town" (1:23), but clues allow a somewhat more precise mapping. Ellen's journey there from New York City requires a day-long steamboat ride up the Hudson River followed by another full day in a stagecoach. According to an 1850 guidebook, the steamboat trip from New York to Albany took 10 hours; the "city" (1:98) Ellen lands at after her day on the steamboat is undoubtedly Albany. Van Zandt notes that stagecoaches running between New York and Albany from 1835 to 1845 typically made 8 miles per hour (*Catskill Mountain House*, 52), giving Ellen's day-long stage ride perhaps a fifty- to seventy-five-mile radius from Albany. It seems likely, then, that the locale of Thirlwall is not the "Hudson River mountains" as Kim suggests ("Puritan Realism," 799) but the Berkshires near Lenox, Stockbridge, and Pittsfield, Massachusetts, and that Thirlwall is a fictional reconstruction of the nearby town of Canaan, New York (just across the state line), where Warner spent her summers as a child. Foster notes that "Canaan itself was essentially a New England village" and that "although the Canaan homestead was technically located in New York State, the few miles that separated the house from the Massachusetts border did not prevent the family from thinking of themselves as Yankees or New Englanders" (*Susan and Anna*, 42). For steamer schedules, see *Wilson's Illustrated Guide to the Hudson River*, 8th ed. (New York: H. Wilson, 1850), 9.

25. For a discussion of the novel in this context, see Balaam, *Misery's Mathematics*, chap. 2.

26. Ronald M. Green, "Theodicy," in Jones, *Encyclopedia of Religion*, 13:9114.

27. Abrams, *Natural Supernaturalism*, 97, 107.

28. Hodder, *Emerson's Rhetoric*, 24, 26, 48.

29. Jeffrey Stout, *Democracy and Tradition* (Princeton: Princeton University Press, 2004), 19–20.

30. See P. Miller, "The Augustinian Strain of Piety," in *New England Mind*, 3–34.

31. Robert D. Richardson Jr., *Emerson: The Mind on Fire* (Berkeley: University of California Press, 1995), 23–28.

32. Charles Taylor, *Sources of the Self: The Making of the Modern Identity* (Cambridge, MA: Harvard University Press, 1989), 63.

33. Foster, *Susan and Anna*, 36; Jackson, *Word and Its Witness*, 142, 149; Kim, "Puritan Realism," 785, 789–90; Ruth K. MacDonald, *Christian's Children: The Influence of John Bunyan's The Pilgrim's Progress on American Children's Literature* (New York: Peter Lang, 1989), 46–59; Tompkins, *Sensational Designs*, 183–84.

34. Jackson, *Word and Its Witness*, 23, 151.

35. Bunyan, *Pilgrim's Progress*, 59–60.

36. Kim, "Puritan Realism," 798.

37. Balaam, *Misery's Mathematics*, 107; Emerson, *Collected Works*, 1:10, 9.

38. Kim, "Puritan Realism," 803.

39. For Warner's tract distribution, see Anna B. Warner, *Susan Warner ("Elizabeth Wetherell")* (New York: G. P. Putnam's Sons, 1909), 207, 214–17, 220–21; and Foster, *Susan and Anna*, 31.

40. A. Warner, *Susan Warner*, 252.

41. Emerson, *Collected Works*, 1:26.

42. Green, "Theodicy," 9114.

43. Reynolds, *Faith in Fiction*, 10, 5, 38.

44. See Reynolds, *Faith in Fiction*, chap. 3.

45. For the novel, see Reynolds, *Faith in Fiction*, 75, 79–81, 231; for Melville, see Merton M. Sealts, *Melville's Reading*, revised and enlarged ed. (1966; Columbia: University of South Carolina Press, 1988), 190.

46. G., "A Review of *Justina, or the Will*," *American Monthly Magazine*, June 1824, 527, 524.

47. For the orphan bildungsroman, see Amy L. Kort, "Speculating in Intimacy: Daughters, Sons, and Citizens in Early Domestic Fictions" (PhD diss., University of Wisconsin-Madison, 2000), 108.

48. D. Bruce Hindmarsh, "Wesley Agonistes and the Calvinist Sublime: The Early Evangelical Movement as a Devotional School" (lecture, Nicholson Center for British Studies, University of Chicago, October 13, 2009); [Susan DeWitt?], *Justina; or, The Will, A Domestic Story*, 2 vols. (New York: Charles Wiley, 1823), 1:14, 16 (hereafter cited in the text as *JTW*).

49. Schuyler, *Sanctified Landscape*; for weaned affections, see P. Miller, *New England Mind*, 42–43; and Abram C. Van Engen, *Sympathetic Puritans: Calvinist Fellow Feeling in Early New England* (New York: Oxford University Press, 2015), 19–20.

50. Sarah Ann Evans, *Resignation*, 2 vols. (Boston: John B. Russell, 1825), 2:443.

51. [Anne Tuttle Bullard,] *The Wife for a Missionary*, 3rd ed. (Cincinnati: Truman and Smith, 1835 [1834]), 42–43.

52. Joseph Alden, *Alice Gordon; or, The Uses of Orphanage* (New York: Harper & Brothers, 1847), 37.

53. Reynolds, *Faith in Fiction*, 81, 79.

54. Stokes, *Altar at Home*, 106–7.

55. Emerson, *Collected Works*, 1:10–11, 3:29.

56. Emerson, *Collected Works*, 6:19, 26.

57. Emerson, "Compensation," in *Collected Works*, 2:55–57.

58. Hodder, *Emerson's Rhetoric*, 134, 133.

59. Stanley Hauerwas and David B. Burrell, "From System to Story: An Alternative Pattern for Rationality in Ethics," in Stanley Hauerwas, Richard Bondi, and David B. Burrell, *Truthfulness and Tragedy: Further Investigations in Christian Ethics* (Notre Dame, IN: University of Notre Dame Press, 1977), 15–39; Edmund Pincoffs, "Quandary Ethics," *Mind* 80.320 (October 1971): 552–71.

60. For the modern essay and its relationship to the classic life and moral philosophy, see Stout, *Democracy and Tradition*, 164–66.

61. Tompkins, *Sensational Designs*, 183 ("trials of faith"); Emerson, *Collected Works*, 6:114.

62. Quoted in Tompkins, *Sensational Designs*, 184.

63. Reynolds, *Faith in Fiction*, 5, 75, 94, 121.

64. For readers' emphasis on plot, see Baym, *Novels, Readers, and Reviewers*, chaps. 4 and 6.

65. Taylor, *Secular Age*, 2–3; see also Stout, *Democracy and Tradition*, 97.

66. See Tompkins's influential account of "The Other American Renaissance" (*Sensational Designs*, chap. 6).

67. For a work that focuses on the valley, see Sanford Robinson Gifford's *Catskill Mountain House* (1862), in Wilton and Barringer, *American Sublime*, 119.

68. My thanks to Anthony M. Speiser for identifying the tree as a birch (email message to author, September 3, 2019).

69. Howat, *American Paradise*, 205.

70. See William S. Talbot, *Jasper F. Cropsey, 1823–1900* (Washington, DC: Smithsonian Institution Press, 1970), 76–77; Howat, *American Paradise*, 205; and Wilton and Barringer, *American Sublime*, 84.

71. See Sweeney, "Advantages of Genius"; and note 11 in this chapter.

72. Davis, *Landscape of Belief*; A. Miller, *Empire of the Eye*, 107–10, 155–56.

73. For the "Letters" and naturalism, see Ferber, "Asher B. Durand," 171–81 (quote on 171).

74. Veith, *Painters of Faith*, 28, 24.

75. Asher B. Durand, "Letters on Landscape Painting: Letter IX," *The Crayon*, July 11, 1855, 16–17.

76. Cropsey's drawings of the site include three views on an undated page titled "Note to Mt. Holyoke" (page labeled number 42) and "View from Mt. Holyoke" dated July 8, 1853 (number 72), Cropsey Papers, reel 337.

77. "A Visit to Cattskills [sic]," *The Atlantic Souvenir; A Christmas and New Year's Offering* (Philadelphia: Carey, Lea & Carey, 1828), 274, 276, 281.

78. "Visit to the Cattskills [sic]," 280.

79. Gatta, *Making Nature Sacred*, 73–74; Hodder, *Emerson's Rhetoric*, 12–13.

80. Doreen M. Rosman, *Evangelicals and Culture* (London: Croom Helm, 1984), 44–47.

81. [Park Benjamin,] "Cattskill [sic] Mountain House," *New World*, August 12, 1843, 183.

82. James Pierce, "A Memoir on the Catskill Mountains with Notices of Their Topography," *American Journal of Science and Arts* 6.1 (January 1, 1823): 91. The quote is a slight paraphrase of the biblical verse.

83. Willis Gaylord Clark, *The Literary Remains of the Late Willis Gaylord Clark*, ed. Lewis Gaylord Clark (New York: Burgess, Stringer, & Co., 1844), 209, 211, 213.

84. Harriet Martineau, *Society in America*, 2 vols. (New York: Saunders and Otley, 1837), 1:181, 180. The allusion apparently refers to Book 4 of *Paradise Lost*, lines 131–357.

85. Harriet Martineau, *Retrospect of Western Travel*, 3 vols. (London: Saunders and Otley, 1838), 1:85, 89–90.

86. Charles Lanman, *Letters from a Landscape Painter* (Boston: James Munroe & Co., 1845), 9–10, 45, 47.

87. Cropsey records his reading of *Paradise Lost* in an entry dated July 27 in a notebook titled "Journal of Travels &c 1845 Vol. 3," Cropsey Papers, reel 4086.

88. [David Murdoch,] "Catskill Mountain House," in *The Scenery of the Catskill Mountains*, [ed. David Murdoch] (New York: D. Fanshaw, 1860? [1846]), 32–34. For the anthology, see Myers, *Catskills*, 68.

89. [James Fenimore Cooper,] *The Pioneers; or, The Sources of the Susquehanna: A Descriptive Tale*, 2 vols. (New York: Charles Wiley, 1823), 2:107–8.

90. Martineau, *Retrospect*, 1:87.

91. Myers, *Catskills*, 51–54; Sears, *Sacred Places*, 5–6.

92. Sears, *Sacred Places*, 6, 66, 71.

93. Sears, *Sacred Places*, 10.

94. Myers, *Catskills*, 45–46, 49–50.

95. "Visit to the Cattskills [sic]," 276; T. Addison Richards, "The Catskills," *Harper's New Monthly Magazine*, July 1854, 153, 151; T. Addison Richards, *Appletons' Illustrated Hand-Book of American Travel* (New York: D. Appleton & Co., 1857), 147.

96. [James Kirke Paulding,] *The New Mirror for Travellers; and Guide to the Springs* (New York: G. & C. Carvill, 1828), 146, 145. The words are attributed to a local alderman.

97. Nathaniel Parker Willis, *American Scenery; or, Land, Lake, and River*, 2 vols. (London: George Virtue, 1840), 1:106.

98. Robert Sands, "Association," *Talisman*, January 1, 1830, 208–9; Richards, "Catskills," 149; Frances S. Osgood, "A Remonstrance. Written at the Catskill Mountain House," *Poems* (New York: Clark & Austin, 1846), 64.

99. Richards, "Catskills," 150.

100. English evangelical leaders warned against attending resorts and spas for precisely this reason. See Rosman, *Evangelicals and Culture*, 70.

101. Rev. Theodore L. Cuyler, "A Sabbath on the Catskills," in Murdoch, *Scenery*, 47.

102. "Catskill," *New-York Christian Inquirer*, September 15, 1860, 2. Rpt. in Murdoch, *Scenery*, 47.

103. [Maria S. Cummins], *The Lamplighter* (Boston: John P. Jewett, 1854) (hereafter cited in the text as *L*). For the novel's popularity, see Mott, *Golden Multitudes*, 124–25, 308.

104. For a classic discussion of these issues, see Peter L. Berger, *The Sacred Canopy: Elements of a Sociological Theory of Religion* (New York: Anchor, 1969).

105. Kilde, "Approaching Religious Space," 188. For a fuller discussion, see the introduction.

106. Sands, "Association," 209; Richards, "Catskills," 151; Richards, *Appletons'*, 147.

107. Quoted in Myers, *Catskills*, 121.

108. Bedell, *Anatomy of Nature*, 55.

109. Alasdair MacIntyre, *After Virtue: A Study in Moral Theory* (Notre Dame, IN: University of Notre Dame Press, 1981), 175. My understanding of this conflict in the antebellum period has been informed by Harris, *Artist in American Society*; and Baym, *Novels, Readers, and Reviewers*.

Chapter Five: Cosmic Modernity: Henry David Thoreau, the Missionary Memoir, and the Heathen Within

1. An earlier version of this chapter appeared as Jerome Tharaud, "'So far heathen': Thoreau, the Missionary Memoir, and *Walden*'s Cosmic Modernity," *ESQ: A Journal of the American Renaissance* 59.4 (2013): 618–61, © 2013 by the Board of Regents of Washington State. *The Correspondence of Henry David Thoreau*, ed. Walter Harding and Carl Bode (New York: New York University Press, 1958), 283–84 (hereafter cited in the text as *C*).

2. Because of the frequency with which "heathen" and its cognates are discussed in this chapter, subsequent uses of this term will not be placed in scare quotes, but they are always implied.

3. Henry D. Thoreau, *Walden*, ed. J. Lyndon Shanley (1854; Princeton: Princeton University Press, 1971), 77 (hereafter cited in the text as *W*).

4. For the genre, see Irene Quenzler Brown, "Death, Friendship, and Female Identity during New England's Second Great Awakening," *Journal of Family History* 12.4 (1987): 367–87; Mary Kupiec Cayton, "Canonizing Harriet Newell: Women, the Evangelical Press, and the Foreign Mission Movement in New England, 1800–1840," in *Competing Kingdoms: Women, Mission, Nation, and the American Protestant Empire, 1812–1960*, ed. Barbara Reeves-Ellington, Kathryn Kish Sklar, and Connie A. Shemo (Durham, NC: Duke University Press, 2010), 69–93; Lisa Joy Pruitt, *A Looking-Glass for Ladies: American Protestant Women and the Orient in the Nineteenth Century* (Macon, GA: Mercer University Press, 2005), chap. 2; Malini Johar Schueller, "Nation, Missionary Women, and the Race of True Womanhood," in *Messy Beginnings: Postcoloniality and Early American Studies*, ed. Malini Johar Schueller and Edward Watts (New Brunswick, NJ: Rutgers University Press, 2003), 155–74.

5. Michael P. Conzen and Diane Dillon, *Mapping Manifest Destiny: Chicago and the American West* (Chicago: Newberry Library, 2007), 76; for "hierarchies of heathenism," see Conroy-Krutz, *Christian Imperialism*, chap. 1.

6. See Buell, *Environmental Imagination*, 397–423; Linck C. Johnson, "Revolution and Renewal: The Genres of *Walden*," in *Critical Essays on Henry David Thoreau's Walden*, ed. Joel Myerson (Boston: G. K. Hall, 1988), 215–35; and Michael G. Ziser, "*Walden* and the Georgic Mode," in *More Day to Dawn: Thoreau's Walden for the Twenty-First Century*, ed. Sandra Harbert Petrulionis and Laura Dassow Walls (Amherst: University of Massachusetts Press, 2007), 171–88.

7. Warner, "Evangelical Public Sphere."

8. This figure was calculated using the bibliography in Edwin Munsell Bliss, *The Encyclopaedia of Missions*, vol. 1 (New York: Funk & Wagnalls, 1891), 647–55. See Leonard Woods, *A Sermon, Preached at Haverhill, (Mass.) in Remembrance of Mrs. Harriet Newell, Wife of the Rev. Samuel Newell, Missionary to India*, 4th ed. (Boston: Samuel T. Armstrong, 1814) (hereafter cited in the text as *HN*); and Margarette Woods Lawrence, *Light on the Dark River; or, Memorials of Mrs. Henrietta A. L. Hamlin, Missionary in Turkey* (Boston: Ticknor, Reed, and Fields, 1854).

9. They included his paternal grandmother (Rebecca Thoreau) and at least three of his aunts, Jane, Maria, and Sarah Thoreau. See Kenneth W. Cameron, "Thoreaus in the Evangelical Missionary Society of Concord," *Emerson Society Quarterly* 7 (1957): 52–53. For Thoreau's religious background more generally, see Laura Dassow Walls, *Henry David Thoreau: A Life* (Chicago: University of Chicago Press, 2017), 47–49.

10. For women and evangelical periodicals, see Cayton, "Canonizing Harriet Newell," 76, 79, 85.

11. Henry D. Thoreau, *Journal*, ed. Elizabeth Hall Witherell et al., 8 vols. (Princeton: Princeton University Press, 1981–2002), 6:41 (hereafter cited in the text as *PJ*).

12. With one exception, none of these memoirs appears on Robert Sattelmeyer's list of nearly 1,500 published works that Thoreau is known to have read. (The exception is Convers Francis's *Life of John Eliot: The Apostle to the Indians* [Boston: Hilliard, Gray; London: R. J. Kennett, 1836],

published as vol. 5 of Jared Sparks's ten-volume *Library of American Biography* [1836–39]). But as Sattelmeyer notes, "Thoreau did not leave a record of everything he read: . . . many works that he read simply did not register in such a way as to cause him to refer to them in his writings, despite the fact that they exerted a considerable influence." Robert Sattelmeyer, *Thoreau's Reading: A Study in Intellectual History, with Bibliographical Catalogue* (Princeton: Princeton University Press, 1988), 271, xiii (quote).

13. For Thoreau's localism, see Buell, *Environmental Imagination*, 132–33, 258, 276–78; for *Walden* as individualistic and antimodern, see Michael T. Gilmore, *American Romanticism and the Marketplace* (Chicago: University of Chicago Press, 1985), chap. 2. Recent studies of Thoreau that inform my argument include: on Thoreau's globalism, Dimock, *Through Other Continents*, chap. 1; and Laura Dassow Walls, "Walking West, Gazing East: Planetarity on the Shores of Cape Cod," in *Thoreauvian Modernities: Transatlantic Conversations on an American Icon*, ed. François Specq, Laura Dassow Walls, and Michel Granger (Athens: University of Georgia Press, 2013), 21–42. On communitarianism, Shannon L. Mariotti, *Thoreau's Democratic Withdrawal: Alienation, Participation, and Modernity* (Madison: University of Wisconsin Press, 2010); Christian Maul, "'A Sort of Hybrid Product': Thoreau's Individualism between Liberalism and Communitarianism," in *Thoreauvian Modernities*, 157–70; and Michelle C. Neely, "Embodied Politics: Antebellum Vegetarianism and the Dietary Economy of *Walden*," *American Literature* 85.1 (March 2013): 33–60; and on modernity, the essays in Specq, Walls, and Granger, *Thoreauvian Modernities*.

14. Harriet A. Jacobs, *Incidents in the Life of a Slave Girl*, ed. Jean Fagan Yellin (1861; Cambridge, MA: Harvard University Press, 2000), 73. See also William Apess, *Eulogy on King Philip* (1836), in Apess, *On Our Own Ground*, 287, and chapter 1 (above); Herman Melville, *Typee: A Peep at Polynesian Life*, ed. Harrison Hayford, Hershel Parker, and G. Thomas Tanselle (Evanston, IL and Chicago: Northwestern University Press and the Newberry Library, 1968), 125–26; and Stowe, *Uncle Tom's Cabin*, 2:34, 92, 138.

15. Earlier studies that probed popular religion include Douglas, *Feminization*; Franchot, *Roads to Rome*; Reynolds, *Beneath*; and Tompkins, *Sensational Designs*. More recent work in hemispheric American Studies, for instance, has taught us a great deal about literary and political encounters between the United States and Latin America but has said relatively little about how religious difference inflected those encounters. See Anna Brickhouse, *Transamerican Literary Relations and the Nineteenth-Century Public Sphere* (Cambridge: Cambridge University Press, 2004); Gruesz, *Ambassadors of Culture*; Caroline F. Levander and Robert S. Levine, eds., *Hemispheric American Studies* (New Brunswick, NJ: Rutgers University Press, 2008); and Streeby, *American Sensations*.

16. Fessenden, *Culture and Redemption*, 6.

17. Dimock, *Through Other Continents*, 32.

18. Hack, "Close Reading."

19. Hickman, "Globalization and the Gods," 147. For the "horizontal" aspects of globalization, see Anthony Giddens, *The Consequences of Modernity* (Stanford: Stanford University Press, 1990).

20. Laura Dassow Walls, *The Passage to Cosmos: Alexander von Humboldt and the Shaping of America* (Chicago: University of Chicago Press, 2009), 220. For Thoreau's reading of Humboldt's *Cosmos*, see Laura Dassow Walls, *Seeing New Worlds: Henry David Thoreau and Nineteenth-Century Natural Science* (Madison: University of Wisconsin Press, 1995), 119–21.

21. This latter tradition concerns what Max Weber called "a conception of the world as a meaningful totality" that exists in tension with "empirical reality." As developed by Mircea Eliade and others, the cosmic signifies a religious orientation toward a "transcendent reality" mediated by myths and rituals that interrupt profane time and space by recapitulating the primordial founding of sacred order. While several twentieth-century theorists associated this orientation with "primitive," "archaic," and non-Western religions, more recently Thomas A. Tweed has argued that the cosmic remains an integral part of modern religions as they facilitate processes of "dwelling" in and "crossing" between a number of domains including "the body, the home, the homeland, and the cosmos." Max Weber, *The Sociology of Religion*, trans. Ephraim Fischoff (1922; Boston: Beacon Press, 1963), 59; Mircea Eliade, *Cosmos and History: The Myth of the Eternal Return*, trans. Willard R. Trask (1954; New York: Harper, 1959), 5; Tweed, *Crossing and Dwelling*, 74.

22. See Alan D. Hodder, *Thoreau's Ecstatic Witness* (New Haven: Yale University Press, 2001).

23. Taylor, *Secular Age*, 345–46; Bruno Latour, "Whose Cosmos, Which Cosmopolitics?: Comments on the Peace Terms of Ulrich Beck," *Common Knowledge* 10.3 (2004): 454, 456.

24. Abzug, *Cosmos Crumbling*; Tomoko Masuzawa, *The Invention of World Religions; or, How European Universalism Was Preserved in the Language of Pluralism* (Chicago: University of Chicago Press, 2005), 22.

25. For the historical construction of "religion" as an analytic category in the West, see Talal Asad, *Genealogies of Religion: Disciplines of Power in Christianity and Islam* (Baltimore: Johns Hopkins University Press, 1993), chap. 1.

26. For travel narratives, see John Aldrich Christie, *Thoreau as World Traveler* (New York: Columbia University Press and the American Geographical Society, 1965); for "religious universalism," see Hodder, *Thoreau's Ecstatic Witness*, 140–43 (quote on 143); for "nature religion," see Catherine L. Albanese, *Nature Religion in America: From the Algonkian Indians to the New Age* (Chicago: University of Chicago Press, 1990), 87–93; for the divinity of man, see Hodder, *Thoreau's Ecstatic Witness*, 171–72.

27. Sir Thomas Browne, *Religio Medici*, in *Sir Thomas Browne's Works: Including His Life and Correspondence*, vol. 2, ed. Simon Wilkin (London: William Pickering, 1835), 21. For Thoreau's reading of Browne, see Sattelmeyer, *Thoreau's Reading*, 140; and F. O. Matthiessen, *American Renaissance: Art and Expression in the Age of Emerson and Whitman* (London: Oxford University Press, 1941), 110–12, 117–18. Hodder notes that Thoreau's use of the microcosm/macrocosm correspondence was inflected by his reading of Hindu texts (*Thoreau's Ecstatic Witness*, 221).

28. Browne, *Religio Medici*, 21. The phrase "home-cosmography" comes from another Renaissance figure, English poet William Habbington. See Henry David Thoreau, *Walden: A Fully Annotated Edition*, ed. Jeffrey S. Cramer (New Haven: Yale University Press, 2004), 310.

29. Ronald Earl Clapper, "The Development of *Walden*: A Genetic Text" (PhD diss., UCLA, 1967), 46. I have reproduced the earliest version of the passage evident in the draft, retaining struck material and omitting interlined phrases added later.

30. Daniel H. Bays and Grant Wacker, "Introduction: The Many Faces of the Missionary Enterprise at Home," in *The Foreign Missionary Enterprise at Home: Explorations in North American Cultural History*, ed. Daniel H. Bays and Grant Wacker (Tuscaloosa: University of Alabama Press, 2003), 2. For an account that interprets the passage in terms of secular travel literature, see Christie, *Thoreau as World Traveler*, 230. Thoreau may have in mind here specific works such as Rev. William Ellis's *Polynesian Researches* (1829), which contains (in addition to Ellis's reports

on his missionary labors in the Pacific) extensive observations and commentary on the culture and religious practices of "Sandwich Islanders" and other Polynesian peoples, and which Thoreau excerpted in his *Journal* in 1848 (*PJ*, 3:8–9).

31. For the shift of the Anglo-American Protestant missionary field to Asia in the early nineteenth century, see Conroy-Krutz, *Christian Imperialism*, 20–34. For missionary memoirs as a form of "pseudoknowledge," a mix of observation and cultural misconceptions that served to tout "the supposedly obvious advantages of the American ways of life, which were superior to the ways of the 'heathen,'" see Rennie B. Schoepflin, "The Mythic Mission Lands: Medical Missionary Literature, American Children, and Cultural Identity," in *Religion and the Culture of Print in Modern America*, ed. Charles L. Cohen and Paul S. Boyer (Madison: University of Wisconsin Press, 2008), 97.

32. Quoted in Bradley P. Dean and Ronald Wesley Hoag, "Thoreau's Lectures before *Walden*: An Annotated Calendar," in *Studies in the American Renaissance 1995*, ed. Joel Myerson (Charlottesville: University of Virginia Press, 1995), 161–62.

33. Anderson, *Imagined Communities*; King, *Imagined Spiritual Communities*, 7, 11.

34. Cayton, "Canonizing Harriet Newell," 85; Jackson, *Word and Its Witness*, 113–14, 125.

35. William R. Hutchison, *Errand to the World: American Protestant Thought and Foreign Missions* (Chicago: University of Chicago Press, 1987), 4.

36. For memorial prints, see Harry T. Peters, *Currier & Ives: Printmakers to the American People* (Garden City, NY: Doubleday, Doran & Co., 1943), 36, plate 66; and Bernard F. Reilly Jr., comp., *Currier and Ives: A Catalogue Raisonné*, 2 vols. (Detroit: Gale Research, 1984), 1:342, 2:657. I thank David Morgan for calling these to my attention.

37. "Memoir of Mrs. Harriet Newell, Wife of the Rev. Samuel Newell, Missionary to India," in *PATS*, 6:123, 109, 118, 123, 114.

38. Laurel K. Gabel, "'I Never Regretted Coming to Africa': The Story of Harriet Ruggles Loomis' Gravestone," *Markers* 16 (1999): 141, 145, 160–61 (inscription on 161).

39. James D. Knowles, *Memoir of Mrs. Ann H. Judson, Late Missionary to Burmah*, 3rd ed. (Boston: Lincoln & Edmands, 1829), 58 (hereafter cited in the text as *AJ*).

40. Brown, "Death," 372.

41. See P. Miller, *Errand into the Wilderness*, 1–15; and Bercovitch, *American Jeremiad*, 3–30. For missionary use of the "errand into the wilderness" trope, see Hutchison, *Errand to the World*, 4–9. For a memoir that makes frequent use of this trope, see Miron Winslow, *A Memoir of Mrs. Harriet Wadsworth Winslow, Combining a Sketch of the Ceylon Mission* (New York: Leavitt, Lord, 1835), 133, 307, 326, 364.

42. For the traditional jeremiad, see Harry S. Stout, *The New England Soul: Preaching and Religious Culture in Colonial New England* (New York: Oxford University Press, 1986), 62–63, 74–76, 96.

43. William Ellis, *Memoir of Mrs. Mary Mercy Ellis, Wife of Rev. William Ellis, Missionary in the South Seas* (Boston: Crocker & Brewster, 1836), 25 (hereafter cited in the text as *ME*).

44. See, for example, Knowles, *Ann H. Judson*, 128; Lawrence, *Henrietta A. L. Hamlin*, 192; Joseph Mitchell, *The Missionary Pioneer; or, A Brief Memoir of the Life, Labours, and Death of John Stewart, (Man of Colour)* (New York: J. C. Totten, 1827), 30–36.

45. Maul, "Hybrid Product," 167–70.

46. ABCFM, *A Narrative of Five Youth from the Sandwich Islands, Now Receiving an Education in This Country* (New York: J. Seymour, 1816), 13, 40, 42, 43.

47. Lyman Beecher, *A Sermon Delivered at the Funeral of Henry Obookiah, A Native of Owhyhee, and a Member of the Foreign Mission School in Cornwall, Connecticut, February 18, 1818* (Elizabethtown, NJ: Edson Hart, 1819), 32.

48. [Edwin W. Dwight and] Henry Obookiah, *Memoirs of Henry Obookiah, A Native of Owhyhee, and a Member of the Foreign Mission School; who Died at Cornwall, Conn. Feb. 17, 1818 Aged 26 Years* (Philadelphia: American Sunday School Union, 1830) (hereafter cited in the text as *HO*).

49. Demos, *Heathen School*, 84.

50. Forbes quoted in Jeffrey K. Lyons, "Memoirs of Henry Obookiah: A Rhetorical History," *Hawaiian Journal of History* 38 (2004): 36–37, 41 (expedition figure).

51. Melville, *Typee*, 125; Conroy-Krutz, *Christian Imperialism*, 20.

52. For the diversity of the Foreign Mission School, for example, see Demos, *Heathen School*, 70–71, 87–88, 98, 114–17.

53. Lance Newman, *Our Common Dwelling: Henry Thoreau, Transcendentalism, and the Class Politics of Nature* (New York: Palgrave MacMillan, 2005), 135.

54. C. Brown, *Word in the World*, 2; Gruesz, *Ambassadors of Culture*, 20.

55. Hodder, *Thoreau's Ecstatic Witness*, 139–48, 174–78; for the Oriental Renaissance, see Masuzawa, *Invention*, 149–55.

56. Quoted in Hodder, *Thoreau's Ecstatic Witness*, 139; for Clarke and Parker, see Masuzawa, *Invention*, 77–79, 92.

57. John Lardas Modern, *Secularism in Antebellum America* (Chicago: University of Chicago Press, 2011), 72, 85–87.

58. Henry D. Thoreau, "A Plea for Captain John Brown," in *Reform Papers*, ed. Wendell Glick (Princeton: Princeton University Press, 1973), 121 (hereafter cited in the text as *RP*).

59. Greeson, *Our South*, 4, 25, 172 (quote).

60. For "cosmic drama," see Abzug, *Cosmos Crumbling*, 5, 30–31; and Hickman, "Globalization and the Gods," 147.

61. Anderson, *Imagined Communities*, 19, 24.

62. Latour, *We Have Never*, 47. A "semiotic form" refers to a system of signification that includes "not only language but also music, visual imagery, food, architecture, gesture, and anything else that enters into actual semiotic practice [that] functions within perceptible experience by virtue of its material properties." Webb Keane, *Christian Moderns: Freedom and Fetish in the Mission Encounter* (Berkeley: University of California Press, 2007), 21.

63. See Dana Luciano, *Arranging Grief: Sacred Time and the Body in Nineteenth-Century America* (New York: New York University Press, 2007); on mediums, see Cathy Gutierrez, *Plato's Ghost: Spiritualism in the American Renaissance* (New York: Oxford University Press, 2009), chaps. 2 and 3.

64. For Millerite charts, see Morgan, *Protestants and Pictures*, chap. 4; for obeah, see Toni Wall Jaudon, "Obeah's Sensations: Rethinking Religion at the Transnational Turn," *American Literature* 84.4 (December 2012): 715–41.

65. Taylor, *Secular Age*, 146, 207–11.

308   NOTES TO CHAPTER FIVE

66. Latour, *We Have Never*, 4, 10. Cosmic collectives would include the transcendent "nonhumans" Latour emphasizes in "Whose Cosmos?" as discussed earlier. The emphasis on individuals is exemplified by Taylor's account of the personal experience of "fullness" (*Secular Age*, 5–6); see the editors' introduction to *Varieties of Secularism in a Secular Age*, ed. Michael Warner, Jonathan VanAntwerpen, and Craig Calhoun (Cambridge, MA: Harvard University Press, 2010), 10–12.

67. Taylor, *Secular Age*, 38–39, 27.

68. Henry D. Thoreau, *A Week on the Concord and Merrimack Rivers*, ed. Carl F. Hovde, William L. Howarth, and Elizabeth Hall Witherell (Princeton: Princeton University Press, 1980), 279, 43. See also Hodder, *Thoreau's Ecstatic Witness*, 134–36.

69. J. Lyndon Shanley, *The Making of Walden; with the Text of the First Version* (Chicago: University of Chicago Press, 1957), 139.

70. "Homer. Ossian. Chaucer.," in *Early Essays and Miscellanies*, ed. Joseph J. Moldenhauer and Edwin Moser, with Alexander C. Kern (Princeton: Princeton University Press, 1975), 157–58.

71. For the "world bible," see Alan Hodder, "Asian Influences," in *The Oxford Handbook of Transcendentalism*, ed. Joel Myerson, Sandra Harbert Petrulionis, and Laura Dassow Walls (New York: Oxford University Press, 2010), 32, 35. For "Ethnical Scriptures," see Hodder, "Asian Influences," 32; and Robert Kuhn McGregor, "Henry David Thoreau: The Asian Thread," in *Thoreau's Importance for Philosophy*, ed. Rick Anthony Furtak, Jonathan Ellsworth, and James D. Reid (New York: Fordham University Press, 2012), 204–6. Keane, *Christian Moderns*, 54.

72. *The Journal of Henry D. Thoreau*, ed. Bradford Torrey and Francis H. Allen, 14 vols. bound as 2 (1906; New York: Dover, 1962), 3:266 (hereafter cited in the text as *J*).

73. See, for example, Alvan Bond, *Memoir of the Rev. Pliny Fisk, A.M., Late Missionary to Palestine* (Boston: Crocker and Brewster, 1828), 249.

74. Neill Matheson, "Thoreau's Inner Animal," *Arizona Quarterly* 67.4 (Winter 2011): 16, 17.

75. Albanese, *Nature Religion*, 82–83, 93, 89, 87, 92. "Confusion" is Albanese's characterization (87); she quotes "vacillation" (92) from Donald Worster.

76. Dunch, "Beyond Cultural Imperialism," 301, 322.

77. Saba Mahmood, "Can Secularism Be Other-wise?" in Warner, VanAntwerpen, and Calhoun, *Varieties of Secularism*, 286–87.

78. Latour, *We Have Never*, 10–11.

79. D. Bruce Hindmarsh, *The Evangelical Conversion Narrative: Spiritual Autobiography in Early Modern England* (New York: Oxford University Press, 2005), 342, 344, 346, 343, 341.

80. See, for example, Robert N. Bellah et al., *Habits of the Heart: Individualism and Commitment in American Life*, with a new preface (1985; Berkeley: University of California Press, 2008), 55–56; and Robert D. Putnam, *Bowling Alone: The Collapse and Revival of American Community* (New York: Simon & Schuster, 2000), 24.

81. Taylor, *Secular Age*, 299, 595.

82. Taylor, *Secular Age*, 299.

83. Stoll, *Inherit the Holy Mountain*.

84. Ralph Waldo Emerson, *Nature*, in *Collected Works*, 1:29. For Thoreau's adoption of the concept, see Hodder, *Thoreau's Ecstatic Witness*, 93–94.

85. Hodder, *Emerson's Rhetoric*, 100, 79, 78.

86. Hodder, *Thoreau's Ecstatic Witness*, 94.
87. Jaudon, "Obeah's Sensations," 716.
88. Fessenden, *Culture and Redemption*, 33.
89. Akeel Bilgrami, "What Is Enchantment?" in Warner, VanAntwerpen, and Calhoun, *Varieties of Secularism*, 152, 157, 156.
90. Latour, "Whose Cosmos?" 457, 453.

Chapter Six: The Sensational Republic: Catholic Conspiracy and the Battle for the Great West

1. Ray A. Billington, "Anti-Catholic Propaganda and the Home Missionary Movement, 1800–1860," *Mississippi Valley Historical Review* 22.3 (December 1935): 361–84; Ray Allen Billington, *The Protestant Crusade, 1800–1860: A Study of the Origins of American Nativism* (1938; Chicago: Quadrangle Books, 1964), chap. 5; Bryan Le Beau, "'Saving the West from the Pope': Anti-Catholic Propaganda and the Settlement of the Mississippi River Valley," *American Studies* 32.1 (Spring 1991): 101–14.

2. For the evangelical role in the anti-Catholic movement, see Billington, "Anti-Catholic Propaganda"; Billington, *Protestant Crusade*, 41–42, 47–48, 67, 70, 129, 166–68, 173–78, 181–85; Franchot, *Roads to Rome*, 100–103, 109, 131; and Carwardine, *Evangelicals and Politics*, 30, 33, 35, 47, 66, 80–84, 129, 199–204, 273.

3. For the "city-mysteries" novel, see Michael Denning, *Mechanic Accents: Dime Novels and Working-Class Culture in America*, rev. ed. (1987; London: Verso, 1998), chap. 6. For Klauprecht's *Cincinnati* as an example, see Werner Sollors, *Beyond Ethnicity: Consent and Descent in American Culture* (New York: Oxford University Press, 1986), 141–48.

4. Emil Klauprecht, *Cincinnati; or, The Mysteries of the West*, trans. Steven Rowan, ed. Don Heinrich Tolzmann (1854–55; New York: Peter Lang, 1996), 623 (hereafter cited in the text as CMW).

5. For progressive nineteenth-century frontier histories, see William Cronon, "A Place for Stories: Nature, History, and Narrative," *Journal of American History* 78.4 (March 1992): 1352–54.

6. A. Miller, *Empire of the Eye*, 154. For city views in the regional press, see Katz, *Regionalism and Reform*, 19–20, 91–109; for Klauprecht's lithography, see Richard F. Askren, "Emil Klauprecht—Ohio Valley German American," in *Art as Image: Prints and Promotion in Cincinnati, Ohio*, ed. Alice M. Cornell (Athens: Ohio University Press, 2001), 57–71.

7. For producer ideology, see Steven J. Ross, *Workers on the Edge: Work, Leisure, and Politics in Industrializing Cincinnati, 1788–1890* (New York: Columbia University Press, 1985), 15, 57–61.

8. See John Barrell, *English Literature in History, 1730–80: An Equal, Wide Survey* (London: Hutchinson, 1983), 32–33, 35–36, and chap. 1.

9. See Billington, *Protestant Crusade*, chap. 5; Elizabeth Fenton, *Religious Liberties: Anti-Catholicism and Liberal Democracy in Nineteenth-Century U.S. Literature and Culture* (New York: Oxford University Press, 2011), chaps. 1–2; Franchot, *Roads to Rome*, chap. 3; and Le Beau, "'Saving the West.'"

10. For Protestant anxieties about (and admiration of) Catholic built space, see R. Smith, *Gothic Arches*, esp. chap. 2.

11. Accusations leveled in the nativist press since the 1830s that Benton was a Catholic conspirator (thanks to his role in establishing Saint Louis University, a Jesuit institution that his own sons later attended) reinforce the sense that Benton himself has merged with the foreign minions of popery. See Beecher, *Plea for the West*, 57; and Le Beau, "'Saving the West,'" 107.

12. David Anthony, *Paper Money Men: Commerce, Manhood, and the Sensational Public Sphere in Antebellum America* (Columbus: Ohio State University Press, 2009), 21.

13. See Timothy J. Gilfoyle, *City of Eros: New York City, Prostitution, and the Commercialization of Sex, 1790–1920* (New York: Norton, 1992); Amy Gilman Srebnick, *The Mysterious Death of Mary Rogers: Sex and Culture in Nineteenth-Century New York* (New York: Oxford University Press, 1995); and Upton, *Another City*, chap. 6.

14. Notable exceptions include Coleman, *Preaching*, chap. 3; Fenton, *Religious Liberties*; Franchot, *Roads to Rome*; and Susan M. Griffin, *Anti-Catholicism and Nineteenth-Century Fiction* (Cambridge: Cambridge University Press, 2004).

15. Steven J. Ross, "The Transformation of Republican Ideology," *Journal of the Early Republic* 10.3 (Autumn 1990): 325, 324.

16. For "alternative republicanism," see Andy Doolen, "Early American Civics: Rehistoricizing the Power of Republicanism," *American Literary History* 19.1 (Spring 2007): 132; Sandra M. Gustafson, *Imagining Deliberative Democracy in the Early American Republic* (Chicago: University of Chicago Press, 2011), chap. 2.

17. Gustafson, *Imagining Deliberative Democracy*, 152.

18. For "direct-access societies," see Charles Taylor, "Modes of Secularism," in *Secularism and Its Critics*, ed. Rajeev Bhargava (Delhi: Oxford University Press, 1998), 39–40; and Taylor, *Secular Age*, 207–11.

19. Asad, *Formations*, 4, 5.

20. For anti-Catholicism as an expression of secular concerns, see Billington, *Protestant Crusade*, 32–35, 68; David Brion Davis, "Some Themes of Counter-Subversion: An Analysis of Anti-Masonic, Anti-Catholic and Anti-Mormon Literature," *Mississippi Valley Historical Review* 47.2 (September 1960): 205–24; Franchot, *Roads to Rome*, 5–6, 141–43; and R. Smith, *Gothic Arches*, 5. Not all of these authors reduce anti-Catholicism to exclusively secular causes; Davis is perhaps the most inclined to see it as a symptom of non-religious causes.

21. For the prospect poem and the picaresque novel, see Barrell, *Equal, Wide Survey*, chaps. 1, 3; see also Michael Warner, *The Letters of the Republic: Publication and the Public Sphere in Eighteenth-Century America* (Cambridge, MA: Harvard University Press, 1990), 29–30, 52–53. For visual forms, see John Barrell, *The Political Theory of Painting from Reynolds to Hazlitt: "The Body of the Public"* (New Haven: Yale University Press, 1986); Wendy Bellion, *Citizen Spectator: Art, Illusion, and Visual Perception in Early National America* (Chapel Hill: University of North Carolina Press, 2011), 42, 156–57, 165; Wendy Bellion, "'Extend the Sphere': Charles Willson Peale's Panorama of Annapolis," *Art Bulletin* 86.3 (September 2004): 529–49; and Alexander Nemerov, *The Body of Raphaelle Peale: Still Life and Selfhood, 1812–1824* (Berkeley: University of California Press, 2001), 43–57, 176–78. For architecture, see Loughran, *Republic in Print*, 246–47; Laura Rigal, *The American Manufactory: Art, Labor, and the World of Things in the Early Republic* (Princeton: Princeton University Press, 1998), chap. 1; and Eric Slauter, *The State as a Work of*

Art: The Cultural Origins of the Constitution (Chicago: University of Chicago Press, 2009), 41, 63–72, 79–85.

22. James Thomson, *The Seasons*, ed. James Sambrook (New York: Oxford University Press, 1981), 46, 16; see Barrell, *Equal, Wide Survey*, 59–63.

23. For examples of these phrases used by various Federalists, see Lorri Glover, *The Fate of the Revolution: Virginians Debate the Constitution* (Baltimore: Johns Hopkins University Press, 2016), 62; Michael J. Klarman, *The Framers' Coup: The Making of the United States Constitution* (New York: Oxford University Press, 2016), 365; Bernard Bailyn, ed., *The Debate on the Constitution*, 2 vols. (New York: Library of America, 1993),1:140, 411, 161; and Slauter, *State as a Work*, 137. On the Federalist "comprehensive view," see Bellion, "'Extend the Sphere,'" 544–45.

24. "Marcus," *Daily Advertiser* (New York), October 15, 1787, reprinted in Bailyn, *Debate on the Constitution*, 1:128. The passage is (mis)quoted in Bellion, "'Extend the Sphere,'" 544.

25. Bellion, " 'Extend the Sphere,'" 529. The panorama was never completed, but Peale's preparatory sketches survive.

26. Tony Bennett, "The Exhibitionary Complex," *new formations* 4 (Spring 1988): 76.

27. Barrell, *Equal, Wide Survey*, 33.

28. The Cincinnati Observatory was erected in 1843 on land donated to the Cincinnati Astronomical Society by real estate mogul Nicholas Longworth. See Urania, "The Lighthouse of the Skies," *Cleveland Daily Herald*, November 13, 1843, 2; and Charles Cist, *Sketches and Statistics of Cincinnati in 1851* (Cincinnati: Wm. H. Moore, 1851), 107.

29. William Cronon, *Nature's Metropolis: Chicago and the Great West* (New York: W. W. Norton, 1991).

30. See Phyllis Lee Levin, *The Remarkable Education of John Quincy Adams* (New York: Palgrave Macmillan, 2015), 83, 380–81, 459; and Nina Burleigh, *The Stranger and the Statesman: James Smithson, John Quincy Adams, and the Making of America's Greatest Museum: The Smithsonian* (New York: William Morrow, 2003), 187, 194, 207, 218–20, 228–30.

31. J. H. Elliott, *Empires of the Atlantic World: Britain and Spain in America, 1492–1830* (New Haven: Yale University Press, 2006), 187.

32. Franchot, *Roads to Rome*, 88–89.

33. See, for example, the narratives of Hannah Dustan and Elizabeth Hanson in *Women's Indian Captivity Narratives*, ed. Kathryn Zabelle Derounian-Stodola (New York: Penguin, 1998), 59, 65, 77, 79 (quote on 59). See also Franchot, *Roads to Rome*, 94–97; and Wai Chee Dimock, "Early American Literature as a Networked Field: Mary Rowlandson, Louise Erdrich, Sherman Alexie," *Early American Literature* 50.1 (2015): 119–20.

34. Fenton, *Religious Liberties*, 52.

35. Thomas D'Arcy McGee, *The Catholic History of North America* (Boston: Patrick Donahoe, 1855), 101; Franchot, *Roads to Rome*, 36.

36. Franchot, *Roads to Rome*, 23.

37. Franchot, *Roads to Rome*, 4. On fears of overextension, see Reginald Horsman, "The Dimensions of an 'Empire for Liberty': Expansion and Republicanism, 1775–1825," *Journal of the Early Republic* 9.1 (Spring 1989): 1–20.

38. Marryat quoted in Billington, *Protestant Crusade*, 122. Le Beau, "'Saving the West,'" 102–3.

39. "The Great and Good Work," *Home Missionary*, August 1839, 73, misquoted in Billington, "Anti-Catholic Propaganda," 373.

40. Albert Barnes, *Home Missions; A Sermon in Behalf of the American Home Missionary Society: Preached in the Cities of New York and Philadelphia, May, 1849* (New York: American Home Missionary Society, 1849), 19, misquoted and mis-cited in Billington, "Anti-Catholic Propaganda," 375.

41. R. Smith, *Gothic Arches*, 20.

42. Jody M. Roy, *Rhetorical Campaigns of the 19th Century Anti-Catholics and Catholics in America* (Lewiston, NY: Edwin Mellen, 2000), 75; [Samuel F. B. Morse,] *Foreign Conspiracy against the Liberties of the United States* (New York: Leavitt, Lord & Co., 1835), 174–75.

43. "Popery at the West," *Vermont Chronicle* (Windsor, VT), December 6, 1843, 193.

44. Butler, *Awash*, 271; W. C., "Topics of Correspondence," *Scioto Gazette* (Chillicothe, OH), September 12, 1844, 1.

45. R. Smith, *Gothic Arches*, 8–11, 21 (quote on 8).

46. "Bishop Bappe—Temperance—Free School—Female Seminary—Cathedral," *Cleveland Herald*, March 16, 1848, 2.

47. "St. John's Cathedral," *Milwaukee Daily Sentinel*, July 16, 1853, 2.

48. "Consecration of St. John's Cathedral, Milwaukee," *Milwaukee Daily Sentinel*, August 2, 1853, 2.

49. "A Plea for the West," *Western Monthly Magazine*, May 1835, 320–21, 323–25. For Beecher as the rare anti-Catholic writer who had lived in the West, see Le Beau, "'Saving the West,'" 112.

50. "On Western Character," *Western Monthly Magazine*, February 1833, 51.

51. Billington, *Protestant Crusade*, 138n48.

52. Asad, *Formations*, 5.

53. Fessenden, *Culture and Redemption*, 4–6.

54. Quoted in R. Smith, *Gothic Arches*, 26–27.

55. [Benjamin F.] Tefft, "A Day with the Catholics," *Ladies' Repository*, September 1847, 283; see also R. Smith, *Gothic Arches*, 35–37.

56. For a related discussion, see Franchot, *Roads to Rome*, 43–45.

57. R. Smith, *Gothic Arches*, 15.

58. See John Davis, "Catholic Envy: The Visual Culture of Protestant Desire," in *The Visual Culture of American Religions*, ed. David Morgan and Sally M. Promey (Berkeley: University of California Press, 2001), 114.

59. See, for example, Wallach, "Making a Picture," 83.

60. See Michel Foucault, *Discipline and Punish: The Birth of the Prison*, trans. Alan Sheridan (1975; New York: Vintage, 1995), 139–40; Bennett emphasizes the modern state and the secular institutions (museums, galleries, etc.) associated with it ("Exhibitionary Complex," 79).

61. For sources on the "Infernal Regions," sacred dioramas, and apocalyptic paintings, see the introduction.

62. Griffin, *Anti-Catholicism*, 96.

63. George Lippard, *New York: Its Upper Ten and Lower Million* (Cincinnati: H. M. Rulison, 1853), 283–84 (hereafter cited in the text as *NY*).

64. Frederick Jackson Turner, "The Significance of the Frontier in American History," in *Rereading Frederick Jackson Turner*, ed. John Mack Faragher (New Haven: Yale University Press, 1998), 31. For agrarianism, see H. Smith, *Virgin Land*, esp. chaps. 11–22; for Turner specifically, see pp. 3–4, 250–60.

65. For artisan republicanism, see Sean Wilentz, *Chants Democratic: New York City & the Rise of the American Working Class, 1788–1850* (New York: Oxford University Press, 1984), chap. 2; for city-mysteries, see Denning, *Mechanic Accents*, 103–17; Denning cites Dermoyne as an early version of "the producer hero, the honest mechanic of working class republicanism" (111). For a critique of this perspective, see David M. Stewart, *Reading and Disorder in Antebellum America* (Columbus: Ohio State University Press, 2011), 22–23.

66. Wilentz, *Chants Democratic*, 242–43.

67. Streeby, *American Sensations*; Jesse Alemán and Shelley Streeby, eds., *Empire and the Literature of Sensation: An Anthology of Nineteenth-Century Popular Fiction* (New Brunswick, NJ: Rutgers University Press, 2007).

68. Richard White, *The Middle Ground: Indians, Empires, and Republics in the Great Lakes Region, 1650–1815* (New York: Cambridge University Press, 1991).

69. My use of the term "men of letters" follows Gruesz, *Ambassadors of Culture*, 16–17.

70. Bethel Saler, *The Settlers' Empire: Colonialism and State Formation in America's Old Northwest* (Philadelphia: University of Pennsylvania Press, 2015), 2.

71. Lippard's first trip occurred from June to October 1851 and was apparently prompted in part by the deaths of his sister, two children, and wife to tuberculosis in the span of less than three years; it included public lectures in Cleveland and Columbus. Lippard returned to Ohio in the summer and fall of 1852, and again in the summer of 1853. For the first trip, see "Mr. Lippard" and "Empire Hall," *Cleveland Herald*, June 25, 1851, 2; *Daily Scioto Gazette* (Chillicothe, OH), August 6, 1851, 2; "Wayside Gatherings," *Gleason's Pictorial Drawing Room Companion*, November 8, 1851, 447; and [John Bell Bouton,] *The Life and Choice Writings of George Lippard* (New York: H. H. Randall, 1855), 72–79, 90. For the second, see the *Cleveland Daily Plain Dealer*, July 13, 1852, 3; "Geotge [sic] Lippard," *Daily Cleveland Herald*, September 3, 1852, 2. For the third, see "Personal Intelligence," *Daily Cleveland Herald*, August 13, 1853, 3; [Bouton,] *Life and Choice*, 117–19; and David S. Reynolds, *George Lippard* (Boston: Twayne, 1982), 23.

72. A published letter attributed to Lippard indicates that he began writing *New York* before the 1851 trip. "Mere Mention," *Home Journal* (New York), March 25, 1854, 2. For the novel's composition, see [Bouton,] *Life and Choice*, 93, 116.

73. "George Lippard," *Cleveland Daily Plain Dealer*, September 13, 1853, 3. See also Reynolds, *George Lippard*, 22.

74. Rulison's 284-page double-columned edition cost 50 cents. Mendenhall's edition was marketed more for the "Upper Ten" than the "Lower Million": it was "printed in new type, on the best paper, bound in embossed muslin, in a beautiful volume of about 300 pages. Price $1." *Cincinnati Daily Enquirer*, November 19, 1853, 2. For Rulison and Mendenhall, see Walter Sutton, *The Western Book Trade: Cincinnati as a Nineteenth-Century Publishing and Book-Trade Center* (Columbus: Ohio State University Press for the Ohio Historical Society, 1961), 329, 336.

75. Ads in Ohio include the *Cincinnati Daily Enquirer*, November 19, 1853, 2; *Daily Ohio Statesman* (Columbus), November 30, 1853, 3; *Daily Cleveland Herald*, December 13, 1853, 2;

Columbian & Great West (Cincinnati), December 17, 1853, 4; *Daily Commercial Register* (Sandusky), December 22, 1853, 2; and *Cleveland Daily Plain Dealer*, December 31, 1853, 3. Ads outside of Ohio include the *Public Ledger* (Philadelphia), December 21, 1853, 2; *Philadelphia Inquirer*, December 24, 1853, 3; *New York Daily Tribune*, December 28, 1853, 1; *The Sun* (Baltimore), December 31, 1853, 2; and *New York Times*, March 11, 1854, 4.

76. "George Lippard," *Columbian & Great West*, February 18, 1854, 2; see also [Bouton,] *Life and Choice*, 128.

77. *Cleveland Daily Plain Dealer*, March 25, 1854, 3; *Albany Evening Journal*, April 10, 1854, 1. A similar ad to the former ran in the *Columbian & Great West*, August 5, 1854, 4. For further evidence of demand, see "Too Late," *Philadelphia Inquirer*, February 16, 1854, 2.

78. *Milwaukee Daily Sentinel*, April 25, 1854, 3; *Albany Evening Journal*, April 10, 1854, 1; *Alexandria* [Virginia] *Gazette*, January 12, 1854, 3; *Charleston Courier*, May 23, 1854, 3; *Charleston Courier, Tri-Weekly*, October 21, 1854, 4; *Charleston Mercury*, January 1, 1855, 1; and the ads from the *Philadelphia Inquirer*, *New York Daily Tribune*, and Baltimore *Sun* in note 75 in this chapter.

79. *Cincinnati Daily Enquirer*, November 19, 1853, 2.

80. Quoted in *Public Ledger* (Philadelphia), December 21, 1853, 2. This group of quotations, among others, appears in nearly every Mendenhall ad for *New York* in 1853 and 1854.

81. For absorptive reading, see Michael Millner, *Fever Reading: Affect and Reading Badly in the Early American Public Sphere* (Durham: University of New Hampshire Press, 2012), xvii.

82. Saler, *Settlers' Empire*, 1–2.

83. Fredric Jameson, "Postmodernism; or, The Cultural Logic of Late Capitalism," *New Left Review* 146 (1984): 89, 84.

84. Fredric Jameson, *The Geopolitical Aesthetic: Cinema and Space in the World System* (Bloomington: Indiana University Press, 1992), 3–4, 10.

85. Bernard DeVoto, "The West: A Plundered Province," *Harper's Monthly Magazine*, August 1934, 355–64.

86. Jack P. Greene, "Colonial History and National History: Reflections on a Continuing Problem," *William and Mary Quarterly*, 3rd ser., 64.2 (April 2007): 248–49.

87. See, for example, Rowland Berthoff, "Independence and Attachment, Virtue and Interest: From Republican Citizen to Free Enterprise, 1787–1837," in *Uprooted Americans: Essays to Honor Oscar Handlin*, ed. Richard L. Bushman et al. (Boston: Little, Brown, 1979), 97–124; and Horsman, "'Empire for Liberty.'" For other reappraisals, see Doolen, "Early American Civics," and Ed White, "The Ends of Republicanism," *Journal of the Early Republic* 30.2 (Summer 2010): 179–99.

88. These writings are collected in Turner, *Rereading*.

89. For critical response to Turner dating back to the 1920s, see John Mack Faragher, "Afterword: The Significance of the Frontier in American Historiography," in Turner, *Rereading*, 225–41.

90. William Cronon, George Miles, and Jay Gitlin, "Becoming West: Toward a New Meaning for Western History," in *Under an Open Sky: Rethinking America's Western Past*, ed. William Cronon, George Miles, and Jay Gitlin (New York: Norton, 1992), 6. See also Stephen Aron, "Lessons in Conquest: Towards a Greater Western History," *Pacific Historical Review* 63.2 (May 1994): 125–47.

91. See Erik Altenbernd and Alex Trimble Young, "Introduction: The Significance of the Frontier in an Age of Transnational History," *Settler Colonial Studies* 4.2 (2014): 127–50.

92. Cronon, Miles, and Gitlin, "Becoming West," 18.

93. Streeby, *American Sensations*, 23.

94. George Lippard, *George Lippard, Prophet of Protest: Writings of an American Radical, 1822–1854*, ed. David S. Reynolds (New York: Peter Lang, 1986), 62.

95. David S. Reynolds, introduction to George Lippard, *The Quaker City; or, The Monks of Monk Hall*, ed. David S. Reynolds (Amherst: University of Massachusetts Press, 1995), xii–xiii; for Brotherhood circles in the West, see David S. Reynolds, introduction to Lippard, *Prophet of Protest*, 37.

96. "Death of George Lippard," *Cleveland Plain Dealer*, February 10, 1854, 2.

97. See Benjamin Drake, *The Life and Adventures of Black Hawk: With Sketches of Keokuk, the Sac and Fox Indians, and the Late Black Hawk War* (Cincinnati: George Conclin, 1838); Benjamin Drake, *Life of Tecumseh, and of His Brother the Prophet; with a Historical Sketch of Shawanoe Indians* (Cincinnati: E. Morgan, 1841).

98. Turner, *Rereading*, 19.

99. Turner, "Significance of the Frontier," 39, 57–58. For a later study that did undertake it, see T. Scott Miyakawa, *Protestants and Pioneers: Individualism and Conformity on the American Frontier* (Chicago: University of Chicago Press, 1964).

100. Fessenden, *Culture and Redemption*, 6; for the "Bible Wars" in Cincinnati public schools, see Fessenden, chap. 3.

101. Turner, "Significance of the Frontier," 38.

102. Turner, "Significance of the Frontier," 33, 47, 32.

103. Streeby, *American Sensations*, 51–52.

104. The motto ran regularly at the top of page 2, beginning with the first issue on May 6, 1848. For an overview of the *Great West*, which merged with the *Columbian* in March 1850 to form the *Columbian & Great West*, see Sutton, *Western Book Trade*, 197–99. All references to the *Great West* and the *Columbian & Great West* refer to the microfilm copy owned by the Ohio Historical Society. Subsequent citations will be abbreviated *GW* or *CGW* with the date in numerical form.

105. "Our Paper," *GW*, 5/6/1848: 2; "For 1850! The Great West!" *GW*, 1/5/1850: 3.

106. "The Western Cities," *GW*, 5/6/1848: 2.

107. The June 23, 1849, issue is the earliest extant number that lists offices in Pittsburgh, St. Louis, and Louisville; on January 5, 1850, Detroit replaces Louisville, but by January 19, 1850, Louisville has returned and Detroit is no longer listed on the masthead. By May 7, 1853, Cincinnati is the only city listed and remains so until the last extant issue on April 28, 1855. The division between "Eastern Cities" and "Western Cities" was present in both extant issues from 1848 and 1849, but by January 5, 1850, news briefs from U.S. cities were combined under a single "Metropolitan Items" heading.

108. "Introductory," *GW*, 5/6/1848: 2.

109. L. A. Hine, "The West: Its History and Resources, No. III," *GW*, 6/23/1849: 2.

110. See, for example, the accounts of New York vagrancy in "Youthful Depravity" (*GW*, 1/26/1850: 2); labor strife in Boston in "Good Results" (*GW*, 1/26/1850: 2); and riots in "Philadelphia" (*GW*, 2/2/1850: 3). Reports of violence involving Catholics include the stoning of a

Catholic church in Lexington, Massachusetts ("Brief Mention," *CGW*, 9/9/1854: 2), and a "fracas" in Jersey City "between the Priest and Young Irelanders" ("The News," *CGW*, 1/7/1855: 4).

111. For the "safety-valve," see H. Smith, *Virgin Land*, 7; David Harvey, "The Spatial Fix: Hegel, Von Thünen and Marx," in *Spaces of Capital: Towards a Critical Geography* (New York: Routledge, 2001), 288, 293, 299.

112. "Eastern Propagation," *GW*, 2/9/1850: 2.

113. See, for example, the reports from Cincinnati, Pittsburgh, Dayton, and St. Louis in *CGW*, 3/9/1850: 3; the mob violence in "Cincinnati," *CGW*, 3/30/1850; and "Murder on Walnut Street," *CGW*, 11/9/1850: 3.

114. "Cincinnati," *GW*, 3/9/1850: 3.

115. "Cincinnati," *CGW*, 6/8/1850: 3; "Cincinnati," 6/15/1850: 3.

116. "The Laboring Poor," *CGW*, 4/6/1850: 2.

117. "The Poor and Their Homes," *CGW*, 11/26/1853: 2.

118. F. Lindo, "Sketches of Travel in Central America: Part I," *GW*, 5/6/1848: 2.

119. Griffin, *Anti-Catholicism*, 139–40.

120. Hine, "The West."

121. Horsman, "'Empire for Liberty.'"

122. "The Catholic Element in America," *CGW*, 4/1/1854: 2.

123. "Keep Clear of Cities," *GW*, 3/2/1850: 2.

124. "Eastern Propagation."

125. Cincinnati fiction included Fred Freenould, "The False Accusation," *CGW*, 8/3/1850: 1; and Walter Whitmore, "Ella Winston; or, The Adventures of an Orphan Girl. A Romance of Cincinnati," *CGW*, 11/30/1850: 1.

126. "Spicy Literature," *CGW*, 8/31/1850: 2.

127. *CGW*, 11/12/1853: 1.

128. Foreign city-mysteries included "Annette; or, The Fatal Elopement," *CGW*, 11/26/1853: 4; urban sketches included Ignis, "Scenes of London Life," *CGW*, 4/13/1850: 1, and the series of Cincinnati "City Scenes" that ran in the paper from December 1853 to May 1854; sensational crime reports include "Horrible Murder—Another Deed of Blood," *CGW*, 3/4/1854: 2; and "Further Particulars of the Late Fiendish Atrocity! Dying Declarations!" *CGW*, 7/1/1854: 3.

129. "The Queen City—Its Mysteries and Miseries," *CGW*, 2/24/1855: 2.

130. "The Queen City—Its Mysteries and Miseries," *CGW*, 3/10/1855: 2.

131. C. P. Bickley, "The Queen City: Its Mysteries and Miseries! A Story of Life in the Western Metropolis," *CGW*, 3/17/1855: 1.

132. [C. P. Bickley,] *The Mock Marriage; or, The Libertine's Victim: Being a Faithful Delineation of the Mysteries and Miseries of the Queen City* (Cincinnati: E. Mendenhall, [1855]) (hereafter cited in the text as *MM*). Four Cincinnati firms published editions of *The Mock Marriage*: Barclay & Co., U. P. James, Mendenhall, and Rulison.

133. My use of "panoramic" here encompasses several distinct visual and literary modes, including panoramic views, moving panoramas, and literary prospects. As Alan Wallach notes, the "panoramic" or "panoptic mode" during this period combined "a complex set of interrelated, and mutually reinforcing, cultural practices" that included "landscape painting and landscape drawing," as well as "landscape tourism, landscape literature, and landscape aesthetics." Wallach, "Making a Picture," 80–81.

134. For antebellum urban "sporting culture," see Srebnick, *Mysterious Death*, 53–54; Gilfoyle, *City of Eros*, chap. 5; and Patricia Cline Cohen, Timothy J. Gilfoyle, and Helen Lefkowitz Horowitz, eds., *The Flash Press: Sporting Male Weeklies in 1840s New York* (Chicago: University of Chicago Press, 2008), 6–7, 9–10.

135. See, for example, Lippard, *Quaker City*, 49, 56; and George Thompson, *Venus in Boston and Other Tales of Nineteenth-Century City Life*, ed. David S. Reynolds and Kimberly R. Gladman (Amherst: University of Massachusetts Press, 2002), 113.

136. Taylor, "Modes of Secularism," 39.

137. Denning, *Mechanic Accents*, 105–6.

138. Taylor, "Modes of Secularism," 39–40.

139. Taylor, "Modes of Secularism," 39.

140. Franchot, *Roads to Rome*, 74.

141. For the ways in which the midcentury expansion of federal power legally dismantled "the local, regional, and state-based identities for which the Revolution had been fought" and established a new, direct relationship to the citizen epitomized by the Fourteenth Amendment, see Loughran, *Republic in Print*, 443–44.

142. Gustafson, *Imagining Deliberative Democracy*, 2, 5. See Saul Cornell, *The Other Founders: Anti-Federalism and the Dissenting Tradition in America, 1788–1828* (Chapel Hill: University of North Carolina Press, 1999); Alison L. LaCroix, *The Ideological Origins of American Federalism* (Cambridge, MA: Harvard University Press, 2010), chap. 5; Loughran, *Republic in Print*, chaps. 3–5; and Slauter, *State as a Work*, chap. 3.

143. Taylor, *Secular Age*, 542.

Epilogue

1. Mark Twain, *Mark Twain's Letters, Volume 1: 1853–1866*, ed. Edgar Marquess Branch, Michael B. Frank, and Kenneth M. Sanderson (Berkeley: University of California Press, 1988), 117.

2. Mark Twain, *Mark Twain Speaking*, ed. Paul Fatout (Iowa City: University of Iowa Press, 1976), 237 ("shams"); Twain quoted in Harold K. Bush Jr., *Mark Twain and the Spiritual Crisis of His Age* (Tuscaloosa: University of Alabama Press, 2007), 1 ("Christianity"). For examples of the first approach, see Van Wyck Brooks, *The Ordeal of Mark Twain* (New York: Dutton, 1920); Bernard DeVoto, *Mark Twain's America* (Cambridge, MA: Houghton Mifflin, 1932); and John T. Frederick, *The Darkened Sky: Nineteenth-Century American Novelists and Religion* (Notre Dame, IN: University of Notre Dame Press, 1969), chap. 4. For the second, see Bush, *Spiritual Crisis*; Lawrence Berkove, *Heretical Fictions: Religion in the Literature of Mark Twain* (Iowa City: University of Iowa Press, 2010); and William E. Phipps, *Mark Twain's Religion* (Macon, GA: Mercer University Press, 2003).

3. Fessenden, *Culture and Redemption*, 143, 139, 140.

4. A. Miller, *Empire of the Eye*, 287–88, 258.

5. Kelly, *Frederic Edwin Church*, 126; see also Rachael Ziady DeLue, *George Inness and the Science of Landscape* (Chicago: University of Chicago Press, 2004), 10, 25, 37–38.

6. Raab, *Frederic Church*, 40–41.

7. Tim Barringer, "The Course of Empires: Landscape and Identity in America and Britain, 1820–1880," in Wilton and Barringer, *American Sublime*, 63.

8. Marsden, *Evangelical Mind*, 210.

9. George M. Marsden, *Fundamentalism and American Culture: The Shaping of Twentieth-Century Evangelicalism, 1870–1925* (New York: Oxford University Press, 1980), 11, 17–18.

10. Holifield, *Theology in America*, 508.

11. For Beecher's "New Theology," see Marsden, *Fundamentalism*, 22–26.

12. Morgan, *Protestants and Pictures*, 268.

13. Quoted in Marsden, *Fundamentalism*, 36, 38.

14. Glenn W. Shuck, *Marks of the Beast: The Left Behind Novels and the Struggle for Evangelical Identity* (New York: New York University Press, 2005), 34, 36.

15. For the popularization of dispensationalism in America, see Marsden, *Fundamentalism*, 46–48, 51–71; Ernest R. Sandeen, *The Roots of Fundamentalism: British and American Millenarianism, 1800–1930* (Chicago: University of Chicago Press, 1970), 38, 62–80; and Shuck, *Marks of the Beast*, 30–37.

16. Nord, *Faith in Reading*, 157–58.

17. Moorhead, "Millennium and the Media," 223–24 (quotes), 228. For the Moody Press, see Shuck, *Marks of the Beast*, 36.

18. Morgan, *Protestants and Pictures*, 267, 269, 344.

19. Shirley Jackson Case quoted in Moorhead, "Millennium and the Media," 235.

20. Hickman, "Globalization and the Gods," 153–54.

21. Moorhead, "Millennium and the Media," 236–37.

22. Louisa M. Alcott, *Little Women; or, Meg, Jo, Beth and Amy*, ed. Anne K. Phillips and Gregory Eiselein (New York: Norton, 2004), 117.

23. Obenzinger, *American Palestine*, xii.

24. Davis, *Landscape of Belief*, 46.

25. Obenzinger, *American Palestine*, 165, 176, 168.

26. Mark Twain, *The Innocents Abroad; or, The New Pilgrim's Progress* (Hartford, CT: American Publishing Company, 1869), 106, 204 (hereafter cited in the text as *IA*).

27. Miller's followers were famously disappointed when his predictions of the Second Coming failed to materialize in 1844, but a group of them led by Clorinda S. Minor established the short-lived colony of Mount Hope in Palestine in the early 1850s. See Davis, *Landscape of Belief*, 38–39.

28. See William Feaver, *The Art of John Martin* (London: Clarendon Press, 1975), plate 4, p. 195, and plate 7.

29. Mark Twain, *Roughing It* (Hartford, CT: American Publishing Company, 1872), 19–20 (hereafter cited in the text as *RI*).

30. Jackson, *Word and Its Witness*, 264; John Muir, *My First Summer in the Sierra* (Boston: Houghton Mifflin, 1911), 354, 65.

31. Nell Irvin Painter, *Exodusters: Black Migration to Kansas after Reconstruction* (New York: Knopf, 1977), 195; for the relationship to Native land, see Quintard Taylor, *In Search of the Racial Frontier: African Americans in the American West, 1528–1990* (New York: Norton, 1998), 137, 144.

32. Louis S. Warren, *God's Red Son: The Ghost Dance Religion and the Making of Modern America* (New York: Basic Books, 2017), 12.

33. See Mark David Spence, *Dispossessing the Wilderness: Indian Removal and the Making of the National Parks* (New York: Oxford University Press, 1999).

34. [Fitz Hugh Ludlow,] "Seven Weeks in the Great Yo-Semite," *Atlantic Monthly*, June 1864, 740, 746.

35. Quoted in Nancy K. Anderson, "Chronology," in *Albert Bierstadt: Art & Enterprise*, ed. Nancy K. Anderson and Linda S. Ferber (New York: Hudson Hills Press with the Brooklyn Museum, 1990), 178.

36. For Bierstadt's travels and paintings of Yosemite, see Anderson and Ferber, *Albert Bierstadt*, 90–91, 198–201, 203, 206–7, 224–26; and Wilton and Barringer, *American Sublime*, 236–39, 184.

37. For the allusion to Cole, see Andrew Wilton's catalogue entry for *Yosemite Valley* (1868) in Wilton and Barringer, *American Sublime*, 236.

38. Wilton and Barringer, *American Sublime*, 238.

39. Wilton and Barringer, *American Sublime*, 229.

40. Quoted in Nancy K. Anderson, "'Wondrously Full of Invention': The Western Landscapes of Albert Bierstadt," in Anderson and Ferber, *Albert Bierstadt*, 87.

41. Quoted in Gordon Hendricks, *Albert Bierstadt: Painter of the American West* (New York: Harry M. Abrams with the Amon Carter Museum of Western Art, 1974), 164.

42. Mark Twain, "Letter from 'Mark Twain,'" *Daily Alta California*, August 4, 1867, 1.

43. Veith, *Painters of Faith*, chap. 2.

44. Anderson, "'Wondrously Full,'" 79.

45. See Thomas Starr King, *A Vacation among the Sierras: Yosemite in 1860* (San Francisco: Book Club of California, 1962). For King and other Protestant figures who helped publicize Yosemite, see Stoll, *Inherit the Holy Mountain*, 98–100.

46. Peter H. Hassrick, "Art, Agency, and Conservation: A Fresh Look at Albert Bierstadt's Vision of the West," *Montana: The Magazine of Western History* 68.1 (Spring 2018): 13.

47. Sedgwick, *Atlantic Monthly*, 38.

48. For exhibition schedules, see Anderson, "Chronology," 181–85.

49. See Helena E. Wright, "Checklist of Nineteenth-Century Prints after Paintings by Albert Bierstadt," in Anderson and Ferber, *Albert Bierstadt*, 274, 276–77, 279, 281.

50. See Tom Gunning, "Phantom Images and Modern Manifestations: Spirit Photography, Magic Theater, Trick Films, and Photography's Uncanny," in *Fugitive Images: From Photography to Video*, ed. Patrice Petro (Bloomington: Indiana University Press, 1995), 42–71.

51. John Muir, "The Treasures of the Yosemite," *Century Illustrated Magazine*, August 1890, 483–500; Muir, "Features of the Proposed Yosemite National Park," *Century Illustrated Magazine*, September 1890, 656–67.

52. See Donald Worster, *A Passion for Nature: The Life of John Muir* (New York: Oxford University Press, 2008), 310–15. The 1864 Yosemite Grant Act had set the land aside, but it was initially ceded to California to be administered as a state park.

53. Muir, "Treasures of the Yosemite," 483.

54. For Cole's *Oxbow*, see chapter 1.

55. Muir, "Treasures of the Yosemite," 489, 492, 499.

56. John Muir, *Our National Parks* (Boston: Houghton, Mifflin, 1901), preface.

57. For the bill's passage, see Worster, *Passion for Nature*, 320, 314. For the proposed boundaries, see Muir, "Features," 666.

58. Stoll, *Inherit the Holy Mountain*.

59. Todd Wilkinson, "Are We Loving Yellowstone to Death?" *National Geographic*, May 2016, https://www.nationalgeographic.com/magazine/2016/05/yellowstone-national-parks-land-use/.

60. For "environmental apocalypticism," see Buell, *Environmental Imagination*, chap. 9.

61. Matthew Avery Sutton, *American Apocalypse: A History of Modern Evangelicalism* (Cambridge, MA: Belknap Press of Harvard University Press, 2014), 351, 346; for the "Tribulation," see Shuck, *Marks of the Beast*, 41–52.

62. See Sutton, *American Apocalypse*, chap. 11.

63. Shuck, *Marks of the Beast*, 1–2.

64. Lisa Vox, *Existential Threats: American Apocalyptic Beliefs in the Technological Era* (Philadelphia: University of Pennsylvania Press, 2017), 110; for a particularly revealing example involving Billy Graham, see Sutton, *American Apocalypse*, 362.

65. Wahlberg quoted in Lisa Vox, "Why Don't Conservative Evangelicals Worry about Climate Change? God," *Washington Post*, June 2, 2017, Gale General OneFile, https://link.gale.com/apps/doc/A493942098/ITOF?u=mlin_m_brandeis&sid=ITOF&xid=0117f38e. For "One World Government," see Amy Johnson Frykholm, *Rapture Culture: Left Behind in Evangelical America* (Oxford: Oxford University Press, 2004), 121.

66. William Bradford Nichols, "What's Really behind Evangelicals' Climate Denial?" *The Humanist* 79.3 (May/June 2019): 25.

67. Bill McKibben, *The End of Nature*, 10th anniversary ed. (New York: Anchor, 1999 [1989]), cover, 147.

68. David Wallace-Wells, *The Uninhabitable Earth: Life after Warming* (New York: Duggan, 2019), 152, 208, 143, 175, 207.

69. Vox, *Existential Threats*, xii.

70. McKibben, *End of Nature*, 216–17; Wallace-Wells, *Uninhabitable Earth*, 227.

71. *An Inconvenient Truth: A Global Warning*, dir. David Guggenheim (Hollywood, CA: Paramount, 2006), DVD.

72. Wallace-Wells, *Uninhabitable Earth*, 13.

SELECTED BIBLIOGRAPHY

Abrams, M. H. *Natural Supernaturalism: Tradition and Revolution in Romantic Literature*. New York: Norton, 1971.

Abzug, Robert H. *Cosmos Crumbling: American Reform and the Religious Imagination*. New York: Oxford University Press, 1994.

American Tract Society. *The Evangelical Family Library*. 45 vols. New York: American Tract Society, 1832–?

———. *The Publications of the American Tract Society*. 12 vols. New York: American Tract Society, n.d.

Anderson, Benedict. *Imagined Communities: Reflections on the Origin and Spread of Nationalism*. 1983. Rev. ed. London: Verso, 2016.

Apess, William. *On Our Own Ground: The Complete Writings of William Apess, A Pequot*. Ed. Barry O'Connell. Amherst: University of Massachusetts Press, 1992.

Appadurai, Arjun. *Modernity at Large: Cultural Dimensions of Globalization*. Minneapolis: University of Minnesota Press, 1996.

Asad, Talal. *Formations of the Secular: Christianity, Islam, Modernity*. Stanford: Stanford University Press, 2003.

Barnes, Gilbert Hobbs. *The Antislavery Impulse, 1830–1844*. New York: D. Appleton-Century, 1933.

Bedell, Rebecca. *The Anatomy of Nature: Geology & American Landscape Painting, 1825–1875*. Princeton: Princeton University Press, 2001.

Beecher, Lyman. *A Plea for the West*. Cincinnati: Truman and Smith, 1835.

Bercovitch, Sacvan. *The American Jeremiad*. Madison: University of Wisconsin Press, 1978.

Boyer, Paul. *Urban Masses and Moral Order in America, 1820–1920*. Cambridge, MA: Harvard University Press, 1978.

Brooks, Joanna. *American Lazarus: Religion and the Rise of African-American and Native American Literatures*. New York: Oxford University Press, 2003.

Brown, Candy Gunther. *The Word in the World: Evangelical Writing, Publishing, and Reading in America, 1789–1880*. Chapel Hill: University of North Carolina Press, 2004.

Brückner, Martin. *The Geographic Revolution in Early America: Maps, Literacy, and National Identity*. Chapel Hill: University of North Carolina Press, 2006.

Buell, Lawrence. *The Environmental Imagination: Thoreau, Nature Writing, and the Formation of American Culture*. Cambridge, MA: Belknap Press of Harvard University Press, 1995.

Bunyan, John. *The Pilgrim's Progress from This World to That Which Is to Come; Delivered Under the Similitude of a Dream*. 1678. Evangelical Family Library, vol. 4. Reprint, New York: American Tract Society, 1832–?

Butler, Jon. *Awash in a Sea of Faith: Christianizing the American People*. Cambridge, MA: Harvard University Press, 1990.

Carwardine, Richard J. *Evangelicals and Politics in Antebellum America*. New Haven: Yale University Press, 1993.

Coleman, Dawn. *Preaching and the Rise of the American Novel*. Columbus: Ohio State University Press, 2013.

Collins, John J. "Apocalypse: An Overview." In Jones, *Encyclopedia of Religion*, 1:409–14.

Conroy-Krutz, Emily. *Christian Imperialism: Converting the World in the Early American Republic*. Ithaca: Cornell University Press, 2015.

Davis, Hugh. *Joshua Leavitt: Evangelical Abolitionist*. Baton Rouge: Louisiana State University Press, 1990.

Davis, John. *The Landscape of Belief: Encountering the Holy Land in Nineteenth-Century American Art and Culture*. Princeton: Princeton University Press, 1996.

De Certeau, Michel. *The Practice of Everyday Life*. Trans. Steven F. Rendall. Berkeley: University of California Press, 1984.

Demos, John. *The Heathen School: A Story of Hope and Betrayal in the Age of the Early Republic*. New York: Knopf, 2014.

DeRogatis, Amy. *Moral Geography: Maps, Missionaries, and the American Frontier*. New York: Columbia University Press, 2003.

Dimock, Wai Chee. *Through Other Continents: American Literature across Deep Time*. Princeton: Princeton University Press, 2006.

Douglas, Ann. *The Feminization of American Culture*. 1977. New York: Farrar, Straus, and Giroux, 1998.

Douglass, Frederick. *The Frederick Douglass Papers, Series One: Speeches, Debates, and Interviews*. Ed. John W. Blassingame and John R. McKivigan. 5 vols. New Haven: Yale University Press, 1979–92.

Dunch, Ryan. "Beyond Cultural Imperialism: Cultural Theory, Christian Missions, and Global Modernity." *History and Theory* 41.3 (October 2002): 301–25.

Edwards, Jonathan. *A History of the Work of Redemption*. 1739. Ed. John F. Wilson. New Haven: Yale University Press, 1989.

Emerson, Ralph Waldo. *The Collected Works of Ralph Waldo Emerson*. Ed. Robert E. Spiller, Alfred R. Ferguson, Joseph Slater, Jean Ferguson Carr, Wallace E. Williams, Douglas Emory Wilson, Philip Nicoloff, et al. 10 vols. Cambridge, MA: Belknap Press of Harvard University Press, 1971–2013.

Fessenden, Tracy. *Culture and Redemption: Religion, the Secular, and American Literature*. Princeton: Princeton University Press, 2007.

Fields, Annie, ed. *Life and Letters of Harriet Beecher Stowe*. Boston: Houghton, Mifflin, 1897.

Franchot, Jenny. *Roads to Rome: The Antebellum Protestant Encounter with Catholicism*. Berkeley: University of California Press, 1994.

Gatta, John. *Making Nature Sacred: Literature, Religion, and Environment in America from the Puritans to the Present*. New York: Oxford University Press, 2004.

Giles, Paul. *The Global Remapping of American Literature*. Princeton: Princeton University Press, 2011.

Gilroy, Paul. *The Black Atlantic: Modernity and Double Consciousness*. Cambridge, MA: Harvard University Press, 1993.

Gould, Stephen Jay. "Church, Humboldt, and Darwin: The Tension and Harmony of Art and Science." In Franklin Kelly, Stephen Jay Gould, James Anthony Ryan, and Debora Rindge, *Frederic Edwin Church*, 94–107. Washington, DC: National Gallery of Art, 1989.

Greeson, Jennifer Rae. *Our South: Geographic Fantasy and the Rise of National Literature*. Cambridge, MA: Harvard University Press, 2010.

Gruesz, Kirsten Silva. *Ambassadors of Culture: The Transamerican Origins of Latino Writing*. Princeton: Princeton University Press, 2002.

Gutjahr, Paul C. *An American Bible: A History of the Good Book in the United States, 1777–1880*. Stanford: Stanford University Press, 1999.

Hack, Daniel. "Close Reading at a Distance: The African Americanization of *Bleak House*." *Critical Inquiry* 34.4 (Summer 2008): 729–53.

Hambrick-Stowe, Charles E. *Charles G. Finney and the Spirit of American Evangelicalism*. Grand Rapids, MI: Eerdmans, 1996.

Hardman, Keith J. *Charles Grandison Finney, 1792–1875: Revivalist and Reformer*. Syracuse, NY: Syracuse University Press, 1987.

Harris, Neil. *The Artist in American Society: The Formative Years, 1790–1860*. New York: George Braziller, 1966.

Harvey, David. *Cosmopolitanism and the Geographies of Freedom*. New York: Columbia University Press, 2009.

———. "Space as a Keyword." In *David Harvey: A Critical Reader*, ed. Noel Castree and Derek Gregory, 270–92. Malden, MA: Blackwell, 2006.

Hatch, Nathan O. *The Democratization of American Christianity*. New Haven: Yale University Press, 1989.

Hickman, Jared. "Globalization and the Gods, or the Political Theology of 'Race.'" *Early American Literature* 45.1 (2010): 145–82.

Hodder, Alan D. *Emerson's Rhetoric of Revelation: Nature, the Reader, and the Apocalypse Within*. University Park: Pennsylvania State University Press, 1989.

Holifield, E. Brooks. *Theology in America: Christian Thought from the Age of the Puritans to the Civil War*. New Haven: Yale University Press, 2003.

The Holy Bible. Authorized King James Version. Grand Rapids, MI: Zondervan, 1962.

Howe, Daniel Walker. *What Hath God Wrought: The Transformation of America, 1815–1848*. New York: Oxford University Press, 2007.

Hsu, Hsuan L. *Geography and the Production of Space in Nineteenth-Century American Literature*. Cambridge: Cambridge University Press, 2010.

Huhtamo, Erkki. *Illusions in Motion: Media Archaeology of the Moving Panorama and Related Spectacles*. Cambridge, MA: MIT Press, 2013.

Husch, Gail E. *Something Coming: Apocalyptic Expectation and Mid-Nineteenth-Century American Painting*. Hanover, NH: University Press of New England, 2000.

Jackson, Gregory S. *The Word and Its Witness: The Spiritualization of American Realism*. Chicago: University of Chicago Press, 2009.

Jones, Lindsay, ed. *The Encyclopedia of Religion*. 2nd ed. 15 vols. Detroit, MI: Macmillan Reference USA, 2005. Gale Virtual Reference Library. https://go-gale-com.resources.library.brandeis.edu/ps/i.do?u=mlin_m_brandeis&p=GVRL&it=etoc&id=GALE%7C9780028659978&v=2.1&sw=w.

Katz, Wendy Jean. *Regionalism and Reform: Art and Class Formation in Antebellum Cincinnati*. Columbus: Ohio State University Press, 2002.

Kelly, Franklin. *Frederic Edwin Church and the National Landscape*. Washington, DC: Smithsonian Institution Press, 1988.

Kilde, Jeanne Halgren. "Approaching Religious Space: An Overview of Theories, Methods, and Challenges in Religious Studies." *Religion & Theology* 20 (2013): 183–201.

———. *When Church Became Theatre: The Transformation of Evangelical Architecture and Worship in Nineteenth-Century America*. New York: Oxford University Press, 2002.

King, Joshua. *Imagined Spiritual Communities in Britain's Age of Print*. Columbus: Ohio State University Press, 2015.

Kirkham, E. Bruce. *The Building of Uncle Tom's Cabin*. Knoxville: University of Tennessee Press, 1977.

Knott, Kim. *The Location of Religion: A Spatial Analysis*. London: Equinox, 2005.

Lane, Belden C. *Landscapes of the Sacred: Geography and Narrative in American Spirituality*. 1988. Expanded ed. Baltimore: Johns Hopkins University Press, 2002.

Larson, John Lauritz. *The Market Revolution in America: Liberty, Ambition, and the Eclipse of the Common Good*. New York: Cambridge University Press, 2010.

Latour, Bruno. *We Have Never Been Modern*. Trans. Catherine Porter. 1991. Cambridge, MA: Harvard University Press, 1993.

Lefebvre, Henri. *The Production of Space*. Trans. Donald Nicholson-Smith. 1974. Malden, MA: Blackwell, 1991.

Loughran, Trish. *The Republic in Print: Print Culture in the Age of U.S. Nation Building, 1770–1870*. New York: Columbia University Press, 2007.

Marsden, George M. *The Evangelical Mind and the New School Presbyterian Experience: A Case Study of Thought and Theology in Nineteenth-Century America*. New Haven: Yale University Press, 1970.

May, Cedric. *Evangelism and Resistance in the Black Atlantic, 1760–1835*. Athens: University of Georgia Press, 2008.

McGill, Meredith L. *American Literature and the Culture of Reprinting, 1834–1853*. Philadelphia: University of Pennsylvania Press, 2003.

Miller, Angela. *Empire of the Eye: Landscape Representation and American Cultural Politics, 1825–1875*. Ithaca: Cornell University Press, 1993.

Miller, David C. *Dark Eden: The Swamp in Nineteenth-Century American Culture*. Cambridge: Cambridge University Press, 1989.

Miller, Perry. *Errand into the Wilderness*. Cambridge, MA: Belknap Press of Harvard University Press, 1956.

———. *The New England Mind: The Seventeenth Century*. 1939. Cambridge, MA: Belknap Press of Harvard University Press, 1954.

Mitchell, W. J. T. "Imperial Landscape." In *Landscape and Power*. 2nd ed. Ed. W. J. T. Mitchell, 5–34. 1994. Chicago: University of Chicago Press, 2002.

Moorhead, James H. "Between Progress and Apocalypse: A Reassessment of Millennialism in American Religious Thought, 1800–1880." *Journal of American History* 71.3 (December 1984): 524–42.

———. "The Millennium and the Media." In *Communication and Change in American Religious History*, ed. Leonard I. Sweet, 216–238. Grand Rapids, MI: Eerdmans, 1993.

Morgan, David. *The Lure of Images: A History of Religion and Visual Media in America*. London: Routledge, 2007.

———. *Protestants and Pictures: Religion, Visual Culture, and the Age of American Mass Production*. New York: Oxford University Press, 1999.

———. *Visual Piety: A History and Theory of Popular Religious Images*. Berkeley: University of California Press, 1998.

Noll, Mark A. *America's God: From Jonathan Edwards to Abraham Lincoln*. New York: Oxford University Press, 2002.

Nord, David Paul. *Faith in Reading: Religious Publishing and the Birth of Mass Media in America*. New York: Oxford University Press, 2004.

Obenzinger, Hilton. *American Palestine: Melville, Twain, and the Holy Land Mania*. Princeton: Princeton University Press, 1999.

Raab, Jennifer. *Frederic Church: The Art and Science of Detail*. New Haven: Yale University Press, 2015.

Reynolds, David S. *Beneath the American Renaissance: The Subversive Imagination in the Age of Emerson and Melville*. Cambridge, MA: Harvard University Press, 1988.

———. *Faith in Fiction: The Emergence of Religious Literature in America*. Cambridge, MA: Harvard University Press, 1981.

Robinson, Douglas. *American Apocalypses: The Image of the End of the World in American Literature*. Baltimore: Johns Hopkins University Press, 1985.

Schantz, Mark S. "Religious Tracts, Evangelical Reform, and the Market Revolution in Antebellum America." *Journal of the Early Republic* 17.3 (Autumn 1997): 425–66.

Sedgwick, Ellery. *The Atlantic Monthly, 1857–1909: Yankee Humanism at High Tide and Ebb*. Amherst: University of Massachusetts Press, 1994.

Smith, Henry Nash. *Virgin Land: The American West as Symbol and Myth*. Cambridge, MA: Harvard University Press, 1950.

Smith, Ryan K. *Gothic Arches, Latin Crosses: Anti-Catholicism and American Church Designs in the Nineteenth Century*. Chapel Hill: University of North Carolina Press, 2006.

Stokes, Claudia. *The Altar at Home: Sentimental Literature and Nineteenth-Century American Religion*. Philadelphia: University of Pennsylvania Press, 2014.

Stoll, Mark R. *Inherit the Holy Mountain: Religion and the Rise of American Environmentalism*. New York: Oxford University Press, 2015.

Stowe, Harriet Beecher. *Uncle Tom's Cabin; or, Life among the Lowly*. 2 vols. Boston: John P. Jewett, 1852.

Streeby, Shelley. *American Sensations: Class, Empire, and the Production of Popular Culture*. Berkeley: University of California Press, 2002.

Sweeney, J. Gray. "The Advantages of Genius and Virtue: Thomas Cole's Influence, 1848–58." In Truettner and Wallach, *Thomas Cole*, 113–35.

Taylor, Charles. *A Secular Age*. Cambridge, MA: Belknap Press of Harvard University Press, 2007.

Tompkins, Jane. *Sensational Designs: The Cultural Work of American Fiction, 1790–1860*. New York: Oxford University Press, 1985.

Truettner, William H., and Alan Wallach, eds. *Thomas Cole: Landscape into History*. New Haven: Yale University Press; Washington, DC: Smithsonian Institution, 1994.

Tuveson, Ernest Lee. *Redeemer Nation: The Idea of America's Millennial Role*. Chicago: University of Chicago Press, 1968.

Tweed, Thomas A. *Crossing and Dwelling: A Theory of Religion*. Cambridge, MA: Harvard University Press, 2006.

Upton, Dell. *Another City: Urban Life and Urban Spaces in the New American Republic*. New Haven: Yale University Press, 2008.

Veith, Gene Edward. *Painters of Faith: The Spiritual Landscape in Nineteenth-Century America*. Washington, DC: Regnery, 2001.

Vines, Michael E. "The Apocalyptic Chronotope." In *Bakhtin and Genre Theory in Biblical Studies*, ed. Roland Boer, 109–17. Atlanta: Society of Biblical Literature, 2007.

Wallach, Alan. "Making a Picture of the View from Mount Holyoke." In *American Iconology: New Approaches to Nineteenth-Century Art and Literature*, ed. David C. Miller, 80–91. New Haven: Yale University Press, 1993.

———. "Thomas Cole: Landscape and the Course of American Empire." In Truettner and Wallach, *Thomas Cole*, 23–111.

Warner, Michael. "The Evangelical Public Sphere." University of Pennsylvania Libraries A. S. W. Rosenbach Lectures in Bibliography for 2009. Van Pelt Library, University of Pennsylvania, Philadelphia, March 23–26, 2009. MP3 audio file. June 16, 2017, http://repository.upenn.edu/rosenbach/2/.

Wilton, Andrew, and Tim Barringer, eds. *American Sublime: Landscape Painting in the United States, 1820–1880*. Princeton: Princeton University Press, 2002.

INDEX

Numbers in italics refer to illustrations.

AASS. *See* American Anti-Slavery Society
Abbott, Jacob, 41–43
abolitionism, 70, 95; in artworks, 133; geography of, 70, 77–89, 95–97, 103–6, 108; mediascape of, 69–70, 72–73, 92–93, 99–101, 106, 108, 160; the millennium and, 72, 78–79; publications, 69, 71, 72–79, 80, 106–8, 113–14, 117–18, 283n6; as spiritual practice, 72, 78–79. *See also* American Anti-Slavery Society; anti-abolitionism; slavery
ABS. *See* American Bible Society
Abrams, M. H., 154, 155
Abzug, Robert H., 117, 190
Africa: enslaved people's memories of, 92–93; evangelical views of, 71–72, 78, 89–92, *105*, 138; missionaries in, 194–97; representations of, 125
Agamben, Giorgio, 208
Albanese, Catherine L., 208–9, 308n75
Alden, Joseph, 163
Alemán, Jesse, 230
Alice Gordon (Alden), 163
Allston, Washington, 44
almanacs, 49–53, *51–52*, *84*, *100*, *102*
American and Foreign Anti-Slavery Society, 108
American Anti-Slavery Society (AASS), 22, 72–77, 81, *86*, 89, *105*; almanacs, 81, 82–83, *84*, *100*, 101, *102*, 283n6; anti-colonizing stance of, 91–92, 96; 1840 split of, 108; libraries, 74–76; on missionary work, 98–99; publishing program, 69, 72–74, 76–77, 88, 106–8, 283n6, 285n34; and West Indian emancipation, 97–105. *See also* abolitionism
American Bible Society (ABS), 40, 49, 284n23
American Slavery as It Is (Weld/Grimké), 69, 106–8; influence on Stowe, 109
American Sunday School Union, 49, 284n23
American Tract Society (ATS), publications of, 10, *11*, 46–49, *47*, *50*, 52–53, *52–59*, *56–58*, 65–66, 78, 194, *195*, 279n25, 284n23
Ames, Julius Rubens, 84–85, *86*, *105*
Anderson, Alexander, 46–48, *47*
Anderson, Benedict, 4, 113, 204
Anthony, David, 217
anti-abolitionism, 73
anti-Catholicism, 17, 214, 215–17, 222–29, 240–41, 242–43, 249–50, 252, 310nn11 and 20; in fiction, 231, 232–33, 236–37, 242, 253; responses to, 225–28; Thoreau and, 198–99. *See also* Catholicism
anti-slavery. *See* abolitionism; American Anti-Slavery Society
Apess, William, 61–65
apocalypse: in artworks, 4–5, 8–9, 24–25, 34, 44–45, 147, 169–71; climate, 270–72; definition of, 2–3; geography/landscape and, 24–25, 70, 79, 150; in literature, 3–4, 22, 125–38, 152–55, 158–67, 261–65, 270; of the mind, 211; slavery and, 24, 68, 70, 79. *See also* apocalypticism; geography, apocalyptic; landscape, as apocalyptic medium; millennium

327

apocalypticism: conservative, 131, 269–71; environmental, 211, 269, 271–72; naturalized, 155; theistic, 155
Appadurai, Arjun, 14, 70
architecture: in artworks, 168; civic status and, 224–25; cosmic, 2–3; personal interactions with, 119; sacred, 16, 119, 208, 223–27
artists: lifestyle of, 176; Protestant view of, 141, 150, 266; naturalism and, 169–71, 256; secularism and, 147, 169, 182–83
Asad, Talal, 23, 219, 227, 237, 251–52
Asia, evangelistic views of, 78, 197; Thoreau on, 192
ATS. *See* American Tract Society

Baigell, Matthew, 43
Ball, Charles, 82
Ball, James P., 127
Barnes, Gilbert H., 276n66, 285n42
Baxandall, Michael, 35
Bebbington, D. W., 114
Bedell, Rebecca, 9, 39
Beecher, Henry Ward, 10, 257
Beecher, Lyman, 17, 19, 21, 121, 141, 200, 226–27; Turner on, 236
Bellion, Wendy, 220–21
Bennett, Emerson, 242
Bennett, Tony, 221, 222, 228, 312n60
Bennett, William James, 30
Benton, Thomas Hart, 310n11; as fictional character, 216–17, 221–22
Bestor, Arthur, 122
Betjemann, Peter, 132–33
Bible: in evangelicalism, 17–18, 60, 129, 173; illustrations, 40–41, 42; in missionary work, 99; vs nature, 173; Thoreau on, 206–7; Uncle Tom as representation of, 124–25, 132; world, 206–7
Bickley, C. P., 245–51
Bierce, Ambrose, 265
Bierstadt, Albert, 263–67; *The Last of the Buffalo*, 256; *Sunset in the Yosemite Valley*, 264–65, 265, 267, *pl.8*; Twain on, 265–66; *Yosemite Valley*, 264, *pl.7*

Bilgrami, Akeel, 212
Bjelajac, David, 34
black Atlantic, evangelical, 72, 89–97
Bowen, Abel, 50, *51*
Boyer, Paul, 122
Brainerd, David, 46, 210
Brooks, Joanna, 96–97
Brooks, Lisa, 61
Brown, Candy Gunther, 59, 117, 143
Brown, Charles Brockden, 222
Brown, Henry Box, 127, 294n92
Brown, Irene Quenzler, 197
Brown, Matthew P., 55–56
Brown, Thomas C., 91–92
Browne, Thomas, 190–91
Brückner, Martin, 3, 6
Buell, Lawrence, 21
Bullard, Anne Tuttle, 163
Bunyan, John, 8–9, 10, *11*, 55. See also *The Pilgrim's Progress*

Calvinism. *See* Edwards, Jonathan; fiction, Calvinist
Camp, Stephanie M. H., 79, 88
Carey, Mathew, 40–41
Carrera, Rafael, 240–41
Carretta, Vincent, 95
Catholicism: assimilation, 243–44; churches, 223–27; influence on Native Americans, 263; religious services, 227–28; wilderness, 241. *See also* anti-Catholicism
Catskill Mountain House, 147, *148*, 171–74, 177, *181*.
Catskill Mountain House (Cropsey), 147–49, *148*, 168–72, *170*, 180–83, 297n2, *pl.6*
Certeau, Michel de, 24
Chapman, J. G., 42
Cheever, George Barrell, 3
Chidester, David, 20
Child, Lydia Maria, 65, 92, 103, 160, 218
Church, Frederic Edwin, 7–8, 256; *Cotopaxi*, 24–25, *25*, *pl.3*; *Heart of the Andes*, 8–14, *9*, *13*, 254–55, *pl.2*; interpretations of, 9–13,

24–25; *New England Scenery*, 14; *Twilight in the Wilderness*, 8, pl.1
Cincinnati; or, The Mysteries of the West (Klauprecht), 214–17
citizenship, US: direct access vs mediated, 219, 251–52, 317n141; in the spatial imagination, 217, 220–21, 230
Civil War, US; apocalyptic imagery and, 24–25, 256–57; secularization/multireligiosity and, 151, 255, 256–59, 263, 298n14
Clark, Eliot Candee, 279n25
Clark, Elizabeth B., 108, 283n11
Clemens, Samuel L. *See* Mark Twain
Clukey, Amy, 70
Cole, Thomas, 36, 147; *Course of Empire*, 35–36, 82; "Essay on American Scenery," 34; evangelical culture and, 33–41, 44–46, 59–60, 68; *Expulsion from the Garden of Eden*, 36–37, 37, 264–65; *Subsiding of the Waters of the Deluge*, 39, 40; *View from Mount Holyoke ... The Oxbow*, 22, 31–32, 31, 33–46, 38, 44, 54, 59–60, 62, 63, 65, 170–71, 268, pl.4; *View of the Two Lakes and Mountain House, Catskill Mountains, Morning*, 148
Coleman, Dawn, 111, 120
Collins, John J., 2
Columbian & Great West, The, 238–53
Cooper, James Fenimore, 175, 218
Cordell, Ryan, 69
cosmic, the, 189, 190, 202, 211–12, 258–59, 305n21; in apocalypticism, 2–3, 5, 79. *See also* cosmos, the; geography, cosmic; mapping, cognitive; modernity, cosmic, the; self, cosmic
cosmos, the, 189–90, 204, 212, 305n21. *See also* cosmic, the
Cotopaxi (Church), 24–25, 25, pl.3
Crane, Gregg, 122
Cropsey, Jasper Francis, 57, 147, 169, 174, 180–81, 296n1, 297n2; apocalyptic themes in, 147, 149; *Catskill Mountain House*, 147–49, 148, 168–72, 170, 180–83, 297n2, pl.6; *Millennial Age*, 149, 171; *Pilgrim of the Cross*, 147, 149; *Starrucca Viaduct, Pennsylvania*, 11, 12
Cummins, Maria S., 153; *The Lamplighter*, 153, 172, 177–82
Curtin, Philip, 105–6
Cuyler, Theodore Ledyard, 8–9, 176

Darby, John Nelson, 257
Davis, David Brion, 310n20
Davis, Rebecca Harding, 1–2, 3–4, 259, 263
Denning, Michael, 251, 313n65
DeWitt, Susan, 161
Dillon, Elizabeth Maddock, 4
Dimock, Wai Chee, 4, 153, 189
Douglass, Frederick, 24–25, 87, 98
Douglass, Grace, 103
drama, cosmic, 17, 32
Duncanson, Robert S., 82, 111; *Uncle Tom and Little Eva*, 132–34, 134, pl.5
Dunch, Ryan, 209
Durand, Asher B., 49, 50, 182; "Letters on Landscape Painting," 169–70; *Progress (The Advance of Civilization)*, 11, 215; *Sunday Morning*, 101

Edwards, Jonathan, 17, 33, 43–44, 45–49, 47, 90–91, 279n47
Edwards, Justin, 49
Eliade, Mircea, 20, 305n21
Elliott, J. H., 222
emancipation, 72–73; geography of, 70, 80–84; millennium as, 71, 98; West Indian, 68, 95, 97–103. *See also* abolitionism
Emancipation in the West Indies (Thome and Kimball), 97–98
Emerson, Ralph Waldo, 98, 157, 189, 206–7, 211; on abolition, 106; apocalypticism of, 155, 211; ethics of, 165–66; on good and evil, 165–66; on the landscape, 164–65; Warner on, 158
enslaved people: autobiographical works by, 82, 85–88, 92–93; biographies of, 93–94; as colonists, 91–92; fictional,

enslaved people (*continued*)
110–11, 124–25, 126–28, 129–39; as missionaries, 91–92; West Indian, 98–99. *See also* abolition; slavery
Equiano, Olaudah, 92
eschatology: and creative works, 12–13, 110–12, 130–31, 134, 153, 159–60, 164–65, 169–71, 180; definition of, 2, 17; landscape and, 149; missionary memoirs and, 197–98; spatialization of, 65–66, 108, 110–11, 134, 159–60. *See also* space, evangelical
Eulogy on King Philip (Apess), 63–65
evangelical, definition of, 114
evangelicalism, 17–18, 31–33, 48, 97, 108, 204, 256–58
Evans, Sarah Ann, 163
Everett, Edward, 63
expansionism, US, 62–65; in art and literature, 59–61

Fanuzzi, Robert, 69, 97
Fessenden, Tracy, 188–89, 211–12, 227, 236, 255
fiction: apocalyptic, 3–4, 22, 125–38, 152–67, 261–65; Calvinist, 160–64; liberal, 160; regionalist, 214–18; secular-religious, 153; sensationalist, 217–18, 245–53
Fields, James T., 1
Finney, Charles Grandison, 29, 56, 69, 117–21, 142
Finseth, Ian Frederick, 81
Forbes, David W., 200
Foucault, Michel, 210, 228
Franchot, Jenny, 223, 252

Garrison, William Lloyd, 95, 104
Gaudio, Michael, 33
geography: abolitionist, 70, 77–89, 95–97, 103–6, 108; apocalyptic, 2–4, 17, 19, 65–66, 69, 80–82, 125, 138, 211, 214, 222–23, 263, 267–68; in artworks, 10–12; Catholics and, 217, 222–23, 226, 241–42; colonial, 63–64, 222–23, 242; cosmic, 2–3, 271–72; definition of, 3, 15; economic, 242; global, 185, 186–87, 193, 203, 241, 272; of health, 95; Holy Land and, 40–41, 43; inner, 191; landscape and, 15–16; in literature, 110, 130–31, 150–51, 164–65, 230–31, 234–35; moral (*also* moral mapping), 6, 18, 31–32, 50–54, 61–65, 70, 71, 78, 84–85, 86, 103–4, 121, 164, 184–85, 186–87, 197–200; national, 79, 84–88; sacred, 13–14, 18–21, 60–61, 63–65, 70, 83–87, 88, 89–91, 95, 98, 110, 150, 176–77, 217–18, 222–23, 255–56, 263; slavery and, 70, 79, 82–87, 88, 110. *See also* landscape; space
Ghost Dance Religion, 263
Gifford, Sanford Robinson, 147, 256, 301n67
Giles, Paul, 6
Gilroy, Paul, 96
Gore, Al, 272
Greeson, Jennifer Rae, 79, 88, 125, 203
Griffin, Susan, 241
Grimké, Angelina, 69, 78–80, 103–4, 106–8, 109
Grimké, Sarah, 106–7
Gustafson, Sandra M., 139, 218, 252

Harvey, David, 16, 77, 239, 276n70
Hawthorne, Nathaniel, 142, 182
Hayden, Robert M., 20
Heart of the Andes (Church), 8–14, *9*, *13*, 254–55, pl.2
heathenism: geography of, 78, 88, 103, 130, 185, 186–87, 244; hierarchy of, 185, 200–1; missionary view of, 63, 64, 90–91, 103, 188, 197–98, 200–1; Thoreau on, 184–85, 192–93, 198–99, 201–13
Hegel, Georg, 239
Hickman, Jared, 189, 258
Hindmarsh, D. Bruce, 161, 210
Hine, L. A., 239, 241–42
Hirschkind, Charles, 15
Hitchcock, Edward, 37–38
Hodder, Alan D., 155, 165, 211, 305n27
Holbrook, John, 41
Hope Leslie (Sedgwick), 60
Horton, George Moses: 96

How the Other Half Lives (Riis), 4
Hsu, Hsuan L., 6
Humboldt, Alexander von, 12–13, 189
Humphrey, Z. M., 9–10
Huntington, David C., 8

identity, 210, 219, 237, 317n141; birth, 92, 94; national, 219, 227–28, 237, 253; regional, 225, 231, religious, 202–3, 227–28, 231, 237, 241. *See also* self
Innocents Abroad, The (Twain), 255, 259–62, 261

Jackson, Gregory S., 4, 54, 156, 193
Jacobs, Harriet A., 188
Jameson, Fredric, 233–34
Jaudon, Toni Wall, 211
Jenkins, Jerry B., 270
Johnson, Paul E., 123
Jones, Lindsay, 119
jubilee, 71, 81, 97
Judson, Ann H., 197–98
Justina; or, The Will, 161–64

Kaufman, Allen, 43
Keane, Webb, 204, 207, 307n62
Kilde, Jeanne Halgren, 20, 119
Kim, Sharon, 153, 157, 299n24
Kimball, J. Horace, 97–98, 103, 107
Klauprecht, Emil, 214–17
Knott, Kim, 20

LaHaye, Tim, 270
Lamplighter, The (Cummins), 153, 172, 177–82
landscape: as apocalyptic medium, 16, 22, 41–56, 131–34, 147–50, 59, 150, 160, 163, 164, 168–71, 173–74, 211, 214–18, 255–56, 264–65; built, 223–28; commercialization of, 150; definition of, 15; as form of geography, 15–16; homiletic, 54–56, 59, 62–63, 87, 158, 164, 172, 179–80, 194; millennial, 54, 56–57, 59, 78–79, 169, 174, 182; moral, 8–9, 31–32, 34, 48, 62–63, 101;

pastoral, 35–36, 50–52, 54, 81, 83; sacralization of, 10, 16, 32–33, 77–78, 166, 169–70, 175, 182–83, 263; slavery and, 70, 81–84; theodicy and, 154–55, 159–60, 164–65, 180; therapeutic, 182; US expansion and, 59–60. *See also* space
Lane, Belden C., 20–21
Lanman, Charles, 174
Latour, Bruno, 190, 204, 210, 212
Leavitt, Joshua, 76, 117–18, 120, 121
Lefebvre, Henri, 19–20, 32, 276n70
Left Behind novels (LaHaye/Jenkins), 270
Leja, Michael, 15
"Life in the Iron-Mills" (Davis), 1–2, 3–4
Lindo, F., 240–41
Linenthal, Edward T., 20
Lippard, George: 219–20, 251–52, 313n71; *New York: Its Upper Ten and Lower Million*, 229–35, 237, 240, 245, 251, 253, 313nn72 and 74; *The Quaker City*, 235; *Washington and His Generals*, 235
Loomis, Harriet Ruggles, 194–97, 196
Loughran, Trish, 104, 108, 125, 258, 317n141
Luxon, Thomas H., 44, 55
Lyon, Mary, 45

MacIntyre, Alasdair, 182
Mahmood, Saba, 209–10
mapping: cognitive, 16, 68, 70, 163, 190–91, 217, 233–35; moral. *See* geography, moral
maps: in Bibles, 40–41; geopolitical space and, 4; moral, 84–85, 86, 185, 186–87. *See also* mapping, cognitive
Marsden, George, 256–57
Martin, John, 7, 261; *Adam and Eve Driven out of Paradise*, 36–37, 39
Martineau, Harriet, 174, 175, 179
Marx, Karl, 239, 242
Mason, Erskine, 31–32, 36, 54
Mather, Cotton, 21
Matheson, Neill, 208, 209
Mathews, Donald G., 131–32
Maul, Christian, 199

May, Cedric, 96–97
McCarthy, Timothy Patrick, 71
McKibben, Bill, 270, 271–72
McLuhan, Marshall, 113
media: definition of, 113; people and
  characters as, 124, 125, 134, 143
mediascape, 14–15; abolitionist, 69–109;
  evangelical, 111, 112, 116–25, 141, 143,
  149–50, 171–72, 182–83, 190–91, 200–1,
  255–60, 266–70; regional, 217
Melville, Herman, 97, 161, 201
Memoir and Poems of Phillis Wheatley, 89,
  90, 92–96, 287n86, 288nn90 and 91
millennium, the, 45, 48–49, 91, 117, 185, 257;
  abolitionism and, 67–68, 70, 71, 78–81,
  82–83, 98, 101, 104; Cole and, 34, 45, 54,
  59; Edwards on, 17, 45–46, 48–49; Stowe
  and, 137; Thoreau and, 211. *See also*
  landscape, millennial; postmillennialism;
  premillennialism
Miller, Angela, 6, 35–36, 169, 215, 256,
  298n14
Miller, George, 50,
Miller, Perry, 155
Miller, William, 137, 318n27. *See also*
  Millerites
Millerites, 108, 260–61, 318n27. *See also*
  Miller, William
Milton, John, 142, 173–74
missionaries, 51–52, 54, 91–92, 98–99;
  fictional, 124, 130, 136, 137–38, 163;
  memoirs of, 89–90, 185, 188, 192–98, *195*,
  200–1; slavery and, 101–6; Thoreau on,
  184, 192–93; in the United States, 50, 62,
  101–4, 129, 188, 197, 201, 223
Mitchell, W. J. T., 15
Mock Marriage, The (Bickley), 245–53
modernity, cosmic, 189–91, 193, 202–5
Moody, Dwight L., 257
Moorhead, James H., 136, 258–59
Morazan, Francisco, 240–41
More, Hannah, 142
Morgan, David, 15, 34, 258
Morse, Samuel F. B., 223–24, 228

mourning rituals, 194
movement: within creative works, 8–10,
  11–12, 124–25, 126–27, 153–54, 156–59,
  168, 171, 191, 215; piety and, 15–16, 177;
  transatlantic, 89; within religions, 14
Muir, John, 263, 267–69
Murdoch, David, 174–75
Myers, Kenneth, 175

National Academy of Design, 265, 279n25
National Park System, 264, 266–69
Native Americans, 60–65, 263
nature: vs human progress, 36; observed,
  169–70; as sacred space, 33–34, 46–48,
  150, 163, 169–70, 173, 180–81; Thoreau
  and, 190, 199, 208–9, 212–13. *See also*
  apocalypticism, environmental;
  landscape; National Park System
Newell, Harriet, 193–94, *195*
New York: Its Upper Ten and Lower Million
  (Lippard), 229–35, 240, 245, 253, 313nn72
  and 74
Niagara Falls, 29–30, *30*
Noll, Mark A., 18
Nord, David Paul, 132, 258, 279n25

Obookiah, Henry, 200–2
Odell, Margaretta Matilda, 93, 94,
  287n86
'Ōpūkaha'ia. *See* Obookiah, Henry
Oxbow, The. See Cole, Thomas: *View from
  Mount Holyoke . . . The Oxbow*

panoramas, 127
Paradise Lost (Milton), 173–74
Parry, Ellwood C., 59
Peale, Charles Willson, 220–21, 311n25
Pelletier, Kevin, 111, 125
Pilgrim's Progress, The (Bunyan), 8–9, 10, *11*,
  55; artistic interpretations of, 8–9, 57, 87,
  149, 156–58, 161, 167, 168, 180
postmillennialism: 17, 48–49, 65–66, 116,
  256–57, 258; print and, 33, 49, 116, 125;
  Stowe and, 111, 125, 137, 164

premillennialism, 137, 166, 257, 270–71
Progress (The Advance of Civilization) (Durand), 11

Reed, Luman, 30, 34, 36
religions, world, 204, 211, 263; Thoreau on, 205–12
Resignation (Evans), 163
revivalism, 29, 45, 48–49, 69, 77, 108, 118–120
Reynolds, David S., 153, 160, 163–64, 167
Richmond, Legh, 55
Riis, Jacob A., 4, 263, 267
Roberts, Jennifer L., 10, 12
Robinson, Douglas, 3, 131
Rosman, Doreen M., 173
Ross, Steven J., 218
Roughing It (Twain), 262–63
Ruskin, John, 150, 169

Saler, Bethel, 231, 233, 244
Scarlet Letter, The (Hawthorne), 142
Schantz, Mark S., 122
Schoolman, Martha, 104
Sears, John F., 175
secularism, 7, 70, 147, 150–51, 167, 188–90, 219, 227, 228, 236, 249, 251–52; and artworks, 65, 182, 258; and literature, 1, 153, 155, 163–64, 167, 188–89, 255, 260; space and, 20, 21, 191, 236–37; Turner on, 236–37
Sedgwick, Catharine Maria, 60–61, 142, 160, 222
self, the: buffered, 205, 212; cosmic, 204–13; evangelical sense of, 210; landscape and, 15, 32–33, 155; religion and, 23, 191; space and, 190–91; Thoreau on, 190–91, 203, 205, 208–11, 212–13
senses, the: arts/media and, 113, 227, 228; spiritual, 15–16, 119, 165, 211, 227–28
Sinha, Manisha, 71
slave narratives, 82, 85–88, 92–93
slavery: Child on, 92; Douglass on, 24–25; evangelical views of, 65–66, 68–69, 80, 91; in fiction, 110–11, 124–39; and geography, 70, 79, 82–87, 88, 110; and the landscape, 70, 81–84; Thoreau on, 207; US attitudes toward, 65–68, 104. *See also* abolitionism; *American Slavery as It Is*; emancipation; enslaved people; slave narratives
slaves. *See* enslaved people
Smith, John Rubens, 180, *181*
Smith, Jonathan Z., 20
Soja, Edward, 20
space: absolute, 16–17, 77, 276n70: American Studies and, 21; built, 16, 119, 223–25; Catholic, 217, 222–28, 242; conceived, 19; evangelical, 14, 18–19, 32–56, 59, 61–66, 68–69, 77–78, 80, 81–82, 84, 88, 101–6, 150, 166–67, 259, 263–69; frontier (*also* Turner, Frederick Jackson), 219, 222–23, 231, 235–37; Harvey on, 16–17, 77–78, 276n70; heathen, 78, 88, 130, 244; homiletic. *See under* landscape: Lefebvre on, 19, 32; lived, 19, 32, 89; material, 19, 32, 79, 276n70; millennial; Native, 61–63; produced, 19, 32; relational, 65, 276n70; religious, 19–20; represented, 2, 19, 32, 166; sacred, 16–17, 19–21, 65, 112, 151, 153, 175–76, 178, 227–28, 229, 260, 262; social, 14, 123, 143, 182; urban, 15, 123–24. *See* space, frontier; *See also* landscape; spatial fix, sacred; Turner, Frederick Jackson
space-time, 16–17, 77–78. *See also* spacetime
spacetime, 16–17, 77. *See also* space-time
spatial fix, sacred, 220, 239–42, 244, 251, 253
spiritualism, Thoreau on, 184
Stauffer, John, 71
Stein, Jordan Alexander, 97
Stokes, Claudia, 111, 164
Stoll, Mark R., 33–34, 211, 269
Stout, Jeffrey, 155
Stowe, Harriet Beecher, 3, 19, 21, 108–9, 291n18; apocalyptic/millennial themes in, 126–37, 164; "Drunkard Reclaimed, The," 123–24; *Primary Geography for Children*, 128–29; "Tea Rose, The," 124; "Uncle Enoch," 115, 121–22; "Which Is the Liberal Man?," 124. *See also Uncle Tom's Cabin*

Streeby, Shelley, 230, 235, 237
sublime: Calvinist, 161; evangelical, 29, 34, 58–59, 165; nature as, 190
Sunset in the Yosemite Valley (Bierstadt), 264–65, 265, 267, *pl.8*

Talbot, Charles N., 32, 34, 40, 45
Tappan, Arthur, 45, 116, 117
Tappan, Lewis, 45, 73, 107, 116, 117
Taylor, Charles, 151, 153, 156, 175, 189–90, 204, 205, 210–11, 249, 251, 252, 253, 308n66
temperance, 121; Stowe on, 121–24
theodicy, definition of, 126, 154; educative, 154; eschatological, 160; landscape, 152–60, 164–65, 179–80
Thomas, Isaiah, 40
Thome, James A., 72–73, 97–98, 103, 107
Thoreau, Henry David, 184–213; books read by, 303n12, 305n30; religion and, 189–91, 212–13. See also *Walden*
Thünen, Johann von, 239
time, apocalyptic, 3, 4, 101, 110, 173, 202, 272; deep, 4; Industrial Revolution and, 7; as "irreversible arrow," 150; nation-state and, 97, 204. See also space-time; spacetime
Tompkins, Jane, 111
tourism: artists and, 176, 182–83; commercialization and, 150, 176–77; evangelical, 46, 149–50, 175, 182–83, 259–60; landscape, 149–50, 175, 180–81, 182–83, 316n133. See also Catskill Mountain House
Transcendentalism, 185, 188–91, 206–7, 210
Turner, Edith, 20, 175
Turner, Frederick Jackson, 219, 229–30, 234–37
Turner, Victor, 20, 175
Twain, Mark (*also* Samuel L. Clemens), 254–55, 259–63; on Bierstadt, 265–66; on Christianity, 255; on Church, 254–55
Tweed, Thomas A., 14, 20, 305n21

Uncle Tom's Cabin (Stowe), 108–13, 124–28, 129–41, 143; as apocalyptic text, 3, 19, 126–27, 129–37. See also Duncanson, Robert S.; Stowe, Harriet Beecher

Valencius, Conevery Bolton, 95
View from Mount Holyoke … The Oxbow (Cole), 22, 31–32, 31, 33–46, 38, 44, 54, 59–60, 62, 63, 65, 170–71, 268, *pl.4*
Vines, Michael E., 3, 126
virtue, civic, 220
Vox, Lisa, 270, 271

Walden (Thoreau), 184, 204–13; as missionary memoir, 184–85, 188, 192–93, 198–99, 201–4
Wallace-Wells, David, 271, 272
Wallach, Alan, 33, 316n133
Walls, Laura Dassow, 189
Warner, Michael, 21, 72, 96–97
Warner, Susan (*also* Elizabeth Wetherell), 142; *The Wide, Wide World* 152–67, 299n24
Weber, Max, 305n21
Weld, Angelina Grimké. See Grimké, Angelina
Weld, Theodore Dwight, 69, 111. See also abolitionism; American Anti-Slavery Society; Grimké, Angelina
West, Benjamin, 41–42
Wetherell, Elizabeth. See Warner, Susan
Wheatley, Phillis, 90, 92–97. See also Memoir and Poems of Phillis Wheatley
White, Richard, 230
Whittier, John Greenleaf, 74, 81, 83–85, 87–88
Wide, Wide World, The (Warner), 152–67, 299n24
Wife for a Missionary, The (Bullard), 163
Wilkins, Shadrach. See Williams, James
Williams, James (*also* Shadrach Wilkins), 85–88
Willis, Nathaniel Parker, 172, 176
Wordsworth, William, 155

Yellin, Jean Fagan, 128
Yosemite Valley (Bierstadt), 264–65, 264, *pl.7*

Zboray, Ronald J., 123
Zuba, Clayton, 64–65

A NOTE ON THE TYPE

This book has been composed in Arno, an Old-style serif typeface in the classic Venetian tradition, designed by Robert Slimbach at Adobe.